The Complete
10-DAY
DETOX
Diet Plan &
Cookbook

Karen Barnes, MSc, ND

Robert
ROSE

For complete cataloguing information, see page 325.

Disclaimer

This book is a general guide only and should never be a substitute for the skill, knowledge and
experience of a qualified medical professional dealing with the facts, circumstances and symptoms
of a particular case.

The nutritional, medical and health information presented in this book is based on the research,
training and professional experience of the author, and is true and complete to the best of her
knowledge. However, this book is intended only as an informative guide for those wishing to know
more about health, nutrition and medicine; it is not intended to replace or countermand the advice
given by the reader's personal physician. Because each person and situation is unique, the author
and the publisher urge the reader to check with a qualified health-care professional before using any
procedure where there is a question as to its appropriateness. A physician should be consulted before
beginning any exercise program. The author and the publisher are not responsible for any adverse
effects or consequences resulting from the use of the information in this book. It is the responsibility
of the reader to consult a physician or other qualified health-care professional regarding his or her
personal care.

This book contains references to products that may not be available everywhere. The intent of the
information provided is to be helpful; however, there is no guarantee of results associated with
the information provided. Use of brand names is for educational purposes only and does not imply
endorsement.

The recipes in this book have been carefully tested by our kitchen and our tasters. To the best of our
knowledge, they are safe and nutritious for ordinary use and users. For those people with food or other
allergies, or who have special food requirements or health issues, please read the suggested contents
of each recipe carefully and determine whether or not they may create a problem for you. All recipes
are used at the risk of the consumer. We cannot be responsible for any hazards, loss or damage that
may occur as a result of any recipe use. For those with special needs, allergies, requirements or health
problems, in the event of any doubt, please contact your medical adviser prior to the use of any recipe.

Design and Production: Daniella Zanchetta/PageWave Graphics Inc.
Indexer: Gillian Watts
Nutrient analysis: Magda Fahmy
Illustrations: Kveta/threeinabox.com
Cover image: smoothie © iStockphoto.com/knape
Cover recipe: Vanilla Raspberry Dessert Smoothie (see variation, page 324)

The publisher gratefully acknowledges the financial support of our publishing program by the
Government of Canada through the Canada Book Fund.

Published by Robert Rose Inc.
120 Eglinton Avenue East, Suite 800, Toronto, Ontario, Canada M4P 1E2
Tel: (416) 322-6552 Fax: (416) 322-6936
www.robertrose.ca

Printed and bound in Canada

1 2 3 4 5 6 7 8 9 MI 24 23 22 21 20 19 18 17 16

Contents

Introduction 4

Part 1: Exposure to Toxins 7
Chapter 1: Environmental Toxins 9
Chapter 2: Pesticides 25
Chapter 3: Heavy Metals: Arsenic, Lead and Cadmium 41
Chapter 4: Mercury 53
Chapter 5: Iron Toxicity 61
Chapter 6: Detoxifying the Bowel and Liver 71

**Part 2: Food Allergies, Sensitivities
and Intolerances 103**
Chapter 7: Food Allergies 105
Chapter 8: Food Intolerances, Celiac Disease
and Gluten Sensitivity 113
Chapter 9: Common Food Sensitivities 129
Chapter 10: Human Consumption:
Effects on the Environment 143

**Part 3: The Cleansing Detox Diet:
Meal Plans and Recipes 155**
The 10-Day Detox Diet 156
The 10-Day Cleansing Detox Meal Plan 159
About the Nutrient Analysis 160
Breakfast 161
Juices and Smoothies 177
Breads and Muffins 185
Snacks and Appetizers 197
Dips, Spreads and Sauces 211
Salads and Dressings 227
Soups 247
Beans, Peas and Lentils 265
Vegetables and Grains 287
Desserts 309

Contributing Authors 326
References 328
Resources 339
Health Index 340
Recipe Index 344

Introduction

There are many things in today's society that make our bodies toxic. Environmental toxins, pesticides, heavy metals and inflammatory foods cause oxidative damage to cells, impact the immune system and, together with stress and hormones, can overwhelm the liver. Detoxifying and cleansing to eliminate harmful substances from the body is treatment and preventive medicine for a host of medical conditions, including arthritis, cancer, constipation, skin disease, hormone imbalance, insomnia, irritable bowel syndrome and weight, mood and energy disorders. The Cleansing Detox Diet will help get you on a path to wellness by increasing the nutrients vital to each cell, organ and gland in the body.

Manufactured chemicals, such as pesticides, contaminate the food we eat, disrupt hormone balance and have the potential to destroy insects, such as bees, on which we depend to pollinate our food crops. Hormone-mimicking compounds in pesticides disrupt the natural hormone rhythm, leading to mood, hormone and sleep problems. Some of the hormone-like structures in pesticides have been linked to breast and other cancers. This book will help you sort out which foods contain high levels of pesticides — and, therefore, should only be purchased organic — and which foods are lower in toxic pesticides.

Heavy metals that are released from the burning of coal for manufacturing, transportation, heat and electricity end up in the environment and affect aquatic food chains. The long-term effects of consuming fish and shellfish that are contaminated with heavy metals, such as lead, cadmium and mercury, may include a long list of ailments, from allergies and arthritis to attention deficit disorder (ADD) and psoriasis. This book will help you understand the relationships between human consumption levels and pollution in the lakes, rivers, oceans and biosphere.

Excessive iron levels create a health risk especially for men over 40 and postmenopausal women over 60 years old. Iron overload from consuming too much iron from food and genetic hemochromatosis have been linked to an increased risk of cancers, liver and heart disease, diabetes, Alzheimer's disease and immune system dysfunction.

Foods can be a primary source of inflammation. When the body's immune system has a reaction to foods, it can affect many systems in the body, including the thyroid, immune system, skin, liver, kidney and digestion. In addition, food sensitivities can cause low energy level, joint pains, sleep disturbance, low mood, hormone imbalance and chronic infections. In this book, you'll learn which foods cause inflammation in the body, how to get tested for individual food sensitivities and how to avoid eating these food culprits.

To help you identify and remove harmful substances like chemicals, heavy metals and certain foods from your daily life, the book provides action plans at the end of several chapters. You will also get a big-picture perspective on environmental concerns, and how your food and lifestyle choices can have a direct and positive impact on the health of the planet.

Detoxification is a natural function that is accomplished through the bowels, liver and kidney. The liver is the major organ of detoxification, but excessive alcohol, hepatitis viruses and iron overload can all have an effect on the liver. So can hormones, stress hormones, chemicals, pesticides and heavy metals, and depending on the body's retention and absorption of toxins, your body may need help in the detoxification process. Identifying which nutrients are needed and how to get them from foods and supplements is a key step in aiding the detoxification process. The Cleansing Detox Diet will help you understand the best ways to get rid of toxins in the body through diet, nutrients, herbs and lifestyle changes.

In this book, you will find a 10-day cleansing detox menu plan, complete with easy recipes for breakfast, snacks, lunch and dinner, to help you put a simple diet into action. Choosing foods high in nutrients essential for liver and bowel health is the first step on the path to feeling great. You will find 150 recipes to help you incorporate low-allergen, gluten-free, dairy-free and corn-free recipes into planning meals for you and your family. Eating an organic plant-only diet, choosing locally grown produce and reducing your overall consumption of products are essential to creating a healthy planetary biosphere for future generations.

Food and lifestyle choices can have a direct and positive impact on the health of the planet.

PART 1

Exposure to Toxins

Benefits of Reducing Toxins

While the main source of exposure to PCBs and dioxins is through our diet, many other environmental toxins are found in manufactured products that individuals use daily, such as formaldehyde, BPA, phthalates, brominated flame retardants and others. Minimizing exposure to these toxins may help prevent hormone disruption and cancer as well as minimize damage to the immune, nervous and endocrine systems.

CHAPTER 1

Environmental Toxins

Before the growth of the chemical industry, which began around the time of the Industrial Revolution in the late 18th century, many of the toxins we are exposed to today were not found in the environment. By the 1940s and 1950s, the chemical revolution was in full swing with the invention and widespread use of pesticides. Today, we find environmental toxins in many of the synthetic chemicals and household products we use every day. Among the most persistent and well-known toxins are PCBs (polychlorinated biphenyls) and dioxins. Other environmental toxins include formaldehyde, bisphenol A (BPA), brominated flame retardants, phthalates, perfluorinated compounds (PFCs), parabens, sunscreens and organic solvents such as xylene, toluene, styrene and perchloroethylene.

Polychlorinated Biphenyls (PCBs)

PCBs are synthetic organic chemicals, known as chlorinated hydrocarbons, that were once used in electrical, heat transfer and hydraulic equipment; as plasticizers in paints, plastics and rubber products; and in pigments and dyes. They were manufactured from 1929 until 1979, when they were first banned. Despite their ban, PCBs can persist in the environment for decades because they do not break down and do not readily dissolve in water — rather, they bind to sediments, where they are taken up by plants. The chemicals enter the food chain when smaller fish eat plants that then become food for other fish and larger marine animals such as whales, seals and dolphins. In marine mammals, chemical levels can be thousands of times higher than the concentrations found in water.

Intake of PCBs

About 90% to 98% of the average exposure of PCBs comes from dietary intake. PCBs that are in the environment end up in waterways and the toxins build up the food chain as smaller

> **DID YOU KNOW?**
>
> **Chemical Release**
> Environmental toxins have largely been found to disrupt the hormonal system and can increase our risk of cancer. Some toxins accumulate in fatty tissue and take decades to break down. Because these chemicals are stored in the fat cells, they can be released during weight loss, so it is recommended to have the right nutrients and diet during a weight-loss program to mediate this effect.

fish that feed on plant matter get eaten by larger fish, then consumed by people. Besides being found in fish, PCBs are most commonly found in the fat of meat and in milk products.

PCBs in Fish Feed

The main dietary source of PCB contamination comes from fish. PCBs are found in high concentrations in farmed fish. In most cases, fish pellets that are fed to farmed fish have added fish oil, which contains PCBs. This makes fish that come from these farms more toxic. The fish oil added to fish pellets has been found to contain between 9 and 30 times more PCBs than those from fish meal alone. The fish oil comes from wild fish, which have bioaccumulated toxins in the wild. It takes approximately 7 pounds (3 kg) of fish pellets to make 1 pound (450 g) of farmed fish, such as salmon or sea bass. Studies have shown that farmed sea bass have higher concentrations of PCBs than wild sea bass, indicating that commercial fish pellets are a major source of PCBs. Humans are also known to ingest more of the PCBs in fish because fish oil is being strongly promoted for its health benefits.

Farmed or Wild Fish Contamination

Even wild-caught fish are not exempt from the effects of PCBs. People who regularly eat fish from the North Shore of the St. Lawrence River, for example, are exposed to a mean PCB level of 6 parts per million (ppm). In comparison, Inuit populations that rely on seafood have a PCB level of 4.1 ppm. The average North American has 5 to 10 times lower PCB levels than an Inuit because they do not eat as much fish, but any farmed or wild-caught fish, especially from the Great Lakes, is likely to be contaminated with PCBs. Because PCBs accumulate in humans, especially in the fat tissues, the less fish, dairy or meat products consumed, the less likely your chances of being contaminated with PCBs.

DID YOU KNOW?

Limits of PCBs in Fish

The United States and Canada have adopted maximum allowable limits of PCBs in commercial fish caught in the Great Lakes. In the U.S., 0.2 to 3 parts per million (ppm) is acceptable in fish for human consumption, although children and pregnant women are advised to stay closer to the lower limit. In Canada, 2 ppm is the maximum allowable limit for PCBs in fish.

Effects of PCBs on Human Health

A 2015 study in *Environment International* reported that almost all samples of human blood, fat or breast milk show some detectable level of PCBs. Many studies of PCBs in breast milk showed concentrations 4 to 10 times higher than in the mother's blood. Long-term accumulation of PCBs has been shown to cause cancer. These persistent organic pollutants can also exert a variety of other adverse health effects on the immune system, reproductive system, nervous system and endocrine system.

Thyroid Hormones

Thyroid hormones are produced in the thyroid gland, a butterfly-shaped gland in the throat area. These hormones — which regulate bodily functions including breathing, heart rate, body weight, body temperature and cholesterol levels — circulate in the bloodstream by attaching to a transport carrier that takes them through the circulatory system to have an effect in tissues in other parts of the body. If the body lacks thyroid hormones, the body's metabolism slows down, causing symptoms such as weight gain or difficulty losing weight, constipation, low energy, depression, hair loss, dry skin, fatigue, sensitivity to the cold, a slow heart rate and menstrual changes.

PCBs have been shown to affect the endocrine system by reducing thyroid hormones by interfering with hormone transport carriers that take the hormone to where it is used. In studies, it has been shown that PCB levels and consumption of Great Lakes fish was significantly associated with changes in thyroid hormones. When the thyroid is not functioning optimally during pregnancy, it can affect the unborn baby by producing effects such as a low birth weight and autoimmune disease.

DID YOU KNOW?

Bioaccumulation in Fish
Wild fish, especially larger predatory fish, accumulate PCBs by eating smaller fish that have accumulated PCBs from the environment. This process of accumulating more toxins as you move up the food chain to larger fish is known as bioaccumulation of toxins.

DID YOU KNOW?

Avoiding PCBs
Eating a plant-only diet that includes vegetables, grains, nuts, seeds and beans as protein sources instead of meat, fish and dairy can greatly reduce the exposure to PCBs.

Cancer Risk

Eighty PCBs have been classified by the United States Environmental Protection Agency (EPA) and the World Health Organization's International Agency for Research on Cancer (IARC) as probable human carcinogens. In one study, four commercial PCB mixtures induced liver tumors when fed to rats. In another study, capacitor manufacturing workers exposed to PCBs had increased mortality from liver, gallbladder and gastrointestinal cancers. Researchers have found a significant association between non-Hodgkin's lymphoma and PCB concentrations in fat tissues. Women who have the highest amount of PCBs in their breast tissue have twice the risk of breast cancer as compared to those with lower amounts, and this is largely due to fish consumption. Bioaccumulated PCBs appear to be more toxic than the original PCB and more persistent in the body.

Dioxins

Dioxins are almost exclusively produced by industrial processes and take a long time to break down, so they persist in our environment. Dioxins are formed as a result of incineration of municipal solid waste and hospital waste, smelting, chlorine bleaching of paper pulp and the manufacturing of some herbicides, pesticides and fungicides. One way dioxins end up in the food supply is from sewage sludge that is used as a fertilizer for growing crops. Sewage sludge is the solid waste material produced by sewage treatment and contains most of the toxic contaminants, such as dioxins. Although technology is available for controlled waste incineration with low dioxin emissions,

FAQ

Q: How do PCBs affect hormones and pregnancy?

A: Thyroid hormones, as well as ovarian hormones estrogen and progesterone, are affected by PCBs. Thyroid hormone is essential for the normal growth and development of a baby's brain while in the uterus and for proper metabolism in the mother. Prenatal exposure to PCBs through the placenta is thought to play a significant role in the future health of the child. PCBs have been shown to cause neurobehavioral development, such as hyperactivity, impaired learning and memory, while excess accumulation of PCBs in the body is associated with lower IQ and attention and motor deficit.

uncontrolled waste incinerators — namely, solid waste and hospital waste — are often the worst culprits for polluting the environment.

Intake of Dioxins

The highest environmental concentrations of dioxin are found in soil and sediment. Dioxins that are liberated from incineration of waste get deposited in the soil and run into rivers, ending up in the sediment of rivers, lakes and oceans. More than 90% of human exposure to dioxins is through eating meat and dairy products, fish and shellfish, especially from food products containing animal fat. Contaminated animal feed is often the root cause of dioxin contamination of food.

Like PCBs, dioxins bioaccumulate in the food chain. It takes about 8 pounds (4 kg) of dry weight of food to make 1 pound (450 g) of cow meat, 5 pounds (2.5 kg) of dry weight to make 1 pound of pig meat, and 2 pounds (1 kg) of dry weight to make 1 pound of chicken meat. About 50% of daily dietary dioxin intake by the U.S. population is attributable to meat and dairy products.

> Uncontrolled waste incinerators — namely, solid waste and hospital waste — are often the worst culprits for polluting the environment.

Effects of Dioxins on Human Health

Dioxins have a half-life (the time it takes to eliminate half of the toxins from the body) of between 7 and 11 years, although this varies widely with each individual. Other dioxins may be eliminated more or less rapidly with as little as a 6-month half-life, but others can take up to 20 years. Dioxins accumulate in the body with age, an increase in fat stores and the frequency of Great Lakes sport-caught fish eaten. In Japan, for example, the accumulation of dioxins largely depends on a high intake of fish and shellfish because the population there consumes large amounts of fish. Breast milk monitoring programs have been implemented in various countries to monitor the effect of dioxins on infant health. Research shows that breastfed infants can have daily exposures from 10 to 20 times higher than the rest of the population.

DID YOU KNOW?

Fish Feed in Animals

About a third of the total fish caught in the oceans is used to feed farm animals such as chickens and pigs, which further contributes to the accumulation of dioxins in animal products.

Hormone Health

The functioning of hormones, such as sex, thyroid and adrenal hormones, is thought to be greatly affected by exposure to environmental toxins early in life. The reproductive function of humans and animals is most affected prenatally by environmental toxins because sex hormones play a critical role in sexual differentiation at this time. The thyroid hormones play a critical role in brain development, both prenatally and in infancy. Studies of exposed populations have found that dioxins can cause reproductive and developmental problems. Dioxins have also been shown to affect the synthesis of adrenal hormones.

Dioxins interfere with hormones by inhibiting enzymes that break down hormones. When dioxins interfere with estrogen breakdown, this in turn elevates the estrogen circulating in the bloodstream and affects target organs. Elevated estrogen has also been associated with increased risk of prostate cancer in men.

Cancer Risk

There is an increased risk of cancer with high levels of dioxins. Chronic exposure of animals to dioxins has resulted in several types of cancer. Studies have also shown that chemical workers who are exposed to high levels of dioxins have an increased risk of cancer. The International Agency for Research on Cancer (IARC) has classified dioxins as a known human carcinogen, based on animal and human studies.

The World Health Organization has determined that most people have a background level of dioxins and "due to the high toxic potential of this class of compounds, efforts need to be undertaken to reduce current background exposure."

Organochlorine Compounds

Organochlorides are chemicals that contain chlorine. They are found in plastics, pesticides, solvents and dry-cleaning agents. By-products of industry, such as the bleaching of paper, the incineration of waste that contains chloride and the chlorination of drinking water, produce organochlorides when released into the environment. Organochlorides concentrate in the fatty tissue of animals. Meat, dairy and fish eaters have higher body stores of these chemicals than vegetarians.

Breast Cancer and Endometriosis Link

A 2015 meta-analysis in the *International Journal of Molecular Sciences* found a link between breast cancer, endometriosis and PCBs. The study examined three endocrine-disrupting chemicals that work by blocking or mimicking estrogen in the body: PCBs, bisphenol A (BPA) and phthalates. The study specifically examined the role of these chemicals in altering genes, which would increase the odds of getting breast cancer. Several hundred genes, including five common genes, were found to be altered by exposure to PCBs, BPA and phthalates. Researchers noted that breast and uterine tumors and endometriosis were all affected by PCBs, BPA and phthalates and that only PCB exposure, not BPA and phthalates, increased the summary odds ratio for breast cancer and endometriosis. It concluded that breast cancer and endometriosis share some common environmental risk factors.

Dioxins and PCBs and Breast Cancer

The New York University Women's Health Study, with 14,274 participants enrolled between 1985 and 1991, examined the effects of dioxins and PCBs in relation to breast cancer, among other goals. The researchers found mean levels of blood dioxins and PCBs were higher for breast cancer patients than for control subjects. Those who had a dioxin concentration in their blood of 2 ng/mL (nanograms per milliliter) had the lowest risk of breast cancer. For women with a value of 19 ng/mL of dioxins in their blood, the risk of getting breast cancer was four times as high. The study concluded that breast cancer was strongly associated with dioxin concentrations in the blood, but not with PCBs.

Effects of Organochlorides on Human Health

Cancer Risk

Women with the highest concentrations of organochloride pesticides have a 4 to 10 times greater risk of breast cancer than those with the lowest levels. Organochlorine compounds, such as DDT (dichlorodiphenyltrichloroethane), DDE (dichlorodiphenyldichloroethylene) and PCBs, are often found in cancer biopsies of women with breast cancer. People who use chlorinated water for 35 years have a 1.5 times greater cancer risk. Composting toilets that recycle human waste reduce the need to use chlorine to treat sewage.

Endocrine Disruptors

Endocrine glands produce hormones at one area of the body that function at another location. Endocrine disruptors are chemicals that interfere with the process of synthesis, secretion, transport, binding and/or elimination of hormones in the body. The body's endocrine system includes the thyroid, adrenal and pituitary glands and hormones, such as estrogen, progesterone and testosterone. Organochlorines have been linked to breast cancer because they exert estrogenic effects on breast tissue. Some mixtures of organochlorines found in breast cancer patients also have an anti-androgenic effect in that they block male hormones produced by the adrenal glands or ovaries in women.

> Organochlorines have been linked to breast cancer because they exert estrogenic effects on breast tissue.

Other Environmental Toxins

There are many other environmental toxins in manufactured products that most people use daily. These toxins include formaldehyde, bisphenol A (BPA), phthalates, brominated flame retardants, perfluorinated compounds, parabens, ultraviolet filters and organic solvents such as xylene, toluene, styrene and perchloroethylene. Minimizing exposure to these toxins may help prevent hormone disruption and cancer.

Formaldehyde

Formaldehyde is a preservative often found in carpets, paper towels, pesticides, plastics, plywood, particle board, rodent poison, shoe polish, wood stains and preservatives. It is considered a volatile organic compound and becomes a gas at room temperature. Formaldehyde can off-gas from carpets or plywood for up to a year. When materials like natural gas, wood, gasoline or tobacco are burned, formaldehyde gas is also released during combustion.

Formaldehyde is also used as part of a mixture for embalming and preserving corpses after death. The preservative found in corpses is between 18% and 35% formaldehyde, which is significant because it is released into the environment over decades. In the United States, modern embalming started around the time of the Civil War. Soldiers who died on the battlefront were shipped home for burial, and to make sure they didn't decay before getting there, up to 12 pounds (5.5 kg) of arsenic was used to preserve the body. More recently, preservatives use a formaldehyde solution. When the body decays, it releases formaldehyde, mercury from fillings in teeth and varnish from caskets into the water table. Embalming is not a common practice outside of the United States and Canada.

DID YOU KNOW?

Air It Out
Formaldehyde gets into the air and is absorbed by the lungs, so it is important, when buying new furniture or rugs that contain the preservative, to let them sit and air out. Store them in a garage for several weeks, or buy the floor model that has already released its formaldehyde.

Toxicity Symptoms

Common symptoms are eye, nose and throat irritation, coughing, headaches, dizziness and nausea. Long-term exposure to high levels of formaldehyde has been shown to cause cancer. The United States Environmental Protection Agency (EPA) has listed formaldehyde as a "probable human carcinogen," while the International Agency for Research on Cancer (IARC) has classified formaldehyde as "carcinogenic to humans" based on nose and throat cancers in those who work in the industry.

Bisphenol A (BPA)

BPA is a synthetic substance used in the production of polycarbonate plastics and epoxy resins. It is found in plastic bottles and containers, as a lining in food containers such as cans, and in coffee cup lids. In a recent screening by the Centers for Disease Control and Prevention, BPA was detected in the urine of 93% of the U.S. population. Health Canada recently reported that 95% of Canadians have measurable levels of BPA in their blood or urine, with the highest levels found in children. BPA has been shown in studies to block thyroid development, which can lead to thyroid resistance syndrome and attention deficit/hyperactivity disorder (ADHD). The substance has also been shown to have an effect on pancreatic cells, where it causes high insulin levels in the short term and insulin resistance and high insulin levels in the long term, both of which are factors in the development of diabetes. Research has shown BPA to mimic estrogen — as a synthetic estrogen that disrupts the hormone system, even small exposure increases the risks for breast cancer, prostate cancer, infertility, early puberty and type 2 diabetes.

Brominated Flame Retardants

Brominated flame retardants are used in many household products, such as furniture and mattresses, as well as in thermoplastics, electronics, textiles and building materials, to prevent household items from catching fire easily. These chemicals migrate from products and contaminate the dust and air and accumulate in the environment.

Some forms of flame retardants can inhibit the growth of plankton and algae and suppress the reproduction of zooplankton, the microscopic animals in the water column that eat plankton. Lab tests on rats and mice have shown nervous system damage and liver disturbances as the result of these substances. Brominated flame retardants have also been found to disrupt hormones.

Phthalates

Phthalates, also known as plasticizers, are used to soften plastics and are found in plastics, nail polish, fragrances and building materials. In 2008, they were prohibited from use in children's toys due to their toxicity. Among the harmful effects, phthalates are known to cause hormonal disruption, are linked to DNA damage of sperm and lower sperm count in men and cognitive behavior problems in children and youth.

Perfluorinated Compounds (PFCs)

Perfluorinated compounds are used to make products more resistant to stains. They are found in nonstick pan coatings, food containers, electronics, cosmetics, food packaging and cooking utensils. PFCs are also used to reduce friction in automotive and construction materials. PFCs are known to disrupt hormones and, in animal studies, have been shown to disrupt endocrine function and affect the liver and pancreas.

Parabens

Parabens are found in cosmetics, shampoos, creams and some pharmaceuticals. A recent study found that 96% of Americans showed parabens in their urine samples due to its widespread use in regular personal care items. Parabens mimic estrogen, a female sex hormone. While the European Union restricts the concentrations of parabens in cosmetics, there are no restrictions in the U.S. or Canada. The U.S. Cosmetic Ingredient Review Expert Panel concluded in 2012 that parabens were safe as a preservative in cosmetics at current concentrations. Health Canada continues to monitor paraben research.

DID YOU KNOW?

Parabens in Cosmetics
Women can be exposed to up to 50 mg of parabens a day from cosmetics use.

Ultraviolet Filters (Sunscreens)

The American Academy of Dermatology states that prevention of sunburns and skin cancer through the use of sunscreens outweighs any "unproven claims of toxicity or human health hazard from ingredients in sunscreens." According to the AAD, individuals should be using a sunscreen even on a cloudy day, since 80% of the sun's harmful UV rays can penetrate skin.

The Environmental Working Group (EWG), an environmental organization, annually reviews sunscreens in its *Sunscreen Guide* to evaluate the exposure and toxicity levels of more than 1,000 products with 9 FDA-approved sunscreen chemicals, such as oxybenzone, octyl methoxycinnamate and homosalate. Oxybenzone acts like estrogen in the body and can be detected in nearly every American due to widespread use in sunscreens. Chemicals that mimic estrogen have been associated with endometriosis in women. The chemical UV filter octyl methoxycinnamate has hormone-like activity and has been shown in animal studies to affect thyroid and behavior. Homosalate is known to disrupt estrogen, testosterone and progesterone.

According to the EWG, UV filters with lower toxicity concerns include mineral sunscreens, such as titanium dioxide, zinc oxide, avobenzone and Mexoryl SX. These UV filters are not usually absorbed through the skin so show little evidence of hormone disruption in studies.

If you choose to avoid the sun or cover up during sun exposure, it is important to check your vitamin D level. Vitamin D is produced on the skin from sun exposure, and those who avoid the sun will need to check with their doctor about taking a vitamin D supplement.

Organic Solvents

Organic solvents, such as xylene, toluene, styrene, and perchloroethylene, are used as degreasing agents in industrial machinery and dry cleaning and are present in plastics, paints, adhesives, nail salons, cigarette smoke and exhaust fumes. Occupational exposure is the most likely place to become susceptible to these compounds. The occupations with the highest exposure include chemical factory workers, dry cleaners, painters, tannery workers, nail salon workers and gas station workers. Organic solvents mainly affect the endocrine system as hormone disruptors.

Endocrine Disruptors and Environmental Chemicals

The endocrine glands secrete a hormone at one location and the hormones then act at a different location in the body. Examples of endocrine glands are the adrenals, thyroid, ovaries and testes. Endocrine disruptors that mimic or block the functioning of hormones include polychlorinated biphenyls (PCBs), polybrominated biphenyls (PBBs), dioxins, plastics such as bisphenol A (BPA), phthalates (plasticizers), pesticides such as methoxychlor, chlorpyrifos, dichloro-diphenyltrichloroethane (DDT) and fungicides such as vinclozolin.

Endocrine disruptors are known to cause problems with reproduction in animal populations. Seals in the Baltic Sea have been adversely affected by PCBs with lower fertility, PCB exposure in blue herons affects fertility, and mink fed fish contaminated with PCBs at high levels die or, at lower levels of PCB exposure, are infertile. DDT that accumulates in eagles and gulls when they consume fish from the Great Lakes affects reproduction by causing egg shell thinning, high rates of deformities and death of embryos.

Endocrine disrupters are also tied to weight gain. According to the World Health Organization's 2014 statistics, 39% of the adult population, or 1.9 billion adults worldwide, are overweight and 13%, or 600 million, are obese. The epidemic of obesity coincides with the exponential increase in exposure to endocrine disrupting toxins during the past 40 years. Some researchers have used the term "obesogens" for those endocrine-disrupting chemicals (EDCs) that cause people to gain weight even though they are limiting calories and increasing physical activity. Animal and human studies indicate that obesogens such as tributyltin, bisphenol A, lead, perfluorooctanoic acid, phthalates, PCBs, DDT and tobacco smoke can lead to weight gain later in life. Minimizing exposure to these toxins, especially early in life, is thought to be a sensible part of a preventative strategy for maintaining a healthy weight.

The potential effects of these contaminants on human health highlight the need to reduce our use of chemicals in our everyday lives to help protect not just our own health but also that of our children and wildlife. The overview of toxins on the following page will help you minimize or eliminate exposure.

DID YOU KNOW?

Bioaccumulation

Polychlorinated biphenyls (PCBs), dioxins and organochlorinated pesticides bio-accumulate in fat cells.

Environmental Toxin Overview

Toxin	History	Used in	Exposure Risk	Health Risks
Bisphenol A (BPAs)	• Banned in baby bottles in 2012	• Plastics • Lining of metal cans • Baby bottles • Toys • Plastic containers	• Passed in breast milk • Seafood • Fish oil • Found in 50% of people	• Hormone disruptor • Made worse by heating
Brominated flame retardants		• Thermoplastics • Electronics • Textiles • Building materials	• Fatty fish, dust and air	• Hormone disruptor
Organic solvents (xylene, toluene, styrene, perchloro-ethylene)		• Industrial degreasing • Dry cleaning • Plastics • Paint • Adhesives • Nail salon products • Cigarette smoke • Exhaust fumes	• Occupational exposure: - chemical factory workers - dry cleaners - using plastics - painters - tannery workers - nail salon workers - gas station workers - smoking	• Hormone disruptors
Parabens		• Cosmetics • Pharmaceuticals • Personal care		• Detected in breast tumors • 96% of Americans show exposure in urine samples • Higher in women and girls due to use of cosmetics
Perflu-orinated compounds (PFCs)		• Coating on pans • Food containers • Electronics • Cosmetics • Food packaging • Cooking utensils	• Contaminated air • Water	• Hormone disruptor
Phthalates (plasticizers)	• Banned in children's toys in 2008	• Plastics • Nail polish • Fragrances • Building materials	• Infants susceptible to higher levels than adults because of chewing on plastic toys	• Hormone disruptor
Poly-chlorinated biphenyls (PCBs)	• Banned in the late 1970s • Current emissions in developing countries	• Oils • Pesticides • Electric transformers • Coolants	• Fish, dairy products and meat	• Increased cancer risk • Hormone disruptor
Ultraviolet filters (sunscreens)		• Sunscreens • Cosmetics	• 96% of Americans show exposure in urine samples	• Hormone disruptors

Action Plan

❑ Avoid eating marine fish and farmed fish, especially fatty fish, such as salmon, which can be contaminated with PCBs.

❑ Avoid eating meat, fish, poultry and dairy products.

❑ Use glass or lead-free ceramic containers instead of plastic containers.

❑ Filter water with a charcoal or reverse osmosis filter.

❑ Avoid use of cosmetics and personal care products with parabens.

❑ Stay out of the sun, especially during high UV times of 10 a.m. to 2 p.m. Cover up with hats and protective clothing and minimize sun exposure in order to limit the use of sunscreen.

❑ Avoid buying food in plastic or cardboard packaging; avoid plastic food wraps and nonstick coatings on cookware.

❑ Avoid eating food from cans with BPA lining.

❑ Use unbleached recycled paper.

❑ Install composting toilets in your home.

❑ Buy books printed on recycled paper, like this one.

❑ Take measures to avoid occupational exposure, such as working as or in a tannery, dry cleaner, painter, gas station, chemical factory, nail salon, hair dresser, incinerator, the pulp and paper industry or hazardous waste sites.

❑ Consider leaving a will that states your intention to be cremated to reduce the toxicity from formaldehyde used in embalming or opt for natural burial.

❑ Learn more about toxins in the environment from active organizations in this field (see Resources, page 339).

Unintended Consequences

The most persistent and well-known toxins are PCBs, used for decades in North America to increase the productivity of crops. Today, recent pesticides used in lawn care and agriculture, while thought to be more target-specific and to have shorter half-lives in the environment, are being blamed for some of the catastrophic effects now being seen on some wildlife not intended as targets, including sea life, birds, amphibians, dogs and bugs (see chapter 10).

Pesticides

The United Nations Food and Agriculture Organization (FAO) defines a pesticide as "Any substance, or mixture of substances, or micro-organisms including viruses, intended for repelling, destroying or controlling any pest, including vectors of human or animal disease, nuisance pests, unwanted species of plants or animals causing harm during or otherwise interfering with the production, processing, storage, transport, or marketing of food, agricultural commodities, wood and wood products or animal feeding stuffs, or which may be administered to animals for the control of insects, arachnids or other pests in or on their bodies." Pesticides have been used since the adoption of agriculture, when humans moved away from being part of the natural ecosystem of gatherers and hunter-gatherers, and its use has intensified since the 1940s.

The History of Agriculture

The practice of agriculture first began about 11,000 years ago when hunter-gatherers in the Middle East cultivated wheat, barley, peas, lentils, chickpeas, bitter vetch and flax. In China, rice and millet were domesticated. In Africa, rice and sorghum were farmed, while in North and South America, corn, squash, potato and sunflowers were cultivated. Many diverse cultures came to rely on farming as the population grew.

Before agriculture, people on Earth were gatherers and hunter-gatherers. This way of life kept human populations in check within the limits of the carrying capacity of the environment. "Carrying capacity" refers to the maximum population size of the species that the environment can sustain indefinitely given the amount of food, water and habitat available.

Farming allowed for an abundance of food and allowed human populations to grow, which is now on an exponential growth curve. It is estimated that the world population reached 1 billion for the first time in 1804. It took 123 years to reach 2 billion in 1927. Roughly 33 years later, the population reached 3 billion in 1960 and then 4 billion 14 years later in 1974. In 1987, in just 13 years, the population was at 5 billion. Just 12 years later, in 1999, the population ballooned to 6 billion. The most recent landmark of 7 billion humans on Earth was reached in 2011 or, by some accounts, 2012.

DID YOU KNOW?

Early Estimates
Up until agriculture was adopted, the population of humans on Earth was estimated to be about 10 to 15 million people.

Thomas Malthus, a scholar of demography, predicted in 1798 that geometric (exponential) population growth and arithmetical (linear) food production increases would lead to chronic food shortages, with dire consequences for the future of humanity. The Green Revolution of the 1960s increased agricultural productivity through the use of pesticides, increasing the area of land used for crops, the mechanization of farming and the planting of hybrid crops. To increase crop yield, massive amounts of pesticides were needed. The use of pesticides created an increased food supply for humans, allowing populations to continue on an exponential path.

Global Impact of Consumption of Animals

Humans are currently having devastating effects on the biosphere through the consumption of animals, a process that depletes water and uses up land that could be reforested or used to grow plants that go directly to feeding humans. The raising of animals for human consumption is by some accounts one of the largest contributors to greenhouse gas emissions, deforestation, soil and water depletion, dead zones in the oceans, loss of habitat and extinction of species (see chapter 10).

Global Impact of Farming Practices

Modern mechanized farming often relies heavily on monoculture (growing one crop), pesticides and herbicides, fertilizers and machinery. Monoculture crops can deplete the soil of nutrients. To overcome this obstacle, fertilizers high in nitrogen and phosphorus are used; however, their run-off leads to more algae growth in streams and disrupts

Meat/Fish Consumption

The total numbers of animals and fish consumed worldwide in 2010, according to the United Nations Food and Agriculture Organization, are as follows (figures have been rounded off):

- Beef and buffalo: 328 million
- Poultry: 59 billion
- Pork: 1.3 billion
- Fish and marine animals: 1 to 3 trillion

the stream and coastal ocean ecosystems. When algae blooms proliferate in water that is high in nitrogen and phosphorus, this process prevents sunlight from getting to the bottom and limits the amount of oxygen available for fish. This has a devastating effect on coral reefs in coastal areas of the oceans. The result is dead zones in the ocean areas, devoid of oxygen, where nothing can live and fish die if they swim into them.

Instead, farmland could be used to produce organically grown crops for direct human consumption and can help sequester carbon from the atmosphere instead of contributing to it. Growing only food plants to feed humans and using farming techniques that involve crop rotation, increasing diversity, plowing under and composting plant material, along with planting legumes that fix nitrogen in the soil, can help end the need for harmful fertilizers.

The History of Pesticides

Pesticides have not only affected the "pests" intended to be the targets but also reduced populations of beneficial species of insects, other animals and even humans. Arsenic pesticides were used in the 1920s and 1930s and resulted in human deaths due to toxicity. In the 1940s, sodium chlorate and sulfuric acid were used as pesticides, and ammonium sulfate and sodium arsenate were used as herbicides.

That same decade saw the discovery of synthetic pesticides, including DDT (dichlorodiphenyltrichloroethane), BHC (benzene hexachloride), aldrin, dieldrin, endrin, chlordane, parathion, captan and 2,4-D (2,4-dichloro-phenoxyacetic acid). DDT was used to reduce insect-borne diseases, such as malaria, yellow fever and typhus, and to rid crops of unwanted bugs. These pesticides killed all bugs indiscriminately, but years later it was discovered that there was also harm to non-target plants and animals and problems with residues.

Meanwhile, targeted pests began developing resistance to pesticides, leading to the need for heavier doses to control them. The potential "solution" caused an even bigger problem — because these pesticides also killed many beneficial species that helped to naturally control any outbreak of other species, new pesticides were then introduced to control the exploding population growth of secondary pests. This led to an increase in pesticide use.

There seemed to be little concern among governments about the potential health risks of using pesticides with DDT despite the mounting evidence of harm in the decades that preceded their eventual ban. In her 1962 book, *Silent Spring*,

DID YOU KNOW?

Pesticide Names
Some types of pesticides are called a herbicide, insecticide, fungicide, bactericide, algaecide and molluscicide, among others.

Rachel Carson first brought attention to how DDT enters the food chain and accumulates in the fatty tissues of animals, including human beings, and causes cancer and genetic damage. Her work highlighted what the world later came to know: a single application of DDT killed insects for weeks or months, including the beneficial species; DDT remained toxic in the environment even after it was diluted by rainwater; and DDT and other pesticides had irrevocably harmed birds, fish and animals and contaminated the entire world food supply. Her research helped ban DDT in the United States and spurred on the creation of the Environmental Protection Agency (EPA).

In the decades that followed, many herbicides and insecticides were being developed that were thought to be more target-specific or have shorter half-lives in the environment, including glyphosate, sulfonylurea and imidazolinone herbicides, as well as dinitroanilines and the aryloxyphenoxypropionate and cyclohexanedione families. Insecticides of the time included pyrethroids, avermectins, benzoylureas and *Bacillus thuringiensis* used as a spray treatment. In the 1990s, triazolopyrimidine, triketone and isoxazole herbicides and chloronicotinyl, spinosyn, fiprole and diacylhydrazine insecticides were produced and used.

Today, the genetically engineered crops that have been developed produce their own insecticides. Some varieties of corn are resistant to corn borer, a known pest to the crop. Other crops are genetically engineered to be resistant to herbicides or pesticides. Soybeans, corn, canola and cotton are herbicide-tolerant — so when these crops are sprayed with herbicides, they kill the weeds but not the crop plants.

Pesticide Use in Lawn Care

Nearly 80 million pounds (36 million kg) of pesticide active ingredients are used annually on U.S. lawns. Homeowners who apply their own pesticides are directly exposed to chemicals and use up to 10 times more pesticides per acre than farmers apply to their crops, according to the U.S. Fish and Wildlife Service. In the U.S., it is estimated that 30 million acres of lawn are treated with chemicals each year.

Pesticide Bans

The Stockholm Convention on Persistent Organic Pollutants, which was adopted on May 22, 2001, and entered into force on May 17, 2004, is a global treaty whose purpose is to safeguard human health and the environment from highly harmful chemicals that persist in the environment and affect the well-being of humans and wildlife. At this convention, the following pesticides were banned:

- Aldrin
- Alpha-hexachlorocyclohexane
- Beta-hexachlorocyclohexane
- Chlordane
- Chlordecone
- DDT
- Dieldrin
- Endrin
- Heptachlor
- Hexachlorobenzene
- Lindane
- Mirex
- Pentachlorobenzene
- Technical endosulfan and its related isomers
- Toxaphene

Lawn Pesticide Ban: Leading the Way

In June 2008, the Ontario legislature took a leading role by passing the Cosmetic Pesticide Ban Act, which amended the provincial Pesticide Act to ban the use and sale of lawn and garden pesticides. This act prohibits the use for cosmetic reasons of 295 products containing certain active ingredients. Products that are not to be used on lawns and gardens include WeedOut and Later's outdoor insecticide, weed and feed fertilizer and pesticide combinations. The active ingredients glyphosate and glufosinate, found in Roundup and Wipe-Out herbicides, are prohibited generally but can be used to control poisonous plants such as poison ivy. Commercially, companies that use pesticides under an exemption will be required to post warning signs. Lawn bowling, cricket, lawn tennis and croquet are exempt from the ban, as are golf courses; however, they must submit

DID YOU KNOW?

Lawn Pesticides Targeted

In 2010, 171 municipalities in Canada placed restrictions on the cosmetic use of synthetic lawn pesticides. New Brunswick and Prince Edward Island adopted legislation in 2009 and 2010, respectively, banning the herbicide 2,4-D.

annual reports about the amount of pesticides used and be certified in integrated pest management. Wasp sprays and insect repellants are exempt from the ban.

Types of Pesticides

There are many types of pesticides that work against different pests. The suffix *-cide* comes from the Latin word "to kill." Pesticides can be classified by the target organism they kill or by the chemical compounds they contain. Four categories of pesticides that target organisms, for example, are fungicides, herbicides, insecticides and bactericides. Fungicides kill molds and fungus, herbicides kill unwanted plants, insecticides kill unwanted insects, and bactericides kill bacteria. Pesticides classified by the compound they contain or their chemical nature include organochlorides, organophosphates, carbamates and pyrethroids, microbial insecticides and insect growth regulators.

Organochlorides

Commonly used decades ago in agriculture in North America, organochlorine pesticides work by disrupting the sodium/potassium balance in nerve fibers in insects. Organochlorines, such as DDT (dichlorodiphenyl-trichloroethane), were banned by the U.S. Environmental Protection Agency; however, they still have ecological ramifications (see the history of pesticides in this chapter for more information).

Organophosphates

Organophosphates, which also act as nerve toxins, are used to kill different insects, including termites, mosquitoes and roundworms. They are used on golf courses and included in products that are used to treat wood fences and utility poles. Chlorpyrifos, commonly used on agriculture and feed crops, is an example of an organophosphate insecticide. Organophosphates degrade faster than organochlorides, such as DDT, but have greater acute nervous system toxicity.

Effects in Children

In general, children are more sensitive to exposure than adults. Organophosphates are found in higher concentrations in children than adults; it is found in 90% of children's urine because it is a pesticide that is commonly consumed. In studies, children who had chlorpyrifos in their blood had more developmental delays and disorders than children who did not have chlorpyrifos in their blood. Exposed children also had more attention deficit disorders and hyperactivity disorders.

Toxic Effects of Repeated Exposure

- Impaired memory and concentration
- An increased risk (55% to 72%) of attention deficit disorder (ADD) in children
- Disorientation
- Severe depression
- Irritability
- Confusion
- Headache
- Speech difficulties
- Delayed motor reactions
- An increased risk of Alzheimer's disease
- Fetal brain development problems, especially in boys

Carbamates

Carbamates are less toxic than organophosphate pesticides. They work by affecting the transmission of nerve signals in pests and are used throughout the world to kill insects, foliage, nematodes, fungus, and birds. Carbamate compounds are generally short-lived in the environment. An acute pesticide dose can paralyze the nervous system and lead to death due to respiratory failure.

Human Exposure

Human exposure to carbamate pesticides can result in serious illness or even death. Exposure can occur by breathing it in, absorbing it through the skin or ingesting it. Initially, individuals may experience incoordination, and symptoms can progress to moderate to severe muscle weakness and paralysis.

Pyrethroids

Synthetic pyrethroid pesticides are made by imitating the structure of natural pyrethrins. This class of pesticides is highly toxic to insects but deemed only slightly toxic to mammals. Pyrethroids are used to control pest insects and have been used in agriculture, restaurants and schools and for the treatment of fleas in dogs and topical head lice in humans. The pesticide is made by extracting compounds from a species of chrysanthemum and works by penetrating insects and paralyzing their nervous system. The pyrethroid resmethrin is used to kill flying and crawling insects in homes, greenhouses, processing plants, commercial kitchens and airplanes and for government mosquito control programs. Resmethrin is found in consumer insecticide brands like Scourge and Raid Flying Insect Killer.

In toxicity studies on laboratory animals, chronic exposure has shown benign and cancerous liver tumors. Resmethrin is extremely toxic to fish, other aquatic life and bees.

Immediate or Acute Toxic Effects

- Headache
- Nausea
- Incoordination
- Tremors
- Convulsions
- Facial flushing and swelling
- Burning and itching sensations

Neonicotinoid Pesticides

Neonicotinoids are a relatively new class of insecticides in use today. These substances are applied to plant seeds to coat them, but these pesticides travel systemically through the plants and end up in their pollen and nectar. Neonicotinoids are much more water-soluble than other pesticides, so plants have an easier time absorbing them from the soil. Neonicotinoid pesticides are currently registered for use on more than 140 crops in over 120 countries.

Neonicotinoids and the Decline of Bees

In the United States, 25% of honey bee populations have disappeared since 1990. A similar situation exists in Canada, which saw an average decline of 26% from 2007 to 2015. Some of the major factors associated with the decline include mites, pesticides, pathogens, loss of habitat and nutritional deficiencies. While neonicotinoids were once thought to be less toxic to insects and bees, researchers are now discovering that the low levels of contamination over a

FAQ

Q: Why are we so concerned about the health of bees and how neonicotinoids may affect their health?

A: More than $15 billion a year in U.S. crops and over 30% of the food we eat is pollinated by bees. Crops that are pollinated by bees include apples, berries, cantaloupes, cucumber and almonds. Other crops, such as cereals, canola (oilseed rape), corn, cotton, sunflower and sugar beets, are routinely treated with neonicotinoid insecticides on the seeds before planting and the insecticide is absorbed by all parts of the plant, including the flowers that the bees will later pollinate.

Governments in Italy, Germany, France and elsewhere have already taken action against neonicotinoids to protect their pollinators and beekeepers. Despite growing evidence of this effort's effect, the U.S. is still not restricting its use. The Ontario government is the first jurisdiction in North America to implement a phase-out of neonicotinoid pesticides as part of its Pollinator Health Action Plan, which took effect July 1, 2015. The regulations will reduce the use of seeds treated with neonicotinoids. By 2017, the use of neonicotinoid-treated soy and corn seeds will be reduced by 80%.

period of time may be impairing the memory of bees when foraging for nectar and pollinating plants. Bees may have trouble finding and remembering which flowers have nectar and how to find their way back to their hives to communicate to other bees where to find pollen.

Sulfoxaflor

Another neonicotinoid pesticide called sulfoxaflor has been approved for use in North America. Several beekeeping organizations and beekeepers have filed a legal action to stop its use. There is concern that waterways are being affected by neighboring soils that contain neonicotinoids. In one study, after sampling nine Midwestern stream sites during the 2013 growing season, neonicotinoids were detected at all sites sampled. After spring planting, the levels of pesticides were above what is deemed too toxic to aquatic animals.

Glyphosate

Glyphosate is used extensively as a herbicide on lawns. This weed killer blocks the proteins essential to plant growth and selectively kills broad-leaf weeds but not grasses. About 1.4 billion pounds (635 million kg) of this herbicide are applied each year in more than 160 countries. Roundup,

DID YOU KNOW?

Neonicotinoid Treatment
The EPA has recently concluded that seed treatments with this insecticide provide little or no overall benefits to soybean production in most situations.

Pesticides and "Pests"

In nature, there is no such thing as a pest. Every species exists for a reason and is important to the health of the ecosystem. Nature self-regulates without the need for chemicals to keep populations in check. Here are some reasons why pesticides should not be used on lawns and why foods grown with pesticides should be avoided:

- Pesticides are persistent chemicals that take decades to break down.
- Pesticides are known to be implicated in breast cancer risk.
- Pesticide toxicity is far-reaching to wildlife species in the ecosystem.
- Pesticides have been implicated in bee and butterfly decline as well as in the death of birds.

the common name for this herbicide, is one of the most used lawn and garden weed killers. In agriculture, it is primarily applied to most of the corn, soy and cotton grown in the U.S., where 90% of soy is found to contain traces of glyphosate.

Lack of Testing

Glyphosate is not included in the U.S. government's testing of food for pesticide residues. Because it is not tested, there is no information on exposure or risk from eating food that contains glyphosate.

Limitations to Pesticide Testing

A report by the U.S. Government Accountability Office (GAO) found that the Food and Drug Administration (FDA) and U.S. Department of Agriculture (USDA) should strengthen the pesticide residue monitoring programs. According to the FDA's 2011 annual monitoring report, the tests are able to detect the majority of about 400 pesticides with the Environmental Protection Agency's established tolerances. In imported foods, the FDA tested less than 1% of shipments of a particular food or imported food that came through the country's ports. In 2012, the FDA tested a small amount — 1,167 samples — of pesticide residues in domestic foods, which represents a quarter of the imported goods tested. To better inform the public about pesticides, the GAO recommended that the pesticide monitoring program report be published and the pesticides that are not tested identified.

Toxicity of Active Ingredients

The toxicity levels of pesticides are currently tested based on the active ingredient only. Pesticide formulations, however, include mixtures of ingredients, and the adjuvants — the ingredients, known as the inert elements, that help the principal ingredients — are not included in the toxicity tests.

Pesticides in Produce

The Environmental Working Group's (EWG) *Shopper's Guide to Pesticides in Produce* analyzes more than 34,000 samples from laboratory tests done by the USDA and FDA. The annual guide ranks pesticide contamination on 48 popular fruits and vegetables after they have been washed or peeled to replicate what people would normally do before eating a fruit or vegetable. It looks at different measures of pesticide contamination, including the percentage tested with detectable pesticides, the percentage of samples with two or more detectable pesticides, the average number of pesticides found on a single sample, the average amount of pesticides found, the maximum number of pesticides found on a single sample and the total number of pesticides present.

The result of its findings make up their two popular lists — the Dirty Dozen and Clean Fifteen.

Growing Crops without Pesticides

There are many ways to grow food without the use of pesticides; for example, permaculture and biointensive farming. Each one involves working with nature in order to promote healthy, fertile soil without pesticides.

Permaculture: Farming with an Ecological Perspective

Permaculture is a way of designing an agricultural system that works with nature. The idea is to create an alternative agricultural system to be sustainable over the long term, like a forest ecosystem. If you are growing your own backyard garden, here is an example of the way permaculture gardening works.

Permaculture can be done on a small scale in your own backyard or in a local field or as part of an eco-village community. The fundamental principle of permaculture is to care for the earth through practicing biodiversity, restoring

Dirty Dozen Plus

This EWG guide is meant for individuals who want to reduce their exposure to pesticides in produce but find it expensive to buy all organic fruits and vegetables. Known as the Dirty Dozen Plus, it includes produce that is best purchased organic because it contains higher levels of pesticide residue when compared to other produce. This list is helpful, although buying organic is always best when possible.

- Apples
- Peaches
- Nectarines
- Strawberries
- Grapes
- Celery
- Peaches
- Spinach
- Sweet bell peppers
- Cucumbers
- Cherry tomatoes
- Snap peas (imported)
- Potatoes

Plus Category
These contain highly toxic pesticides:

- Hot peppers
- Collard greens
- Kale

Clean Fifteen

The fruits and vegetables that form the Clean Fifteen contain the least amount of pesticides in the edible part. Pesticides may still be used on these crops but are found in low concentrations. It is still advisable to buy all fruits and vegetables organic when possible, as pesticides have far-reaching effects on the ecosystem, wildlife and human health.

- Avocados
- Sweet corn
- Pineapples
- Cabbage
- Onions
- Sweet peas (frozen)
- Asparagus
- Mangos
- Papayas
- Kiwi
- Eggplant
- Grapefruit
- Cantaloupe (domestic)
- Cauliflower
- Sweet potatoes

DID YOU KNOW?

Purchasing Power
Buying local, organic fresh fruits and vegetables and completely avoiding all animal products is the best way to improve your health and your survival by ensuring the long-term health of the planetary biosphere.

soil and creating habitat for species. The second principle is to see people as nature and weave human needs into the functioning health of a wider ecosystem. Sharing the surplus is the third principle, which involves sharing resources with other people and species and not overconsuming and hoarding.

A simple illustration of permaculture is the way Native North Americans grew corn, beans and squash as companion plants. An Iroquois legend explains the relationship well. The "three sisters" are inseparable and grow and thrive together. The corn stalk provides a climbing structure for the beans to grow, while the beans fertilize the soil with

FAQ

Q: **What should I look for when buying organic?**

A: The USDA-certified organic label means that the fruit or vegetable is grown without pesticides or fertilizers. Organic also means that it is not made with synthetic ingredients and that sewage sludge is not used as a fertilizer. A third-party government-approved inspector determines whether the farm is in compliance with the regulations before a product is labeled USDA-certified organic.

In Canada, the Organic Products Regulations came into effect on June 30, 2009. All organic products bearing the Canada Organic logo or represented as organic in interprovincial and international trade must comply with these regulations. The Canadian Food Inspection Agency (CFIA) is responsible for the monitoring and enforcement of the regulations. British Columbia, Quebec and Manitoba have created their own legislation to enforce the federal regulations for products that are sold within their own provinces.

their nitrogen-fixing ability and stabilize the corn plant. The squash provides shade for her other two sisters, preventing the moisture in soil from evaporating, and her spiny vines discourage predators. The biomass from this crop is incorporated back into the soil to improve organic matter for the next year.

Organics: Community or Backyard Gardening

If you currently don't grow your own food, there are many ways to get involved in a more local and sustainable way of eating. You can join a local organic food co-op, which will deliver food to your door or to a local place for weekly pickup. Visit your local farmers' market and ask vendors if they sell organic produce, or talk to your grocer about providing a wider selection of organic food. The way you spend your money has the biggest impact on what is sold.

When gardening, start small: fill some pots with soil and seeds that you can put next to a windowsill. Go a little bigger by planting easy-to-grow plants, such as beans, carrots, lettuce or herbs, near a window throughout the year, then move things outside by planting a small vegetable garden in your backyard. If you have squirrels or rabbits, fence off the area with chicken wire and secure it into the ground 1 to 2 feet (30 to 60 cm) deep to keep the critters out. Plan to expand your garden each year by adding more plants.

DID YOU KNOW?

Permaculture Is...
"The conscious design and maintenance of agriculturally productive eco-systems which have the diversity, stability and resilience of natural ecosystems."
— Bill Mollison, co-developer of modern permaculture

"Consciously designed eco-systems, which mimic patterns and relationships found in nature, while yielding an abundance of food, fiber and energy for provision of local needs."
— David Holmgren, co-developer of modern permaculture

DID YOU KNOW?

Sustainability
Biointensive agriculture is a sustainable way to grow your own food.

If you are interested in expanding your knowledge of permaculture, look for classes offered in your area and see the references in the back of this book. A greenhouse can give you more flexibility to grow crops all year round. It has other advantages, too, such as the ability to recycle water and regulated conditions to help plants grow well. Plant fruit trees in your front- or backyard or consider spaces

Permaculture Design Principles

1. Consider thoughtful observation of the landscape, soil conditions, sunlight, water and wildlife.
2. Start small and scale up.
3. Obtain a material yield, such as food, water, energy, medicine, fiber, building materials, biodiversity, soil and biomass. It is also possible to obtain a non-material yield, including beauty, learning, wisdom, solitude, recreation and community.
4. Allow for multiple functions — for example, planting a tree to provide food, shade, cooling, biomass, beauty, building materials, a structure for other plants to climb and habitat for many species.
5. Grow many different things and rotate your crops; for example, annual vegetables, mushrooms, edible forest gardens.
6. Allow for vertical and horizontal planting to maximize the biomass in a small space. There also needs to be a succession in time for maximum productivity.
7. Maximize diversity of crops to create resilience.
8. Recycle the energy by using waste. For example, compost vegetable scraps and use a composting toilet to help fertilize next year's crop.
9. Use local resources, such as planting legumes to build soil fertility.
10. Produce no waste. In natural systems, the output of one organism becomes food for another organism.
11. Consider relative location: create functional relationships between diverse elements in the design; for example, a tree can cool the house, shade the greenhouse and provide biomass for the garden.
12. Practice the law of return: leave some vegetation, such as compost made from the stalks of plants grown the previous year, for the garden to replenish the soil.
13. Maximize the edge: a dynamic place where two different ecosystems meet can have a higher diversity, such as where the meadow meets the forest.
14. Remember: "The problem is the solution." If you encounter a problem, see it as an opportunity.
15. Plan for decreasing intervention over time. Good designs will require less work because they are following nature's rules.

in your community to plant them. Many communities, for example, have organized to use green spaces provided by churches or fields near them to grow a community garden. Talk to your municipality, businesses or child's school about volunteering to put a garden next to it. In the case of the school, the children can participate in looking after it.

Action Plan

- ❏ Buy organic foods.
- ❏ Eat foods grown locally.
- ❏ Eat a plant-based diet.
- ❏ Grow vegetables, such as string beans, carrots and lettuce, in your house near a window.
- ❏ Grow your own backyard garden. Learn about or take a course on permaculture agriculture and transform your backyard into a permaculture garden.
- ❏ Start a community organic garden. Get together with others to plant locally in your own local green spaces. Make a community garden at a local church or in your neighborhood.
- ❏ Avoid the use of pesticides and herbicides for lawns, gardens and fruit trees or to kill bugs.
- ❏ Talk to your friends and neighbors about not using pesticides.
- ❏ Meet with your local politicians to discuss not spraying fields and not mowing green spaces to allow native flowering plants for bees and butterflies and to permit natural vegetation to grow near roadways and parks. Talk to politicians about banning neonicotinoid pesticides (see chapter 10).
- ❏ Feed your pet a vegan diet (dried vegan kibble is available at pet food stores).
- ❏ Buy food without packaging.
- ❏ Avoid food and cosmetic products that contain palm oil, palm kernel or palm.

Health Threats

It takes 10 hours for half the arsenic in the body to exit. The liver detoxifies arsenic through a process called methylation. At a low dose, 70% of arsenic is excreted in the urine; the other 30% is taken up by the tissues. This is just one example of the threat posed to human health by heavy metals.

CHAPTER 3

Heavy Metals: Arsenic, Lead and Cadmium

The main threats to human health from heavy metals are associated with exposure to arsenic, lead, cadmium and mercury. These metals are released during mining and smelting, the burning of fossil fuels, waste incineration, agriculture and manufacture of electronics.

Sources of Exposure

Coal-fired power plants are currently the dominant emitters of mercury (50%), acid gases (more than 75%) and many other toxic metals (20% to 60%) in the United States. Mercury that is released into the atmosphere rains down onto the ground and ends up in streams, lakes and oceans, where it accumulates in aquatic ecosystems and contaminates fish. (See Chapter 4 for more information on mercury toxicity.)

Agriculture contributes to arsenic exposure from pesticides. Arsenic remains in the soil and does not break down. Arsenic-containing pesticides have been used in Australia, New Zealand and the United States.

Gold mining affects local areas through the release of arsenic and mercury. When gold is mined, arsenic that coexists with it is mobilized, and mercury is released during the refining process. The Ashanti region of central Ghana, for example, is at risk for local contamination due to its gold mining activities.

> **DID YOU KNOW?**
>
> **Mercury Release**
> Major sources of mercury worldwide include gold mining, steel production, boilers, incinerators and cement plants.

Air Pollution from Power Plants

The Environmental Protection Agency (EPA) provides a look at the portion of U.S. air pollution that comes from power plants:

- Acid gases: 77%
- Arsenic: 63%
- Sulfur dioxide: 60%
- Mercury: 50%
- Nickel: 28%
- Chromium: 22%
- Mono-nitrogen oxides: 13%

Power Plants and Carbon Dioxide

Burning fossil fuels, such as coal, oil and natural gas, at power plants for heat and industry releases carbon dioxide into the atmosphere. This activity alone releases about 10 billion tons of carbon annually. Fifty percent of the carbon dioxide gas remains in the atmosphere, leading to climate change. Of the remaining carbon dioxide gas, approximately 25% or more is dissolved into oceans, where it is making them more acidic, and the remaining 25% is used during photosynthesis by plants and sequestered into plant material.

Ocean acidification has the potential to harm everything from the coral reef ecosystems — which house up to 25% of the fish in the ocean — to the open water ecosystems unless there are dramatic changes in fossil fuel use. When oceans become more acidic, corals, fish and shelled organisms, such as the microscopic phytoplankton and zooplankton, and shelled creatures like clams, oysters and mussels, cannot make shells. Some of these creatures are the basis of the food chain in the oceans.

Heavy Metal Toxicity

Arsenic, lead, cadmium and mercury are known to affect the body's nerves and genes and cause diseases such as cancer, Alzheimer's and heart disease through a process called oxidative stress. Oxidative stress is the body's reaction to oxygen that comes from breathing and normal cellular processes involved in the production of energy. Highly reactive oxygen species known as free radicals are produced because of this activity. When free radicals interact with the membranes of cells, proteins and genes, oxidative damage occurs. Exposure to environmental toxins and heavy metals increases the free radicals in the body. To counteract the process of oxidative stress, the body produces antioxidants. Antioxidants, which neutralize free radicals and prevent harm to cells, are also obtained from eating plants.

Oxidative Damage

Heavy metals contribute to oxidative damage in the body. The oxidative damage is like rusting in a car — the more it accumulates, the older you look. It also causes a host of conditions, including rapid aging, heart disease, cancer, Alzheimer's disease, inflammation and diabetes. Oxidation can damage cell membranes, which leads to heart disease.

When cholesterol is oxidized, it sticks to the wall of the arteries, which causes the formation of plaques, further contributing to heart disease risk. Mercury has been shown to have neurological and immune effects and cause intestinal lining damage. This can lead to memory problems, a lowered resistance to infection and more food sensitivities and allergies. Arsenic, lead and cadmium bond to proteins in the body. This depletes an antioxidant in the body known as glutathione. This antioxidant is found in the liver and is responsible for helping the body detoxify. When glutathione is depleted, the body cannot detoxify other toxins effectively.

Arsenic Toxicity
The History of Arsenic

From the late 19th and throughout the entire 20th century, arsenic compounds were used in agriculture as a pesticide. The compound Paris green, which contained arsenic, was used as a pigment in green paint. Lead arsenate was popular in the 1890s and was spread on fruits and vegetables as a pesticide, while calcium arsenate was used as a pesticide against the cotton boll weevil. Between 1890 and 1900, reports of arsenic poisoning were quite frequent. Opposition to arsenic and lead in pesticides grew in response to reports of poisonings. By the 1930s, more than 100 million Americans suffered from mild to severe arsenic and lead poisoning, while many farm children died of arsenic poisoning. During that same time, pests were showing resistance to lead and arsenic pesticides and the public was increasingly opposed to their use. Still, companies sold the pesticides, farmers continued to use them, and the government did not ban their use. After the Second World War, arsenical pesticides were replaced by DDT and other organochlorides, which were subsequently banned.

Arsenic in Food and Drinking Water

Human exposure to arsenic is mainly via the intake of food and drinking water, with food being the most common source. Arsenic contamination of both soil and water comes from the burning of coal and pesticide use in agriculture. Despite the eventual ban of certain arsenic-containing compounds, old agricultural soils may still contain high levels of arsenic from pesticides previously used on the land.

Banning Arsenic-Containing Pesticides

In 2006, the United States Environmental Protection Agency (EPA) banned arsenic-containing chemicals from use as a pesticide in the United States because the agency showed these chemicals convert over time to a more toxic form of metal, changing to inorganic arsenic. This inorganic form of arsenic compound had the potential to contaminate drinking water through soil runoff. Because animals were fed cotton by-products, the EPA identified that there could be human contamination through milk or meat consumption.

In the two years following the decision, stakeholders lobbied the EPA to keep the arsenical pesticides. In 2009, the EPA overturned its previous decision and continued to allow arsenical compounds in the growing of cotton. However, pesticides containing arsenic could not be applied to residential lawns, citrus trees and in forestry. Use of arsenic-containing pesticides was still allowed on golf courses, sod farms and highway rights-of-way until 2012.

In Canada, in 2013 the Canadian Food Inspection Agency tested food products, including rice and rice products, infant cereals, fruit products, bottled water and seaweed, for arsenic. A total of 1,071 domestic and imported samples were evaluated for organic and inorganic arsenic, and it was found that most had detectable levels of total arsenic. The established arsenic tolerance in beverages is 0.1 parts per million (ppm); however, the tolerance limit is under review by Health Canada. It was concluded that none of the samples were expected to pose a health concern to consumers.

In 2014, the Canadian Food Inspection Agency tested 213 samples of pear and rice products for arsenic. All rice samples contained levels of total arsenic, with brown rice having the highest amounts at 0.24 ppm, white rice 0.14 at ppm, rice drinks at 0.02 ppm and sake (a rice-based alcoholic beverage) at 0.01 ppm. Seventy to 80% of the arsenic in brown and white rice is in the inorganic form, which is thought to be more harmful than the organic form of arsenic. Because there is no established maximum level for total arsenic in rice, the Canadian Food Inspection Agency does not think that the levels of arsenic detected would pose a human health risk to the Canadian public.

RESEARCH SPOTLIGHT

FDA Study of Arsenic in Rice

The FDA conducted a study in 2012 of inorganic arsenic, the more toxic form of arsenic, found in various rice and rice product samples. The average levels of inorganic arsenic in the rice ranged from 2.6 to 7.2 micrograms of inorganic arsenic per serving. Instant white rice was at the low end of the range and brown rice was at the higher end because arsenic tends to concentrate in the outer coating of rice, which is ground off when making white rice. The range of products containing rice, including rice milks, crackers, flours and others, was found to have average levels of inorganic arsenic that ranged from 0.1 to 6.6 micrograms of inorganic arsenic per serving.

FAQ

Q: **Why is some rice more contaminated with arsenic than other plants and in different regions?**

A: Rice grown in recent years has been found to be contaminated in particular because it is grown in water paddies and therefore may be exposed to higher amounts of arsenic than plants grown in drier soils. The highest levels of arsenic in U.S.-grown rice comes from the southern states and the lowest levels come from rice grown in California. Cotton farmers in the U.S. South once used arsenic-based pesticides to control bugs in their cotton fields. The rice now grows in paddies where cotton once grew and uptakes the arsenic found in the soil. Arsenic does not degrade.

Arsenic in Coal and Coal Waste

Arsenic is found in coal and coal waste and is one of the most common causes of acute heavy metal poisoning in adults. A 2010 EPA report, *Human and Ecological Risk Assessment of Coal Combustion Wastes*, found that people who live near coal ash impoundments and drink from nearby wells have as much as a 1 in 50 chance of getting cancer from arsenic contamination. A 2011 Environmental Integrity Project (EIP) monitor identified 19 new sites across the U.S. where groundwater near coal ash dumps was found to be contaminated with arsenic and other pollutants and identified an urban rail trail in Indiana, which uses recycled coal ash, where the soil is contaminated with arsenic at levels 900 times greater than the federal screening level.

Effects on Human Health

Arsenic and Cancer

Arsenic is a known human carcinogen. The World Health Organization cites "overwhelming evidence from epidemiological studies that consumption of elevated levels of arsenic through drinking-water and other sources is causally related to the development of cancer at several sites, particularly skin, bladder and lung." The International Agency for Research on Cancer has stated that arsenic causes cancer of the lung, urinary bladder and skin. Long-term exposure to arsenic in drinking water is mainly related to increased risks of skin cancer, but also some other cancers, as well as other skin lesions, such as hyperkeratosis and pigmentation changes. Arsenic is linked to cancers of the kidney, liver and prostate.

Arsenic and the Nervous System

Arsenic toxicity has been shown to cause neurotoxic effects in the developing brain as it crosses the placenta from the mother to the fetus, affecting intelligence and memory at levels below the current safety guidelines. Studies have shown that urinary arsenic levels were higher in boys than girls despite comparable exposures.

Lead Toxicity

The History of Lead

The Roman Empire was the first society to use lead extensively in plumbing and as an additive in wine to enhance its taste and preserve its shelf life. Reports indicate that lead at that time caused severe colic, anemia and gout.

In the 1800s, lead was added to paint to increase durability. Because of lead's naturally sweet taste, children

Tolerable Weekly Intake Withdrawn

The World Health Organization (WHO) and the Joint Food and Agriculture Organization of the United Nations (FAO)/WHO Expert Committee on Food Additives (JECFA) established that the previous provisional tolerable weekly intake (PTWI) of 15 μg/kg body weight (equivalent to 2.1 μg/kg body weight a day) for inorganic arsenic was no longer appropriate due to the potential carcinogenicity of arsenic. The PTWI limit was withdrawn by the committee and no new limit was established.

often ate paint chips and were subsequently exposed to high levels of lead, which was discovered to cause lead poisoning later. When lead is absorbed, it crosses into the brain and causes neurological damage that can lead to Alzheimer's disease. Many European countries banned the use of interior lead-based paints in 1909, but the United States did not adopt a similar ban until 1971, when it finally began to phase out lead-based house paint.

Lead in Gasoline

From the time leaded gasoline was first introduced in 1921 to its phase-out in 1986 and ban between 1996 and 2000, it is estimated that 7 million tons of lead have been released into the atmosphere from gasoline in the United States alone. The history of these events shows how long it can take to stop an environmental toxin once it has gained momentum in use.

- In 1854, a specific type of lead was discovered.
- In 1921, lead was added to gasoline to prevent engine knock. During this period, there was enormous growth in the automotive, oil and gas, and chemical industries.
- In 1922, the U.S. Public Health Service issued a warning about the potential hazards associated with lead.
- In 1923, lead workers died from exposure in factories and leaded gasoline went on sale.
- In 1924, five workers died from lead poisoning at a factory.
- In 1925, sales were suspended while the U.S. Surgeon General reviewed the safety of lead. The next year, a committee approved use of lead in gasoline and sales resumed.

DID YOU KNOW?

Harmful Lead Stores
During pregnancy and breastfeeding, the body can mobilize lead stores, increasing the level of lead in the blood. It takes between 28 and 36 days for half of the lead to get out of the body. The bones and teeth of adults contain about 94% of stored lead, or body burden.

- By 1936, 90% of the gasoline sold in the U.S. contained lead.
- In 1965, a report came out highlighting that high levels of lead were caused by human use.
- In 1972, the EPA gave notice of an intended phase-out of lead in gasoline and was promptly sued by the lead manufacturer.
- In 1979, the effects of lead on the intellectual development of children were first documented by researchers.
- In 1980, the National Academy of Sciences reported that leaded gasoline was the greatest source of environmental lead contamination.
- In 1986, the primary phase-out of lead from gasoline was completed in the U.S.
- In 1996, the World Bank called for a ban on leaded gasoline.
- In 2000, the European Union banned leaded gasoline.

Although there had been warning signs of lead toxicity in the early 1920s, and significant research into deleterious health effects in the 1960s and 1970s, it took decades for a ban on the use of lead in gasoline.

Lead Leaching into Food

In 2010, the U.S. Food and Drug Administration (FDA) received reports that traditional pottery from several manufacturers in Mexico labeled as lead-free contained levels in excess of the FDA's levels for lead in ceramic tableware. They found that lead was found in the glazes or decorations covering the surface of some traditional pottery. Lead found in pottery leaches into food and drink that is prepared or stored in these dishes.

Lead in Children

Children are particularly susceptible to lead exposure — their bodies have high gastrointestinal absorption and their brains are more permeable to toxins. In the 1960s, the threshold for blood lead levels thought to cause toxicity was 60 µg/dL (micrograms per deciliter), but three decades later it was 10 µg/dL. The Centers for Disease Control and Prevention has reported that it no longer considers any blood lead levels safe in children. There has been a decrease in blood lead levels in the U.S. and Canada in the past 30 years, since the ban on lead in gasoline and paints, but the same cannot be said about children in other parts of the world. For example, in China, 7% to 10% of children had blood lead levels above 10 µg/dL when tested in a study between 2004 and 2006. In Egypt, 44% of children also exceeded levels beyond 10 µg/dL between 2007 and 2008. Of those, 37% had cognitive dysfunction.

Cadmium Toxicity

Cigarette smoking is a major source of cadmium exposure. In non-smokers, food is the biggest source of exposure. Cadmium emissions have increased dramatically during the 20th century. One reason that cadmium is present in the environment has to do with the fact that cadmium compounds used in rechargeable nickel–cadmium batteries are rarely recycled and the batteries are often dumped together with other household waste. The waste gets into landfills and leaches into the soil and water table.

> Cadmium compounds used in rechargeable nickel–cadmium batteries are rarely recycled and the batteries are often dumped together with other household waste.

Cadmium Exposure and Human Health

- 2% to 6% of the cadmium that people ingest through food is absorbed in their digestive tracts.
- 30% to 64% of inhaled cadmium is absorbed.
- 50% of intake of cadmium comes from smoking cigarettes.
- 98% of the ingested cadmium comes from food.

Cadmium from Cigarette Smoking

Mass marketing and the availability of cigarettes at the end of the 19th century encouraged people to smoke. In 1912, it was proposed that smoking might be responsible for an increase of tumors in the lungs. By the 1920s, surgeons noticed an increased frequency of lung cancer, and pathologists later discovered that smokers had a deadening of the hair-like structures in the upper airway passages that are responsible for removing bacteria, dust and other larger particles from the lungs.

The evidence against smoking and its link to health harms continued in the decades that followed. In the 1940s and 1950s, studies showed a connection between cigarette smoking and lung cancer. A study in 1954 concluded that smokers of 35 or more cigarettes a day increased their odds of dying from lung cancer by a factor of 40. Even though repeated studies concluded that there was a cancer risk with cigarette smoking, popular knowledge at the time still did not share this view. In a Gallup poll asking, "Do you think cigarette smoking is one of the causes of lung cancer?" only 41% answered yes.

Naturally, cigarette manufacturers disputed the mounting evidence with a campaign to reassure the public that the companies were in fact doing more research on possible risks and links to health hazards. It worked. The public increased consumption of cigarettes in the 1960s and 1970s, with a peak use in 1982 despite the fact that a Surgeon General's report in 1964 recognized smoking as a cause of lung cancer in men.

Currently, consumption rates of cigarettes are falling in most of the richer countries but remain high in poorer countries such as many in Africa as well as in China. China is now manufacturing about 2.4 trillion cigarettes a year, close to 40% of the global total.

History shows that there is a lag time between knowing something causes harm to the public and accepting this knowledge. Even though scholars and medical professionals recognized tobacco's harm as early as the 1920s, the public was slow to react and governments worldwide have yet to ban the sales of cigarettes.

Toxins in Cigarettes

Among the toxins, polycyclic aromatic hydrocarbons, arsenic, chromium, nickel and cadmium have been identified in cigarette smoke. The majority of cadmium exposure in humans who are smokers comes from tobacco smoke. Smokers have up to four times as much cadmium in their blood as non-smokers.

Cadmium from Industry

Exposure to cadmium also comes from industry. These are the most significant industrial sources to human exposure:

- Phosphate fertilizers: 41.3%
- Fossil fuel combustion: 22.0%
- Iron and steel production: 16.7%

Action Plan

- ❑ Reduce fossil fuel combustion by not purchasing unnecessary products, driving less and taking more vacations close to home.
- ❑ Reuse by buying clothing and books, for example, at second-hand stores and by organizing community swaps for clothing and other items so you don't consume things that need to be manufactured using fossil fuels.
- ❑ Recycle items you don't need by donating them to charities or selling them on a website.
- ❑ When you consume products, make sure that they are grown or made locally.
- ❑ Dispose of batteries appropriately or recycle them. Batteries are considered hazardous waste and should not be put in the regular garbage.
- ❑ Avoid cigarette smoking and second-hand smoke.
- ❑ Reduce your rice consumption from the U.S. South where cotton once grew.
- ❑ Lobby your governmental officials to stop the use of coal-fired power plants due to heavy metal toxicity and carbon dioxide emissions.
- ❑ Avoid living close to mines, smelters and industrial sites.
- ❑ Avoid using pressure-treated lumber that contains arsenic.
- ❑ Avoid the use of glazed pottery that may contain lead and avoid wearing jewelry that may contain lead.
- ❑ Avoid stripping lead-based paints or wear a protective mask and suit.
- ❑ Use protective equipment when making stained glass to prevent lead exposure.
- ❑ Avoid fishing with old, lead-based sinkers.
- ❑ Avoid working on radiator repairs or battery recycling.
- ❑ Replace polyvinyl chloride (PVC) plastic mini-blinds with other window coverings. New mini-blinds are no longer made with lead.

Mercury Accumulation

Once methylmercury is consumed, 90% is absorbed in the digestive tract. The mercury is distributed throughout the body within hours of absorption. On average, it takes 50 days for the body to excrete 50% of the mercury that is consumed.

CHAPTER 4

Mercury

Coal-fired power stations, burning coal for heating in homes, industrial manufacturing processes, waste incinerators and gold mining all contribute to the liberation of mercury into the environment. It is found naturally in several elements on Earth, and it is liberated into the atmosphere from volcanoes and found in geological deposits. Although rocks, sediments and water contain small amounts of mercury, the dominant source of mercury in the environment is release by human activities.

Mercury in the Environment

The burning of fossil fuels for energy or for manufacturing of products is the primary method in which mercury enters into the environment and subsequently into our food chain, particularly in fish, shellfish and seafood that have been contaminated. Mercury that enters the environment becomes methylmercury, which is bioaccumulated in aquatic food chains and found in higher concentrations in larger carnivorous fish. Human exposure therefore occurs mostly from eating contaminated fish from lakes, as well as fish, shellfish and other wildlife from the oceans.

Sources of Exposure

We can be exposed to mercury in various forms under different circumstances, either chronically (regular exposure over long-term contact) or acutely (high levels for a short time). Exposure to even small amounts can bring serious health effects.

Chronic Exposure

High levels of mercury exposure over a long period may result from a reliance on fish for food or occupational exposure. The nervous system is most affected by chronic or acute exposure. Symptoms include tremors, irritability, insomnia, memory loss, headaches, speech difficulty and problems with cognition.

DID YOU KNOW?

Mercury Exposure
Mercury is the third-most-toxic heavy metal noted by the U.S. Agency for Toxic Substances and Disease Registry, behind arsenic and lead. Coal-fired power plants contribute to 50% of the mercury toxicity in the atmosphere. The other 50% of exposure comes from incineration of medical waste, dental amalgam fillings, broken mercury thermometers, batteries in landfills that leach into the waterways and latex paints used before 1990.

Acute Exposure

Neurological problems can occur from acute exposure
to mercury. Tremors, insomnia, memory loss, headaches
and cognitive dysfunction are common. Acute exposure
to inorganic mercury (from old latex paints, pesticides or
disinfectants) by the oral route may result in effects like
nausea, vomiting and severe abdominal pain.

Effects of Mercury
The Developing Fetus

Methylmercury exposure in the womb can result from a
mother's consumption of fish and shellfish while pregnant.
Fetuses and small children are more vulnerable to the
neurotoxic effects of methylmercury and can be 5 to
10 times more sensitive to mercury than an adult. During
fetal development, the combination of a lack of selenium,
a nutrient that protects against mercury toxicity, and the
presence of high levels of mercury leads to inadequate

RESEARCH SPOTLIGHT

Fish Consumption and Methylmercury in Asian Americans

A study published in the *Journal of Occupational and Environmental Medicine* in
2015 aimed to examine the risk of elevated mercury level from fish consumption
by Asians in Chicago. The amount of fish eaten and hair samples were measured.
Of the 71 participants, at least 28% had mercury levels above 1 µg/g and 20%
of participants ate fish four or more times a week. Tuna consumption was
associated with higher mercury levels. This study revealed that Asians who
typically ate more fish than the general U.S. population are at higher risk of
elevated methylmercury.

Mercury in Great Lakes and Commercial Fish

A study published in 2015 by the Wisconsin departments of Health Services
and Natural Resources aimed to assess the risks associated with long-term
fish consumption in male anglers over the age of 50 in that state. Blood and
hair samples were taken and questionnaires completed about the amount of
fish eaten. On average 54.5 fish meals were eaten in a year, and most were
from locally caught fish. Participants had somewhat higher mercury levels
compared with the U.S. general population. Commercial fish consumption was
also associated with both hair and blood mercury. Great Lakes fish were also
associated with higher levels of PCBs.

brain development in the baby. The baby's nervous system can be affected, with impaired neurological development, including attention, language, memory and fine motor skills. Infants born to women who have ingested high levels of methylmercury are at risk of developmental delay or disability, problems with coordination, reduced vision or blindness and cerebral palsy.

Candida Albicans

Candida albicans is a yeast, or fungus, found in the gastrointestinal lining. The lining of the intestines contains a vast amount of probiotics, or beneficial bacteria, as well as yeast. When there is an imbalance of bacteria due to a number of factors, including mercury toxicity, antibiotic use, an imbalance of hormones or an excess of sugar and carbohydrates in the diet, the gut's ecosystem is thrown off balance and the yeast can take over and grow. An imbalance of good bacteria and overgrowth of candida has been linked to allergies, chronic inflammation in the digestive tract and joints, chronic bladder inflammation, brain fog, chronic fatigue and an inability to concentrate.

Mercury toxicity is thought to be a cause of chronic yeast infections and yeast-related illness. It is also believed that yeast grows preferentially when metals are present.

DID YOU KNOW?

Most Vulnerable

Fetuses and small children are more vulnerable to the neurotoxic effects of methylmercury, which people are mainly exposed to from the consumption of contaminated fish. Research shows that the fetus is 5 to 10 times more sensitive to mercury than adults.

In his book *The Yeast Syndrome*, Dr. John Trowbridge specifies that 98% of patients with chronic candida also had mercury toxicity. Detoxifying mercury — and ensuring it is not ingested — is important to deal with the underlying cause of yeast overgrowth in the body. Sometimes, individuals report feeling worse after taking antibiotics or doing a "cleanse" to kill yeast or bacteria in the digestive tract because there is a release of metals from the yeast when it dies.

The following are candida symptoms that mimic mercury toxicity symptoms:

- Inability to focus
- Memory problems
- Brain fog
- Irritability
- Depression
- Fatigue
- Hyperactivity
- Poor coordination

Thyroid Problems

The thyroid gland controls how quickly the body burns energy (metabolism), makes protein and secretes important hormones. There have been inverse associations between mercury and thyroid levels — when mercury levels are high, the circulating thyroid hormones will be low. When mercury accumulates in the thyroid, it reduces iodine uptake by binding to iodine. Iodine is essential for the formation of thyroid hormones. Mercury can also inhibit the ability of the enzyme that draws iodine from the target tissues, which is necessary for the thyroid hormone to work properly.

If mercury blocks either one of these processes, it can bring on symptoms of low thyroid, such as

- Constipation
- Unexplained weight gain or difficulty losing weight
- Depression
- Hair loss
- Dry skin
- Fatigue
- Being more sensitive to cold
- Slow heart rate
- Carpal tunnel syndrome
- Menstrual cycle changes

Tolerable Intakes of Mercury

Allowable limits vary depending on the research and knowledge of the science of the time. In 1972, a provisional tolerable daily intake (PTDI) for methylmercury of 0.47 microgram per kilogram (µg/kg) of body weight a day was established by the Joint FAO/WHO Expert Committee on Food Additives (JECFA) and adopted by Health Canada. JECFA cautioned that pregnant women and nursing mothers were at greater risk, so the provisional tolerable daily intake was lowered to 0.2 µg/kg a day for pregnant women, women of childbearing age and young children. In 2003, Health Canada adopted guidelines that set 0.23 µg/kg a day or 1.6 µg/kg a week as the PTDI for methylmercury. In the U.S., between 0.1 and 0.4 µg/kg a day is recommended for pregnant and childbearing women.

RESEARCH SPOTLIGHT

Mercury in Dental Fillings

A study published in 2014 in the journal *Environmental Health* did a longitudinal analysis of the removal of dental amalgams and improvement of symptoms. The study found that people with such fillings have double the measured urine mercury compared with those who have never had amalgam fillings. Removal of amalgam fillings decreases measured urine mercury to levels found in persons without these fillings. Removal of amalgam fillings had a positive health impact, with symptoms improved in comparison to people who retained their amalgam fillings. Mercury exposure from amalgam fillings could be considered a health risk and the use of safer alternative materials for dental fillings should be encouraged. The study did not discuss risks of removing mercury fillings.

Combined Heavy Metals in Fish and Seafood

Cadmium, lead and mercury levels were investigated in fish and seafood products in Italy as part of a pilot project in 2012 to evaluate food contamination in seafood. It found that the concentrations of mercury in swordfish, Atlantic bluefin tuna and red mullet accounted for 50%, 30% and 30% of the maximum levels of cadmium, lead and mercury, respectively. Cadmium exceeded the maximum levels in squid, red mullet, European hake and Atlantic cod. Squid and blue mussels showed the highest lead concentrations and accounted for 60% and 10% of the maximum levels, respectively.

In another Italian study published in 2015 in *Food Additives & Contaminants*, lead, cadmium and mercury were simultaneously studied in samples of fish and shellfish. Of the 342 samples, the study found higher-than-acceptable limits of lead and cadmium for two samples of bivalve mollusk and higher-than-acceptable levels of mercury in 14 fish samples.

Fish and Mercury

Eating smaller fish to avoid ingesting more mercury from larger ones promotes overfishing of smaller fish in the food web, and that affects the food supply for the bigger fish.

The methylmercury content of large, long-lived fish, such as swordfish, shark, tuna and marlin, is likely higher because they eat smaller fish that have ingested mercury from their food supply. Mercury remains a pollutant of major concern in the Great Lakes region and in fish and shellfish in the oceans. While several websites, such as the Natural Resources Defense Council (www.nrdc.org), the Monterey Bay Aquarium (www.montereybayaquarium.org) and the David Suzuki Foundation (www.davidsuzuki.org), include listings of fish that are ranked from the lowest to highest mercury levels, they fail to provide the whole picture in terms of food webs and ecosystem interactions that occur in the wild. Eating smaller fish to avoid ingesting more mercury from larger ones promotes overfishing of smaller fish in the food web, and that affects the food supply for the bigger fish. The imbalance may lead to the demise of both large and small fish (see chapter 10).

Ocean Ecosystems and Human Health

The oceans can be considered the lungs of the Earth — more so than its forests. At least 50% to 70% of the oxygen we breathe comes from phytoplankton in the oceans, compared to approximately 20% from forests. Phytoplankton are microscopic organisms that use energy from the sun to grow, much like plants do on land. The phytoplankton are regulated in a complex food web with zooplankton (microscopic ocean animals) that feed on phytoplankton, the fishes that feed on zooplankton and fishes that feed on them, all the way up to top predators like sharks, swordfish, salmon and tuna. When one species in the food web is reduced, it causes its prey to increase and that leads to an imbalance that ripples throughout the entire ecosystem (see chapter 10).

Action Plan

- ❑ Avoid consumption of fish, especially if you are a woman of childbearing age — to help prevent bioaccumulation of mercury and its negative health effects, and to help avoid potential harm to underwater ecosystems.

- ❑ Consider removal of dental amalgams, but *only* with a qualified dentist who takes extra precautions, such as removing the particles in the air and using a rubber dam. If you are considering removal, ask your naturopathic doctor about supplementation while getting amalgams removed.

- ❑ Buy rechargeable batteries or batteries that are labeled "mercury free."

- ❑ Use digital or red-line thermometers instead of mercury thermometers.

Excess Iron Stores

It is believed that excess iron contributes to chronic disease by fostering excess production of free radicals. The result is oxidative stress and has been implicated in the development of atherosclerosis, cancer, liver failure and diabetes. Having the highest ferritin levels from eating the more absorbable iron from animal sources is correlated with higher iron stores.

CHAPTER 5

Iron Toxicity

Iron is a necessary element that forms part of the body's red blood cells. It allows the body to pick up oxygen in the lungs and deliver it to the tissues. Like other metals, however, iron can cause oxidative damage to tissues in the same way that water or moisture in the air coming into contact with iron causes rusting. A genetic condition known as genetic hemochromatosis causes the body to absorb too much iron and is cause for concern because it can increase the risk of damage to cells. Even in individuals who don't have the hereditary condition, iron overload in the body, accumulated over years, can lead to damage to their cells. This chapter explores the balance of getting enough iron to prevent anemia but not so much that it leads to chronic conditions like heart disease, cancer and diabetes.

> **DID YOU KNOW?**
>
> **Antioxidant Power**
>
> The antioxidants that are found in colored fruits, in particular purple fruits, help bond to iron, making it less toxic and preventing the oxidation of tissue.

Ferritin Levels
Understanding Ferritin

Ferritin is the protein structure that stores iron in a nontoxic form, protecting the cells from oxidizing. It also acts as a carrier and a buffer to keep iron levels in check. The amount of ferritin in a healthy person reflects the body's total iron stores. Ferritin can be abnormally elevated in a wide range of diseases, such as infection, inflammation, chronic iron overload and cancer, and is thought to be an inflammation marker.

Acceptable Range

The reference range (normal values) for ferritin varies depending on the lab used to analyze the blood work and is generally 10 to 250 ng/mL (U.S. values of nanograms per milliliter) or 22 to 561 pmol/L (Canadian values of picomole per liter). Currently, a wide range of ferritin levels are viewed as acceptable by a lab reference range. Ranges are determined by some labs from sampling the general population, so they sometimes reflect samples from that population and not what is best for optimal health.

FAQ

Q: **What are the optimal ferritin levels to help prevent disease?**

A: A goal in the prevention of diabetes, heart disease and cancer is to maintain an optimal ferritin level. The question of what ferritin levels are optimal, however, is still open to debate. One thing we know from research is that having the highest ferritin levels from eating the more absorbable iron from animal sources is correlated with higher iron stores, heart attack, higher cholesterol levels, elevated blood sugar and cancer risk. Because there is no definite answer with regard to optimal ferritin level, it is best to consider what clinical studies are revealing about the healthier individuals and working with your medical or naturopathic doctor to keep ferritin levels within an optimal range, which will vary depending on energy level, age, pregnancy and gender. In one study, the men who did not get cancer had a ferritin level of 76.4 to 81.4 ng/mL. In another study, of U.S. women, an average ferritin level ranged from 43.3 and 58.93 µg/L. As more studies are published, we will come to a better understanding of ideal, or optimal, levels of ferritin for the population in general.

High Ferritin Levels

A rise in ferritin levels in body stores may be due mainly to an increase in the absorption of dietary iron in the body. This can happen when someone has the genetic condition known as hemochromatosis or from consuming too much iron through meals. When the body has an excess of iron, it will cause oxidative damage and deposits of fibrous tissue in the body, which contribute to inflammation.

The following is a list of diseases that may be correlated to a high ferritin level:

- Amyotrophic lateral sclerosis (ALS, or Lou Gehrig's disease)
- Atherosclerosis
- Cancer
- Cirrhosis of the liver
- Coronary artery disease
- Hypertension
- Lupus
- Metabolic syndrome
- Multiple sclerosis (MS)
- Myocardial infarction (heart attack)
- Non-alcoholic fatty liver disease
- Preeclampsia
- Rheumatoid arthritis
- Stroke
- Type 2 diabetes

Excess Iron

Genetic Hemochromatosis

Hereditary hemochromatosis is a genetic mutation that affects approximately 2% of the North American population and as many as 24% of people in Ireland. Type 1 hemochromatosis, which involves inheritance of genes from both parents, affects approximately 1 in 300 people of Northern European descent in Canada and is one of the most common genetic disorders in the United States. Lab results showing high ferritin is a potential marker for hemochromatosis. There is a correlation between serum ferritin and cellular damage found in cardiovascular disease, cancer and inflammation.

DID YOU KNOW?

Reporting Symptoms
As many as half the people who have genetic hemochromatosis don't have signs or symptoms.

Signs and Symptoms

Early symptoms, such as stiff joints and fatigue, are common and may be mistaken for other, more common conditions. Hereditary hemochromatosis leads to iron affecting the cells of various organs, such as the liver, heart, pancreas and endocrine glands, resulting in cellular toxicity, tissue injury and organ fibrosis.

Iron Chelation

Iron chelation or donating blood can help reduce ferritin levels and improve glucose tolerance in those with metabolic syndrome or type 2 diabetes in those with high ferritin levels or hemochromatosis. Iron chelators such as deferoxamine (Desferal or desferrioxamine), deferiprone and deferasirox are used to bind to iron and prevent it from doing damage to tissue.

Associated Disease

Iron Toxicity and the Liver

Too much iron in the liver causes oxidative damage to the fats in cell membranes. The result can be an enlarged liver, liver failure, liver cancer or cirrhosis, which is a disease of the liver whereby scar tissue blocks the flow of blood and the organ's proper functioning. It is also possible that the liver will experience hemorrhaging, inflammation and scarring as the liver tries to manage the excess iron by storing it.

Iron Toxicity and Cardiovascular Disease

It is thought that excess iron contributes to chronic disease by fostering excess production of free radicals. The result is oxidative stress, and it is a contributor to the development of atherosclerosis, a condition in which plaque deposits line the inner walls of the arteries. Recent studies have shown that iron is deposited in atherosclerotic plaques and bound with a highly oxidized fat and protein. This means that iron, like other metals, can affect the walls of the arteries and lead to plaques that narrows arteries, eventually leading to high blood pressure and blockage of the arteries.

Iron Toxicity and Cancer

Excess iron has been implicated in cancer risk through increased free-radical-mediated oxidative stress. Recent research shows that for each increment of $3\frac{1}{2}$ ounces (100 g) of red meat consumed daily, there is an estimated 29% increased risk of developing colon cancer. When ferritin levels are high, reducing them through blood donation is known to lower the risk of cancer and mortality.

Anemia

Anemia can develop if there is too little iron obtained or absorbed from the diet. Among the symptoms for the condition are tiredness, poor concentration, irritability and shortness of breath on exertion. The Centers for Disease Control and Prevention (CDC) estimate the prevalence of iron deficiency in 1999–2000 was greatest among toddlers aged 1 to 2 years (7%) and females aged 12 to 49 years (9% to 16%). Iron deficiency was approximately two times higher among non-Hispanic black and Mexican-American females (19% to 22%) than among non-Hispanic white females (10%).

In children, anemia can lead to developmental delays and behavioral disturbances, while in pregnant women, iron-deficiency anemia can cause preterm delivery and low birth weight.

Assessing Iron Levels
Anemia

Assessment of anemia is straightforward and is achieved by measuring iron, hemoglobin and ferritin levels in the blood. In a person without an inflammatory process, serum ferritin levels are more or less closely related to body iron liver stores. Measuring ferritin levels in the blood can help determine whether someone is lacking in iron stores. If this number is low, adding more iron through supplementation or diet is beneficial.

Iron Deficiency

While there is a concern about excess iron, having an optimal range of iron in the body is equally important and can be checked by measuring ferritin in the blood. In fact, the CDC claims that iron deficiency is one of the most common known forms of nutritional deficiency among Americans.

A vegetarian needs to consume 1.8 times as much iron as a meat eater does because iron from meat is more bioavailable than iron from plants.

Recommended Dietary Allowances (RDAs) for Iron

Age	Iron Intake
Birth to 6 months	0.27 mg
7–12 months	11 mg
1–3 years	7 mg
4–8 years	10 mg
9–13 years	8 mg
14–18 years males	11 mg
14–18 years females	15 mg
19–50 years males	8 mg
19–50 years females	18 mg
51+ years	8 mg

Source: Adapted from Institute of Medicine. Food and Nutrition Board. Dietary Reference Intakes for Vitamin A, Vitamin K, Arsenic, Boron, Chromium, Copper, Iodine, Iron, Manganese, Molybdenum, Nickel, Silicon, Vanadium, and Zinc: A Report of the Panel on Micronutrients. Washington, DC: National Academy Press, 2001.

Food Sources of Iron

There are some very important reasons to eat a plant-only diet, including your long-term health and that of the environment. Eating plants instead of meat reduces heart disease risk in men by almost 50%. Plant sources of iron include nuts, beans, vegetables and fortified grain products. Vitamin C enhances the bioavailability of vegetarian iron.

Sources of Iron

Food	Per Serving	Percent Daily Value
Breakfast cereals, fortified with 100% of the DV for iron, 1 serving	18 mg	100%
White beans, canned, 1 cup (250 mL)	8 mg	44%
Chocolate, dark, 45% to 69% cacao solids, 3 oz (90 g)	7 mg	39%
Lentils, cooked, ½ cup (125 mL)	3 mg	17%
Spinach, cooked and drained, ½ cup (125 mL)	3 mg	17%
Tofu, firm, ½ cup (125 mL)	3 mg	17%
Kidney beans, canned, ½ cup (125 mL)	2 mg	11%
Chickpeas, cooked, ½ cup (125 mL)	2 mg	11%
Tomatoes, canned stewed, ½ cup (125 mL)	2 mg	11%
Potato, with skin, baked, 1 medium	2 mg	11%
Cashew nuts, oil-roasted, 1 oz (30 g), about 18 nuts	2mg	11%

Source: Adapted from USDA National Nutrient Database for Standard Reference, Release 26, 2013.

Added Benefits of Getting Iron from Plants

Meat and dairy production accounts for greater than 80% of all greenhouse gas emissions from the food sector.

Eating a plant diet is one of the ways to reduce the environmental cost of food on the global ecosystem and attain sustainability. Meat and dairy production accounts for greater than 80% of all greenhouse gas emissions from the food sector. Raising animals for food is less efficient than directly eating plants. It takes approximately 13 pounds (5 kg) of food and 40 times the energy use to make 1 pound (500 g) of beef as compared to plant protein. Climate change prevention, avoiding environmental degradation, preserving natural habitats for other animals, maintaining biodiversity of life on earth and preventing nitrogen and phosphorus runoff into rivers, lakes and oceans are all benefits that come from getting iron from plants or taking supplemental plant-based iron when prescribed by a medical or naturopathic doctor.

FAQ

Q: **How do I know if my stored iron, or ferritin, is too high?**

A: If you don't have an inflammatory disease, getting your ferritin levels checked is a good way to measure the amount of iron stored in the body. This test can help you determine whether you should reduce vitamin C or iron-rich foods that may cause cellular damage or whether you should get chelation therapy to get rid of excess iron. Iron tends to accumulate as people age, and too much dietary iron can be a problem especially for men over 40 and women over 60. Ideally, to prevent the risks of common North American diseases such as heart disease, cancer and diabetes, monitor your ferritin levels with your naturopathic or medical doctor and get informed about optimal ferritin levels to help you make better dietary decisions.

Action Plan

- ☐ Get ferritin levels checked by your family doctor or naturopathic doctor and ask about a preventive optimal range to prevent anemia and chronic diseases.
- ☐ Get iron from plant sources. If you are deficient in iron and eating only plant sources, increase your intake of vitamin C to enhance absorption of plant-based iron.
- ☐ Take iron supplements only under the supervision of a medical or naturopathic doctor.
- ☐ If you are taking iron supplements, take them at least 2 hours before or after ingesting foods or supplements with calcium.
- ☐ Consider being checked for bowel cancer or celiac disease, especially if anemia is not getting better from supplementation.

Detox Solutions

A clean, nutrient-dense diet of organic plant-based foods and some key vitamin and mineral supplements can help the body's detoxification process. Fiber is also crucial, as it binds to toxins within the intestine to ensure elimination from the body and prevent them from entering into the bloodstream. The best long-term solution is to minimize the toxins entering the body.

CHAPTER 6

Detoxifying the Bowel and Liver

Promoting healthy bowels and liver detoxification, together with eliminating exposure to environmental toxins, is the best way to optimize health and vitality.

What Is Detoxification?

Detoxification is a natural function that is accomplished through the bowels, liver and kidney and, to a smaller extent, on the skin through sweating. Depending on the body's exposure to and retention of toxins, or body burden, and the amount of toxins that are absorbed by the body, the natural detoxification process may need some assistance. Nutrients from food or supplements play an important role in the process, together with herbs and fiber from food or supplements.

Detoxification in the liver is a two-stage process that involves modifying the toxin into a water-soluble compound and then excreting it through urine or into the stool via bile. Both phases are designed to modify toxins into more neutral and less damaging compounds. A number of nutritional cofactors help ensure the process works optimally.

Phases of Detoxification

The first phase of detoxification involves taking a toxin and making it more toxic. All toxic compounds, such as those found in cigarette smoke or charbroiled meats, stimulate the first phase of detoxification in the liver, and this results in a more potentially harmful metabolite.

The intermediate metabolites are highly reactive molecules called free radicals, which can increase oxidation and damage liver cells and tissues (free radicals and oxidation are also implicated in the growth of cancer). Fortunately, the body has defense mechanisms to help protect itself from free radicals: those it produces itself and those derived primarily from plant foods (antioxidants).

> **DID YOU KNOW?**
>
> **Adverse Effects of Herbs or Vitamins**
>
> Adverse symptoms such as headaches, irritability, flu-like symptoms or worsening of other symptoms is possible when pushing the body to detoxify too quickly. A supportive treatment plan that includes dietary changes, supplements and herbs can help ensure your body is getting the nutrients it needs to detoxify. Exercise that promotes sweating is additionally beneficial since some toxins are excreted through sweat. A complete treatment plan of diet, vitamins and exercise is best done under the supervision of a naturopathic doctor.

Detoxifying Foods

1. Turmeric promotes bile flow from the gallbladder and assists the body in eliminating toxins.
2. Green tea can help promote detox enzymes during the second phase of detoxification.
3. Artichokes, watercress, cilantro and apples have been found to help the body detoxify.

The second phase of liver detoxification helps make the toxin more water-soluble so it can be excreted. Sulphur-containing cruciferous vegetables, such as broccoli, cabbage, cauliflower, kale, onions and garlic, for instance, help the second phase of liver detoxification.

A Plan for Detoxification

A clean, nutrient-dense diet of organic plant-based foods and some key vitamin and mineral supplements can help the body's detoxification process.

Today, humans are continually bombarded with toxic compounds. There is evidence to suggest that a clean, nutrient-dense diet of organic plant-based foods and some key vitamin and mineral supplements can help the body's detoxification process. Fiber is also important to bind toxins within the intestine to ensure elimination in the stool and prevent them from being uptaken into the intestines and into the bloodstream.

The best long-term solution is to minimize the toxins entering the body and consume a diet high in plant fibers and fluids to promote the bowels to move regularly and eliminate waste. Some vitamins in supplemental doses might also be helpful if the body is lacking them.

An overall healthful diet is the foundation of any detoxification regime. Generally, eating more cruciferous vegetables, eating foods that are high in antioxidants, choosing organic foods, drinking green tea, eating more fiber, sweating through exercise or saunas and reducing consumption of toxins are all beneficial in preventing long-term body burden of toxins and helping the natural detoxification process. Eliminating smoking, second-hand smoke exposure and recreational drug use; reducing refined sugars, saturated fats and trans fats from the diet; removing foods high in pesticides, PCBs and heavy metals from the diet; keeping alcohol consumption to no more than one glass a day for women and two a day for men; and eating a variety of vegetables, fruits, nuts, seeds, beans, whole grains, herbs and spices are all key in assisting daily detoxification. Probiotics are also showing a promising role in helping the body detoxify.

There are several ways to detoxify the body that include elimination of certain foods from the diet and the addition of some supplements. Your naturopathic doctor is the best source of advice on what to purchase and what dietary changes are necessary.

Your naturopathic doctor is the best source of advice on what to purchase and what dietary changes are necessary.

Detox Cautions

There are a number of conditions that are not favorable when pulling toxins out of the body and bringing them into circulation during detoxification:

• During pregnancy or breastfeeding, the toxins can be released into the mother's blood and go to the baby.

• Young children and people taking medication must be monitored carefully or should not detoxify with supplements unless followed by a naturopathic doctor.

• The process may not be feasible for those with impaired nutrition from celiac disease, Crohn's or colitis, in particular if they are experiencing a flare-up.

- People going through a lot of emotional upheaval or extreme stress should not focus on detoxification until they feel well enough mentally to do so.
- Caution is indicated for individuals taking medications, unless supervised by a qualified medical professional. For example, some nutrients, such as N-acetylcysteine, can reduce the circulating levels of drugs.

Bowel Health

The body rids itself of solid waste through the large intestine. When elimination does not occur at least daily, toxins that are stuck in the colon can be reabsorbed into the bloodstream and then need to be detoxified in the liver again. Fiber is an effective way to bulk up the stool, trap toxins and allow the bowels to move more regularly. Regular exercise, drinking enough water and maintaining the right balance of good bacteria (probiotics) in the digestive system help ensure proper functioning of the bowels.

The typical North American gets only about 11 grams of fiber in their daily diet, yet it is recommended that adults get about 30 grams of fiber a day. A diet rich in foods like whole grains, vegetables, fruits, nuts, seeds and legumes ensures an adequate level of fiber. When individuals are not receiving enough fiber from their diet, they may need assistance from fiber supplements and laxative herbs to encourage proper elimination. These products may be used for short periods of time — you should not rely on them over the long term.

Symptoms of Bowel (Large Intestine) Toxicity

- Stiff back
- Frequent yawning
- Thirst
- No taste for food
- Headaches
- Poor digestion
- Heaviness of body
- Constipation
- Mental fatigue
- Acne on chin, jawline and back
- Abdominal bloating
- Hemorrhoids
- Irritability

Fiber Sources

It is recommended for women to consume 21 to 25 grams of fiber a day and men 30 to 38 grams a day. Here are some suggested sources. Note that fiber content can vary among brands.

Food	Serving Size	Total Fiber
Fruits		
Raspberries	1 cup (250 mL)	8.0 g
Pear, with skin	1 medium	5.5 g
Apple, with skin	1 medium	4.4 g
Banana	1 medium	3.1 g
Orange	1 medium	3.1 g
Strawberries (halves)	1 cup (250 mL)	3.0 g
Figs, dried	2 medium	1.6 g
Raisins	1 ounce (30 g), about 60	1.0 g
Grains, Cereal and Pasta		
Oat bran muffin	1 medium	5.2 g
Oatmeal, instant, cooked	1 cup (125 mL)	4.0 g
Brown rice, cooked	1 cup (125 mL)	3.5 g
Legumes, Nuts and Seeds		
Split peas, cooked	1 cup (125 mL)	16.3 g
Lentils, cooked	1 cup (125 mL)	15.6 g
Black beans, cooked	1 cup (125 mL)	15.0 g
Lima beans, cooked	1 cup (125 mL)	13.2 g
Baked beans, vegetarian, canned, cooked	1 cup (125 mL)	10.4 g
Sunflower seed kernels	¼ cup (60 mL)	3.9 g
Vegetables		
Artichoke, cooked	1 medium	10.3 g
Green peas, cooked	1 cup (125 mL)	8.8 g
Broccoli, cooked	1 cup (125 mL)	5.1 g
Turnip greens, cooked	1 cup (125 mL)	5.0 g
Brussels sprouts, cooked	1 cup (125 mL)	4.1 g
Potato, with skin, baked	1 small	3.0 g
Tomato paste	¼ cup (60 mL)	2.7 g
Carrot, raw	1 medium	1.7 g

Source: Adapted from USDA National Nutrient Database for Standard Reference, 2012.

Good Gut Bacteria

Another important aspect of bowel health, in addition to getting enough fiber, is maintaining a balance of good bacteria in the intestines. Probiotics, live bacteria that are good for digestive health, help maintain a healthy colon by reducing other bacteria and yeast that potentially create toxins.

Preliminary studies are also showing the role of probiotic species in helping to detoxify heavy metals. A study published in the *Canadian Journal of Microbiology* in 2006 revealed that specific probiotic bacteria may be able to bind toxins like cadmium and lead from food and water. *Lactobacillus rhamnosus* LC-705 and *Propionibacterium freudenreichii* subsp. *shermanii* JS have been shown to bind to cadmium and lead.

Reducing Allergic Reactions

Gut bacteria, known as intestinal microflora, are an important part of the mucous membrane of the intestinal tract. Probiotics help increase the IgA (immunoglobulin A) immune system reaction as a barrier to unwanted bacteria and reduce the chances of proteins getting past the lining of the intestines into the bloodstream. When proteins from food enter the bloodstream from the intestines, the body has an immune system reaction to the food. This causes inflammation. The food protein then needs to be removed from the body by being broken down and detoxified in the liver.

Beneficial intestinal bacteria have a number of positive health effects, including reducing lactose intolerance and

RESEARCH SPOTLIGHT

Probiotics and Detoxification

A 2006 study revealed that Melanesian horticulturists, who consume a diet rich in fiber and probiotics, show an absence of cancer and cardiovascular disease. The study indicates that four out of five are daily smokers and are exposed to smoke from indoor air pollution from the use of fire to cook meals. Because they preserve their food by fermenting, however, it is speculated that the probiotics in these foods may help increase immune cells called natural killer cells, which help the body defend against cancer and aid the detoxification process of the liver and kidney. More research was recommended to see if the routine use of probiotics could be used to help the body during its natural detoxification process.

making nutrients more available to the body. The probiotic bacteria colonize the intestinal tract and reduce inflammatory response.

Childhood Allergies and Probiotics

Research has shown that allergic children have different bacteria in their intestines than non-allergic children. Allergic children have higher amounts of clostridia and lower levels of bifidobacteria. Non-allergic children have more of the bifidobacteria and lactobacillus species in their intestines. Lactobacillus bacteria are correlated with protection against skin disease, asthma and runny nose. It has also shown to improve allergic runny nose and allergic eczema.

Probiotics in Infants

When babies are born, the immune system is poorly developed, so the time after birth is critical in its development. The function of the gut-mediated immune system cells is assisted by the types of bacteria in the intestines, vitamin A and secretory IgA, an immune system complex that enhances a baby's immune system and is found in the mother's breast milk. Secretory IgA from breast milk has been shown to reinforce the layer of the mucous membrane that lines the intestines. In bottle-fed infants in the Western world, there is a reduction of certain types of good bacteria, such as bifidobacteria, and an increase in pathogenic species like clostridia, which is associated with producing toxins.

In addition, in a study of infants with eczema, adding probiotics (lactobacillus) to their diets reduced inflammation in the lining of their intestinal tract. It was suggested that lactobacillus may be a useful tool in helping alleviate food allergy.

RESEARCH SPOTLIGHT

Allergic Dermatitis and Lactobacillus Probiotics

A preliminary study published in 2015 in *Clinical & Experimental Allergy* examined the role of probiotics in the treatment of an allergic skin condition known as atopic dermatitis. The study used a randomized controlled study of children aged 1 to 18 who had moderate to severe symptoms and gave some groups probiotics *Lactobacillus paracasei* and *Lactobacillus fermentum*. Children who received the probiotics had less severe symptoms, and this continued up to 4 months after discontinuing the probiotics. Researchers concluded that supplementing with probiotics decreased the severity of allergic dermatitis in the children.

Anatomy of the Digestive Tract

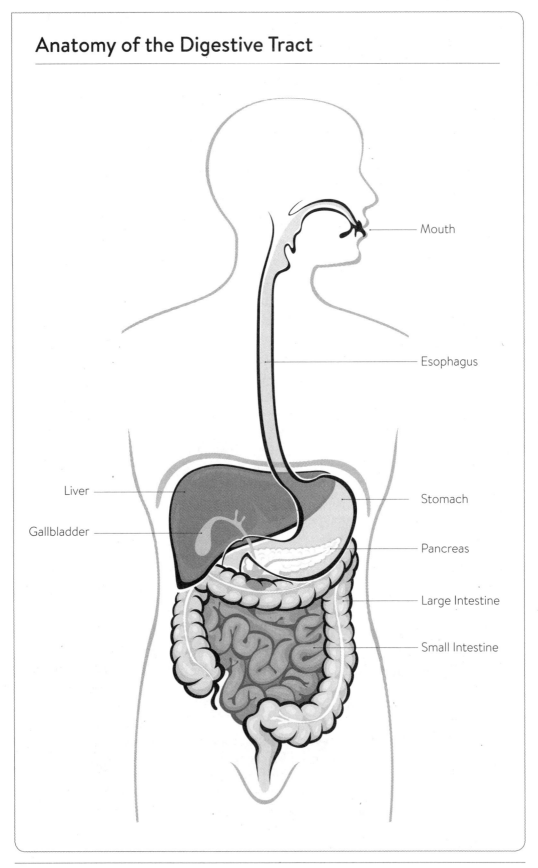

Mouth

Esophagus

Liver

Gallbladder

Stomach

Pancreas

Large Intestine

Small Intestine

Overgrowth of Bacteria or Yeast

When the bacteria in the digestive system are not balanced because of either a hormonal imbalance, use of antibiotics, a lack of lactobacillus bacteria or a high-sugar diet and excess carbohydrates, you may experience symptoms like gas and bloating, constipation or diarrhea. Symptoms like these can spur irritable bowel syndrome.

The digestive tract is one of the primary organs of detoxification. The elimination and barrier function are crucial in preventing the reabsorption of toxins into the bloodstream. When the colon functions normally, detoxification can be enhanced.

Treating Digestive Bacteria

Clinically, it is often a necessary first step to cleanse the colon of unwanted bacteria and boost it with probiotics, such as lactobacillus, while avoiding food sensitivities in order to rebalance the intestines. When the bowels are moving regularly and there is a good amount of probiotics in the intestines, it takes the burden of dealing with toxins off the liver alone.

Foods and food derivatives can also have positive effects. For example, oregano, garlic, caprylic acid and grapefruit seed extract can be used separately or in combination to get rid of unwanted bacteria or yeast in the intestines, together with taking a probiotic supplement such as lactobacillus for good bacteria species. The foods and food derivatives on the following page have been shown to have therapeutic effects in treating gut bacteria.

> When the bowels are moving regularly and there is a good amount of probiotics in the intestines, it takes the burden of dealing with toxins off the liver alone.

Die-Off Reactions

Reduce or stop taking a supplement that kills bacteria or yeast in the digestive tract if you experience headaches, fatigue, brain fog, gas, bloating, skin rash, pain in the muscles or joints, or symptoms similar to flu. These symptoms may be a sign of yeast die-off reactions but can also signify an underlying problem with heavy metal toxicity. Consult with your naturopathic or medical doctor if you experience any adverse reactions to determine the best course of action.

- **Caprylic acid:** Caprylic acid is derived from coconut, among other sources, and has antifungal properties against candida overgrowth by interfering with the organism's cell walls. Caprylic acid is usually taken in a dose of approximately 600 mg twice a day. *Caution:* Pregnant or breastfeeding women, as well as children, should not take caprylic acid.

- **Citricidal (grapefruit seed extract):** Citricidal is a brand-name supplement that contains grapefruit seed extract. Its antibacterial and antiviral properties help rid the body of candida. *Caution:* Citricidal should not be taken with cholesterol-lowering medications, immunosuppressant drugs or antihistamines.

- **Garlic:** Garlic is considered a potent food in the prevention of disease. One to three cloves of fresh or cooked garlic can have a beneficial influence on the bacteria balance in the digestive tract and help reduce the numbers of candida species of yeast, as well as bacteroides and clostridium species. When a disturbance to the gut microflora upsets the balance of bacteria in the digestive tract, such as when you take antibiotics, otherwise harmless bacteria can grow out of control. For instance, the bacterium *Clostridium difficile (C. diff)*, one of the most frequent causes of diarrhea in North America, can grow after taking antibiotics and release toxins that attack the lining of the intestines, causing colitis.

- **Oregano:** Oil of oregano is an antifungal and antibacterial agent. It can help treat parasitic infections such as giardia. It treats overgrowth of bacteria in the digestive tract such as salmonella, *E. coli* and candida species of yeast. Check with your naturopathic doctor before using oil of oregano and follow the dosage instructions carefully on the package of capsules or drops. *Caution:* Do not use oil of oregano if you are pregnant or breastfeeding.

Combination Treatment

Collectively, caprylic acid, Citricidal, oil of oregano and garlic are known as "yeast cleansing," although they will have an effect on bacteria balance in the intestines as well. Part of any detoxification plan involves getting systems, such as the digestive tract, into balance. These products must be taken in low doses at first, in particular if there is a suspicion of heavy metal toxicity in the body based on a history of fish consumption or mercury fillings in the teeth.

Antimicrobial Properties of Garlic Powder

A garlic powder at concentrations of 0.1% and 1% was evaluated to determine its antimicrobial properties to four specific strains of bacteria, including lactobacilli, bacteroides, bifidobacteria and clostridia. In culture, lactobacilli were found to be resistant to the garlic powder. To further test this, a colonic model was used to look at the effects of garlic powder on a mix of bacteria resembling the microbiota of the distal colon. The garlic powder temporarily reduced the bacterial count of most of the bacteria with the exception of lactobacilli, which were largely resistant, suggesting that the consumption of garlic powder may favor this type of bacteria in the digestive tract.

If bacteria and yeast are killed too quickly, there can be a die-off reaction, which liberates mercury into the system. It is not recommended that these products be used during pregnancy or breastfeeding and, if used in children, they should be monitored by a health care provider. Consult your naturopathic doctor about whether targeting bad bacteria and yeast and increasing probiotics is right for you.

Nutrients for Healing the Digestive Tract

The digestive tract of people with gastrointestinal disease, such as celiac disease, Crohn's disease or colitis, may need some assistance in healing. In these situations, there is inflammation and damage to the tissue of the intestinal lining, but with proper therapeutic doses of the following vitamins and nutrients — in addition to removing inflammatory foods that cause food sensitivities, allergies or intolerances and rebalancing intestinal microflora — the intestinal lining has a better opportunity to heal itself.

- **L-glutamine:** An amino acid that the cells of the digestive tract can use as fuel to help repair and maintain the lining of the digestive tract. Glutamine is also used to make glutathione, the master detoxifying antioxidant. Taking supplemental L-glutamine may be beneficial under certain circumstances. Consult with a naturopathic doctor or follow the guidelines on the label. The usual dose is between 500 to 2000 mg a day.

DID YOU KNOW?

Maintain Daily Detoxification

Eating a clean diet of organic fruits, vegetables, seeds and beans and taking a few supplements recommended by your naturopathic doctor to enhance removing toxins out of the body daily can act as prevention. Eating high-fiber foods, drinking adequate fluids and encouraging sweating can also help maintain daily detoxification.

- **Pantothenic acid:** Reduces inflammation in the intestines. In supplement form, pantothenic acid (also known as vitamin B5) is often used in 250 to 500 mg doses.

- **Probiotics:** Active beneficial bacteria that help maintain a balance against harmful yeast and bacteria, aid in the digestion of food and regulate the immune system. In supplement form, you may see them labeled as *Lactobacillus acidophilus*, *Lactobacillus sporogenes* or *Lactobacillus bifidus*. A naturopathic doctor can help you determine which probiotic is right for you. They can be purchased in capsules, powder or liquid and taken as directed. Keep in mind that probiotics (live bacteria) are encouraged to grow in a healthy body that is given foods containing fiber. Rely on plant-based diets for added fiber to maintain good bacteria in the intestinal tract and overall good health.

- **Quercetin:** An anti-allergic bioflavonoid that helps reduce food sensitivity reactions by reducing the amount of histamine released by immune cells. By doing so, quercetin reduces inflammation, allowing the intestines to heal. Generally, people need from 1 to 3 capsules of 500 mg a day. *Caution:* Quercetin may cause nausea, headache or tingling of the extremities in doses above 1000 mg a day.

- **Selenium:** A mineral that the body needs to make glutathione, an antioxidant referred to as the master detoxifier. As an antioxidant, glutathione also helps protect the intestines against free-radical damage. A typical dose is 200 µg (micrograms) a day.

- **Vitamin A:** Commonly known as the anti-infective vitamin. This vitamin plays an essential role in vision, wound healing and cell division and differentiation. It is also needed to lengthen and strengthen the walls of the intestinal tract. There is some evidence that vitamin A and breastfeeding can protect against the development of harmful responses to dietary proteins in babies. When nutrient-deficient infants are given vitamin A, some studies show an improvement in gut integrity. *Caution:* Vitamin A is not to be taken above 10,000 IU in pregnancy. Excess vitamin A is stored in the liver, where it can become toxic in high doses. Consult with your naturopathic doctor about the proper dosage, which varies from person to person.

- **Zinc:** A nutrient that helps heal the skin and membranes in the oral, nasal and digestive tract. To increase zinc to a good level, supplementation may be required for up to a few months at a dosage of 30 to 60 mg a day. If you experience nausea or vomiting when taking zinc, reduce the dose and make sure you take zinc with food.

Herbs for Healing the Digestive Tract

- **DGL (deglycyrrhizinated licorice):** Soothes inflamed mucous membranes and is used to help heal stomach and duodenal ulcers, Crohn's disease, celiac disease, colitis, stomach ulcers, stomach inflammation. DGL is typically found in 500 mg capsules and, depending on the level of severity of the condition, it may be necessary to take between 1 and 3 DGL capsules a day.

- **Marshmallow root:** An anti-inflammatory herb for stomach and intestines. It coats the mucous membranes and is useful in treating diarrhea, stomach ulcers, constipation and inflammation of the lining of the stomach. Follow package directions for dosing.

- **Slippery elm:** Soothes the mucous membranes of the stomach and intestines. Slippery elm can help relieve inflammation in the bowels and increase mucus production to protect the stomach against ulcer formation. Useful for gastritis, reflux, colitis, diverticulitis, diarrhea and irritable bowel syndrome. Capsules of 400 to 500 mg each should be taken with a full glass of water three to four times daily. It is recommended to take slippery elm 2 hours before taking any other herbs and medications. *Caution:* Do not take slippery elm when pregnant or breastfeeding unless you consult with your health care provider first.

> Slippery elm can help relieve inflammation in the bowels and increase mucus production to protect the stomach against ulcer formation.

- **Aloe vera gel:** Jelly-like substance found in the leaves of the aloe vera plant. Aloe is soothing and healing to the mucous membranes, in particular those with ulcerative colitis and stomach ulcers. Typical dosage is 1 to 3 tbsp (15 to 45 mL) a day. *Caution:* Avoid taking aloe by mouth if you are having surgery within 2 weeks. Aloe may decrease blood sugar, so it should be used with caution if you have diabetes.

Laxatives

Laxative Herbs

Laxative herbs must only be taken as needed. They are meant to be used occasionally for constipation, when there is no bowel movement at least every day or every other day. These herbs stimulate the bowels to move and should not be taken if you have diarrhea. Individuals who rely on laxatives could have a nutritional deficiency, an imbalance of good bacteria in the intestines, not enough fiber or water, food sensitivities or possibly even colon cancer. Colon cancer may manifest as chronic constipation or diarrhea, or it can be found when reporting any change in bowel habits to your medical doctor. Follow the recommended dosage of laxative herbs, since too much may cause diarrhea and too little won't work. If constipation persists, consult your family physician because it can be a sign of a more serious problem.

- **Senna:** Tones the gastrointestinal tract and increases the function of elimination. Senna is a stimulating laxative, which works to stimulate the lining of the intestine to accelerate the passage of stool through the colon. For that reason, senna should not be taken for more than 7 days unless directed by your health care physician. It may take 6 to 12 hours before senna works for constipation. Take as directed.

Laxative Vitamins and Minerals

- **Vitamin C:** Stimulates the bowels when taken in high doses. Taking 1000 mg and increasing it until you get loose stools and then taking 1000 mg less the next day is the way to tell how much vitamin C your bowels will tolerate. Although this is a nutritional way to make the bowels move, it is usually better to take magnesium instead to help the bowels move.

Magnesium Toxicity

It is rare to experience toxicity symptoms from taking magnesium, unless you have kidney disease. The symptoms of taking too much magnesium and a possible overdose include:

- Cardiac arrest
- Irregular heartbeat
- Lethargy
- Low blood pressure
- Muscle weakness
- Nausea and vomiting
- Respiratory distress
- Urine retention

- **Magnesium:** Helps the bowels move when taken in low supplemental doses. Magnesium taken in high doses can cause loose stools or diarrhea. Daily recommended intakes of magnesium from either food or supplements is about 300 mg a day for an adult for optimal health. More may be taken to stimulate the bowels only under the direction of a naturopathic doctor. *Caution:* Magnesium may not be safe for people taking diuretics, heart medication or antibiotics. Consult your medical doctor, pharmacist or naturopathic doctor. People with diabetes, kidney disease, heart disease or intestinal disease should also speak with their health care practitioner before starting to take supplemental magnesium, as it may pose a risk to their health.

Liver Detoxification

The liver is the primary source of detoxification for all toxins that are produced by the body and outside the body. There are two phases of liver detoxification. The first phase involves taking toxins and making them fat-soluble. This process makes substances more toxic to the body. The second phase aims at making toxins less toxic and water-soluble so that they can be removed through the urine, bile or stool. Several key nutrients are involved in the phases of detoxification — without them, the detoxification process will not work and can lead to liver toxicity.

DID YOU KNOW?

Weight Loss and Detoxification

Because certain toxins get stored in fat cells, it is important that you take the proper supplements to ensure the liver can get rid of these toxins while you're on a weight-loss diet.

Magnesium Content in Food

Food	Serving Size	Magnesium
Vegetables and Fruits		
Prickly pear	1 fruit	88 mg
Spinach, cooked	½ cup (125 mL)	83 mg
Swiss chard, cooked	½ cup (125 mL)	80 mg
Tamarind pulp	½ cup (125 mL)	58 mg
Edamame/baby soy beans, cooked	½ cup (125 mL)	52 mg
Potato, with skin, cooked	1 medium	47–52 mg
Okra, cooked	½ cup (125 mL)	50 mg
Grain Products		
Quinoa, cooked	½ cup (125 mL)	47 mg
Legumes (Dried Beans, Peas and Lentils)		
Peas, black-eyed peas/cowpeas, cooked	¾ cup (175 mL)	121 mg
Tempeh/fermented soy product, cooked	5 oz (150 g)	116 mg
Soybeans, mature, cooked	¾ cup (175 mL)	109 mg
Beans (black, lima, navy, adzuki, white kidney, pinto, great northern, cranberry, chickpeas), cooked	¾ cup (175 mL)	60–89 mg
Tofu, prepared with magnesium chloride or calcium sulfate	5 oz (150 g)	45–80 mg
Baked beans, with pork, canned	¾ cup (175 mL)	64 mg
Lentils, split peas, cooked	¾ cup (175 mL)	52 mg
Nuts and Seeds		
Pumpkin or squash seeds, shelled	¼ cup (60 mL)	317 mg
Sunflower seed butter	2 tbsp (30 mL)	120 mg
Sunflower seeds, shelled	¼ cup (60 mL)	119 mg

Source: Adapted from Dietitians of Canada. 2014. Food Sources of Magnesium, www.dietitians.ca/Your-Health/Nutrition-A-Z/Minerals/Food-Sources-of-Magnesium.aspx.

Signs and Symptoms of Liver Toxicity

- Acne, skin rashes, eczema, psoriasis
- Chronic headaches
- Chronically tight trapezius muscles
- Cirrhosis of the liver
- Constipation
- Depression
- Fatty liver
- Feeling sick
- Feeling sick around fumes
- General moodiness
- High cholesterol/high triglycerides
- Joint pains
- Menstrual migraines
- Migraines
- Pimples on shoulders and back
- PMS
- Prone to headaches
- Spells of low energy

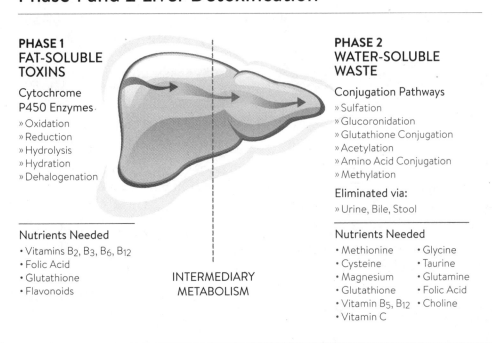

Phase 1 and 2 Liver Detoxification

PHASE 1
FAT-SOLUBLE
TOXINS

Cytochrome
P450 Enzymes
» Oxidation
» Reduction
» Hydrolysis
» Hydration
» Dehalogenation

Nutrients Needed
• Vitamins B_2, B_3, B_6, B_{12}
• Folic Acid
• Glutathione
• Flavonoids

INTERMEDIARY
METABOLISM

PHASE 2
WATER-SOLUBLE
WASTE

Conjugation Pathways
» Sulfation
» Glucoronidation
» Glutathione Conjugation
» Acetylation
» Amino Acid Conjugation
» Methylation

Eliminated via:
» Urine, Bile, Stool

Nutrients Needed
• Methionine • Glycine
• Cysteine • Taurine
• Magnesium • Glutamine
• Glutathione • Folic Acid
• Vitamin B_5, B_{12} • Choline
• Vitamin C

Nutrients for Liver Detoxification

Nutrients like whole foods are necessary for the first phase of liver detoxification. During this phase, toxins in the body are converted into an intermediate metabolite before the second phase of liver detoxification can take place. The intermediate phase is more toxic than when the detoxification process started — toxins must undergo the second phase before they are rendered harmless and eliminated through the kidneys or the gallbladder into the small intestine and finally eliminated through the bowels. Phase 2 requires some of the same vitamins and nutrients as Phase 1 of liver detoxification, as well as additional nutrients to complete the liver detoxification process.

Nutrients may be needed in higher doses than the amounts found in foods when the body is overwhelmed with toxins, such as PCBs, dioxins, pesticides, hormones and heavy metals. If you are planning to take supplements, check with your naturopathic doctor first because dosing varies from person to person. The most common supplementation series used to help detoxify the body includes the following: chlorella, spirulina, cilantro, B_6, B_5, choline, N-acetylcysteine, B_{12}, folic acid and flavonoids such as quercetin.

DID YOU KNOW?

Vitamins for the Liver

Identifying which nutrients are needed and how to get them from foods and supplements is a key step in aiding the detoxification process. The liver needs vitamins such as zinc, B_6, B_5, B_3, folic acid, plant pigments, magnesium, B_{12} and choline to help it function effectively.

Liver-Cleansing Foods

Several nutrient-boosting foods are known to naturally help cleanse the liver because they assist the body through either Phase 1 or Phase 2 of a liver detoxification program.

- **Apples** promote detoxification because of their high fiber content and powerful antioxidants known as flavonoids. Apples help stimulate bile production and are needed for Phase 1 of liver detoxification. Buy only organic apples to limit exposure to pesticides.

- **Artichokes** contain phytonutrients known as cynarin and silymarin that aid the liver in producing bile and protecting and regenerating liver cells.

- **Asparagus** contains plant pigments known as flavonoids, including kaempferol, quercetin and rutin, which are necessary for Phase 1 of liver detoxification.

- **Beets** are high in plant flavonoids that help the first phase of liver detoxification.

- **Broccoli**, **cabbage** and **Brussels sprouts**, also known as cruciferous vegetables, contain sulfur-based substances, such as sulforaphanes, indole-3-carbinol and calcium-D-glucarate, that help stimulate the production of enzymes that detoxify cancer-causing toxins in the body. When broccoli is sprouted, it offers more benefit — up to 20 times more sulforaphane than broccoli florets.

- **Carrots** are high in plant flavonoids, which aid the first phase of liver detoxification.

- **Garlic** is useful for its sulfur content, which stimulates the liver to produce glutathione, an antioxidant that prevents damage to certain cellular components caused by heavy metals and free radicals, among other factors.

- **Green tea** contains catechins, antioxidant flavonoids that are between 25 and 100 times more potent than vitamin C and aid in the first phase of liver detoxification. Its antioxidant property makes it useful for protecting the body from oxidative damage.

- **Lemons** contain vitamin C, which helps stimulate both phases of liver detoxification by aiding in the production of glutathione. Vitamin C is also useful for making bile the right consistency during production as it flows from the gallbladder to aid fat digestion. A common naturopathic prescription is to squeeze the juice of half a lemon in a cup of hot water first thing in the morning to stimulate bile flow and aid detoxification.

- **Seaweed**, such as nori or kelp, contains sodium alginate, which can help remove heavy metals from the digestive tract.

- **Spinach** contains large amounts of chlorophyll, a green plant pigment that converts the sun's rays into plant energy, a process known as photosynthesis. Chlorophyll helps eliminate environmental toxins and metals by binding with them to prevent absorption in the digestive tract.

> Chlorophyll helps eliminate environmental toxins and metals by binding with them to prevent absorption in the digestive tract.

Liver Detoxification: Phase 1 Nutrient Sources

Vitamin B2

Uses: B2 is essential for liver detoxification and metabolism of proteins and carbohydrates. It is essential for growth of skin, nails and hair.

Found in: Almonds, mushrooms, sesame seeds, sunflower seeds, leafy green vegetables, cabbage, avocados.

Therapeutic dose: 50–100 mg/day.

Food Sources of Vitamin B2	
Food	mg per 100 g
Almonds	1.10
Mushrooms	0.49
Sesame seeds	0.47
Sunflower seeds	0.36
Spinach	0.24
Cabbage	0.25
Avocados	0.14

Source: Adapted from Whitbread, D. 2015. Top 10 Foods Highest in Vitamin B2 (Riboflavin), www.healthaliciousness.com/articles/foods-high-in-riboflavin-vitamin-B2.php.

Vitamin B3

Uses: B3 is essential for liver detoxification, circulation, regulating the nervous system, breaking down estrogen, aiding in the formation of adrenal hormones and reducing cholesterol levels.

Found in: Nuts, sunflower seeds, brown rice, bran, yeast extract, hemp seeds, potatoes, almonds.

Therapeutic dose: 50–100 mg/day.

Caution: If doses exceed 50 mg per day, a niacin flush may occur, where the blood vessels dilate on the surface of the skin and cause a flushing reaction.

Food Sources of Vitamin B3

Food	µg per 100 g
Sunflower seeds	8.3
Portobello mushrooms	6.3
Fresh green peas	2.1
Baked potato	2.1
Sweet potato	5.1

Source: Adapted from Whitbread, D. 2015. Top 10 Foods Highest in Vitamin B3 (Niacin), www.healthaliciousness.com/articles/foods-high-in-niacin-vitamin-B3.php; Diet & Fitness Today. 2016. Niacin Content in Baked Potato, www.dietandfitnesstoday.com/niacin-in-baked-potato.php; Diet & Fitness Today. 2016. Niacin Content in Sweet Potato, www.dietandfitnesstoday.com/niacin-in-sweet-potato.php.

Vitamin B6

Uses: B6 is essential for liver detoxification; regulation of hormones and mood; metabolism of fats, carbohydrates and proteins; regulation of swelling; metabolism of essential fatty acids; and the production of hydrochloric acid for digestion. Vitamin B6 is effective in reducing accumulation of lead in tissue, to chelate lead before it is absorbed.

Found in: Brown rice, sunflower seeds, pistachios, prunes, bananas, cabbage, potatoes, leafy green vegetables, avocados, carrots.

Therapeutic dose: 50–100 mg/day.

Caution: Side effects such as numbness and tingling in the fingers and toes can occur with doses that exceed 50 mg and will reverse when the vitamin is stopped.

Food Sources of Vitamin B6

Food	mg per 100 g
Brown rice	4.1
Sunflower seeds	1.4
Pistachios	1.1
Prunes	0.8
Potatoes, with skin	0.6
Bananas	0.4
Avocados	0.3
Cabbage	0.3
Potatoes, peeled	0.3
Carrots	0.2
Spinach	0.2

Source: Adapted from Whitbread, D. 2015. Top 10 Foods Highest in Vitamin B6, www.healthaliciousness.com/articles/foods-high-in-vitamin-B6.php.

Vitamin B$_{12}$

Uses: B$_{12}$ is essential for growth, red blood cell formation, energy, memory, production of DNA and RNA (a nucleic acid that acts as a messenger carrying instructions from DNA that control the synthesis of proteins), conversion of beta-carotene to vitamin A and longevity.

Found in: Animal protein; vegans are deficient and need to supplement the diet with vitamin B$_{12}$.

Therapeutic dose: 500–2000 µg/day.

Caution: If you are following the diet in this book for the long term, it is essential to take B$_{12}$ supplements. Ask your naturopathic doctor how much is ideal for you.

Folic Acid

Uses: Folic acid, which is recommended to be taken before pregnancy, is essential in the prevention of neural tube defects during pregnancy. It is also essential for red blood cell formation and the production of RNA, which is one type of nucleic acid and acts as a messenger carrying instructions from DNA that control the synthesis of proteins. Folic acid is also needed for proper formation and repair of DNA, a carrier of genetic information.

Found in: Legumes, green leafy vegetables, asparagus, broccoli, avocados, Brussels sprouts, dates.

Food Sources of Folic Acid	
Food	µg per 100 g
Black-eyed peas	208
Spinach, raw	194
Lentils	181
Asparagus	149
Lettuce	149
Broccoli	108
Avocados	80
Mangos	43

Source: Adapted from Whitbread, D. 2015. Top 10 Foods Highest in Vitamin B$_9$ (Folate), www.healthaliciousness.com/articles/foods-high-in-folate-vitamin-B9.php.

Glutathione

Uses: Glutathione is an essential antioxidant for liver detoxification and white blood cell formation.

Found in: Protein-rich foods containing cysteine, glutamic acid and glycine. Sulfur-rich foods, such as garlic, onions and cruciferous vegetables like broccoli, kale, collards, cabbage, cauliflower and watercress, help the body make glutathione. Cysteine-rich foods include oatmeal, sesame seeds and spirulina. Glutamic acid is high in soy and sesame seeds. Sources of glycine, an amino acid found in protein, include beans, soybeans, spinach, pumpkin, kale, cabbage, cauliflower, cucumbers, kiwi and bananas. Magnesium and zinc are necessary to make glutathione. Selenium, alpha-lipoic acid and the herb milk thistle enhance the manufacture of glutathione by the body.

Flavonoids

Uses: Flavonoids are a diverse group of plant chemicals (phytochemicals) that are found in many fruits and vegetables. They serve as an antioxidant to slow cancer growth and strengthen capillary walls.

Found in: Tea, wine and pigmented fruits, such as cherries, grapefruit, apple skins, blueberries, grapes, bell peppers and black currants.

Polyphenols

Many of the health-promoting properties attributed to plant foods are due to the presence of polyphenols. Unlike vitamins and minerals, which are considered essential nutrients, polyphenols are not required for life but rather make the difference between surviving and thriving.

Anthocyanins and Proanthocyanidins

Anthocyanins and proanthocyanidins are a subcategory of polyphenols. Their chemical structure imparts a red to blue-purple color and foods rich in these compounds, such as currants and red, blue and purple berries including bilberry, red and purple grapes, red wine and plums and prunes, are widely recognized for their healthy properties. These unique antioxidants have been shown to improve blood pressure and blood vessel and eye health.

Flavones, Flavonols and Flavanones

Flavonoids are a subgroup of polyphenols, including flavones, flavonols and flavanones, and can be found in foods such as tea, chocolate, grapes, berries, citrus, parsley, thyme and apples. These flavonoid antioxidants are associated with lower rates of chronic disease, such as cardiovascular, including stroke and dementia.

Polyphenol Content of Selected Foods

The figures in this chart are given in mg per 3½ ounces (100 g) fresh weight or 3½ fluid ounces (100 mL) for liquids.

Food	Antho-cyanins	Proantho-cyanidins	Flavones	Flavonols	Flava-nones
Anthocyanin-Rich Foods					
Blackberries	89–211	6–47	-	0–2	-
Blood orange juice	3–10	-	-	0–2	10–2
Blueberries	67–183	88–261	-	2–16	-
Grapes, red	25–92	44–76	-	3–4	-
Plums	2–25	106–334	-	1–2	-
Raspberries, red	10–84	5–59	-	1	-
Red cabbage	25	-	0–1	0–1	-
Red onions	13–25	-	-	4–100	-
Red wine	1–35	24–70	-	2–30	-
Strawberries	15–75	97–183	-	1–4	-
Flavone-Rich Foods					
Celery	-	-	0–15	4	-
Celery hearts, green	-	-	23	-	-
Chile peppers, green	-	-	5	13–21	-
Oregano, fresh	-	-	2–7	-	-
Parsley, fresh	-	-	24–634	8–10	-
Thyme, fresh	-	-	56	-	-
Flavonol-Rich Foods					
Apple, Red Delicious, with peel	1–4	89–148	-	2–6	-
Apricots	-	8–13	-	2–5	-
Black tea	-	4	-	1–7	-
Broccoli	-	-	-	4–13	-
Chocolate, dark	-	90–322	-	-	-
Green tea	-	-	0–1	3–9	-
Kale	-	-	-	30–60	-
Leek	-	-	-	3–22	-
Onions, yellow	-	-	-	3–120	-
Flavanone-Rich Foods					
Grapefruit, fresh	-	-	-	1	55
Grapefruit juice, fresh	-	-	-	-	10–104
Lemon juice, fresh	-	-	-	0–2	2–175
Orange, fresh	-	-	-	-	42–53
Orange juice, fresh	-	-	0–1	-	5–47

Source: Adapted from Flavonoids. Linus Pauling Institute of Micronutrients, http://lpi.oregonstate.edu/mic/dietary-factors/phytochemicals/flavonoids.

Liver Detoxification: Phase 2 Nutrient Sources

Methionine

Uses: Methionine is essential for healing wounds and treating depression, allergies and asthma.

Found in: Spirulina, Brazil nuts, soybeans.

Food Sources of Methionine	
Food	mg per 100 g
Spirulina	1.1
Brazil nuts	1.0
Dried dulse	0.9
Pumpkin seeds	0.6
Sesame seeds	0.6
Flax seeds	0.5
Soybeans	0.5
Oats	0.3

Source: Adapted from Methionine: Richest Foods for Vegans (per 100 g), http://methionine.rich-vegan-foods.com/100g.html.

Cysteine

Uses: Cysteine is a building block of proteins. When taken as a supplement, it is usually in the form of N-acetyl-L-cysteine (NAC). The body takes NAC and converts it into cysteine and then into glutathione, which is useful as an antioxidant and in liver detoxification.

Magnesium

Uses: Magnesium is essential for muscle and nerves, as well as bone and teeth formation. It also regulates heart rhythm.

Found in: Dark green leafy vegetables, seaweed, nuts, seeds, dried fruit such as figs, potatoes, brown rice, apples, avocados, bananas, lima beans.

Food Sources of Magnesium	
Food	mg per 100 g
Pumpkin seeds	534
Dark chocolate	327
Soybeans	86
Dark green leafy vegetables	79
Brown rice	44

Food Sources of Magnesium	
Food	mg per 100 g
Avocados	29
Bananas	27
Dried figs	28

Source: Adapted from Whitbread, D. 2015. Top 10 High Magnesium Foods You Can't Miss, www.healthaliciousness.com/articles/foods-high-in-magnesium.php.

Vitamin B5 (Pantothenic Acid)

Uses: Vitamin B5, also known as pantothenic acid, reduces inflammation in the body, acts as an anti-allergy agent, increases adrenal hormone production and regulates metabolism of fats, proteins and carbohydrates.

Found in: Sunflower seeds, mushrooms, avocados, sweet potatoes.

Therapeutic dose: 250–500 mg/day.

Food Sources of Vitamin B5	
Food	mg per 100 g
Sunflower seeds	7.06
Shiitake mushrooms	3.59
Avocados	1.46
Sweet potatoes	0.88

Source: Adapted from Whitbread, D. 2015. Top 10 Foods Highest in Vitamin B5 (Pantothenic Acid), www.healthaliciousness.com/articles/foods-high-in-pantothenic-acid-vitamin-B5.php.

Vitamin B12

See page 92.

Vitamin C

Uses: Vitamin C is a powerful antioxidant and aids in the absorption of vegetable sources of iron. The body uses it to help maintain healthy skin, cartilage, bones and teeth and to heal wounds and repair blood vessels.

Found in: Guava, yellow and red bell peppers, kale, kiwifruit, broccoli, papaya, peas, strawberries, oranges, cooked tomatoes.

Therapeutic dose (for an adult): 75–120 mg/day.

Caution: Diarrhea or stomach upset can occur at doses larger than 2,000 mg/day.

Food Sources of Vitamin C

Food	mg per 100 g
Guava	228.3
Yellow and red bell peppers	183.5
Kale	120.0
Kiwifruit	92.7
Broccoli	89.2
Papaya	60.9
Peas	60.0
Strawberries	58.8
Oranges	53.2
Cooked tomatoes	22.8

Source: Adapted from Whitbread, D. 2016. Top 10 Foods Highest in Vitamin C, www.healthaliciousness.com/articles/vitamin-C.php.

Glycine

Uses: Glycine is effective in helping to produce human growth hormone, maintain the health of the digestive tract and nervous system, and treat diabetes, chronic fatigue, schizophrenia, stroke and benign prostatic hyperplasia (BPH, or enlarged prostate).

Found in: Soy, spirulina, pumpkin seeds, sesame seeds.

Food Sources of Glycine

Food	mg per 100 g
Soy protein isolate	3.6
Spirulina	3.0
Pumpkin seeds	2.4
Sesame seed flour	2.1
Soybeans	1.88

Source: Adapted from FoodInfo.us. 2016. Best Sources of Glycine, http://foodinfo.us/SourcesUnabridged.aspx?Nutr_No=516.

Taurine

Uses: Taurine is used in the treatment of high blood pressure, high cholesterol, autism, attention deficit/hyperactivity disorder (ADHD), diabetes and alcoholism. Taurine has been shown in studies to lower cadmium levels.

Found in: Manufactured in the body from the amino acid cysteine, vitamin B_6, vitamin A and the amino acid methionine. Methionine is found in sesame seeds and Brazil nuts.

Therapeutic dose: 500–2000 mg/day.

Glutamine

Uses: Glutamine is effective in healing the digestive tract; treating depression, moodiness, irritability, anxiety, ADHD and insomnia; and enhancing exercise performance. Glutamine is important for removing excess ammonia from the body.

Found in: Vegetables such as spinach, cabbage, parley, peas and beets — best consumed raw because glutamine breaks down under high heat.

Therapeutic dose: 500–1500 mg/day.

Folic Acid

See page 92.

Choline

Uses: Choline is effective in the treatment of depression, memory loss, Alzheimer's disease, dementia and seizures and in lowering cholesterol. Choline, together with B_6, B_{12} and folic acid, are responsible for the conversion of homocysteine to cysteine, a protein that plays several important roles in the body.

Found in: Soy lecithin, nuts, beans, peas, spinach.

Therapeutic dose: 100–3000 mg/day.

Other Important Detoxification Nutrients

A number of antioxidants and minerals have been shown to be effective at preventing or treating heavy metal toxicity by limiting oxidative stress or binding to heavy metals. Some herbs, algae and minerals also protect the body from oxidative stress or help the liver function to rid the body of these metals. Here are several to consider.

Alpha-lipoic Acid

Uses: Alpha-lipoic acid (ALA) is an effective antioxidant and detoxification molecule that is both fat- and water-soluble. It helps improve insulin sensitivity and treat pain associated with nerve damage in diabetics. Alpha-lipoic acid can pass into the brain, and it may be protective against free-radical damage in the brain. Studies show that alpha-lipoic acid can bind with mercury, arsenic and iron. Using supplemental alpha-lipoic acid and NAC in combination is the most effective way to prevent oxidative damage to cells by lowering cadmium levels in the body.

Found in: Broccoli, spinach, brewer's yeast, Brussels sprouts, peas, tomatoes, soybeans, sunflower seeds, oats, split peas, quinoa.

Therapeutic dose (for an adult): As an antioxidant, it can be taken in supplemental form at 50–100 mg/day. To help diabetes and nerve pain from diabetes, a time-released dose of between 600–800 mg/day is recommended.

Caution: Do not take alpha-lipoic acid if pregnant or breastfeeding. May cause skin rash, diarrhea or insomnia. Alpha-lipoic acid can lower blood sugar levels, so it should be taken under the supervision of your health care provider. It may interfere with chemotherapy drugs and lower levels of thyroid hormone.

> Alpha-lipoic acid can lower blood sugar levels, so it should be taken under the supervision of your health care provider.

Food Sources of Alpha-lipoic Acid	
Food	mg per gram of dry weight
Spinach	3.2
Broccoli	0.9
Tomato	0.6
Peas	0.4
Brussels sprouts	0.4

Source: Adapted from Hajoway, M. 2006. Alpha Lipoic Acid: A True Anti-Oxidant! http://www.bodybuilding.com/fun/ala2.htm.

Chlorella Vulgaris

Uses: Chlorella is a freshwater algae grown in Japan and Taiwan. It has a wealth of nutrients that make it a potentially potent food source against disease. It has demonstrated significant protective effects against cellular damage and oxidative stress. Chlorella can contain as much as 45% omega-3 essential fatty acids. It also contains polysaccharides, such as N-acetylglucosamine, N-acetyl-galactosamine, rhamnose, mannose and arabinose, which have immuno-stimulating properties against bacteria such as listeria and candida. Chlorella also contains beta 1,3 glucan, which stimulates the immune system, scavenges free radicals and reduces blood cholesterol. This type of microalgae is also known to contain vitamins A, B_1, B_2, B_6, B_{12}, C, E, biotin, folate and pantothenic acid (vitamin B_5), as well as providing a good source of chlorophyll. It has been used to stimulate the immune system, protect the body against heavy metals and help prevent cancer, in particular colon cancer. It must be broken down and purchased as "cracked" chlorella for it to be digestible.

Therapeutic dose (for an adult): It is best to start with a lower dose and work up to a higher dose because chlorella is effective at detoxifying mercury. Tablets are generally sold in 500 mg doses and it is recommended to work up to 4 g/day.

Caution: Some people experience nausea, so chlorella is best taken with food. Mild diarrhea can occur. Chlorella should be purchased as cracked chlorella to ensure it can be readily used by the body.

Selenium

Uses: As an antioxidant, selenium works with vitamin E to protect cell membranes from oxidative damage. In the liver cells, these nutrients are involved in making proteins that help build blood cells. Selenium and vitamin E also help make immune cells. Selenium is necessary for proper functioning of the thyroid gland. A deficiency in the antioxidant can lead to pain in muscles and joints and symptoms of low thyroid function such as tiredness, weight gain and an inability to lose weight.

Found in: Brazil nuts, sunflower seeds.

Therapeutic dose (for an adult): 200 µg/day.

> Selenium is necessary for proper functioning of the thyroid gland.

FAQ

Q: What evidence are we seeing that selenium can help detoxify the body of heavy metals?

A: Recent research has shown the benefits of preventive selenium-enriched diets to prevent mercury toxicity, among others. Toxicity in the brain, nervous system and hormonal systems can be reversed with supplemental selenium. Preventively, selenium found in lentils has been shown to mitigate arsenic toxicity in laboratory mammals. Selenium is also protective against cadmium and lead toxicity — it protects the brain, lungs, liver, kidneys and blood. It is thought that selenium binds to or forms complexes with heavy metals to enhance detoxification.

Emerging evidence also shows a possible protection against aluminum toxicity. Aluminum, which is found in many manufactured foods and medicines and added to drinking water for purification purposes, can be toxic to the nerve cells. In a study on rats, when aluminum was given together with vitamin E or selenium, these nutrients alleviated the toxic effects of aluminum.

Food Sources of Selenium

Food	µg per 100 g
Brazil nuts	1917.0
Sunflower seeds	79.3

Source: Adapted from Whitbread, D. 2015. Top 10 Foods Highest in Selenium, www.healthaliciousness.com/articles/foods-high-in-selenium.php.

Turmeric (Curcumin)

Uses: Turmeric is one of the main components of curry powder. It may help reduce inflammation. Several studies suggest that it might ease symptoms of osteoarthritis and rheumatoid arthritis, such as pain and inflammation. Turmeric, which contains the active ingredient curcumin, functions to protect cells of the liver from damage. It reduces liver toxicity induced by arsenic, cadmium, chromium, copper, lead and mercury. Turmeric has also been used in combination with other supplements to protect against cadmium-induced cell damage like what occurs from smoking.

Therapeutic dose (for an adult): Turmeric can be sprinkled on foods. As a supplement, 400–600 mg in powder form three times a day or 30–90 drops per day of fluid extract are a usual dose.

DID YOU KNOW?

Forms of Turmeric
As a spice, turmeric is a common ingredient in Indian cooking. The spice and supplement come from the underground stems (rhizomes) of the turmeric plant.

Risks Associated with Turmeric Consumption

There are potential risks in consuming too much turmeric, including stomach pains, nausea, indigestion and gas. People sensitive to ginger or yellow food coloring may have an allergic reaction to turmeric.

There is a risk of ulcers, nausea or diarrhea at high doses. Turmeric in supplemental form should also be avoided during pregnancy. Consult a naturopathic doctor if you have gallstones.

It is best to avoid turmeric as a supplement if you have a bleeding disorder or are taking blood thinners, since it can promote bleeding. Avoid turmeric use at least 2 weeks before surgery. Consult your naturopath if you have diabetes, immune system problems or kidney disease. Some medications interact with turmeric, including aspirin, painkillers, statins, blood pressure medications, diabetes drugs and blood thinning medications such as warfarin. There may also be an interaction with other herbal supplements, such as ginseng, garlic and gingko, that thin the blood.

Zinc

Uses: Zinc is involved in immune functioning, wound healing, the body's production of proteins and DNA, and normal growth. A loss of taste and smell, poor wound healing, a weakened immune system or white spots on the nails can signify a zinc deficiency. Zinc helps the body defend itself against oxidation. It also protects the nervous system from damage.

Found in: Seeds, cashews, cocoa.

Therapeutic dose (for an adult): 25–50 mg/day.

Caution: About 1 of 100 people will feel nausea from taking zinc supplements on an empty stomach and in doses higher than 10 mg/day. If this happens, make sure you take zinc with food or in lower doses at a time, or try to get it from food instead.

Sources of Zinc	
Food	mg per 100 g
Pumpkin and squash seeds	10.3
Cashews	5.6
Sunflower seeds	5.0
Cocoa	6.8

PART 2

Food Allergies, Sensitivities and Intolerances

Allergies on the Rise

A food allergy prompts an IgE immediate reaction and can be severe and life-threatening and require emergency medical treatment. While allergies to milk, eggs, wheat and soy may resolve with age, allergies to peanuts, tree nuts, fish and shellfish are generally lifelong. There has been a 50% increase in food allergies among children between 1997 and 2011.

CHAPTER 7

Food Allergies

Certain foods act as toxins in the body by forming immune complexes. Here's how the process works: When the body recognizes a protein in food as foreign (an antigen), it launches an immune system attack where antibodies — the immune system cells that defend the body against foreign substances — attach to the antigen. The antibody-allergen complex then triggers inflammation through the release of histamine from mast cells, which may then lead to mucous membrane swelling or hives in the case of an immediate-type allergic reaction.

Food Allergy Mechanism

Food antigen

IgE antibody

IgE receptor

Binding of allergen with IgE antibodies and mast cell

Release of histamine from mast cells

The Immune System Response

A number of the cells that make up the immune system help protect the body from foreign substances, such as bacteria, viruses and parasites.

There are three main types of allergic reactions: IgE, IgG and IgA. The most serious and acute conditions are caused by the immune system, which launches an IgE reaction. Someone having this reaction may have an anaphylactic response and experience symptoms such as severe swelling of tissue in the eyes, mouth, throat, lips and lungs, difficulty breathing and hives. IgE reactions can be serious and life-threatening.

Antibody Classification

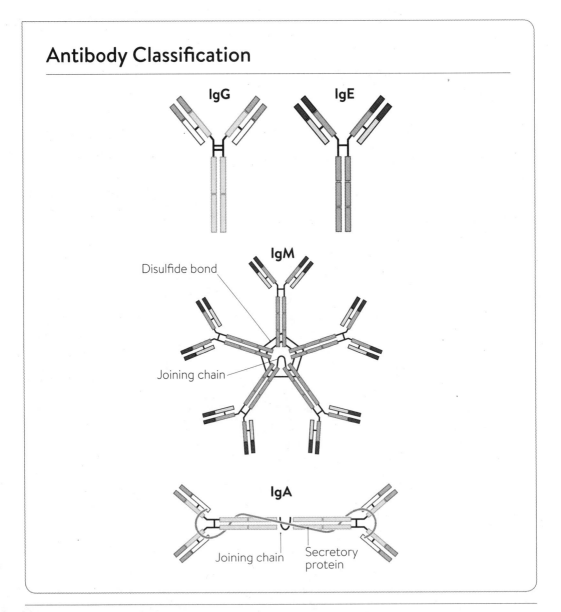

IgG

IgE

IgM

Disulfide bond

Joining chain

IgA

Joining chain

Secretory protein

IgG reactions occur in the digestive tract and can cause delayed symptoms, up to several days later. They may lead to chronic conditions.

IgA reactions can occur in the blood or digestive tract and typically bring on milder reactions than an IgE reaction, but similarly to IgG reactions, they can lead to chronic conditions.

Types of Antibodies

- **Immunoglobulin E (IgE)** is an antibody found in the skin, lungs and mucous membranes and is triggered when the immune system overreacts to the environment or a food (allergic reaction).
- **Immunoglobulin G (IgG)** is an antibody that protects against viral and bacterial infections and is found in all body fluids.
- **Immunoglobulin A (IgA)** is an antibody found in the mucous membranes of the gastrointestinal tract and the airways. It can be measured in the blood and the stool.
- **Immunoglobulin M (IgM)** is an antibody that is found in the blood and lymphatic system and is produced when the body is fighting an infection.

Food Allergy IgE Symptoms

Food allergy symptoms, also known as anaphylaxis or life-threatening allergy, tend to come on immediately after eating a food and up to a half an hour later. Symptoms usually include one or more of the following: swelling and itching in the mouth, tongue or throat, a rash, hives or flushed skin, difficulty in swallowing or speaking, difficulty breathing, abdominal cramps, nausea and vomiting, a feeling of "impending doom," a drop in blood pressure, weakness, collapse or unconsciousness. At the first symptoms of anaphylaxis, it is necessary to seek emergency treatment and call the emergency department, particularly in cases where the person is having trouble breathing or is experiencing throat or mouth swelling — or if any of these signs appear in someone with a previous history of anaphylaxis.

At the first symptoms of anaphylaxis, it is necessary to seek emergency treatment and call the emergency department, particularly in cases where the person is having trouble breathing or is experiencing throat or mouth swelling — or if any of these signs appear in someone with a previous history of anaphylaxis.

Symptoms of Anaphylaxis

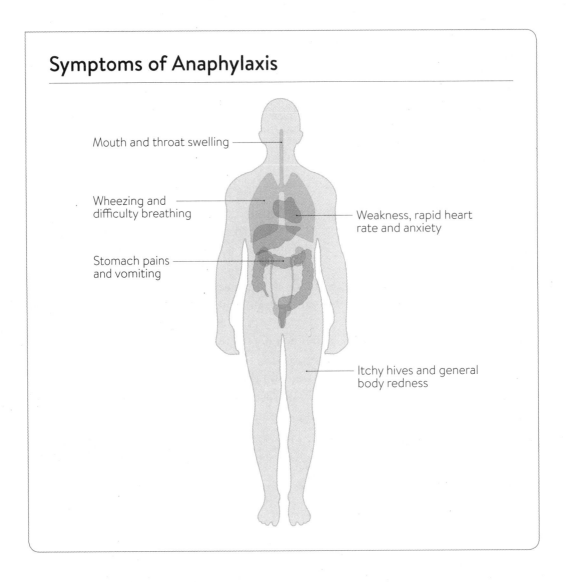

Mouth and throat swelling

Wheezing and difficulty breathing

Weakness, rapid heart rate and anxiety

Stomach pains and vomiting

Itchy hives and general body redness

Follow-Up Medical Treatment

If you have experienced severe allergic symptoms, be sure to notify your medical doctor. Your doctor will likely refer you to an allergist and possibly prescribe an EpiPen, an autoinjector device that administers epinephrine, to have on hand in the event of another serious allergic reaction. Antihistamines may also be prescribed to take either as prevention or in case of a milder allergic reaction. Patients are also recommended to order and wear a MedicAlert bracelet, which contains information about your particular allergies so that a first aid responder is immediately informed of your allergy if you are having a severe reaction or are found unconscious.

FAQ

Q: How do food allergies occur?

A: When a substance that is foreign to the body touches the mucous membranes or lining of the nose, throat, intestines or stomach, IgE antibodies are alerted. Antibodies are proteins found in the blood that detect and destroy bacteria, viruses and parasites. When the body first encounters an allergen, the body makes IgE antibodies to recognize this allergen. The next time this same allergen touches the mucous membranes, the IgE antibody attaches itself to a mast cell — a cell that contains substances that produce an inflammatory response — and releases histamines that trigger inflammation in the body. An immediate reaction can occur within minutes and up to half an hour after inhaling or ingesting an allergen. This reaction causes local inflammation or swelling and an immune system reaction that can be felt all over the body like hives or a rash. There can also be reactions that occur 4 to 6 hours later and can last for days or weeks. This late-phase reaction includes inflammation, swelling and the formation of fibrous tissue.

Prevalence of Food Allergy in North America

An estimated 4% of adults and 8% of children in the U.S. have food allergies. While allergies to milk, eggs, wheat and soy may resolve with age, allergies to peanuts, tree nuts, fish and shellfish are generally lifelong. There has been a 50% increase in food allergies among children between 1997 and 2011. Cow's milk, eggs, peanuts, tree nuts, shellfish and sesame are the most common food allergies.

In Canada, the top 10 food allergens, according to the country's government, are peanuts, tree nuts (almonds, Brazil nuts, cashews, hazelnuts, macadamia nuts, pecans, pine nuts, pistachio nuts and walnuts), sesame seeds, milk, eggs, seafood (fish, crustaceans and shellfish), soy, wheat, sulfites (a food additive) and mustard.

Prevalence of Food Allergies in the U.S. and Canada		
Food	Children	Adults
Cow's milk	2.5%	0.3%
Eggs	1.5%	0.2%
Peanuts	1.4% to 1.7%	0.6% to 0.7%
Wheat, soy	0.4%	0.3%
Tree nuts	1.1% to 1.6%	0.5% to 1.0%
Fish	0.1% to 0.2%	0.4% to 0.6%
Shellfish	0.1% to 0.5%	2.0% to 1.7%
Sesame	0.1% to 0.2%	0.1% to 0.05%

Source: Adapted from Pongracic, J. Patterns of Allergy in North America, www.ilsi.org/Europe/Documents/Food%20Allergy%20Symposium/Present%20Pongracic%20Nice.pdf.

Signs of Anaphylaxis

- Flushed face, hives or a rash with red and itchy skin
- Swelling of the eyes, face, lips, throat and tongue
- Trouble breathing, speaking or swallowing
- Anxiety, distress, faintness, paleness, sense of doom, weakness
- Cramps, diarrhea, vomiting
- A drop in blood pressure, rapid heartbeat, loss of consciousness

The Difference between Allergies, Intolerances and Sensitivities

Food allergies are mediated by the IgE immediate-type response, can be severe and life-threatening and require emergency medical treatment. Someone with a food allergy to milk, for example, typically reacts within minutes to half an hour after exposure, with severe symptoms that are triggered by an IgE immune system reaction — most notably, inflammation with possible hives or swelling of the mouth or throat or airways.

Intolerances involve a reaction to foods that is not an immune system reaction. Using milk as the example again, a lactose intolerance would involve not being able to break down the sugar — lactose — in the milk, and symptoms would include gas, bloating, cramping and possibly diarrhea. The immune system is not triggered with an intolerance.

A food sensitivity may involve an IgG or IgA reaction to a food. The reaction when the body deploys these antibodies can be milder, slower — over hours to days — and chronic and low grade in comparison to IgE reactions. This makes it difficult to identify foods that a person may be sensitive to. If the body reacts to milk with IgG or IgA instead of IgE antibodies, for example, there might be symptoms like excess mucus production, eczema, chronic infections, joint pains, headaches or irritable bowel syndrome. The IgG or IgA reactions are immune system reactions but typically do not cause severe allergic reactions like those found when the IgE immune system reaction is involved.

> The IgG or IgA reactions are immune system reactions but typically do not cause severe allergic reactions like those found when the IgE immune system reaction is involved.

Food Allergy Testing

Testing for allergies involves an IgE scratch test where a medical doctor scratches the arm or back and then places droplets of the possible allergen on the scratches. If the skin reacts by forming a raised welt or hive, an allergic reaction is evident. The test will determine which foods the patient is allergic to, while the size of the hive typically indicates the severity of the allergic reaction. The bigger the hive, the more severe the reaction to the allergen. In addition to the IgE scratch test, blood tests for IgE antibodies may be useful in identifying other relevant food allergies.

Making a Diagnosis

Food intolerances can be difficult to detect because symptoms often mimic those of food sensitivities or allergies. While diagnosis for possible intolerances or other associated conditions can be onerous, there are tests — from antibody blood testing, stool testing, genetic testing or electrodermal testing, as well as lactose or fructose breath tests and food elimination diets — to determine possible intolerances, including lactose intolerance, hereditary fructose intolerance, fructan intolerance, celiac disease and gluten sensitivity.

Food Intolerances, Celiac Disease and Gluten Sensitivity

Food intolerances, celiac disease and gluten sensitivity can all manifest with similar symptoms, including mild digestive problems such as heartburn, gas or bloating. It is important to undergo appropriate testing to determine the cause of the symptoms you are experiencing so you know what foods to avoid for long-term health and vitality.

Food Intolerances

Food intolerances are reactions to foods that are not due to an immune system reaction. They may cause reactions similar to food sensitivities or allergies, such as gas, bloating, nausea, cramping and diarrhea, and can result from a lack of enzymes to break down sugars in the intestines. Intolerances include, for example, lactose intolerance, an inability to properly break down the sugar — lactose — found in cow's milk products, and fructose intolerance, an inability to break down the fruit sugar fructose.

Prevalence of Food Intolerance

It is difficult to determine the number of people who suffer from intolerances because the symptoms resemble those of food sensitivities or food allergies. A German paper published in the *Schweizerische Medizinische Wochenschrift* (*Swiss Medical Weekly*) in 1996 points out some of the discrepancies. The research looked at self-reported prevalence of food allergy or food intolerance in three studies of Dutch and English adults. The three placebo-controlled double-blind studies used a questionnaire to determine that between 12% and 19% of participants reported having symptoms that they thought were due to a food allergy or intolerance. Food allergies were confirmed by an IgE skin prick test in only 0.8% to 2.4% of cases. Food sensitivity testing for IgG- or IgA-mediated immune response or intolerances was not tested but may have accounted for a large part of the reactions that occurred in the participants of these studies.

What Makes Up Lactose

The sugar lactose is made up of two sugars called galactose and glucose. The sugars must be broken apart before being able to be absorbed by the intestines and pass into the bloodstream. The lactase enzyme breaks lactose into galactose and glucose. If lactose is not properly broken down, symptoms of lactose intolerance occur.

Food intolerances may be caused by an underlying condition, including celiac disease (inflammation in the small intestines can cause a lack of enzymes) or Crohn's disease (an inflammatory bowel disease), medication, such as chemotherapy, or an acute bout of diarrhea.

Lactose Intolerance

Lactose intolerance is an inability to break down the sugar found in the milk of mammals and most commonly in dairy products, such as milk, cheese and ice cream. Those with lactose intolerance lack the enzyme — lactase — to digest lactose. Lactose is a complex sugar that needs to be split into two simple sugars, glucose and galactose (see diagram, above), before it is absorbed into the intestinal wall, but when people are deficient in lactase, they cannot break down this complex sugar. Lactase deficiency is common in adulthood and is more likely to be deficient as people age. Prevalence also varies with different ethnic groups.

Most humans, like other mammals, lose the intestinal enzyme lactase after infancy. It is estimated that 70% of the world's population experiences this genetically programmed decrease in the production of the lactase enzyme after weaning. For that reason, lactose intolerance is one of the most common food intolerances.

Tests for Lactose Intolerance

Your medical doctor might first recommend that you avoid dairy to see if your symptoms clear up. A breath test might also be performed to help detect a lactose intolerance. The test involves drinking a lactose-loaded beverage and then breathing into a mechanism at regular intervals to analyze the breath for the amount of hydrogen it contains. Normally, very little hydrogen is detectable in the breath, but undigested lactose produces high levels of hydrogen.

For infants and young children, a stool acidity test is used to determine lactose intolerance. This test measures undigested lactose, which creates the lactic acid that makes the stool acidic.

DID YOU KNOW?

Lactase Deficiency

Lactase deficiency is common with celiac and Crohn's disease, as well as with those who suffer from acute diarrhea. Chemotherapy medication may induce lactase deficiency, and premature infants are more likely to be deficient.

Foods That May Contain Lactose

- Dairy products such as milk, ice cream, cheese, yogurt
- Processed breakfast cereals
- Instant potatoes, soups and breakfast drinks
- Potato chips, corn chips and other processed snacks
- Processed meats, such as bacon, sausage, hot dogs and lunch meats
- Margarine
- Salad dressings that contain milk
- Liquid and powdered-milk-based meal replacements
- Protein powders and bars
- Candies
- Non-dairy liquid and powdered coffee creamers
- Non-dairy whipped toppings
- French fries coated with lactose

DID YOU KNOW?

Fructose in Foods

Fructose is a sugar found naturally in fruits and their juices, some vegetables and honey. Fructose is also a basic component in table or beet sugar (sucrose) and found in the artificial sweetener sorbitol.

Hereditary Fructose Intolerance, Fructose Malabsorption and Fructan Intolerance

Hereditary fructose intolerance (HFI) is a condition in which an individual lacks an enzyme that metabolizes the fruit sugar fructose, table sugar sucrose and the artificial sweetener sorbitol. In contrast, fructose malabsorption is similar to a lactose intolerance where the body is unable to digest the fruit sugar and it results in digestive upset. Individuals with a fructan intolerance are not able to digest larger, more complex branches of sugars that contain fructose and can experience digestive disturbances similar to fructose malabsorption.

DID YOU KNOW?

Prevalence of HFI

Hereditary fructose intolerance affects 1 in 20,000 people, and 1 in 70 people is a possible gene carrier.

Hereditary Fructose Intolerance

Hereditary fructose intolerance, also known as fructosemia or fructose-1,6-biphosphate aldolase deficiency, is a genetic disorder that typically shows symptoms once an infant starts eating formula, fruit, fruit juices or other foods containing fructose. Symptoms may include excessive sleepiness, irritability, jaundice, poor feeding, vomiting and convulsion. Repeated ingestion of fructose-, sucrose- or sorbitol-containing foods can lead to liver and kidney damage, which may result in a yellowing of the skin and whites of the eyes (jaundice), an enlarged liver (hepatomegaly) and chronic liver disease (cirrhosis). Continued exposure to fructose may result in seizures, coma and, ultimately, death from liver and kidney failure.

When people who have this condition eat fruit sugar or sugar, the body cannot change the glycogen (an energy

RESEARCH SPOTLIGHT

Diagnosing HFI

A study detailed the case of a 50-year-old German woman who was diagnosed as an adult with hereditary fructose intolerance. It demonstrated how the intolerance is under-recognized and can be detected after taking a careful and thorough history of diet. The patient told her doctor that she felt nausea, vomiting, pain in her digestive tract and dizziness, and often sweat after eating even the smallest amount of sugar or fruit. She told him that she had never liked sugary foods and that her mother told her that she had refused formula, which contained sucrose, at age 2, when she was weaned. The diagnosis confirmed that she had hereditary fructose intolerance and that she should avoid fructose, sucrose and sorbitol.

RESEARCH SPOTLIGHT

Fructose Malabsorption

A study published in the *Journal of the American Dietetic Association* in 2006 aimed to examine the effects of an elimination diet for patients identified with irritable bowel syndrome and fructose malabsorption. Sixty-two patients with irritable bowel syndrome and fructose malabsorption followed a diet that removed fructose-containing foods, reduced short-chain fructans and included foods in which glucose was balanced with fructose. Patients rated how their symptoms improved following the diet — an improvement of 5 points on a 10-point scale was considered a positive response. The researchers found that 74% of all patients had a positive response to the diet, with marked improvement in their abdominal symptoms by 5 points. Those who tried the diet and followed it — 78% of participants — noted that their symptoms improved by more than 85%. The ones who did not follow the diet as directly only saw a 36% improvement in abdominal symptoms. The study concluded that when participants adhere to a low-fructose/low-fructan diet, there is good symptom improvement.

storage material) into glucose, and harmful substances build up in the liver that lead to a drop in blood sugar. A child, teen or adult with an undiagnosed hereditary fructose intolerance will likely avoid sugary foods, fruit or fruit juice and may feel nauseated, shaky, sick and foggy after eating fruit sugar (fructose) or cane, beet or table sugar (sucrose) or the artificial sweetener sorbitol.

Fructose Malabsorption

Hereditary fructose intolerance should not be confused with a condition called fructose malabsorption. In people with fructose malabsorption, the cells of the intestine cannot break down fructose normally, leading to bloating, diarrhea or constipation, flatulence and stomach pain. Fructose malabsorption is thought to affect approximately 40% of individuals in the Western hemisphere.

Some individuals are unable to absorb the fruit sugar fructose. If an individual cannot absorb about an ounce (25 g) of fructose per sitting, they likely have fructose malabsorption. In comparison, a glass of orange juice has approximately ½ ounce (14 g) of fructose. Symptoms of fructose malabsorption can include diarrhea, cramping, gas and bloating. Up to 30% of those with irritable bowel syndrome may be affected by fructose malabsorption.

To test for fructose malabsorption, health practitioners administer a hydrogen breath test. During this test, an

DID YOU KNOW?

Rise of Sugar

The intake of dietary fructose has increased from 500 years ago with the growth of the sugar industry worldwide and mass production of sugar. Sugar is made up of one glucose and one fructose molecule. Today, most fructose in the American diet comes from high-fructose corn syrup that is found in soft drinks. Soft drink consumption in the United States has increased drastically, from 2 servings a week in 1942 to 2 servings a day in 2000.

individual is asked to blow into an instrument where the breath is analyzed for hydrogen gas. Next, the person is asked to drink 1 cup (250 mL) of fructose dissolved in water. Breath test results are collected every 30 minutes for 3 hours. Similar to the lactose test, if the level of hydrogen rises above the baseline test result, the person is typically diagnosed as having fructose malabsorption.

Fructose-Containing Foods and Foods That May Aggravate Fructose Malabsorption

Fructose malabsorption is thought to affect approximately 40% of individuals in the Western hemisphere.

- Fresh fruit: apples, apricots, cherries, grapes, guava, honeydew, lychee, mangos, peaches, pears, persimmons, plums, watermelon
- Dried fruit
- Fruit juices
- Foods containing apple or pear concentrate
- Plum sauce, sweet and sour sauce
- Fresh vegetables: artichokes, asparagus, leek, onions, tomatoes, peas
- Coconut milk and cream
- Honey
- High-fructose corn syrup or corn syrup solids
- High-sugar foods, such as cakes, cookies, muffins and some breakfast cereals
- Wheat, wheat pasta (because wheat contains fructans; see facing page)
- Soft drinks, fruit juices
- Yogurts with added fruit or fructose
- Sport drinks

Identifying Sugar in the Ingredients List

Sugar isn't always written as "sugar" on the ingredients list of food packaging. The following names indicate added sugar — the higher up on the ingredients list, the more likely the food is high in added sugar.

- Agave
- Brown sugar
- Cane sugar or evaporated cane juice
- Concentrated fruit juice
- Corn syrup
- Dextrose or dextrin
- Fructose
- Galactose
- Glucose
- Glucose-fructose
- High-fructose corn syrup
- Honey
- Invert sugar
- Liquid sugar
- Maltose
- Maple syrup
- Molasses
- Nectar
- Raw sugar
- Sucrose
- Syrup
- White sugar

Source: Adapted from EatRight Ontario, *What You Need to Know about Sugar*, www.eatrightontario.ca

Fructan Intolerance

Fructans are fructose-containing branches of sugars that store carbohydrates in a variety of vegetables and grains. Branches with shorter chains are known as oligosaccharides — a molecule containing three to nine simple sugars — and those with longer chains are polysaccharides, which contain between 200 and 2,500 simple sugars. Fructans are found in wheat, onions, barley, Brussels sprouts, cabbage, broccoli, pistachios, artichokes and chicory root. In the American diet, wheat makes up about 70% and onions 25% of the fructans consumed in the diet. Among the most common symptoms of a fructan intolerance are bloating, abdominal pain and diarrhea.

Fructose Content in Grains	
Food	Fructose per 1 cup (250 mL)
Rice	Trace
Potato chips	0.05 g
Spelt bread	0.07 g
Oats	0.11 g
Dark rye bread	0.60 g
Muesli fruit bar	0.81 g
Wheat	0.96 g
Couscous	1.12 g

Source: Adapted from Biesiekierski J.R., Rosella O., et al. 2011. Quantification of Fructans, Galacto-oligosaccharides and Other Short-chain Carbohydrates in Processed Grains and Cereals. Journal of Human Nutrition and Dietetics, Apr; 24(2):154–76.

An elimination diet for short-chain carbohydrates like fructans and galactans (found in pulses and beans) is the only way to test whether these substances are causing bowel intolerance similar to fructose or lactose intolerance.

Treating Fructan Intolerance with the FODMAP Diet

FODMAP is an acronym for fermentable oligosaccharides, disaccharides, monosaccharides and polyols — short-chain carbohydrates that are poorly absorbed in the digestive tract. In people with digestive problems, such as irritable bowel syndrome, eating foods high in these carbohydrates induces diarrhea, bloating, gas and abdominal pain. The FODMAP diet is commonly prescribed by medical doctors or may be suggested by a naturopathic doctor when a patient is diagnosed with irritable bowel syndrome. An elimination diet for short-chain carbohydrates like fructans and galactans (found in pulses and beans) is the only way to test whether these substances are causing bowel intolerance similar to fructose or lactose intolerance.

Individuals who follow this diet are asked to avoid foods that include fructose, fructans and galactans, among other categories of food. Research suggests that following a low FODMAP diet may help improve symptoms of IBS.

Foods That Should Be Avoided on the FODMAP Diet

- **Fructans:** Wheat, onions, garlic, barley, Brussels sprouts, cabbage, broccoli, pistachios, artichokes, chicory root, inulin
- **Galactans:** Soy, beans, peas, lentils, chickpeas, coffee
- **Lactose:** Ricotta, cottage cheese, milk, yogurt, ice cream
- **Polyols:** Xylitol, sorbitol, apples, plums, cherries, pears, cauliflower, corn, snow peas, mushrooms

Source: Adapted from Fedewa A., Rao S.S. 2014. Dietary Fructose Intolerance, Fructan Intolerance and FODMAPs. Current Gastroenterology Reports, Jan;16(1):370, Table 2.

Celiac Disease

Celiac disease is a lifelong autoimmune reaction to gluten, a protein found in wheat, barley, triticale and rye. Celiac disease is associated with a genetic predisposition — in fact, 95% of those with celiac disease are positive to the human leucocyte antigen HLA-DQ2 or HLA-DQ8, a genetic marker of celiac disease. It is one of the most common genetic diseases in the world, with 1 out of 100 people estimated to have celiac disease. A significant number of individuals remain undiagnosed — only about 10% of people affected by celiac disease are now diagnosed.

Celiac Symptoms

Common symptoms include failure to thrive in infancy, the presence of malabsorption, bloating and cramps, chronic diarrhea, foul-smelling stool and weight loss. In the past decades, however, medical professionals have also been looking for symptoms such as fatigue, anemia, irritable bowel syndrome, gas and constipation.

Less recognized symptoms of celiac disease include joint pains, insomnia, depression, anxiety, iritis (inflammation of the white part of the eye), thyroid problems and weight problems. Often, mild symptoms of constipation, gas and bloating are indistinguishable from other gastrointestinal disorders yet are actually associated with celiac disease.

Diagnosing Celiac

The small intestines, which normally have a finger-like appearance, can get flattened due to an immune system attack.

Small Intestine Lining Under Attack

Stomach

Small intestine

Gluten proteins permeate the intestine wall and damage villi

Submucosa

Mucosa

Villi

Lumen

Gluten proteins break through mucosa into the villi

T-cells produce cytokines

B-cells release antibodies

Antigen-presenting cells

Damaged villi

This autoimmune reaction, where the body attacks itself, causes certain markers to be present in the bloodstream.

Current testing for celiac disease usually involves a screening blood test that looks for the presence of anti-endomysium and tissue transglutaminase antibodies or anti-gliadin antibodies. The most sensitive and specific tests are tissue transglutaminase and deamidated gliadin antibodies. When blood tests are positive, commonly a small intestinal biopsy is recommended to definitively diagnose celiac disease, which is seen under a microscope as a blunted or flat appearance of microvilli, microscopic finger-like projections that are normally found in the small intestines in the absence of celiac disease.

With celiac disease, it is necessary to eliminate all traces of gluten completely from the diet for an individual's entire life (see "Foods That Contain Gluten" on page 126). Patients diagnosed with celiac who eat gluten put themselves at risk for other health complications, including osteoporosis and small bowel lymphoma. To ensure that the body is healing after the removal of gluten from the diet and that there is no unknown contamination of gluten in the diet, another blood test is recommended in 6 to 9 months to measure the presence of antibodies.

An Innovative Diagnostic Approach

Wireless capsule endoscopy is a technique that examines the intestinal lining when a patient swallows a capsule with a camera and it moves through the digestive tract to take a series of images. This technology has been shown in a recent study to identify problems in the small intestine further down than would be seen on a typical endoscopic exam. It is believed that this technology can identify people with celiac disease by examining more of the intestines. Currently, this is an experimental procedure, but it may become part of the diagnostic process in the future.

Associated Conditions
Neurological Symptoms

Emerging research is showing that a number of different conditions — in particular those related to the nervous system — may be related to celiac disease. One recent study

FAQ

Q: I don't experience the same stomach issues as people with celiac disease but notice I have other symptoms when I eat gluten. Could I have celiac disease?

A: The number of people diagnosed with celiac disease is increasing and more and more researchers are finding that some patients do not show the typical gastrointestinal complaints of gas, bloating, constipation and diarrhea. In one study, 200 recently diagnosed celiac patients were evaluated for their health before diagnosis. Of these patients, 58% had gastrointestinal complaints, 35% had non-gastrointestinal symptoms and 7% were silent cases where there was no indication that they had celiac disease.

RESEARCH SPOTLIGHT

Blood Test Screening for Celiac Disease

A study in the *Journal of Clinical Gastroenterology* in 2010 examined whether deamidated gliadin peptide antibodies (IgA and IgG) could be used to improve the blood test screening for celiac disease. The current approach to screen patients for celiac disease uses a combination of tissue transglutaminase, endomysial antibodies and gliadin antibodies. One hundred forty-four patients with gastrointestinal and extra-intestinal signs suggestive of CD were investigated using blood tests and duodenal biopsy. Forty-eight of the 144 patients (33%) had celiac disease with damage to the microvilli as seen by duodenal biopsy. IgA tissue transglutaminase showed 93.7% sensitivity compared with 91.6% for IgA endomysial antibody, 84.3% for IgA deamidated gliadin antibodies and 82.3% for IgG deamidated gliadin antibody. When patients did not show IgA reactions and were deficient in IgA antibodies, the IgG deamidated gliadin antibodies showed high specificity (98.9%) for celiac disease. The addition of IgG markers for celiac disease allows for diagnosis in case of IgA deficiency.

found a higher prevalence of sensory neural hearing loss in pediatric celiac patients than in the healthy control group. The authors suggest a relationship between this type of hearing loss and celiac disease because the body experiences an immune system reaction to the nerves. Multiple sclerosis has also been associated with celiac disease. A recent research article noted that when multiple sclerosis patients who were also diagnosed with celiac disease ate a gluten-free diet, they were in remission after 6 years. New research is showing that other conditions may have a possible link to celiac disease, although further study is necessary.

Autoimmune Disease

A study of first-degree relatives of individuals diagnosed with celiac disease found a significantly higher number of cases were linked to type 1 diabetes and hypothyroidism in those with celiac and their relatives. Rheumatoid arthritis was also more prevalent among first-degree relatives of people with celiac disease. In another study, autoimmune diseases were found in patients with celiac disease — 7.2% of type 1 diabetics, 1.8% of hyperthyroid, 0.9% of vitiligo, 0.9% of rheumatoid arthritis and 2% of primary biliary cirrhosis. The authors suggest that coexistence of celiac disease with other autoimmune diseases is quite frequent.

DID YOU KNOW?

Antibody Testing

According to the Mayo Clinic, testing for IgA and IgG antibodies to unmodified gliadin proteins is no longer recommended. The tests for deamidated gliadin antibodies IgA and IgG replace the older gliadin antibody tests, which have been discontinued at Mayo Clinic.

Type 1 Diabetes

There is an association between celiac disease and type 1 diabetes. The prevalence of gliadin IgG/IgA and transglutaminase IgA antibodies measured through blood tests is shown to be significantly higher in patients with recent-onset type 1 diabetes. In one study, 27.4% of patients also tested positive for antibodies specific to two or more diseases, including type 1 diabetes, autoimmune thyroiditis and celiac disease, compared with 3.1% in the group of first-degree relatives and none of the control subjects. The authors of this study recommend recent-onset type 1 diabetes patients should be routinely screened for autoimmune thyroid disease and additionally for celiac disease.

Autism

> It is recommended that patients with neurological disease, especially with autism, be tested for celiac disease.

A study found that 60% of autism patients showed simultaneous elevations in antibodies against gliadin (a sub-protein of gluten that is measured in the blood) and a brain protein called cerebellar peptides. The authors conclude that a subgroup of patients with autism produce antibodies against Purkinje cells in the brain and gliadin peptides, which may be responsible for some of the neurological symptoms in autism. Another study found high anti-gliadin antibodies in 15 out of 21 autistic children and gluten-sensitivity HLA (human leukocyte antigens) alleles, a measure of genetic predisposition, in 10 of the 10 children tested. It is recommended that patients with neurological disease, especially with autism, be tested for celiac disease.

Gluten Sensitivity

Individuals with a gluten sensitivity may trigger the same reactions to gluten as those who have celiac disease even though they have tested negative for the disease. Symptoms can range from mild to severe, but unlike with celiac, their sensitivity does not damage the intestines.

Once celiac disease has been ruled out, naturopathic doctors may suggest patients eliminate gluten from their diet to gauge whether symptoms improve and determine a gluten sensitivity. IgG and IgA antibody blood testing, IgA stool testing, genetic testing or electrodermal testing have also been used by naturopathic doctors to detect possible gluten sensitivity. From testing genes and stool samples for IgA, some researchers estimate the prevalence of gluten sensitivity in the American population to be 42%. In addition to approximately 1% of the population with celiac disease, there may be more people who need to avoid gluten, such as those with fructan intolerance with irritable bowel syndrome. This may explain why some people who eat gluten-free feel better even though they have ruled out celiac disease when tested.

Certain laboratory companies, such as EnteroLab, offer a genetic test for gluten sensitivity and celiac disease. This test looks for genes that suggest the presence of celiac and can be performed whether or not someone has eaten gluten. Individuals take a swab of the inside of the cheek and collect sample cells, which are sent to the lab to identify genes associated with

DID YOU KNOW?

Gene Pool
When one family member has the gene for gluten sensitivity, they can pass the gene on to the next generation. If the testing reveals that an individual has two copies of the gene, then they received one gene from each parent and all of their children will have at least one copy of the gene from them.

If an individual is diagnosed with a gluten sensitivity, it is recommended that they completely remove gluten from the diet in order to prevent complications.

celiac disease. Although the gene test does not identify an immune reaction to gluten, having the gluten gene indicates a potential to react to gluten. In comparison, blood tests give a better picture of immune reactions, while intestinal biopsies confirm celiac disease by measuring the amount of damage to the small intestine's lining.

If an individual is diagnosed with a gluten sensitivity, it is recommended that they completely remove gluten from the diet in order to prevent complications, such as damage to the nervous system, gastrointestinal system and organs such as the liver, pancreas and lungs.

Gluten Sensitivity Symptoms

The symptoms of gluten sensitivity can be similar to those of general food sensitivity and may include:

- acne
- ADD
- ADHD
- anxiety
- arthritis
- asthma
- bedwetting
- behavior problems
- bronchial infections
- chronic infections
- depression
- dermatitis
- diarrhea
- ear infections
- eczema
- excessive mucus
- fatigue
- gastritis
- gastrointestinal problems
- headaches
- heartburn
- hives
- hyperactivity
- insomnia
- iritis
- irritable bowel syndrome
- itchy skin
- lupus
- migraines
- nasal congestion
- vomiting

Foods That Contain Gluten

- bagels
- biscuits
- beer
- bologna
- bread
- bread crumbs
- breaded fish, chicken, meats
- cake
- candy
- cereal
- cold cuts
- cookies
- crackers
- croissants
- croutons
- doughnuts
- dumplings
- flour
- flour tortillas
- fried vegetables
- graham crackers
- gravy
- hamburger buns
- hot dog buns
- ice cream cones
- Kamut bread
- macaroni
- melba toast
- muffins
- noodles
- pancakes
- pasta
- pastries
- pie crusts
- pizza crust
- potato chips
- pretzels
- rolls
- rye bread
- soup
- soy sauce
- spaghetti
- spelt bread
- stuffing
- tabbouleh
- teriyaki sauce
- waffles

Ingredients That Contain Gluten

- barley
- barley grass
- barley malt
- bleached flour
- bran
- bread
- brewer's yeast
- brown bread
- bulgur wheat
- cookie crumbs
- cookie dough
- couscous
- durum wheat
- enriched bleached flour
- enriched flour
- farina
- flour
- germ
- graham flour
- granary flour
- groats (barley, wheat)
- hard wheat
- hydrolyzed wheat gluten
- hydrolyzed wheat protein
- hydrolyzed wheat starch
- Kamut
- pasta
- pearl barley
- rye
- semolina
- spelt
- sprouted wheat or barley
- wheat bran extract
- wheat germ extract
- wheat grass
- wheat nuts
- wheat protein

Hidden Sources of Gluten

- hydrolyzed wheat protein
- malt
- malt extract
- malt flavoring
- malt syrup
- malt vinegar
- malted barley flour
- malted milk
- starch

Ingredients That Might Contain Gluten

- baking powder
- caramel color
- caramel flavoring
- coloring
- Dextri-Maltose
- dextrins
- dry roasted nuts
- emulsifiers
- enzymes
- fat replacer
- flavoring
- food starch
- glucose syrup
- gravy cubes
- ground spices
- hydrolyzed plant protein (HPP)
- hydrolyzed protein
- hydrolyzed vegetable protein (HVP)
- maltose
- miso
- modified food starch
- modified starch
- natural flavoring
- natural flavors
- non-dairy creamer
- oats
- seasonings
- smoke flavoring
- soy sauce
- starch
- stock cubes
- suet
- vegetable broth
- vegetable protein
- vegetable starch
- vitamins (unless label says free of gluten)

Source: Adapted from American Diabetes Association. 2014. What Foods Have Gluten? www.diabetes.org/food-and-fitness/food/planning-meals/gluten-free-diets/what-foods-have-gluten.html.

Food Reactions

Almost any chronic condition can be tied to a food sensitivity, but because symptoms may not be immediate, and complicated by multiple food reactions, determining the food sensitivity may take some time. Diagnosis is important, however — food sensitivities have been linked to everything from ADD and arthritis to depression and irritable bowel syndrome.

CHAPTER 9

Common Food Sensitivities

Unlike a food allergy, where there is an immediate-type immune system response involving the immunoglobulin E (IgE) antibody, a food sensitivity causes an adverse reaction to a certain food that may involve a different part of the immune system or body. Found in the lining of the mucous membranes in the small intestine, IgA and IgG molecules are considered to play a role in identifying adverse reactions to foods. With food sensitivities, reactions are not immediate or severe in nature. Stool tests measure the IgA antibodies that may have reacted to a suspect food, while blood tests measure IgA or IgG antibodies when a patient has recently eaten the foods tested, usually within the past few weeks.

IgG and IgA Immune System Reactions

Several studies have examined IgG antibodies to determine whether eliminating an offending food(s) has an effect on patient symptoms. The chart on the next page lists several studies that have examined the relationship between reactions like digestive complaints, allergies in children and migraine

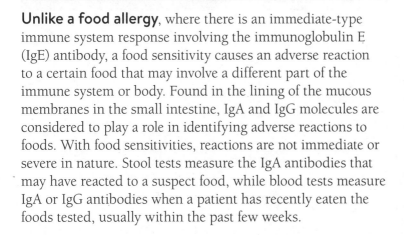

DID YOU KNOW?

Food Triggers
Migraines can be triggered by cheese, chocolate, citrus fruits, hot dogs, monosodium glutamate (MSG), aspartame, fatty foods, ice cream, caffeine withdrawal, alcoholic drinks — especially red wine and beer — histamine, nitrites and sulfites.

FAQ

Q: What symptoms are caused by food sensitivity?

A: Virtually any chronic condition could be a result of food sensitivity. Because symptoms may take a long time to develop, and there may be multiple food sensitivity reactions, it is often hard to pinpoint which foods are causing the reaction. Food sensitivity reactions may contribute to the following conditions or problems: acne, ADD, ADHD, anemia, anxiety, arthritis, asthma, autoimmune disease, bedwetting, behavior problems, bronchial infections, chronic infections, constipation, depression, dermatitis, diarrhea, ear infections, eczema, excessive mucus, fatigue, gastrointestinal problems, headaches, heartburn, hives, hyperactivity, insomnia, iritis, irritable bowel, itchy skin, lupus, migraines, nasal congestion, weight loss, vomiting — and many others.

headaches and positive results to IgG antibodies. These studies show that IgG immune reactions to foods may be a valuable marker to identify foods to eliminate to help relieve patient symptoms.

Condition Studied for IgG Antibodies	Found	Results When Foods Eliminated
Irritable bowel syndrome (IBS)	IgG antibodies to milk, eggs, wheat, beef, pork	Improvement in pain and bloating
Irritable bowel syndrome (IBS)	IgG antibodies to crab, eggs, shrimp, soy	Symptoms associated with IBS improved
Upset stomach	IgG antibodies to eggs and soy	Symptom improved by eliminating foods
Crohn's disease	IgG antibodies to cheese and yeast	Reduced abdominal pain
Migraines with IBS	IgG antibodies to food allergens	Reduced severity and number of headaches and symptoms of IBS
Allergies in children	IgG antibodies to peanuts, milk, eggs	Improvement in allergic symptoms in children

Testing for Food Sensitivity

IgG Blood Testing

The immunoglobulin IgG, which is found in all body fluids to protect against viral and bacterial infections and may indicate a food sensitivity, can be tested in the blood. When IgG antibodies to foods in the blood are eliminated, symptoms may improve.

IgA Stool Testing

The IgG blood test alone tells only part of the story about the immune system's reaction to foods. In addition to IgG blood tests, it may be beneficial to also check for IgA antibody reactions. IgA is an antibody found in the mucous membranes of the gastrointestinal tract and the blood. There are two main ways to test for IgA reactions, either through blood or stool tests.

IgA stool testing may identify the immune system's reaction to a food that is causing a reaction in the body. There are currently tests that measure gluten (the protein in wheat, rye and barley), eggs, soy and casein (the protein in milk) through a stool test for IgA. This test complements the IgG blood testing and is a safeguard in the event that the body's reaction to a food is not showing in the blood work.

Antibody Deficiency

In some cases, an individual can have an antibody deficiency, so measuring antibodies for food sensitivities can be difficult. Up to 25% of children with recurrent respiratory infections can have an IgA and/or IgG deficiency. In contrast, some studies have shown an IgA deficiency in only 1 in 223 to 1 in 1,000 Caucasians in the U.S., and 1 in 333 to 1 in 3,000 among healthy blood donors in the U.S. To make sure that IgA testing is accurate, total IgA should also be tested in the blood before or at the same time a blood or stool test is done, in order to accurately interpret test results. If an individual fails to produce enough IgA, the stool or blood testing for IgA may not show any food sensitivities. Follow-up testing with other methods, such as IgG and IgE, is suggested when the body fails to produce IgA antibodies.

Conflicting Test Results

IgA stool test results differ from IgA blood tests, and these differ from IgG blood and IgE scratch tests (in the case of allergy testing). For example, what does not show up on an allergy scratch test for IgE may be found as a food sensitivity on an IgA or IgG test. The combined results from these tests help to put all the pieces of the puzzle together to understand the complete picture of how foods are affecting your body and whether they provoke a food sensitivity or food allergy reaction. Ask your naturopathic doctor for the most appropriate testing for you. If symptoms do not improve after eliminating foods that show up on IgG tests typically first used for assessment by a naturopathic doctor, for instance, the next step might be to order an IgA stool or blood test, a gene swab test, or an IgE blood or scratch test if this has not already been done by an allergist.

Elimination/Challenge Diets

Elimination and challenge tests are one of the effective ways of knowing whether a food is adversely affecting you without having to test for food sensitivities, but these tests can be time-consuming and symptoms do not always resolve within a short time frame. The elimination phase involves picking one or more foods that may provoke a possible reaction and eliminating them for some time to see if symptoms resolve. After at least 30 days of elimination, the food(s) can be reintroduced to monitor whether symptoms return.

If you have had a severe reaction to a food, such as throat or lip swelling, difficulty breathing, hives or other signs of anaphylaxis, it is best to avoid reintroduction of that food. For example, if an individual is chronically suffering from a stuffy nose or post-nasal drip, they may try excluding all dairy products from their diet. If the person breathes more clearly after that 30-day period of elimination and then the same symptoms return after reintroducing the food back into the diet, it is likely that dairy is a trigger for the immune system. In this case, it is easy to confuse these symptoms with seasonal allergy symptoms, so the elimination challenge is best done before or after the allergy season.

Medical Supervision Required

If an individual has experienced a severe allergic reaction to a food, it is not advisable to test it by elimination and challenge. Foods that prompt severe or life-threatening allergic reactions should be tested by an allergist to confirm food allergies and monitor symptoms. If your medical doctor suggests reintroducing the food, it should be done on the advice of the allergist and under medical supervision at the allergist's office, where an EpiPen and other medications are on hand in the event of severe reactions.

FAQ

Q: How soon can I expect my symptoms to clear completely once I eliminate a food from my diet?

A: The time it takes to see symptoms resolve can vary between individuals and conditions. It could take from days to months, and even years, to see symptoms resolve when foods are eliminated from the diet. For example, it can take up to 6 weeks to see symptoms resolve from eliminating gluten from the diet if you have irritable bowel symptoms, and it may take up to 2 years for sufferers of Crohn's disease or colitis for the same elimination. It may take between 6 to 9 months to see psoriasis clear up and only 3 months for eczema, for example, once foods like wheat, dairy, corn and pork are avoided in the diet. It may also take up to a year to resolve anxiety or depression once gluten is eliminated from the diet and up to 18 months to see an improvement in symptoms from neurological conditions, such as multiple sclerosis, from gluten avoidance.

Limitations of the Test

It may be difficult for most people to know what to eliminate from the diet and for how long. Most people will pick one food at a time to eliminate and see if their symptoms resolve. Without proper knowledge or guidance, it is easy to give up on such a diet because it can be difficult to monitor and follow food intake and reactions, and it can get muddled further if there are multiple food sensitivities.

Often, several foods need to be eliminated at the same time to eliminate symptoms. Some individuals, for example, may be collectively sensitive to corn, wheat, rye, oats, barley, oranges, tomatoes, dairy products, chocolate and pork. If just one food is eliminated at a time, another offending food may be producing the same reaction.

Reintroducing Foods

Most individuals report their symptoms have improved after 1 month of eliminating a suspect food. If they accidentally ingest that food, they may have a reappearance of the initial symptoms or it may affect a different area of the body. There can be a delay of between 3 days and 2 weeks to see the result of a reintroduced food. For that reason, it is best to reintroduce foods one at a time once a day for 3 days, then wait a full week before reintroducing another food, so that you can be certain you are identifying the culprit food in the event that you experience a reaction. In the case of some labs

> **DID YOU KNOW?**
>
> **Reintroduction Symptoms**
> Common reactions when a food is reintroduced can include feeling achy the next day, low mood, low energy, abdominal pains, itching, joint pains, excess gas, bloating, stuffiness, sneezing and skin rashes.

that test for IgG reactions, the foods that are identified by the IgG test should be kept out of the diet for 3 months; then, if the food is reintroduced, it should be monitored for 2 weeks to look for reactions.

Look for gradual changes — including an increase in mucus production; general achiness or lower energy level; trouble sleeping; skin conditions; digestive issues like pain, gas and bloating; headaches; or inflammation in the body, such as in joints — when reintroducing a food that may cause sensitivity. The body does not always show the same symptoms as the original reaction when reintroducing a food.

Look for gradual changes — including an increase in mucus production; general achiness or lower energy level; trouble sleeping; skin conditions; digestive issues like pain, gas and bloating; headaches; or inflammation in the body, such as in joints — when reintroducing a food that may cause sensitivity.

Foods That Provoke Allergies and Sensitivities

When individuals are tested for possible food sensitivities, they often discover that their symptoms are linked to multiple foods. To best evaluate related symptoms, it is often necessary to eliminate all foods marked as sensitive on IgA, IgE, IgG or electrodermal screening tests. Not everyone has the same food sensitivities or as many sensitivities as the foods on this list, but these are the most common. It is important to get tested to determine your individual food sensitivities or allergies and create a plan that is best suited to your situation.

- almonds
- corn
- dairy (cow's milk)
- egg whites
- fish
- gluten (which includes wheat, rye, barley, Kamut, spelt)
- kidney beans
- MSG
- mustard
- oranges
- peanuts
- peppers
- pork
- potatoes
- shellfish
- soy
- sulfites
- tomatoes
- tree nuts

Oral Allergy Syndrome

Oral allergy syndrome is a reaction to certain fruits, vegetables and nuts that occurs due to a cross-reactivity between proteins in fresh fruits or vegetables and pollens in trees, grasses and weeds. In 50% to 75% of adults in the U.S. who are allergic to birch pollen, oral allergy syndrome is present. In Central and North Europe, up to 80% of birch pollen allergic subjects suffer from oral allergy syndrome to fruits, nuts and vegetables. The symptoms are an itchy mouth or swelling in the mouth when eating an uncooked food. Other reactions can include hives or itchy skin on the hands of those handling raw fruits, nuts and vegetables. Generalized itchiness can also occur after eating the raw fruit, vegetable or nut. Typically, oral allergy syndrome does not produce severe IgE immediate-type allergies, except for hazelnuts. Itching in the mouth may only occur when the cross-reactive foods are consumed during that allergy season and more rarely when cross-reactive foods are eaten outside of the season. If a food is cooked, the process changes its makeup so it can be eaten without triggering the syndrome.

It is best to check with an allergist to make sure the reaction is not a sign of a more serious immediate-type anaphylactic allergy and to monitor your symptoms so they don't get any worse. To avoid symptoms of oral allergy syndrome, it is best to avoid certain raw fruits and nuts during the allergy season and, for some individuals, to avoid them at all times if they have had a reaction at different times.

The American Academy of Allergy, Asthma & Immunology indicates the following food and allergy associations.

Spring Birch Tree Pollen Allergy

- almonds
- apples
- apricots
- Brazil nuts
- carrots
- celery
- cherries
- coconut
- fennel
- hazelnuts
- kiwifruit
- nectarines
- parsley
- parsnips
- peaches
- peanuts
- pears
- plums
- potatoes
- prunes
- soybeans
- walnuts

Summer Grass Pollen Allergy

- kiwifruit
- melons
- oranges
- peanuts
- peaches
- tomatoes
- potatoes

Late Summer and Fall Ragweed Pollen Allergy

- bananas
- cantaloupe
- cucumbers
- honeydew melon
- potatoes
- watermelon
- zucchini

Fall Mugwort Pollen Allergy

- anise
- bell peppers
- black pepper
- broccoli
- cabbage
- caraway
- cauliflower
- chard
- coriander
- fennel
- garlic
- onion
- parsley

Sulfite Allergy/Sensitivity

"Sulfites" is a general term for a group of sulfur-based compounds, including sulfur dioxide, sodium sulfite, sodium and potassium bisulfite, and sodium and potassium metabisulfite. Sulfites are used to maintain food color, to act as an anti-microbial, to prolong shelf-life and to maintain the potency of certain medications. Sulfites also occur naturally in a number of foods and beverages such as wine.

An extremely rapid onset (within minutes) of symptoms consisting of flushing, lung spasm such as asthma, low blood pressure and shock is typical of a sulfite allergic reaction. Other sulfite reactions include anaphylaxis, gastrointestinal complaints and skin reactions. People who have asthma are more at risk of sulfite sensitivity.

Common Symptoms of Sulfite Allergy

Symptoms may include:

- wheezing, labored breathing, chest tightness, cough, shortness of breath, asthma
- felling faint, low blood pressure, loss of consciousness, blue discoloration of skin
- hives, itching, contact dermatitis
- flushing, clammy skin
- swelling of the throat, swelling of hands, feet or eyes
- abdominal cramps, nausea, diarrhea
- anaphylactic shock
- mood changes
- headaches

Common Symptoms of Sulfite Sensitivity

Symptoms include:

- sneezing
- stuffiness
- flushed face

Sulfite-Containing Foods

- Alcoholic and non-alcoholic beer and cider
- Bottled lemon and lime juices and concentrates
- Canned and frozen fruits and vegetables
- Cereal, cornmeal, cornstarch, crackers and muesli
- Condiments; for example, coleslaw, horseradish, ketchup, mustard, pickles, relish, sauerkraut
- Dehydrated, mashed, peeled and precut potatoes, frozen french fries
- Dried fruits and vegetables, such as apricots, coconut, raisins, sweet potatoes
- Dried herbs, spices and teas
- Fresh grapes
- Fruit fillings and syrups, gelatin, jams, jellies, preserves, marmalade, molasses, pectin
- Fruit and vegetable juices
- Glazed and glacé fruits; for example, maraschino cherries
- Starches; for example, cornstarch, potato starch
- Sugar syrups; for example, glucose, glucose solids, syrup dextrose, corn syrup, table syrup
- Tomato pastes, pulps and purées
- Vinegar and wine vinegar
- Wine

Other Possible Sources of Sulfites

- Baked goods, especially with dried fruits
- Deli meats, hot dogs and sausages
- Dressings, gravies, guacamole, sauces, soups and soup mixes
- Fish, crustaceans and shellfish
- Granola bars, especially with dried fruit
- Noodle and rice mixes
- Snack foods; for example, raisins, fruit salad
- Soy products

Non-Food Sources of Sulfites

- Bottle-sanitizing solutions for home brewing
- Cellophane

Note: These lists are not complete and may change. In addition, food and food products from different countries are produced using different manufacturing and labeling standards.

Source: Adapted from Health Canada. 2012. Sulphites — One of the Ten Priority Food Allergens, www.hc-sc.gc.ca/fn-an/pubs/securit/2012-allergen_sulphites-sulfites/index-eng.php.

MSG Toxicity

Monosodium glutamate (MSG) is a common flavor enhancer in canned foods, such as soups, some chips, stuffing and fast foods, and is generally associated with Chinese food. By adding MSG to such foods as soups, the amount of sodium

DID YOU KNOW?

Ruled Non-Toxic

Conventional toxicity studies of MSG find it to be safe from toxic- or cancer-causing effects. The Joint FAO/WHO Expert Committee on Food Additives has stated that "glutamate as an additive in food" is not a health hazard to human beings.

can be decreased without altering the taste. Adding MSG has been found to increase the acceptability and consumption of foods. Glutamate (the ionized form) and glutamic acid are common amino acids found in many foods, but only a fraction include a "free" form that potentially causes symptoms.

MSG Toxicity Reactions

Some individuals have a reaction after ingesting MSG, a known excitotoxin, which excites or overstimulates the neuron receptors in the body. However, such reactions to MSG are not allergic in nature and will not test as positive on allergy tests.

Even though the FAO/WHO has declared MSG not to be a health hazard, various organs can react to MSG when consumed. Individuals may experience heart palpitations or arrhythmias. Gastrointestinal symptoms can include bloating, gas, nausea, vomiting, diarrhea and stomach cramps. Joint pains and stiffness can also occur. MSG can cause neurological symptoms, such as headache, mood swings, dizziness, light-headedness, anxiety, panic attacks and behavior problems in children. Vision may also be compromised, with difficulty focusing or blurry vision. If the respiratory system is affected, MSG can cause asthma or shortness of breath or tightness in the chest. Frequent urination is another sign. On the skin, there may be hives or a flushing reaction. Neurological complications can occur that even mimic multiple sclerosis.

Common Reactions to MSG

Symptoms may include:
- numbness anywhere in the body
- burning sensation anywhere in the body
- tingling anywhere in the body

RESEARCH SPOTLIGHT

MSG Threshold Dose

A research study in the *Journal of Allergy and Clinical Immunology* in 1997 reported on a double-blind controlled oral challenge with 61 MSG-sensitive subjects. It found that when the subjects ingested a threshold dose of 2.5 grams of MSG, it produced headaches, muscle tightness, numbness/tingling, general weakness and flushing more frequently compared to ingesting a placebo (no MSG).

MSG Headaches and Blood Pressure

A study published in *Cephalalgia* in 2010 investigated headaches and blood pressure in healthy men fed 75 or 150 milligrams per kilogram (mg/kg) of MSG. The 154 subjects drank sugar-free soda containing either MSG or salt of 75 mg/kg or 150 mg/kg, or sodium chloride (NaCl) — salt — of 24 mg/kg for the placebo group. The study monitored headaches, heart rate and blood pressure for 2 hours. There was a significant increase in headaches in the MSG group. In the high-MSG group taking in 150 mg/kg, systolic blood pressure was elevated compared to the non-MSG and low-MSG groups.

- facial pressure or tightness
- chest pain
- headache
- nausea
- rapid heartbeat
- drowsiness
- weakness
- difficulty breathing for asthmatics
- diarrhea

MSG Labeling

In the United States, the FDA requires that added MSG be listed in the ingredient panel on the food's packaging. MSG cannot be listed as "spices and flavoring."

MSG occurs naturally in these foods, but the FDA does not require these products to specify that they naturally contain MSG:

- hydrolyzed vegetable protein (HVP)
- autolyzed yeast
- hydrolyzed yeast
- yeast extract
- soy extract
- protein isolate

Foods with any ingredient that naturally contains MSG cannot claim "no MSG" or "no added MSG" on their packaging.

In Canada, MSG must be declared on the label. There are no labeling requirements for naturally occurring free glutamates. When a label on a food claims "contains no MSG," "no MSG added" or "no added MSG," however, it may still contain these glutamates (free amino acids):

- hydrolyzed vegetable protein (HVP)
- hydrolyzed plant protein (HPP)
- hydrolyzed soy protein (HSP)
- soy sauce
- autolyzed yeast extracts

Glutamate-Containing Foods

Foods that contain higher amounts of naturally occurring free glutamate, which is similar to MSG, include:

- tomatoes
- potatoes
- soy sauce
- Parmesan, Cheddar, Swiss and Roquefort cheese
- grapes
- grape juice
- fruit juices
- mushrooms

Protection against MSG Toxicity

In preliminary research, dietary antioxidants have been shown to have a protective effect on oxidative stress caused by the consumption of MSG. Antioxidants such as vitamins C and E and quercetin have all been shown to protect cells from MSG toxicity. Vitamin E was most protective toward liver cells, whereas vitamin C and quercetin have a greater affinity to protect the brain from

RESEARCH SPOTLIGHT

MSG and Aspartame in Migraines and Fibromyalgia

In a case study published in *Annals of Pharmacotherapy* in 2001, four patients who had been diagnosed with fibromyalgia for a period of 2 to 17 years had complete or near complete resolution of their symptoms within months of stopping MSG or MSG and aspartame (an artificial sweetener). When these four individuals reintroduced MSG, their symptoms came back. The study suggests that eliminating MSG or MSG and aspartame excitotoxins from the diet has the potential for dramatic results in those diagnosed with fibromyalgia.

damage. Besides antioxidants, magnesium deficiency, low blood sugar and accumulated mercury all make the body more reactive to MSG.

Latex Allergy Cross-Reactive Foods

It is estimated that less than 1% of the general population is sensitized to latex. The U.S. Occupational Safety and Health Administration (OSHA) estimates that 8% to 12% of health care workers, who are some of the biggest users of latex gloves, are sensitized to them. Symptoms can include itchy skin, runny nose, conjunctivitis (red, itchy eyes), spasm of the airways and severe allergic reactions (anaphylaxis). To confirm a diagnosis, either skin prick testing or blood tests for IgE are used.

Approximately 30% to 50% of individuals who are allergic to latex show an associated allergic response to some plant-derived foods, especially freshly consumed fruits. This cross-reactivity is called latex–fruit syndrome. It is not always clear which came first — the food reaction or latex allergy.

> **Approximately 30% to 50% of individuals who are allergic to latex show an associated allergic response to some plant-derived foods, especially freshly consumed fruits.**

Foods Associated with Latex–Fruit Syndrome

These are some common foods that cross-react to latex:

- avocados
- bananas
- bell peppers
- chestnuts
- custard apples
- eggplant
- kiwifruit
- peaches
- potatoes
- tomatoes

FAQ

Q: I think I might have food sensitivities, but how can I be sure which foods are causing my symptoms?

A: Knowing more about common food sensitivities, oral allergy syndrome, sulfite allergy and sensitivity, MSG reactions and latex allergy cross-reactive foods can help you make sense of your symptoms when you eat certain foods. If you think you have had a reaction to a food or additive, it is best to follow up with your medical doctor, who may refer you to an allergist for further testing. A naturopathic doctor can also help further identify food triggers.

Rethinking Our Place in Nature

Over the last 100 years, humans have had a profound impact on the planet, leading to population overgrowth and use of resources that overshoots the carrying capacity of our life support system. It's vital to know how what you eat and consume affects the earth. When you eat an organic, plants-only diet, reduce overall consumption of products, minimize your exposure to toxins and are proactive in protecting the environment, you are helping to save rainforests, protect wildlife and repopulate marine ecosystems, and are contributing to the sustainability of the planetary biosphere for future generations.

CHAPTER 10

Human Consumption: Effects on the Environment

As we've seen throughout this book, human behavior has influenced not only the outcome of our health but also the health of our environment. Perhaps what is having one of the most serious impacts on our environment is exponential population growth and human consumption. With technology and modern farming, fishing and medicine, the human population has grown out of the control of the ecosystem's checks and balances. We are currently in overshoot, using more than 1.6 times the Earth's resources every year and depleting non-renewable and so-called renewable resources faster than they can be replenished. Our current population demands more from nature than nature can provide and cannot be sustained at our current consumption levels over the long term.

Global Impact of Population

What individuals can do to prevent the devastating effects of human populations on the environment is to reverse the upward trend. Reducing the population's growth by decreasing birth rates is a necessary step to bring global population into balance.

While some current thinkers have pointed to countries like China and India for their burgeoning population growth, it is also crucial to consider consumption rates to get the full picture of the effects on the planet. It is estimated that the consumption of one person in an affluent society is equivalent to 40 to 50 people in poor countries.

> **DID YOU KNOW?**
>
> **Land Mammal Biomass**
> In the year 2000, wild animals made up only 2% of the land mammal biomass compared to 98% biomass of humans and their domesticated animals.

> **DID YOU KNOW?**
>
> **Population Burden**
> The already unsustainably high human population is still growing and is predicted to reach 9 or 10 billion by mid-century.

Food Consumption

One of the largest contributors to climate change and global depletion is humanity's consumption of 70 billion farm animals a year for food. It is estimated that avoiding eating meat, fish and animal products reduces an individual's carbon footprint (the amount of carbon that comes from your consumption) by 50%. Changing to a plant diet and encouraging others to do the same is vital in saving our life-support system.

In Brazil, for example, rainforests are being cut down largely to make room for growing soybeans to feed livestock and provide grazing land for cattle. The beef that comes from Brazil is sold around the world. It takes 2,500 gallons (660 L) of water and 16 pounds (8 kg) of feed to make 1 pound (500 g) of cow meat. The same amount of meat takes 20,000 Kcal (kilocalories) of fossil-fuels-generated electricity to manufacture fertilizers and insecticides, mechanize the production of cattle for food, and for transportation. At this rate of destruction, the Amazon rainforest is predicted to be a desert by the year 2050.

Global Impact of Land Use

Only 5% of land is currently being used worldwide to provide plant foods for direct human consumption. Between 2,000 and 4,000 pounds (1,000 to 2,000 kg) of plant food can be grown on 1 acre of land, whereas only

FAQ

Q: Isn't the burning of fossil fuels for transportation the biggest cause of greenhouse gas emissions?

A: Most people believe that burning fossil fuels for transportation is the biggest cause of global greenhouse gas emissions and the resultant climate change and ocean acidification. But some of the statistics do not reveal the whole picture. According to some organizations, including the Worldwatch Institute, 51% of global greenhouse gases comes from the production of livestock for human consumption. This figure takes into account the methane gas produced in the stomachs of livestock when digesting, the use of fossil fuels to grow and transport crops to feed livestock, the clear-cutting of rainforests to grow food for the livestock, the breakdown of manure by bacteria and the processing, packaging and transportation of the end product.

one 300-pound (136 kg) cow can be grazed on this same amount of land. In the United States, 70% of its land is used to feed livestock, in part because of the recent trend to favor grass-fed beef over beef that has been factory farmed. Unfortunately, grass-fed cows create more greenhouse gases because they have to be grazed twice as long before they are slaughtered.

Livestock and Greenhouse Gases

Livestock farming creates 90 million tons of methane annually. Methane is at least 20 times more potent a greenhouse gas than carbon dioxide, so smaller amounts of methane have a greater impact on climate change. Microorganisms in the stomachs of cows, sheep and goats create 37% of total human-related sources of yearly methane gas emissions. This contributes to climate change, which is predicted to bring worse storms and droughts, contribute to the rise of sea levels and have devastating effects on the survival of the human species. About half of the farmland in the U.S. is being used to grow corn and soy for cattle. Every year, 1.4 billion tons of waste, which accounts for 5 tons per person, are produced from the 7 billion livestock produced in the U.S. meat industry. The waste is largely untreated and contains heavy metals, antibiotics and more than 100 pathogens such as *E. coli* bacteria that have the potential to contaminate food and water supplies.

Fossil Fuel Use in Fishing

The use of fossil fuels for catching fish is up to 14 times larger than for the production of vegetable protein. If fish are caught in gill nets, energy use is 65% larger for fish protein than for vegetable protein.

Sustainability

Sustainability involves looking at the efficiency of food production in terms of inputs and outputs and addresses the preservation of ecosystems, including the biosphere. Preventing climate change, avoiding environmental degradation, preserving natural habitats for other animals, maintaining the biodiversity of life on earth, and preventing nitrogen and phosphorus runoff into rivers, lakes and oceans are of key concern for sustainability.

DID YOU KNOW?

Preventing Extinction
About 54% of the Earth's land has already been cleared to feed and provide grazing for livestock — and that has driven wildlife to critically endangered levels and extinction. Eliminating the consumption of animals for food is a necessary and achievable step in saving wildlife and our life-support systems.

DID YOU KNOW?

Plant Pluses
Organic plant agriculture has the lowest effect on the environment and improves soil quality and biodiversity.

FAQ

Q: **What effects are palm plantations having on particular species in Indonesia's rainforests?**

A: Global food choices impact species such as orangutans and can have detrimental effects. Currently, Indonesian rainforests that are home to orangutans and the Sumatran tiger are being burned or logged and converted to plantations to grow palm oil. Since 1998, the orangutan population in Sumatra has been declining by 1,000 a year. The orangutan population has shrunk by more than 50% in Sumatra since 1993 and could be extinct within 25 years if the rate of loss continues. Consumption of palm oil is the biggest threat to the future of orangutans. Demand for palm oil in the U.S. has tripled in the last five years because of its abundant use — 50% of all consumer goods, from cosmetics and packaged food to body lotions and hair care products to biofuels, contain it. Avoiding the purchase of products with palm oil and supporting companies that don't use palm oil goes a long way to saving the rainforest ecosystem for these endangered species. This unique rainforest ecosystem is also threatened by logging for its wood, which is used as paper for cardboard packaging, fast-food wrappers, printer paper and junk mail.

Crops and Soil Erosion

Soil erosion is associated with growing corn and soy, increases the need for fertilizers that impact the beneficial bacteria and worms in the soil and contributes to excess phosphorus and nitrogen runoff into the rivers and oceans. Fertilizer runoff containing nitrates is responsible for large algal blooms that choke out the coral reefs and cause dead zones along coastal regions in the oceans. Fish and other marine life who swim into these areas die immediately.

DID YOU KNOW?

High Emissions
In meals with the same calories, the greenhouse gas emissions calculated for meat compared to vegetables may differ by a factor of two to nine times as much for animal agriculture.

Saving the Rainforests

Consuming less can save the habitat of species in the rainforest. Not buying things that come in cardboard packaging, not buying paper products such as paper towels, buying only recycled paper, not buying a new house, not buying new furniture and choosing a digital instead of a paper version of the local newspaper are all things you can do to save entire forest ecosystems from destruction.

Foods Containing Palm Oil

- Baked goods
- Candies
- Cakes and cake mixes
- Cereal
- Chips
- Chocolate bars and chocolate candies
- Cookies
- Crackers
- Dried and canned soups
- Doughnuts
- Energy bars
- Frozen meals
- Frozen pies
- Frozen pizza
- Frozen potato products
- Frozen waffles/pancakes
- Granola bars
- Ice cream products
- Instant noodles
- Instant oatmeal
- Margarine
- Microwave popcorn
- Peanut butter
- Pretzels
- Toaster pastries

Other Names for Palm Oil

- Fractionated palm oil (FP(K)O)
- Organic palm kernel oil (OPKO)
- Palm kernel oil (PKO)
- Palm kernel olein (PKOo)
- Palm kernel stearin (PKS)
- Palm oil
- Palmate
- Palmitate — Vitamin A or Asorbyl Palmitate
- Partially hydrogenated palm oil (PHPKO)
- Sodium dodecyl sulfate (SDS or NaDS)
- Sodium laureth sulfate
- Vegetable oil (palm kernel)
- Vegetable oil (palm)

Source: Adapted from the Rainforest Action Network. Palm Oil's Dirty Secret: The Many Ingredient Names for Palm Oil. 2011. www.ran.org/palm_oil_s_dirty_secret_the_many_ingredient_names_for_palm_oil.

Refraining from buying foods and products that contain palm oil will help prevent deforestation in Indonesia and can help save the orangutans from extinction. Not buying new cell phones and recycling cell phones and laptops helps prevent deforestation in the Congo and Columbia where the mineral coltan is being mined. Gorilla habitat is being lost due to mining in the Congo.

Buying recycled toilet paper and tissues, or using a handkerchief instead of tissues, and towels instead of paper towels, can help save the Amazon rainforest. Not eating beef can help save the South American rainforest from further destruction. Other initiatives can also help save the rainforests, such as not buying furniture made from exotic wood, buying recycled paper and paper made of grains instead of wood and buying digital books when they're available.

Environmental Impact on Wildlife

Today, we find environmental toxins in many of the synthetic chemicals and household products we use every day. Among the most persistent and well-known toxins are PCBs (polychlorinated biphenyls) and dioxins. In addition to the effects on humans, in recent years they have been having a catastrophic effect on some wildlife, including sea life, birds, amphibians, dogs and bugs. Consider these case studies.

PCBs, DDT and Other Pesticides

Effects of PCBs in Beluga Whales

Cancers were the main cause of mortality in adult belugas during the 1980s and 1990s. Beluga whales from the St. Lawrence River had been found by scientists to be heavily contaminated with PCBs, as well as polyaromatic hydrocarbons (PAHs) and heavy metals. Between 1983 and 1999, 129 of the 263 beluga whales found dead along the shores of the St. Lawrence were examined in the University de Montreal's Faculty of Veterinary Medicine to determine the cause of death. Six of the 18 cases of cancer detected affected the small intestine, which is rare in animals. It is possible that the high rates of cancer found in these whales were caused by a combination of toxins that include PCBs, DDT, pesticides and PAHs.

Since 1982, samples of fatty tissue have been taken from whale carcasses, and a biopsy program in 1994 found that living beluga whales were just as contaminated as those that had been found dead. During that time, a comparison of beluga whales from the St. Lawrence River to those in the Arctic found that concentrations of heavy metals, such as lead and mercury, were 2 to 15 times higher, and PCBs were up to 25 times higher, due to the whales' diet of fish. Because PCBs are immunosuppressant, they weakened the belugas' immune system, making them more susceptible to cancer. The St. Lawrence belugas showed the highest rates of cancer at 27% — much higher compared to Arctic belugas or any other wild mammal species. Studies have identified cancers of the intestines, mammary glands, ovaries, uterus, skin, stomach, salivary glands, thymus and bladder. Since the 1990s, the levels of contamination have decreased for PCBs and no known beluga born after 1971 has died of cancer.

> **Cancers were the main cause of mortality in adult belugas during the 1980s and 1990s.**

Effects of DDT on Birds

Over the past 30 years, the ecological ramifications of using DDT (dichlorodiphenyltrichloroethane), an organochloride known for its insecticidal properties, have resulted in massive and widespread population declines among many bird species over large geographic areas. In particular, DDT has caused eggshells to thin, which causes poor reproduction and rapid population declines in birds, especially in predatory birds like eagles. The lack of ecological insight and unforeseen damages over the decades is still affecting the recovery of bird populations.

Effects of Pesticide Exposure on Birds and Dogs

In a bird-monitoring program in New York, birds that were suspected of dying from West Nile virus were found to have died instead from pesticide poisoning when later tested. Among these bird deaths, lawn care pesticides were found to be one of the biggest culprits. Another study found that for every acre of farmland, between 3 and 14 bird deaths are believed to occur because of pesticides.

In another recent study, dogs, especially Scottish terriers, who were exposed to lawns sprayed with herbicides were found to be at greater risk of bladder cancer. There is also a greater risk of lymphoma in dogs exposed to pesticides — the use of professionally applied pesticides was associated with a 70% higher risk of canine malignant lymphoma.

Chlorpyrifos Toxicity in Birds, Fish and Bugs

Chlorpyrifos is very toxic to many bird species, such as grackles, pigeons and mallard ducks. A similar effect to that of DDT, where eggshells thin and many young ducklings die, occurs when mallard ducks ingest chlorpyrifos. This pesticide is also very toxic to fish and aquatic invertebrates. It is toxic to bees for up to 24 hours after spraying and toxic to earthworms for up to 2 weeks after it is applied to the soil.

Carbamates, Pyrethroids and Glyphosates

Carbamate compounds were first discovered in the 1930s and used as pesticides in the 1940s. They have been used together with organophosphates, especially since the 1970s, when DDT and dieldrin were banned for use in the United States.

DID YOU KNOW?

Pesticides in Amphibians
Amphibian deformities and declines have been found to be potentially caused by pesticides.

Dogs, especially Scottish terriers, who were exposed to lawns sprayed with herbicides were found to be at greater risk of bladder cancer. There is also a greater risk of lymphoma in dogs exposed to pesticides.

Bird Deaths from Carbamates

More than 100 avian species have been poisoned by carbamates and organophosphate pesticides. Raptors and other bird species become victims of secondary poisoning when they scavenge dead animals poisoned by pesticides or feed on live animals or invertebrates unable to escape predation because of pesticide intoxication.

> **Wild birds are often affected seasonally from pesticide application. If not killed immediately, living birds may exhibit convulsions, lethargy, paralysis or tremors.**

Wild birds are often affected seasonally from pesticide application. If not killed immediately, living birds may exhibit convulsions, lethargy, paralysis or tremors. Birds are exposed to pesticides from treated seeds, pesticide residues and water contamination through runoff or irrigation. Species that commonly die due to carbamate poisoning include the mallard duck, ring-necked pheasant, red-winged blackbird, jays, crows, blackbirds, thrushes, bluebirds, swallows, geese, surface-feeding ducks, diving ducks, eagles, hawks, owls, vultures, falcons, shorebirds, wading birds, gulls and doves.

Pyrethroids and Wildlife

Pyrethroids are a synthetic pesticide similar to a compound that is extracted from the flowers of a species of chrysanthemum known as pyrethrums. Both of these compounds are extremely toxic to fish, lobster, mayfly nymphs and zooplankton. These insecticides have the ability to kill fish in lakes at very low concentrations in the range of 1 part per billion. Pyrethroids are moderately toxic to birds, with waterfowl and small insectivorous birds being the most susceptible. Beneficial bugs and pests are all affected by pyrethroids, which can lead to a lack of natural controls on pest populations.

Glyphosate Pesticides and the Monarch Butterfly

Monarch butterflies have been in decline over the past several years due to the eradication of milkweed in favor of other crops. Pesticides are sprayed on the fields to eradicate milkweed plants. U.S. farms' large-scale use of herbicides that destroy milkweed is a major contributor to the decline of the butterflies. Milkweed is the only plant on which monarch butterflies will lay their eggs, and it is the primary food source for monarch caterpillars. The plant's growth decreased

FAQ

Q: **What sorts of effects have neonicotinoids had on bumblebees?**

A: A recent study of the effects of neonicotinoid insecticides on bumblebees has found that bumblebees exposed to levels that are commonly used in the field of the neonicotinoid imidacloprid had a significantly reduced growth rate and suffered an 85% reduction in production of new queens compared with control colonies. Trace levels of the neonicotinoid pesticide are likely to have an impact on the population level because of the lack of queens being produced, thus affecting the next generation of bees. In 2015, the Ontario government passed regulations that will reduce the use of neonicotinoid-treated soy and corn seeds by 80% by 2017 as part of a Pollinator Action Plan.

by 21% in the United States between 1995 and 2013. About 350 million monarchs have historically made the migration from Canada and the United States to overwinter in Mexico. In 2015, only 60 million made it, a decline of 80%.

Several factors are contributing to the decline, including industrial and illegal logging in Mexico, heat waves and genetically modified crops. Genetically modified crops of soy and corn have been planted that are tolerant to Roundup, a glyphosate herbicide that has killed much of the milkweed over an area of 150 million hectares of farmland in the Midwest.

Pesticides and the Decline of Other Species

Populations of insects, earthworms, fish, birds and small mammals not intended as targets are also negatively affected by the use of pesticides. A study conducted in 2008 found that a combination of five widely used insecticides (carbaryl, chlorpyrifos, diazinon, endosulfan and malathion), in concentrations far below the limits set by the Environmental Protection Agency, killed 99% of leopard frog tadpoles. Furthermore, runoff from pesticides eventually ends up in our waterways — rainwater washes away pesticides that flow downstream into rivers, then lakes, then, ultimately, the ocean. Oysters taken from organochloride-contaminated water have deformities in their shells.

DID YOU KNOW?

Boosting Milkweed Growth

The decline in the growth of milkweed has prompted environmental groups to encourage people to grow the plant as feed for monarch butterfly caterpillars, as well as nectar-producing native flowers, such as wild bergamot, New England aster and black-eyed Susans, as feed for butterflies in yards and gardens.

The Health of Our Marine Ecosystems

Human activity is also contributing to the destruction of the oceans' ecosystem, which can be considered the lungs of the Earth. At least 50% to 70% of the oxygen we breathe comes from phytoplankton in the oceans. The pollutants we put in the air, however, along with the activities in which we engage in our waterways, have a serious impact.

Based on current data, ocean acidification is poised to be one of the largest and most rapid destructive forces affecting life in the sea. One of the biggest challenges facing humans today is to eliminate fossil fuel carbon dioxide emissions and the emission of methane and carbon dioxide from agricultural practices associated with livestock farming.

Fishing that overexploits one level of fish affects all other levels. Top predators manage the oceans by keeping all other levels of the food web in balance. If humans continue to wipe out top predators or fish at other food web levels, it will devastate the ocean food web and disrupt the Earth's oxygen supply. It is important to look at the ecological significance of the ocean to our survival. According to National Geographic Explorer-in-Residence Sylvia Earle, "Fish have other values. They are part of what makes the planet function in our favor. When we extract them, we are taking bites out of our life support system."

DID YOU KNOW?

Alarming Declines

Large predatory species like sharks, swordfishes, salmon and tuna have been reduced in numbers by 90% in the past 30 years.

DID YOU KNOW?

Shrimp Waste

For every pound (500 g) of shrimp fished from the ocean, approximately 25 pounds (12 kg) of other fish are destroyed and wasted. Worldwide, 25% to 50% of the total catch of fish is wasted as bycatch because it was not the targeted species.

Destructive Fishing Methods

Commercial fishermen in North America catch most of the fish brought to market — for example, in grocery stores — through a technique called trawling. Bottom trawl nets scoop up the bottom of the ocean floor, including habitats like corals and sponges and every untargeted fish, skate, ray and other sea creature in the area, in the process of going after a target species. It's like clear-cutting a forest in pursuit of a single species.

Fish have swim bladders in their bodies, filled with air to maintain buoyancy at depth. When fish are brought from the bottom of the ocean, where there is more pressure, to the top under almost no pressure, their swim bladders burst and the fish die. The fish that are caught as bycatch are typically not the most profitable species, so they are thrown back into the ocean, resulting in a wasteful and destructive practice to the ocean ecosystem.

Longlines that are used to catch "dolphin-friendly" tuna are typically filled with bycatch that are not targeted catch, including sea turtles, sea lions and sharks, and end up dying on the line. This fishing method is not very friendly to all these other species, but neither is it to the tuna, which have decreased on average by 90% worldwide and 96% in the North Pacific. Thousands of endangered species like sea turtles and sharks are killed each year on longlines.

Overfishing

Researchers at Dalhousie University, in Halifax, predict that by the year 2048 there will no longer be fish to eat because of overfishing and habitat loss if fishing practices continue as usual. Studies in the scientific journal *Nature* have shown that 90% of fish and ocean life has been exploited by humans in the past 100 years. Fish are being depleted at a rate of between 1 and 3 trillion a year — faster than they can reproduce.

Industrialized fisheries have typically reduced the community biomass of a fish species by 80% within 15 years of that species' exploitation. Fishing fleets then move to another species in a process known as serial depletion. This has a devastating effect on the ocean ecosystems and the dolphins, whales, sea turtles, sea lions and penguins that rely on the ocean food web and are also diminishing in number as a consequence.

There is the very real possibility that if humans continue to consume fish at current levels, many fisheries will be driven to collapse. In the waters off the east coast of Canada, the cod fisheries collapsed in 1992. Local inshore fishermen warned of a drop in the numbers of cod, and despite a recommendation by scientists in 1988 to cut the allowable catch in half, the government put off any action. A moratorium on fishing had to be imposed by the Canadian government, but it was too late — to date, the cod have not recovered their populations to a size that can be commercially fished again.

Farmed Fish

Although farmed fish are becoming popular and make up approximately 50% of all seafood produced for human consumption globally, the industry is proving to be destructive to local ecosystems. Like commercial fishing by boat, huge nets are placed in the ocean and the waste from fish ends up in the bottom of the sea. It takes 7 pounds

Rebalancing the Ocean Ecosystem

There is a way to let the ecosystem rebalance to its natural state of abundance in the oceans. As has been seen with the whaling industry, where many whale species were driven to near extinction until there was a complete ban on whaling in 1982, whales are making a comeback in numbers. Humpback whale populations, for example, have rebounded to up to 90% of pre-whaling numbers in Australian waters.

(3.5 kg) of smaller fish to obtain 1 pound (500 g) of a larger farmed fish. The smaller fish still need to be fished out of the ocean to feed the farmed fish, upsetting the ecosystem balance in the oceans by taking food away from wild animals. Since farmed fish live so closely together, they typically have to be fed antibiotics and are often contaminated with PCBs from the fish pellets they are fed, as described in detail in Chapter 1.

The Future of Our Oceans

Currently, 70% of the ocean, known as the high seas, does not have intergovernmental laws to protect it. Some of the logistical questions of how to police the open ocean to prevent illegal fishing or control fishing quotas are daunting intergovernmental tasks that have yet to be adequately addressed. The political process may take years or decades. Meanwhile, the industry is driven by consumer demand. It is up to informed people to take the initiative to end their consumption of fish and to let others know about the potential devastation of this dietary choice so that they can make informed decisions. Our actions are vital in saving our life-support system.

Action Plan

❑ Reduce your overall consumption of consumer products.

❑ Avoid eating meat, fish and animal products. Consider eating a plant-based diet and encouraging others to do the same.

❑ Get informed about the possible toxins in many household products and their effects on human and wildlife health.

❑ Learn more about our effects on the environment (see Resources, page 339).

PART 3

The Cleansing Detox Diet: Meal Plans and Recipes

The 10-Day Detox Diet

Getting Started: The First 10 Days

The first 10 days of the cleansing detox diet encourage the removal of common food sensitivities and substitution of foods that are least likely to cause an immune reaction, as well as foods that are high in nutrients, to allow for detoxification. You should eat more fruits and vegetables, as well as plant-based proteins, to stimulate the liver enzymes in Phase 1 and 2 of the liver detoxification process and to promote proper elimination from the bowels (see Chapter 6).

If you are experiencing a lot of gas and bloating before starting the diet, you may need to do a yeast, candida or bacteria cleanse. Using one or more of the herbs, such as oregano oil, garlic, Citricidal or caprylic acid, alongside a probiotic can be helpful. Check with your naturopathic doctor to see if these products are right for you. If you have constipation that does not resolve with a change in diet, consult your medical doctor, since this can be a sign of a more serious problem.

If you have been diagnosed with Crohn's disease, colitis or irritable bowel syndrome, your symptoms may resolve on this diet over time. Avoiding foods that may provoke sensitivities and taking probiotics together with herbs to heal the digestive lining can be helpful. Ask your naturopathic doctor whether any of these are recommended for you: vitamin A, L-glutamine, pantothenic acid, quercetin, selenium and a probiotic. Many different probiotics are available, and your naturopathic doctor can guide you in taking the appropriate one for your situation.

The specific supplements you might need to help detoxify the body is individual. Common nutrients that are prescribed by naturopathic doctors in supplemental form to assist in detoxification include the following:

- Choline
- Magnesium
- Quercetin
- Vitamin B_5
- Vitamin B_6
- Vitamin B_{12}
- Zinc

Assessment after 10 Days

If, after following the 10-Day Detox Diet menu, you decide to reintroduce wheat or dairy products into your diet, look for symptoms of intolerance such as the ones listed below. Many of my patients will purchase a cleanse system from a health food store and try it for a couple of weeks and then go back to eating what they used to eat. When they reintroduce the foods eliminated during the cleanse, they feel worse. This makes them believe that they need another cleanse, so they repeat the cycle of detoxing instead of just sticking to the diet that was prescribed during the detox in the first place. What this tells me is that they have food sensitivities that should be eliminated permanently from their diet in order to maintain optimal health. If you choose to eat foods that provoke common sensitivities, be aware of what may be provoking these symptoms or reactions:

- More frequent colds, flu or infections, such as sinus or ear
- Stomach pains
- Gas, bloating, constipation, diarrhea
- Joint pains
- Runny nose or post-nasal drip
- Skin rashes
- Itching

Beyond the 10-Day Detox Diet Plan

The 10-Day Detox Diet is a springboard to eating for long-term health and longevity. The recipes are beneficial for reducing inflammation, preventing bioaccumulation of toxins in the body and contributing to a healthy and sustainable long-term plan.

Choose from the 150 recipes listed at the back of the book to incorporate nutritious and low-allergen, nutrient-dense foods in your diet regularly. When you are able, eat more raw fruits and vegetables in your diet. If you suffer from diarrhea or irritable bowel syndrome, eat more cooked foods that are easier on the digestive tract.

Staying away from foods that promote common sensitivities has helped many people alleviate symptoms such as irritable bowel syndrome, gas, bloating, diarrhea, constipation, hormonal imbalances, autoimmune diseases (such as lupus, rheumatoid arthritis, Graves' disease and Hashimoto's thyroiditis), frequent colds, flu, bronchitis, sinusitis, ear infections, insomnia, joint pains, muscle pains,

> **DID YOU KNOW?**
>
> **Essential Supplements**
> People eating a plant-based diet for a long period of time may also need to supplement their diet with vitamin D, calcium, omega-3 essential oils from flax oil, iron, zinc and the amino acid carnosine. The building blocks of carnosine can be made from soy protein in vegetarians.

fibromyalgia, depression, anxiety and low energy. This preventive diet plan can also help minimize the risk of heart disease, cancer and diabetes. Sticking to an organic plant diet reduces the toxins from pesticides, dioxins and PCBs and is good for the planetary ecosystem. As you feel better, spread the knowledge to friends and family.

Follow-Up Vitamins to Consider

If you follow the diet in this book for the long term, it is essential to take B_{12} supplementation. Talk to your naturopathic doctor about taking doses between 500 and 2000 micrograms (µg) a day as a therapeutic dose and/or make sure that you are eating an adequate amount of gluten-free fortified cereals or non-dairy milks that contain B_{12}.

Common Adult Dosages for Optimal Health

If you plan to follow the Detox Diet long-term, consult with your naturopathic doctor to ensure that these supplements are recommended for you.

Supplement	Adult Dosage
Vitamin D	1000 IU a day
Zinc	10–30 mg a day (*Caution:* take with food to avoid nausea)
Vitamin B_{12}	1000 µg a day
Flax oil	1–3 caps a day
Carnosine	500–1000 mg a day
Iron	variable: depends on the person
Calcium	depends on the person; 600–1000 mg a day

The 10-Day Cleansing Detox Meal Plan

DAY 1

Breakfast: Super Protein Shake (page 184)
Snack: Chewy Coconut Quinoa Bar (page 204)
Lunch: Mixed Green Salad with Zesty Herb Dressing (page 229)
Snack: Herbed Vegetable Spread (page 217) on Moroccan Anise Crackers (page 201)
Dinner: Chickpeas in Tomato Curry (page 275)

DAY 2

Breakfast: Green Juice Detox (page 182)
Snack: Multi-Seed Energy Bar (page 203)
Lunch: Spinach and Sea Vegetable Soup (page 255)
Snack: Garlicky White Bean Spread (page 214) on Wheat-Free Thins (page 199)
Dinner: Onion-Braised Potatoes with Spinach (page 298), served with brown rice

DAY 3

Breakfast: Mango Greens Smoothie (page 184)
Snack: Sunflower Quinoa Snack Square (page 205)
Lunch: Summer Greens and Berries with Apple Cider Vinaigrette (page 230)
Snack: Roasted Vegetable Hummus (page 215) on Multi-Seed Quinoa Crackers (page 200)
Dinner: Sweet Potato Shepherd's Pie (page 282)

DAY 4

Breakfast: Grasshopper Juice (page 181)
Snack: Chocolate Date Protein Bar (page 202)
Lunch: Spinach, Quinoa and Broccoli Bisque (page 260)
Snack: Avocado Spinach Dip (page 212) on Wheat-Free Thins (page 199)
Dinner: Chickpeas and Cauliflower in Tomato Curry (page 276)

DAY 5

Breakfast: Green Juice Detox (page 182)
Snack: Sweet Toasted Pumpkin Seeds (page 198)
Lunch: Greens and Vegetable Salad with Lemon Dressing (page 230)
Snack: Garlicky White Bean Spread (page 214) on Wheat-Free Thins (page 199)
Dinner: Butternut Squash with Snow Peas and Red Pepper (page 299)

DAY 6

Breakfast: Bitter Detoxifier (page 182)
Snack: Sliced apple with sunflower seed butter
Lunch: Butternut Squash and Apple Soup with Ginger (page 254)
Snack: Country-Style Eggplant (page 216) on Multi-Seed Quinoa Crackers (page 200)
Dinner: Caribbean Red Bean, Spinach and Potato Curry (page 272)

DAY 7

Breakfast: Green Tea Metabolizer (page 183)
Snack: Apricot Breakfast Bites (page 175)
Lunch: Watercress, Raspberry and Avocado Salad (page 231)
Snack: Roasted Vegetable Hummus (page 215) on Wheat-Free Thins (page 199)
Dinner: Curried Chickpeas (page 277)

DAY 8

Breakfast: Just Peachy Blueberry Picnic (page 178)
Snack: Sunflower Quinoa Snack Square (page 205)
Lunch: Warm Beet Salad (page 233) and Kale Spring Rolls (page 210)
Snack: Herbed Vegetable Spread (page 217) on Moroccan Anise Crackers (page 201)
Dinner: Two-Bean Chili with Zucchini (page 266)

DAY 9

Breakfast: Beta-Carotene Burst (page 179)
Snack: Multi-Seed Energy Bar (page 203)
Lunch: Maki Rolls with Carrot Rice and Avocado (page 208)
Snack: Avocado Spinach Dip (page 212) on Wheat-Free Thins (page 199)
Dinner: Black-Eyed Peas with Vegetables (page 278)

DAY 10

Breakfast: Iron-Builder Juice (page 180)
Snack: Chocolate Date Protein Bar (page 202)
Lunch: Nori Pinwheels (page 206)
Snack: Country-Style Eggplant (page 216) on Multi-Seed Quinoa Crackers (page 200)
Dinner: Black Bean Burger (page 269)

About the Nutrient Analysis

The nutrient analysis done on the recipes in this book was derived from the Food Processor SQL Nutrition Analysis Software, version 10.9, ESHA Research (2011). Where necessary, data was supplemented using the USDA National Nutrient Database for Standard Reference, Release #28 (2016), retrieved January 2016 from the USDA Agricultural Research Service website: www.nal.usda.gov/fnic/foodcomp/search.

Recipes were evaluated as follows:

- The larger number of servings was used where there is a range.
- Where alternatives are given, the first ingredient and amount listed were used.
- The smaller quantity of an ingredient was used where a range is provided.
- Optional ingredients and ingredients that are not quantified were not included.
- Calculations were based on imperial measures and weights.
- Nutrient values were rounded to the nearest whole number for calories, fat, carbohydrate, fiber, protein, fiber and magnesium.
- Nutrient values were rounded to one decimal point for B_6 and zinc.
- Almond butter was used where the ingredient is listed as nut butter.
- Olive oil was used where the type of fat was not specified.
- Recipes were analyzed prior to cooking.

It is important to note that the cooking method used to prepare the recipe may alter the nutrient content per serving, as may ingredient substitutions and differences among brand-name products.

Breakfast

Ancient Grains Granola 162

Multigrain Cereal with Fruit 163

Breakfast Porridge 164

Cranberry Quinoa Porridge 165

Carrot Cake Baked Amaranth 166

Essential Coconut Pancakes 167

Make-Ahead Coconut Crêpes 168

Chia Pancakes with Maple Syrup 170

Good Morning Grain-Free Waffles 171

Pumpkin Latte Waffles 172

Smoky Sweet Potato Hash 173

Beans and Rice 174

Apricot Breakfast Bites 175

Chocolate Chip Breakfast Bars 176

Ancient Grains Granola

With this crispy and
crunchy granola, the
possibilities for variation
are endless, so have fun
with spices, sweeteners,
nuts, seeds, flaked
coconut and dried fruit.

Tips

An equal amount of
melted virgin coconut oil,
or unsalted butter, melted,
can be used in place of the
olive oil.

For the chopped dried
fruit, try apricots, cherries
or raisins.

- **Preheat oven to 325°F (160°C)**
- **Large rimmed baking sheet, lined with parchment paper**

2 cups	certified gluten-free large-flake (old-fashioned) rolled oats	500 mL
1 cup	amaranth or quinoa, rinsed	250 mL
½ cup	teff or millet	125 mL
½ cup	chia seeds	125 mL
⅓ cup	packed light brown sugar	75 mL
2 tsp	ground cinnamon	10 mL
1 tsp	fine sea salt	5 mL
½ cup	olive oil	125 mL
½ cup	pure maple syrup, liquid honey or brown rice syrup	125 mL
1 cup	chopped dried fruit	250 mL

1. In a large bowl, combine oats, amaranth, teff and chia seeds.

2. In a medium bowl, whisk together brown sugar, cinnamon, salt, oil and maple syrup until well blended.

3. Add the brown sugar mixture to the oat mixture and stir until well coated. Spread mixture evenly on prepared baking sheet.

4. Bake in preheated oven for 22 to 27 minutes or until oats are golden brown. Let cool completely on pan.

5. Transfer granola to an airtight container and stir in dried fruit. Store at room temperature for up to 2 weeks.

Nutrients per ½ cup (125 mL)	
Calories	333
Fat	13 g
Carbohydrate	50 g
Fiber	6 g
Protein	6 g
Vitamin B$_6$	0.1 mg
Magnesium	294 mg
Zinc	0.8 mg

Multigrain Cereal with Fruit

A steaming bowl of this tasty cereal gets you off to a good start in the morning and will help to keep you energized and productive throughout the day.

Tip

If you're having trouble digesting grains such as oats, amaranth, millet or quinoa, try soaking them overnight in warm non-chlorinated water (about 2 parts water to 1 part grain) with a spoonful or so of cider vinegar. Add some seeds, if desired. Drain, rinse and cook in the morning. A bonus is that your cereal will be creamier than usual.

4 cups	water	1 L
¼ tsp	salt (optional)	1 mL
½ cup	long- or short-grain brown rice, rinsed and drained	125 mL
½ cup	wild rice	125 mL
½ cup	Job's tears	125 mL
½ tsp	gluten-free vanilla extract	2 mL
2	apples, peeled and thinly sliced	2
½ cup	chopped pitted soft dates (such as Medjool)	125 mL
	Milk or non-dairy alternative	
	Maple syrup	
	Chopped toasted nuts (optional)	

1. In a large saucepan over medium heat, bring water and salt (if using) to a boil. Gradually stir in rice, wild rice, Job's tears, vanilla and apples and return to a boil. Reduce heat to low. Cover and simmer, placing a heat diffuser under the pot, if necessary, until Job's tears are tender, about 1 hour. Stir in dates. Serve with milk or non-dairy alternative and maple syrup. Sprinkle with nuts (if using).

Nutrients per serving	
Calories	148
Fat	1 g
Carbohydrate	33 g
Fiber	2 g
Protein	4 g
Vitamin B$_6$	0.1 mg
Magnesium	41 mg
Zinc	0.9 mg

Breakfast Porridge

1 cup	filtered water	250 mL
1/4 cup	raw pumpkin seeds	60 mL
3 tbsp	chia seeds	45 mL
3 tbsp	raw agave nectar	45 mL
2 tbsp	raw shelled hemp seeds	30 mL
1/4 tsp	raw vanilla extract	1 mL

Makes 1 serving

A crunchy blend of nutrient-dense seeds makes this porridge a great way to start your day.

Tips

When soaked, chia seeds can swell up to nine times their original size. This typically takes between 10 and 15 minutes, so be patient when working with these seeds.

When purchasing raw vanilla extract, look for alcohol-free extract, to avoid the taste of raw alcohol in your dish.

1. In a bowl, combine water, pumpkin seeds, chia seeds, agave nectar, hemp seeds and vanilla. Mix well. Cover and set aside for about 10 minutes so the chia seeds can absorb the liquid and swell. Serve immediately or cover and refrigerate for up to 2 days.

Variations

Add a dash of ground cinnamon and freshly grated nutmeg right before serving.

Substitute an equal amount of coconut milk for the water, whole raw almonds for the pumpkin seeds, and raw sesame seeds for the hemp seeds.

Nutrients per serving	
Calories	507
Fat	39 g
Carbohydrate	23 g
Fiber	15 g
Protein	24 g
Vitamin B6	0.2 mg
Magnesium	514 mg
Zinc	6.9 mg

Cranberry Quinoa Porridge

If you're not organized enough to make hot cereal ahead of time, here's one you can enjoy in less than half an hour, start to finish, and that doesn't require any attention while it's cooking.

Tip

Unless you have a stove with a true simmer, after reducing the heat to low, place a heat diffuser under the pot to prevent the mixture from boiling. This device also helps to ensure the grains will cook evenly and prevents hot spots, which might cause scorching, from forming. Heat diffusers are available at kitchen supply and hardware stores and are made to work on gas or electric stoves.

3 cups	water	750 mL
1 cup	quinoa, rinsed and drained	250 mL
½ cup	dried cranberries	125 mL
	Maple syrup or honey	
	Milk or non-dairy alternative (optional)	

1. In a saucepan over medium heat, bring water to a boil. Stir in quinoa and cranberries and return to a boil. Reduce heat to low. Cover and simmer until quinoa is cooked (look for a white line around the seeds), about 15 minutes. Remove from heat and let stand, covered, about 5 minutes. Serve with maple syrup and milk or non-dairy alternative (if using).

Variations

Substitute dried cherries or blueberries or raisins for the cranberries.

Use red quinoa for a change.

Nutrients per serving	
Calories	135
Fat	2 g
Carbohydrate	27 g
Fiber	3 g
Protein	4 g
Vitamin B$_6$	0.1 mg
Magnesium	58 mg
Zinc	0.9 mg

Carrot Cake
Baked Amaranth

Hello, autumn. Here, carrots, raisins and fall spices merge effortlessly with amaranth for a warming breakfast that epitomizes cozy.

Tip
If using non-dairy milk, try almond, rice or hemp.

Storage Tip
Let cool completely, cover and refrigerate for up to 2 days. Warm in the microwave.

- **Preheat oven to 375°F (190°C)**
- **9-inch (23 cm) square glass baking dish, sprayed with nonstick cooking spray**

1 tbsp	unsalted butter or virgin coconut oil	15 mL
1 cup	amaranth	250 mL
1/4 cup	fine crystal cane sugar or packed dark brown sugar	60 mL
2 1/2 tsp	pumpkin pie spice	12 mL
1/2 tsp	fine sea salt	2 mL
2 1/2 cups	milk or plain non-dairy milk	625 mL
1 1/4 cups	finely shredded carrots	300 mL
1/2 cup	raisins	125 mL
1 tsp	gluten-free vanilla extract	5 mL

Suggested Accompaniments
Pure maple syrup or liquid honey
Milk or plain non-dairy milk

1. In a medium saucepan, melt butter over medium heat. Add amaranth and cook, stirring, for 2 to 3 minutes or until fragrant and golden. Whisk in sugar, pumpkin pie spice, salt, milk, carrots, raisins and vanilla. Pour into prepared baking dish and cover tightly with foil.

2. Bake in preheated oven for 35 minutes. Transfer to a wire rack and carefully remove foil (steam will be released). Stir and let stand for 5 minutes.

3. Spoon into bowls and serve with any of the suggested accompaniments, as desired.

Variation
Carrot Cake Quinoa: Replace the amaranth with an equal amount of quinoa, rinsed.

Nutrients per serving	
Calories	396
Fat	8 g
Carbohydrate	71 g
Fiber	5 g
Protein	13 g
Vitamin B_6	0.5 mg
Magnesium	150 mg
Zinc	2.2 mg

Essential Coconut Pancakes

Makes 14 pancakes

Few things top home-made pancakes and this coconut variation is a winner with kids and adults alike. You'll stay satisfied for hours, too, thanks to the high protein content of the chickpea flour (10 grams in 1 cup/250 mL, compared to 8 grams in wheat flour) and the high fiber content of the coconut flour.

Tip
Serve the pancakes with any or all of your favorite toppings, such as maple syrup, coconut nectar, fresh fruit or a dab of coconut oil.

Nutrients per pancake	
Calories	107
Fat	8 g
Carbohydrate	9 g
Fiber	2 g
Protein	2 g
Vitamin B6	0.1 mg
Magnesium	20 mg
Zinc	0.3 mg

⅔ cup	chickpea flour	150 mL
6 tbsp	coconut flour	90 mL
1½ tbsp	potato starch	22 mL
2½ tsp	gluten-free baking powder	12 mL
½ tsp	fine sea salt	2 mL
1 cup	well-stirred coconut milk (full-fat)	250 mL
⅔ cup	coconut water or water	150 mL
1 tbsp	psyllium husk	15 mL
2 tbsp	coconut sugar	30 mL
2 tbsp	melted virgin coconut oil	30 mL
1 tsp	gluten-free vanilla extract	5 mL
	Additional melted virgin coconut oil	

1. In a large bowl, whisk together chickpea flour, coconut flour, potato starch, baking powder and salt.

2. In a medium bowl, whisk together coconut milk, coconut water and psyllium. Let stand for 10 minutes to thicken. Whisk in coconut sugar, 2 tbsp (30 mL) coconut oil and vanilla until blended.

3. Add the coconut milk mixture to the flour mixture and stir until just blended.

4. Heat a griddle or skillet over medium heat. Brush with coconut oil. For each pancake, pour about ¼ cup (60 mL) batter onto griddle. Cook until bubbles appear on top. Turn pancake over and cook for about 1 minute or until golden brown. Repeat with the remaining batter, brushing griddle and adjusting heat as necessary between batches.

Variations
Blueberry Coconut Pancakes: After pouring the batter onto the griddle, sprinkle each pancake with 4 to 5 blueberries.

Apple Cinnamon Pancakes: Add 1½ tsp (7 mL) ground cinnamon in step 1. Stir in 1 cup (250 mL) shredded tart-sweet apple at the end of step 2.

Storage Tip
Refrigerate pancakes between sheets of waxed paper, tightly covered in plastic wrap, for up to 2 days or freeze, enclosed in a sealable plastic bag, for up to 1 month. Let thaw at room temperature or defrost in the microwave.

Make-Ahead Coconut Crêpes

The French sure know how to do pancakes. This super-satisfying, high-fiber variation of classic crêpes can be made in advance, then reheated with just about any filling — sweet or savory — that suits your fancy.

½ cup	chickpea flour	125 mL
⅓ cup	coconut flour	75 mL
1 tbsp	potato starch	15 mL
½ tsp	fine sea salt	2 mL
1 cup	coconut water or water	250 mL
⅔ cup	well-stirred coconut milk (full-fat)	150 mL
	Melted virgin coconut oil	

1. In a large bowl, whisk together chickpea flour, coconut flour, potato starch and salt. Whisk in coconut water and coconut milk until smooth. Cover and refrigerate for 1 hour.

2. Heat a large skillet over medium-high heat. Remove from heat and lightly grease pan with coconut oil. Whisk the crêpe batter slightly. For each crêpe, pour about ¼ cup (60 mL) batter into pan, quickly tilting in all directions to cover bottom of pan. Cook for about 45 seconds or until just golden at the edges. With a spatula, carefully lift edge of crêpe to test for doneness. The crêpe is ready to turn when it is golden brown on the bottom and can be shaken loose from the pan. Turn crêpe over and cook for about 15 to 30 seconds or until golden brown.

3. Transfer crêpe to an unfolded kitchen towel to cool completely. Repeat with the remaining batter, greasing skillet and adjusting heat as necessary between crêpes, stacking cooled crêpes between sheets of waxed paper to prevent sticking.

Nutrients per crêpe	
Calories	126
Fat	5 g
Carbohydrate	18 g
Fiber	2 g
Protein	3 g
Vitamin B$_6$	0.2 mg
Magnesium	35 mg
Zinc	0.4 mg

Tip

Fill crêpes with lemon juice and a drizzle of coconut nectar or a sprinkle of coconut sugar; a thin spread of coconut butter or seed butter and fruit-sweetened jam; coconut yogurt and fresh fruit or fruit-sweetened jam; grated gluten-free bittersweet chocolate; sautéed greens (spinach, kale, chard) and a sprinkle of nutritional yeast; or thinly sliced pears sprinkled with coconut sugar.

Variation

Coconut Flour Tortillas: Use a medium skillet. For each tortilla, pour about ⅓ cup (75 mL) batter into a hot skillet that has been lightly greased with melted virgin coconut oil. Cook for about 60 to 75 seconds on the first side and 30 to 45 seconds on the second side. Store in the same manner as the crêpes and use as you would wheat or corn tortillas.

Storage Tip

Refrigerate crêpes between sheets of waxed paper, tightly covered in plastic wrap, for up to 2 days or freeze, enclosed in a sealable plastic bag, for up to 1 month.

Chia Pancakes with Maple Syrup

Chia pancakes are full of fiber and protein, and will keep you fuller longer than regular pancakes.

1 cup	ground chia seeds	250 mL
1 cup	rice flour	250 mL
½ tsp	baking soda	2 mL
2 cups	unsweetened rice milk	500 mL
2 tbsp	olive oil, divided	30 mL
¼ cup	pure maple syrup	60 mL

1. In a large bowl, whisk together chia seeds, rice flour, baking soda and rice milk until blended.

2. In a large skillet, heat a thin layer of oil over medium heat. Pour in ¼ cup (60 mL) batter per pancake and cook for about 3 minutes or until lightly browned on bottom. Flip pancakes over and press down firmly with spatula. Cook for about 3 minutes or until golden brown. Transfer pancakes to a plate. Repeat with the remaining batter, adding oil and adjusting heat between batches as necessary. Serve pancakes with maple syrup.

Nutrients per serving	
Calories	449
Fat	18 g
Carbohydrate	67 g
Fiber	12 g
Protein	8 g
Vitamin B$_6$	0.3 mg
Magnesium	157 mg
Zinc	2.7 mg

Good Morning Grain-Free Waffles

These grain-free waffles are even better than the original! The texture is right in line with classic grain flour waffles, but these are far lower in sugar and higher in protein. The result? You'll feel satisfied and energized for far longer.

Storage Tip

Refrigerate waffles between sheets of waxed paper, tightly covered in plastic wrap, for up to 2 days or freeze, enclosed in a sealable plastic bag, for up to 1 month. Toast in a toaster for 1 to 2 minutes before serving.

Nutrients per waffle	
Calories	165
Fat	13 g
Carbohydrate	11 g
Fiber	3 g
Protein	2 g
Vitamin B$_6$	0.1 mg
Magnesium	25 mg
Zinc	0.4 mg

- **Preheat waffle maker to medium-high**

2 tbsp	psyllium husk	30 mL
1 tbsp	coconut sugar	15 mL
1 cup	well-stirred coconut milk (full-fat)	250 mL
½ cup	water	125 mL
2 tbsp	melted virgin coconut oil	30 mL
1 tbsp	gluten-free vanilla extract	15 mL
1½ tsp	cider vinegar	7 mL
½ cup	chickpea flour	125 mL
¼ cup	coconut flour	60 mL
1 tbsp	potato starch	15 mL
1½ tsp	gluten-free baking powder	7 mL
½ tsp	baking soda	2 mL
⅛ tsp	fine sea salt	0.5 mL
	Additional melted virgin coconut oil	

1. In a medium bowl, whisk together psyllium, coconut sugar, coconut milk, water, 2 tbsp (30 mL) coconut oil, vanilla and vinegar. Let stand for 5 minutes.

2. In a large bowl, whisk together chickpea flour, coconut flour, potato starch, baking powder, baking soda and salt. Add psyllium mixture and stir until just blended.

3. Lightly brush preheated waffle maker with coconut oil. For each waffle, pour about ⅓ cup (75 mL) batter into waffle maker. Cook according to manufacturer's instructions until golden brown.

Variation

Chocolate Chip Waffles: Stir ⅓ cup (75 mL) gluten-free miniature semisweet chocolate chips into the batter at the end of step 2.

Pumpkin Latte Waffles

Pumpkin, spice and everything nice is rejigged into a super-charged, super-easy breakfast reminiscent of your favorite autumn latte — you may never go back to the coffee-house again.

Storage Tip

Refrigerate waffles between sheets of waxed paper, tightly covered in plastic wrap, for up to 2 days or freeze, enclosed in a sealable plastic bag, for up to 1 month. Toast in a toaster for 1 to 2 minutes before serving.

Nutrients per waffle	
Calories	157
Fat	11 g
Carbohydrate	15 g
Fiber	3 g
Protein	2 g
Vitamin B$_6$	0.1 mg
Magnesium	26 mg
Zinc	0.5 mg

- **Preheat waffle maker to medium-high**

3 tbsp	coconut sugar	45 mL
2 tbsp	psyllium husk	30 mL
1 cup	pumpkin purée (not pie filling)	250 mL
1 cup	well-stirred coconut milk (full-fat)	250 mL
½ cup	strong-brewed coffee, cooled	125 mL
2 tbsp	melted virgin coconut oil	30 mL
⅔ cup	chickpea flour	150 mL
⅓ cup	coconut flour	75 mL
4 tsp	potato starch	20 mL
2½ tsp	gluten-free baking powder	12 mL
2 tsp	pumpkin pie spice	10 mL
½ tsp	fine sea salt	2 mL
	Additional melted virgin coconut oil	

1. In a medium bowl, whisk together coconut sugar, psyllium, pumpkin purée, coconut milk, coffee and 2 tbsp (30 mL) coconut oil. Let stand for 5 minutes.

2. In a large bowl, whisk together chickpea flour, coconut flour, potato starch, baking powder, pumpkin pie spice and salt.

3. Add the pumpkin mixture to the flour mixture and stir until just blended.

4. Lightly brush preheated waffle maker with coconut oil. For each waffle, pour about ⅓ cup (75 mL) batter into waffle maker. Cook according to manufacturer's instructions until golden brown.

Variations

Pumpkin Spice Waffles: Replace the coffee with an equal amount of coconut water or water.

Banana Waffles: Decrease the coconut sugar to 2 tbsp (30 mL), replace the pumpkin purée with an equal amount of mashed very ripe bananas, and replace the coffee with an equal amount of coconut water or water.

Smoky Sweet Potato Hash

Sweet potatoes take the place of traditional white potatoes in this smoky, hearty dish. And though this recipe is in the breakfast chapter, it makes a terrific dinner, too.

Tips

To vary the flavor, you can replace the smoked paprika with an equal amount of ground cumin, sweet paprika or chili powder.

An equal amount of pinto or kidney beans can be used in place of the black beans.

2 tbsp	virgin coconut oil	30 mL
1½ cups	chopped onions	375 mL
1	red bell pepper, chopped	1
2	cloves garlic, minced	2
2 tsp	smoked paprika	10 mL
2 cups	diced peeled sweet potatoes	500 mL
1¼ cups	coconut water or water	300 mL
¼ tsp	fine sea salt	1 mL
1 cup	rinsed drained canned black beans	250 mL
	Fine sea salt and freshly cracked black pepper	

Suggested Accompaniments

Chopped fresh cilantro or flat-leaf (Italian) parsley

Chopped fresh chives or green onions

Plain coconut yogurt

Salsa

Hot sauce

1. In a large skillet, melt coconut oil over medium heat. Add onions and red pepper; increase heat to medium-high and cook, stirring, for 6 to 8 minutes or until softened. Add garlic and paprika; cook, stirring, for 1 minute.

2. Stir in sweet potatoes, coconut water and salt; bring to a boil. Reduce heat, cover and simmer, without stirring, for 12 minutes. Uncover and stir with a spatula. Add black beans and cook, stirring, for 4 to 5 minutes or until liquid is absorbed and sweet potatoes are tender and slightly browned. Cover and let stand for 5 minutes.

3. Serve warm with any of the suggested accompaniments, as desired.

Variation

Chickpea Masala Hash: Replace the black beans with rinsed drained canned chickpeas, and replace the smoked paprika with an equal amount of garam masala or curry powder.

Nutrients per serving	
Calories	149
Fat	5 g
Carbohydrate	23 g
Fiber	6 g
Protein	4 g
Vitamin B$_6$	0.3 mg
Magnesium	46 mg
Zinc	0.6 mg

Beans and Rice

This dish is easy to make ahead of time and store in the fridge to reheat for a hearty breakfast.

Storage Tip

Store the cooled rice mixture in an airtight container in the refrigerator for up to 5 days. Reheat on the stovetop over medium heat, with a little water added to the pot, for about 5 minutes or until heated through.

2 cups	brown rice	500 mL
4 cups	water	1 L
1 tbsp	vegetable oil	15 mL
1	onion chopped	1
1	red bell pepper, chopped	1
1	can (14 to 19 oz/398 to 540 mL) black beans, drained and rinsed	1
1 cup	diced tomatoes	250 mL
¼ cup	chopped fresh cilantro	60 mL
½ tsp	salt	2 mL

1. In a saucepan, combine rice and water; bring to a boil over high heat. Reduce heat to low, cover and simmer for 30 minutes or until rice is tender and water is absorbed.

2. Meanwhile, in a large skillet, heat oil over medium heat. Add onion and red pepper; cook, stirring, for 5 to 10 minutes or until tender. Stir in beans, tomatoes, cilantro and salt; cook, stirring often, for 5 minutes or until heated through. Gently stir in cooked rice.

Nutrients per serving	
Calories	231
Fat	2 g
Carbohydrate	47 g
Fiber	6 g
Protein	7 g
Vitamin B_6	0.4 mg
Magnesium	91 mg
Zinc	1.3 mg

Apricot Breakfast Bites

Packed with coconut, assorted seeds, tart-sweet apricots and aromatic cardamom, these portable breakfast bites are far more exciting — and nutritious — than what you'll find on the breakfast bar shelf.

Tips

Ground cinnamon or ginger can be used in place of the cardamom.

An equal amount of other moist dried fruits (such as prunes, raisins or cherries) or fresh dates can be used in place of the apricots.

• Food processor

1 cup	moist, soft dried apricots	250 mL
¾ cup	unsweetened flaked coconut	175 mL
1 tbsp	virgin coconut oil	15 mL
¼ tsp	ground cardamom (optional)	1 mL
¾ cup	assorted raw seeds (sunflower, hemp, chia, sesame, green pumpkin)	175 mL

1. In food processor, combine apricots, coconut, coconut oil and cardamom (if using); pulse until mixture resembles a thick paste. Transfer to a medium bowl.

2. In the same food processor bowl (no need to clean it), pulse seeds until finely chopped. Add seeds to apricot paste and, using your fingers or a wooden spoon, combine well.

3. Roll mixture into twenty 1-inch (2.5 cm) balls. Cover and refrigerate for at least 30 minutes before eating.

Storage Tip

Store balls in an airtight container at room temperature for up to 3 days or in the refrigerator for up to 3 weeks. Or wrap them in plastic wrap, then foil, completely enclosing them, and freeze for up to 6 months. Let thaw at room temperature for 1 hour before serving.

Nutrients per piece	
Calories	67
Fat	5 g
Carbohydrate	6 g
Fiber	2 g
Protein	2 g
Vitamin B$_6$	0.1 mg
Magnesium	26 mg
Zinc	0.4 mg

Chocolate Chip Breakfast Bars

Makes 16 bars

If you are weary of grain-laden, preservative-packed energy bars and granola bars, give these chocolate chip breakfast bars a try.

Tips

Lining a pan with foil is easy. Begin by turning the pan upside down. Tear off a piece of foil longer than the pan, and then mold the foil over the pan. Remove the foil and set it aside. Flip the pan over and gently fit the shaped foil into the pan, allowing the foil to hang over the sides (the overhang ends will work as "handles" when the contents of the pan are removed).

An equal amount of chopped dried fruit (such as prunes, apricots or figs) can be used in place of the chocolate chips.

Nutrients per bar	
Calories	278
Fat	25 g
Carbohydrate	12 g
Fiber	3 g
Protein	5 g
Vitamin B6	0.2 mg
Magnesium	54 mg
Zinc	1.4 mg

- Food processor
- 9-inch (23 cm) square metal baking pan, lined with foil (see tip, at left)

2/3 cup	virgin coconut oil	150 mL
2 cups	sunflower seeds (raw, toasted or roasted)	500 mL
1 cup	unsweetened flaked or shredded coconut	250 mL
1/2 cup	sunflower seed butter or tahini	125 mL
3 tbsp	coconut flour	45 mL
1/2 tsp	fine sea salt	2 mL
1 1/2 tbsp	coconut sugar	22 mL
1 tbsp	gluten-free vanilla extract	15 mL
1/2 cup	gluten-free miniature semisweet chocolate chips	125 mL

1. In a small saucepan, melt coconut oil over medium-low heat.

2. In food processor, pulse sunflower seeds and coconut until chopped (not too fine). Add sunflower seed butter, coconut flour, salt, coconut sugar and vanilla; pulse until mixture begins to hold together as dough.

3. Transfer mixture to prepared pan and press flat with a square of waxed paper.

4. Melt chocolate chips in the microwave according to package directions (or in a heatproof bowl set over a saucepan of hot water). Drizzle or spread over bar mixture. Freeze for 30 minutes. Using foil liner, lift mixture from pan. Peel off foil and place bar mixture on a cutting board. Cut into 16 bars.

Storage Tip

Wrap bars individually and refrigerate for up to 2 weeks.

Juices and Smoothies

Just Peachy Blueberry Picnic 178

Beta-Carotene Burst 179

Iron-Builder Juice 180

Grasshopper Juice 181

Green Juice Detox 182

Bitter Detoxifier 182

Green Tea Metabolizer 183

Berry Chia Smoothie 183

Mango Greens Smoothie 184

Super Protein Shake 184

Just Peachy Blueberry Picnic

This smoothie is a wonderful summertime treat when peaches are in season and perfectly ripe. The addition of ginger is a delicious touch.

Tips

To remove the stone from a peach, slice around the middle with a paring knife, cutting the peach into two equal halves. If the fruit is ripe the stone will come out easily with your fingers.

When any stone fruits such as peaches become ripe, store them in the refrigerator. This stops the ripening process and they will keep for up to a week.

Nutrients per 1 cup (250 mL)

Calories	53
Fat	1 g
Carbohydrate	11 g
Fiber	2 g
Protein	1 g
Vitamin B$_6$	0 mg
Magnesium	9 mg
Zinc	0.2 mg

• **Blender**

½ cup	hemp milk	125 mL
1	large peach, peeled	1
½ cup	blueberries	125 mL
1 tbsp	chopped gingerroot	15 mL
1 tsp	freshly squeezed lemon juice	5 mL

1. In blender, combine hemp milk, peach, blueberries, ginger and lemon juice. Blend at high speed until smooth. Serve immediately.

Variations

Substitute an equal quantity of blackberries or brambleberries for the blueberries.

Substitute a nectarine for the peach.

Substitute almond milk for the hemp milk.

Beta-Carotene Burst

**Makes
2 cups (500 mL)**

This juice is rich in beta-carotene, which your body converts into vitamin A, an especially important nutrient for your eyes.

Tip

Whole vegetables such as carrots can go through the juicer as long as they will fit through the feed tube. Make sure you don't jam the machine by trying to put too much through at one time, and always use the proper tool to push foods through.

Nutrients per 1 cup (250 mL)	
Calories	198
Fat	1 g
Carbohydrate	49 g
Fiber	12 g
Protein	3 g
Vitamin B$_6$	0.4 mg
Magnesium	40 mg
Zinc	0.7 mg

- **Juicer**

8 to 10	medium carrots, sliced if necessary, divided	8 to 10
2	apples, quartered, divided	2
1	leaf romaine lettuce	1
1 tsp	freshly squeezed lemon juice	5 mL

1. In juicer, process 4 carrots, 1 apple and the lettuce. Add the remaining carrots and apple. Add lemon juice through the feed tube. Whisk and divide between two glasses. Serve immediately.

Variation

Substitute 3 slices of sweet potato, each approximately 1 inch (2.5 cm) in diameter, for three of the carrots. This will produce a luscious starchy juice that is also high in beta-carotene.

Iron-Builder Juice

This deep red juice provides both iron and folic acid.

Tips

Bunched beets contain beet greens, which are the leaves attached to fresh (not storage) beets. They are a fabulous dark green.

After juicing, you will be left with pulp. Save the pulp — it can easily be turned into raw crackers. Just be sure to remove the seeds from produce, such as the apple in this recipe, before juicing.

- **Juicer**

3	large red beets, sliced, divided	3
4	medium carrots, sliced, divided	4
½	bunch Swiss chard or beet greens, divided	½
1	small apple, sliced, divided	1

1. In juicer, process one-quarter of the beets, 1 carrot, one-quarter of the chard and one-quarter of the apple. Repeat until all the vegetables have been juiced. Whisk well and serve immediately.

Variation

Substitute 1 head of romaine lettuce or 1 bunch spinach or arugula for the chard.

Nutrients per ½ cup (125 mL)	
Calories	96
Fat	0 g
Carbohydrate	23 g
Fiber	6 g
Protein	2 g
Vitamin B$_6$	0.2 mg
Magnesium	36 mg
Zinc	0.5 mg

Grasshopper Juice

This juice is packed full of vitamins, minerals and other nutrients. It is perfect for a midday pick-me-up when blood sugar levels begin to drop.

Tip

Use any kind of green sprouts, such as sunflower, pea, broccoli or radish sprouts, in this recipe. Take care to wash sprouts especially thoroughly before consuming them, as they are dense and can be a haven for bacteria. Look for sprouts in natural foods stores or well-stocked supermarkets.

Nutrients per 1 cup (250 mL)	
Calories	153
Fat	1 g
Carbohydrate	37 g
Fiber	7 g
Protein	4 g
Vitamin B_6	0.4 mg
Magnesium	52 mg
Zinc	0.7 mg

- **Juicer**

2	medium apples, quartered, divided	2
1	bunch kale, divided	1
½	cucumber, cut into 4 pieces, divided	½
4	stalks celery, divided	4
¼ cup	sprouts (see tip, at left)	60 mL

1. In juicer, process half an apple, one-quarter of the kale, 1 piece cucumber, 1 stalk celery and 1 tbsp (15 mL) sprouts. Repeat three times. Whisk and serve immediately.

Variation

Substitute 2 pears for the apples and/or an equal quantity of another leafy green for the kale.

Green Juice Detox

This juice is loaded with chlorophyll, which is a powerful antioxidant.

Nutrients per serving	
Calories	140
Fat	2 g
Carbohydrate	30 g
Fiber	7 g
Protein	8 g
Vitamin B$_6$	0.6 mg
Magnesium	106 mg
Zinc	1.5 mg

- **Juicer**

2	bunches kale, divided	2
6	stalks celery, divided	6
2	cucumbers, sliced, divided	2
1/4	bunch parsley	1/4
1/4	lemon, skin on	1/4

1. In juicer, process 1 bunch kale, 3 stalks celery, 1 cucumber and the parsley and lemon. Repeat with the remaining kale, celery and cucumber. Whisk and serve immediately.

Bitter Detoxifier

If you're really keen on the benefits of raw food, try this juice.

Nutrients per 1 cup (250 mL)	
Calories	111
Fat	2 g
Carbohydrate	24 g
Fiber	7 g
Protein	7 g
Vitamin B$_6$	0.5 mg
Magnesium	87 mg
Zinc	1.3 mg

- **Juicer**

1	bunch dandelion greens	1
1/2	bunch kale	1/2
1/2	English cucumber, sliced	1/2
4	leaves romaine lettuce	4
1/4	bunch parsley	1/4
1/4	lemon, skin on, sliced	1/4
1	apple, sliced (optional)	1

1. In juicer, process half of each ingredient: dandelion greens, kale, cucumber, lettuce, parsley, lemon and apple (if using). Repeat. Whisk and serve immediately.

Variation

Substitute 1 bunch kale and 1/2 bunch Swiss chard for the dandelion greens.

Green Tea Metabolizer

This lemony blend is perfect for anyone who wants to reduce sugar intake.

Nutrients per ½ cup (125 mL)	
Calories	30
Fat	0 g
Carbohydrate	6 g
Fiber	2 g
Protein	1 g
Vitamin B₆	0.1 mg
Magnesium	21 mg
Zinc	0.3 mg

- **Juicer**

½ cup	warm filtered water (see tip, below)	125 mL
½ tsp	matcha green tea powder	2 mL
1	English cucumber, sliced	1
4	celery stalks	4
2	leaves romaine lettuce	2
½	lemon, skin on	½

1. In a large cup, combine warm water and green tea powder. Set aside to steep for 5 minutes.

2. In juicer, process cucumber, celery, lettuce and lemon. Add to the steeped tea, whisk and serve immediately.

Tip

To heat the water for this recipe, bring to a boil. Remove from heat and set aside to cool slightly, for 2 to 3 minutes. This will ensure that the water is below 105°F (41°C) and won't destroy any of the enzymes in the other ingredients.

Berry Chia Smoothie

Makes 2 servings

This drink is good for people of all ages.

Nutrients per serving	
Calories	386
Fat	20 g
Carbohydrate	44 g
Fiber	10 g
Protein	13 g
Vitamin B₆	0.2 mg
Magnesium	167 mg
Zinc	3.1 mg

- **Blender or food processor**

½ cup	cashews	125 mL
1 tbsp	whole chia seeds	15 mL
2 cups	vanilla rice milk or soy milk	500 mL
1 cup	frozen açaí berries	250 mL
1 cup	frozen raspberries	250 mL
6 to 8	pitted dates	6 to 8

1. In a bowl, combine cashews and chia seeds. Cover with water and let stand for 30 minutes. Drain.

2. In blender, combine rice milk, acai berries, raspberries, dates to taste, and cashew and chia seeds mixture. Blend until smooth.

Mango Greens Smoothie

This recipe is thick, rich and a good way to get greens in your diet. The chlorophyll in dark green leafy vegetables helps the body eliminate environmental toxins and metals.

Nutrients per serving	
Calories	108
Fat	1 g
Carbohydrate	26 g
Fiber	3 g
Protein	2 g
Vitamin B$_6$	0.3 mg
Magnesium	42 mg
Zinc	0.3 mg

• Blender

2 cups	frozen mango chunks	500 mL
2 cups	loosely packed trimmed spinach	500 mL
1 cup	water (approx.)	250 mL
1	small date, pitted	1

1. In blender, combine mango, spinach, water and date; blend until smooth. You may need to add a little extra water to the blender to make sure it mixes well. Serve immediately.

Super Protein Shake

Makes 1 serving

This shake provides antioxidants for liver detoxification.

Nutrients per serving	
Calories	525
Fat	35 g
Carbohydrate	51 g
Fiber	21 g
Protein	11 g
Vitamin B$_6$	0.5 mg
Magnesium	221 mg
Zinc	3.7 mg

• Blender

½	avocado	½
½ cup	frozen blueberries	125 mL
½ cup	frozen raspberries	125 mL
1 tbsp	green pumpkin seeds (pepitas)	15 mL
1 tbsp	chia seeds	15 mL
1 tbsp	ground flax seeds (flaxseed meal)	15 mL
½ cup	unsweetened rice milk	125 mL
¼ cup	freshly squeezed lemon juice	60 mL
1 tbsp	sunflower seed butter	15 mL

1. In blender, combine avocado, blueberries, raspberries, pumpkin seeds, chia seeds, flax seeds, rice milk, lemon juice and sunflower seed butter; blend until smooth. Serve immediately.

Breads and Muffins

Egg-Free, Corn-Free, Dairy-Free, Soy-Free
   Brown Bread 186

Egg-Free, Corn-Free, Dairy-Free, Soy-Free
   Flax Bread. 187

Egg-Free, Corn-Free, Dairy-Free, Soy-Free
   White Dinner Rolls 188

Pizza Crust. 189

Swedish Wraps 190

Coconut "Corn" Bread 191

Pumpkin Bread 192

Favorite Blueberry Muffins. 193

Applesauce Raisin Muffins 194

Carrot Cake Muffins 196

Egg-Free, Corn-Free, Dairy-Free, Soy-Free Brown Bread

Makes 15 slices

Though shorter than some loaves, this is the perfect brown sandwich bread for those who must eliminate eggs, corn, dairy and/or soy from their diet. It carries well, for a tasty lunch.

Variations

For a milder bread, substitute 1 tbsp (15 mL) packed brown sugar for the molasses.

The rice bran can be replaced by an equal amount of gluten-free oat bran or brown or white rice flour.

- 9- by 5-inch (23 by 12.5 cm) loaf pan, lightly greased

¼ cup	ground flax seeds (flaxseed meal)	60 mL
⅓ cup	warm water	75 mL
1¼ cups	brown rice flour	300 mL
¾ cup	sorghum flour	175 mL
⅓ cup	rice bran	75 mL
3 tbsp	tapioca starch	45 mL
1 tbsp	xanthan gum	15 mL
1 tbsp	bread machine or instant yeast	15 mL
1¼ tsp	salt	6 mL
1 cup	water	250 mL
2 tbsp	vegetable oil	30 mL
3 tbsp	liquid honey	45 mL
1 tbsp	light (fancy) molasses	15 mL
1 tsp	cider vinegar	5 mL

1. In a small bowl or measuring cup, combine flax seeds and warm water; set aside for 5 minutes.

2. In a large bowl or plastic bag, combine brown rice flour, sorghum flour, rice bran, tapioca starch, xanthan gum, yeast and salt. Mix well and set aside.

3. In a separate bowl, using a heavy-duty electric mixer with paddle attachment, combine water, oil, honey, molasses, vinegar and flax flour mixture until well blended. With the mixer on its lowest speed, slowly add the dry ingredients until combined. Stop the machine and scrape the bottom and sides of the bowl with a rubber spatula. With the mixer on medium speed, beat for 1 minute or until smooth.

4. Spoon dough into prepared pan. Let rise, uncovered, in a warm, draft-free place for 75 to 90 minutes or until dough has risen almost to the top of the pan. Meanwhile, preheat oven to 350°F (180°C).

5. Bake for 25 minutes. Check to see if loaf is getting too dark and tent with foil if necessary. Bake for 10 to 20 minutes or until internal temperature of loaf registers 200°F (100°C) on an instant-read thermometer. Remove from the pan immediately and let cool completely on a rack.

Nutrients per slice	
Calories	145
Fat	4 g
Carbohydrate	27 g
Fiber	4 g
Protein	3 g
Vitamin B$_6$	0.1 mg
Magnesium	47 mg
Zinc	0.4 mg

Egg-Free, Corn-Free, Dairy-Free, Soy-Free Flax Bread

Makes 15 slices

Don't be alarmed when this one turns out shorter than some loaves.

Tip

To crack flax seeds, pulse in a coffee grinder, blender or food processor just long enough to break the seed coat but not long enough to grind completely.

Variation

Make a dozen dinner rolls by following the method for Egg-Free, Corn-Free, Dairy-Free, Soy-Free White Dinner Rolls (page 188).

Nutrients per slice

Calories	138
Fat	5 g
Carbohydrate	21 g
Fiber	3 g
Protein	3 g
Vitamin B$_6$	0.2 mg
Magnesium	42 mg
Zinc	0.7 mg

• 9- by 5-inch (23 by 12.5 cm) loaf pan, lightly greased

¼ cup	ground flax seeds (flaxseed meal)	60 mL
⅓ cup	warm water	75 mL
1¾ cups	brown rice flour	425 mL
¼ cup	almond flour	60 mL
⅓ cup	tapioca starch	75 mL
2 tbsp	granulated sugar	30 mL
2½ tsp	xanthan gum	12 mL
1 tbsp	bread machine or instant yeast	15 mL
1¼ tsp	salt	6 mL
⅓ cup	cracked flax seeds	75 mL
1⅓ cups	water	325 mL
2 tbsp	vegetable oil	30 mL
2 tsp	cider vinegar	10 mL

1. In a small bowl or measuring cup, combine ground flax seeds and warm water; set aside for 5 minutes.

2. In a large bowl or plastic bag, combine brown rice flour, almond flour, tapioca starch, sugar, xanthan gum, yeast, salt and cracked flax seeds. Mix well and set aside.

3. In a separate bowl, using a heavy-duty electric mixer with paddle attachment, combine water, oil, vinegar and flax flour mixture until well blended. With the mixer on its lowest speed, slowly add the dry ingredients until combined. Stop the machine and scrape the bottom and sides of the bowl with a rubber spatula. With the mixer on medium speed, beat for 1 minute or until smooth.

4. Spoon dough into prepared pan. Let rise, uncovered, in a warm, draft-free place for 60 to 75 minutes or until dough has risen almost to the top of the pan. Meanwhile, preheat oven to 350°F (180°C).

5. Bake for 20 minutes. Check to see if loaf is getting too dark and tent with foil if necessary. Bake for 15 to 20 minutes or until internal temperature of loaf registers 200°F (100°C) on an instant-read thermometer. Remove from the pan immediately and let cool completely on a rack.

Egg-Free, Corn-Free, Dairy-Free, Soy-Free White Dinner Rolls

These rolls are perfect for those who must eliminate eggs, corn, dairy and/or soy from their diet but enjoy a roll with dinner.

Tip

The egg substitutes sold in most supermarkets contain egg products and should not be confused with commercial egg replacer. Egg replacer is a white powder containing a combination of baking powder and starches. It is added with the dry ingredients so that it is well mixed in before it touches the liquids. The oil or other fat in the recipe may have to be increased slightly.

Nutrients per roll	
Calories	226
Fat	7 g
Carbohydrate	37 g
Fiber	3 g
Protein	4 g
Vitamin B$_6$	0.2 mg
Magnesium	53 mg
Zinc	0.9 mg

• Baking sheet, lightly greased

¾ cup	brown rice flour	175 mL
¼ cup	amaranth flour	60 mL
¼ cup	tapioca starch	60 mL
1 tbsp	powdered egg replacer	15 mL
1 tbsp	granulated sugar	15 mL
2½ tsp	xanthan gum	12 mL
1 tbsp	bread machine or instant yeast	15 mL
¾ tsp	salt	3 mL
¾ cup	water	175 mL
2 tbsp	vegetable oil	30 mL
1 tsp	cider vinegar	5 mL

1. In a bowl or plastic bag, combine brown rice flour, amaranth flour, tapioca starch, egg replacer, sugar, xanthan gum, yeast and salt. Mix well and set aside.

2. In a separate bowl, using a heavy-duty electric mixer with paddle attachment, combine water, oil and vinegar until well blended. With the mixer on its lowest speed, slowly add the dry ingredients until combined. Stop the machine and scrape the bottom and sides of the bowl with a rubber spatula. With the mixer on medium speed, beat for 1 minute or until smooth.

3. Using a ¼-cup (60 mL) scoop, drop 5 scoops of dough at least 2 inches (5 cm) apart onto prepared baking sheet. Let rise, uncovered, in a warm, draft-free place for 75 minutes. Meanwhile, preheat oven to 350°F (180°C).

4. Bake for 20 to 22 minutes or until internal temperature of rolls registers 200°F (100°C) on an instant-read thermometer. Remove from the pan immediately and let cool completely on a rack.

Variation

Add ¼ cup (60 mL) unsalted raw sunflower seeds or green pumpkin seeds with the dry ingredients.

Pizza Crust

Tip

If you don't have an 8-inch (20 cm) round pizza pan, use a 12-inch (30 cm) pan. After transferring dough to the pan, top it with waxed paper and roll out to an 8½-inch (21 cm) circle. Form a ¼-inch (0.5 cm) ridge all the way around the edge.

- **Preheat oven to 400°F (200°C), with rack set in the bottom third**
- **8-inch (20 cm) round pizza pan, lightly greased**

¼ cup	sorghum flour	60 mL
¼ cup	quinoa flour	60 mL
1 tbsp	tapioca starch	15 mL
1 tsp	granulated sugar	5 mL
2 tsp	xanthan gum	10 mL
1 tbsp	bread machine or instant yeast	15 mL
¼ tsp	salt	1 mL
⅓ cup	water	75 mL
1 tbsp	extra virgin olive oil	15 mL
1 tsp	cider vinegar	5 mL

1. In a bowl or plastic bag, combine sorghum flour, quinoa flour, tapioca starch, sugar, xanthan gum, yeast and salt. Mix well and set aside.

2. In a separate bowl, using a heavy-duty electric mixer with paddle attachment, combine water, oil and vinegar until well blended. With the mixer on its lowest speed, slowly add the dry ingredients until combined. Stop the machine and scrape the bottom and sides of the bowl with a rubber spatula. With the mixer on medium speed, beat for 1 minute or until smooth.

3. Gently transfer dough to prepared pan. Using a moist rubber spatula, carefully spread to the edges.

4. Bake in preheated oven for 10 minutes or until bottom is golden and crust is partially baked.

5. Use right away to make pizza with your favorite toppings, or wrap airtight and store in the freezer for up to 1 month. Thaw in the refrigerator overnight before using.

Nutrients per serving (1 of 2)	
Calories	245
Fat	9 g
Carbohydrate	38 g
Fiber	6 g
Protein	5 g
Vitamin B$_6$	0.1 mg
Magnesium	44 mg
Zinc	0.7 mg

Swedish Wraps

Use these to make the ever-popular wrap instead of a sandwich for lunch. Roll them around your favorite sandwich fillings.

Tips

Xanthan gum helps prevent baked goods from crumbling, gives them greater volume, improves their texture and extends their shelf life.

Dipping the spatula repeatedly into warm water makes it easier to spread this dough thinly and evenly.

Variation

Try adding dried herbs to the soft dough in place of the three varieties of seeds. To make a plainer variety, omit seeds and herbs.

- **Preheat oven to 400°F (200°C), with rack set in the top third**
- **15- by 10-inch (40 by 25 cm) jelly roll pan, lightly greased and lined with parchment paper**

½ cup	sorghum flour	125 mL
¼ cup	amaranth flour	60 mL
¼ cup	tapioca starch	60 mL
1 tsp	granulated sugar	5 mL
2 tsp	xanthan gum	10 mL
1 tbsp	bread machine or instant yeast	15 mL
¾ tsp	salt	3 mL
1 tsp	anise seeds	5 mL
1 tsp	caraway seeds	5 mL
1 tsp	fennel seeds	5 mL
¾ cup	milk	175 mL
1 tsp	extra virgin olive oil	5 mL
1 tsp	cider vinegar	5 mL

1. In a bowl or plastic bag, combine sorghum flour, amaranth flour, tapioca starch, sugar, xanthan gum, yeast, salt, anise seeds, caraway seeds and fennel seeds. Mix well and set aside.

2. In a separate bowl, using a heavy-duty electric mixer with paddle attachment, combine milk, oil and vinegar until well blended. With the mixer on its lowest speed, slowly add the dry ingredients until combined. Stop the machine and scrape the bottom and sides of the bowl with a rubber spatula. With the mixer on medium speed, beat for 1 minute or until smooth.

3. Transfer dough to prepared pan. Using a moistened rubber spatula, spread evenly to the edges.

4. Bake in preheated oven for 12 to 14 minutes or until edges are brown and top begins to brown. Let cool completely on pan on a rack. Remove from pan and cut into quarters.

Nutrients per wrap	
Calories	188
Fat	3 g
Carbohydrate	36 g
Fiber	4 g
Protein	6 g
Vitamin B$_6$	0.1 mg
Magnesium	40 mg
Zinc	0.7 mg

Coconut "Corn" Bread

It may sound odd — "corn" bread without any corn — but take a bite of this home-style bread and you'll swear you're eating the real thing.

Tip

A glass pan of the same dimensions may also be used. Add 3 to 6 minutes to the baking time.

Storage Tip

Store the cooled bread, wrapped in foil or plastic wrap, in the refrigerator for up to 3 days. Alternatively, wrap it in plastic wrap, then foil, completely enclosing bread, and freeze for up to 3 months. Let thaw at room temperature for 4 to 6 hours before serving.

Nutrients per slice	
Calories	117
Fat	8 g
Carbohydrate	11 g
Fiber	3 g
Protein	3 g
Vitamin B$_6$	0.1 mg
Magnesium	27 mg
Zinc	0.5 mg

- **Preheat oven to 350°F (180°C)**
- **9-inch (23 cm) square metal baking pan, greased with coconut oil**

¾ cup	well-stirred coconut milk (full-fat)	175 mL
½ cup	water	125 mL
3 tbsp	pumpkin purée (not pie filling)	45 mL
2 tsp	cider or white vinegar	10 mL
2 tbsp	psyllium husk	30 mL
1 tbsp	coconut sugar (optional)	15 mL
¾ cup	chickpea flour	175 mL
6 tbsp	coconut flour	90 mL
1½ tbsp	potato starch	22 mL
2 tsp	gluten-free baking powder	10 mL
¼ tsp	baking soda	1 mL
½ tsp	ground cumin	2 mL
½ tsp	fine sea salt	2 mL

1. In a small bowl, whisk together coconut milk, water, pumpkin and vinegar. Let stand for 10 minutes or until mixture appears curdled. Whisk in psyllium and coconut sugar (if using); let stand for 5 minutes to thicken.

2. In a large bowl, whisk together chickpea flour, coconut flour, potato starch, baking powder, baking soda, cumin and salt.

3. Add the coconut milk mixture to the flour mixture and stir until just blended.

4. Spread batter evenly in prepared pan.

5. Bake in preheated oven for 40 to 45 minutes or until top is golden brown and a tester inserted in the center comes out clean. Let cool in pan on a wire rack for 10 minutes, then transfer to the rack to cool completely.

Variation

Calico "Corn" Bread: Gently fold in ⅓ cup (75 mL) chopped green onions and ¼ cup (60 mL) chopped drained jarred roasted red bell peppers at the end of step 3.

Pumpkin Bread

This is a perfect pumpkin bread: moist, flavorful and subtly sweet, it's grand for breakfast, a snack or dessert.

Tips

A glass pan of the same dimensions may also be used. Add 4 to 8 minutes to the baking time.

An equal amount of winter squash or butternut squash purée (canned or thawed frozen) can be used in place of the pumpkin purée.

For a bit of crunch, add ¾ cup (175 mL) lightly toasted green pumpkin seeds (pepitas), coarsely chopped, in step 3.

Nutrients per slice	
Calories	187
Fat	11 g
Carbohydrate	23 g
Fiber	3 g
Protein	2 g
Vitamin B$_6$	0.1 mg
Magnesium	22 mg
Zinc	0.3 mg

- **Preheat oven to 350°F (180°C)**
- **8- by 4-inch (20 by 10 cm) metal loaf pan, greased with coconut oil**

¾ cup	chickpea flour	175 mL
⅓ cup	coconut flour	75 mL
1½ tbsp	potato starch	22 mL
2 tsp	gluten-free baking powder	10 mL
1½ tsp	pumpkin pie spice	7 mL
½ tsp	fine sea salt	2 mL
¼ tsp	baking soda	1 mL
⅔ cup	coconut sugar	150 mL
2 tbsp	psyllium husk	30 mL
1¼ cups	pumpkin purée (not pie filling)	300 mL
½ cup	melted virgin coconut oil	125 mL
½ cup	coconut water or water	125 mL

1. In a large bowl, whisk together chickpea flour, coconut flour, potato starch, baking powder, pumpkin pie spice, salt and baking soda.

2. In a medium bowl, whisk together coconut sugar, psyllium, pumpkin purée, coconut oil and coconut water until well blended. Let stand for 5 minutes to thicken.

3. Add the pumpkin mixture to the flour mixture and stir until just blended.

4. Spread batter evenly in prepared pan.

5. Bake in preheated oven for 55 to 65 minutes or until top is golden and a tester inserted in the center comes out clean. Let cool in pan on a wire rack for 10 minutes, then transfer to the rack to cool completely.

Storage Tip

Store the cooled bread, wrapped in foil or plastic wrap, in the refrigerator for up to 3 days. Alternatively, wrap it in plastic wrap, then foil, completely enclosing bread, and freeze for up to 3 months. Let thaw at room temperature for 4 to 6 hours before serving.

Favorite Blueberry Muffins

Makes 12 muffins

These tender-as-can-be muffins have an easy style, their sapphire, tart-sweet berries harmonizing with a vanilla-scented batter.

- **Preheat oven to 350°F (180°C)**
- **12-cup muffin pan, greased**

2 cups	Brown Rice Flour Blend (page 195)	500 mL
2½ tsp	gluten-free baking powder	12 mL
½ tsp	baking soda	2 mL
½ tsp	salt	2 mL
¾ cup	unsweetened applesauce	175 mL
½ cup	agave nectar or liquid honey	125 mL
½ cup	mashed ripe banana	125 mL
¼ cup	vegetable oil	60 mL
1 tsp	gluten-free vanilla extract	5 mL
2 cups	blueberries	500 mL
2 tbsp	turbinado sugar (optional)	30 mL

1. In a large bowl, whisk together flour blend, baking powder, baking soda and salt.

2. In a medium bowl, whisk together applesauce, agave nectar, banana, oil and vanilla until well blended.

3. Add the applesauce mixture to the flour mixture and stir until just blended. Gently fold in blueberries.

4. Divide batter equally among prepared muffin cups. Sprinkle with turbinado sugar, if desired.

5. Bake in preheated oven for 18 to 22 minutes or until tops are golden brown and a tester inserted in the center comes out clean. Let cool in pan on a wire rack for 3 minutes, then transfer to the rack to cool.

Nutrients per muffin	
Calories	216
Fat	5 g
Carbohydrate	42 g
Fiber	2 g
Protein	2 g
Vitamin B6	0.3 mg
Magnesium	32 mg
Zinc	0.6 mg

Applesauce Raisin Muffins

Makes 12 muffins

Whether you use store-bought applesauce or make your own, these comforting muffins will make it hard to stop after just one.

Tip

Other unsulfured dried fruits, such as chopped dried apricots or cherries, may be substituted for the raisins.

- **Preheat oven to 400°F (200°C)**
- **12-cup muffin pan, greased**

2 cups	Brown Rice Flour Blend (see recipe, opposite)	500 mL
2 tsp	gluten-free baking powder	10 mL
1 tsp	ground cinnamon	5 mL
½ tsp	ground allspice	2 mL
½ tsp	baking soda	2 mL
½ tsp	salt	2 mL
1½ cups	unsweetened applesauce	375 mL
½ cup	liquid honey or agave nectar	125 mL
⅓ cup	vegetable oil	75 mL
1 tsp	gluten-free vanilla extract	5 mL
½ cup	unsulfured raisins	125 mL

1. In a large bowl, whisk together flour blend, baking powder, cinnamon, allspice, baking soda and salt.

2. In a medium bowl, whisk together applesauce, honey, oil and vanilla until blended.

3. Add the applesauce mixture to the flour mixture and stir until just blended. Gently fold in raisins.

4. Divide batter equally among prepared muffin cups.

5. Bake in preheated oven for 25 to 28 minutes or until tops are golden brown and a tester inserted in the center comes out clean. Let cool in pan on a wire rack for 5 minutes, then transfer to the rack to cool.

Nutrients per muffin	
Calories	232
Fat	7 g
Carbohydrate	43 g
Fiber	2 g
Protein	2 g
Vitamin B$_6$	0.2 mg
Magnesium	31 mg
Zinc	0.6 mg

Brown Rice Flour Blend

2 cups	finely ground brown rice flour	500 mL
2/3 cup	potato starch	150 mL
1/3 cup	tapioca starch	75 mL

1. In a bowl, whisk together brown rice flour, potato starch and tapioca starch. Use as directed in recipes.

Tips

You can also make the blend in smaller amounts by using the basic proportions: 2 parts finely ground brown rice flour, 2/3 part potato starch and 1/3 part tapioca starch.

You can double, triple or quadruple the recipe to have it on hand. Store the blend in an airtight container in the refrigerator for up to 4 months, or in the freezer for up to 1 year. Let warm to room temperature before using.

Nutrients per
1/4 cup (60 mL)

Calories	152
Fat	1 g
Carbohydrate	33 g
Fiber	2 g
Protein	3 g
Vitamin B_6	0.3 mg
Magnesium	40 mg
Zinc	0.8 mg

Carrot Cake Muffins

These delectable muffins are moist, heady with spices and just plain good!

Tip

To maximize your nutrient intake, make sure to select an enriched hemp or rice milk.

- **Preheat oven to 400°F (200°C)**
- **12-cup muffin pan, greased**

1½ cups	Brown Rice Flour Blend (page 195)	375 mL
2 tsp	gluten-free baking powder	10 mL
1 tsp	ground cinnamon	5 mL
1 tsp	ground ginger	5 mL
½ tsp	baking soda	2 mL
½ tsp	salt	2 mL
¼ tsp	ground nutmeg	1 mL
1 cup	hemp or rice milk	250 mL
½ cup	agave nectar or liquid honey	125 mL
⅓ cup	virgin coconut oil, warmed	75 mL
1 tsp	gluten-free vanilla extract	5 mL
2 cups	shredded carrots	500 mL
½ cup	unsulfured dried currants or raisins	125 mL

1. In a large bowl, whisk together flour blend, baking powder, cinnamon, ginger, baking soda, salt and nutmeg.

2. In a medium bowl, whisk together hemp milk, agave nectar, coconut oil and vanilla until well blended.

3. Add the milk mixture to the flour mixture and stir until just blended. Gently fold in carrots and currants.

4. Divide batter equally among prepared muffin cups.

5. Bake in preheated oven for 18 to 22 minutes or until tops are golden brown and a tester inserted in the center comes out clean. Let cool in pan on a wire rack for 3 minutes, then transfer to the rack to cool.

Nutrients per muffin	
Calories	208
Fat	7 g
Carbohydrate	37 g
Fiber	2 g
Protein	2 g
Vitamin B6	0.2 mg
Magnesium	28 mg
Zinc	0.5 mg

Snacks and Appetizers

Sweet Toasted Pumpkin Seeds....................198

Wheat-Free Thins.................................199

Multi-Seed Quinoa Crackers......................200

Moroccan Anise Crackers.........................201

Chocolate Date Protein Bars 202

Multi-Seed Energy Bars 203

Chewy Coconut Quinoa Bars.......................204

Sunflower Quinoa Snack Squares..................205

Nori Pinwheels..................................206

Avocado Cucumber Hand Rolls.....................207

Maki Rolls with Carrot Rice and Avocado 208

Kale Spring Rolls...............................210

Sweet Toasted Pumpkin Seeds

**Makes
3 cups (750 mL)**

Healthy pumpkin seeds
are the main ingredient
in this easy-to-make
snack.

- **Preheat oven to 400°F (200°C)**
- **Rimmed baking sheet, lightly oiled**

3 cups	raw pumpkin seeds	750 mL
3 tbsp	olive oil	45 mL
2 tbsp	natural cane sugar	30 mL
¼ tsp	ground cinnamon	1 mL
Pinch	ground nutmeg	Pinch

1. In a bowl, combine pumpkin seeds, oil, sugar, cinnamon and nutmeg. Spread evenly on prepared baking sheet and roast in preheated oven, stirring once or twice, for about 20 minutes, until crisp and puffy.

2. Store toasted pumpkin seeds in an airtight container in the refrigerator for up to 2 weeks.

Nutrients per ¼ cup (60 mL)	
Calories	218
Fat	19 g
Carbohydrate	5 g
Fiber	2 g
Protein	10 g
Vitamin B_6	0.1 mg
Magnesium	191 mg
Zinc	2.5 mg

Wheat-Free Thins

Crispy, crunchy and satisfying, these crackers showcase the complex flavors of ancient grain flours. Excellent on their own, they are also a perfect accompaniment to soups or salads.

Tip

If the dough is too dry or not quite cohesive in step 1, add 1 to 2 tbsp (15 to 30 mL) additional water to achieve the desired consistency.

- **Preheat oven to 450°F (230°C)**
- **Large rimmed baking sheet, lined with parchment paper, leaving an overhang**

1 cup	sorghum flour	250 mL
1/2 cup	teff flour	125 mL
1/4 cup	chia seeds	60 mL
1/4 cup	sesame seeds	60 mL
1 1/4 tsp	gluten-free baking powder	6 mL
1/2 tsp	fine sea salt	2 mL
1/2 cup	water	125 mL
2 tbsp	olive oil	30 mL

1. In a large bowl, whisk together sorghum flour, teff flour, chia seeds, sesame seeds, baking powder and salt. Whisk in water and oil until blended and dough is cohesive (see tip, at left). Let stand for 5 minutes.

2. Place dough in center of prepared baking sheet. Using your fingertips, press out dough to cover most of the pan. Place a large sheet of parchment paper or plastic wrap on top of the dough. Using your palm, smooth out dough to even out the surface and completely cover the pan. (The dough should be about 1/16 inch/2 mm thick.) Remove the top sheet of parchment paper.

3. Bake in preheated oven for 5 minutes. Remove pan from oven, leaving oven on. Using parchment paper overhang, lift cracker from pan onto a cutting board. Cut into 1 1/2-inch (4 cm) squares or irregular pieces of a similar size. Turn crackers over with a spatula and return parchment and crackers to baking sheet.

4. Bake for 3 to 5 minutes or until crackers are crisp at the edges. Transfer crackers, on parchment paper, to a wire rack and let cool completely. Store in an airtight tin at room temperature for up to 2 weeks.

Nutrients per 4 crackers

Calories	120
Fat	5 g
Carbohydrate	16 g
Fiber	3 g
Protein	3 g
Vitamin B$_6$	0.1 mg
Magnesium	38 mg
Zinc	0.8 mg

Multi-Seed Quinoa Crackers

Light, crispy and packed with protein, these delectable crackers are perfect eaten straight up or spread with hummus, nut or seed butter or anything else you fancy.

Tip

Cooked amaranth, cooled, can be used in place of the quinoa.

- Preheat oven to 325°F (160°C)
- Large rimmed baking sheet, lined with parchment paper, leaving an overhang

1/3 cup	chia seeds	75 mL
3/4 cup	water	175 mL
3/4 cup	cooked quinoa, cooled	175 mL
1/3 cup	green pumpkin seeds (pepitas)	75 mL
1/3 cup	sesame seeds	75 mL
1/4 tsp	fine sea salt	1 mL

1. In a medium bowl, combine chia seeds and water. Let stand for 5 minutes to thicken. Stir in quinoa, pumpkin seeds, sesame seeds and salt. Let stand for 2 minutes.

2. Spread quinoa mixture evenly on prepared baking sheet to form a 10- by 8-inch (25 by 20 cm) rectangle.

3. Bake in preheated oven for 30 minutes or until surface feels dry. Remove pan from oven, leaving oven on. Using parchment paper overhang, lift cracker from pan onto a cutting board. Cut into 2-inch (5 cm) squares. Turn crackers over with a spatula and return parchment and crackers to baking sheet.

4. Bake for 25 to 30 minutes or until crackers are golden at the edges. Transfer crackers, on parchment paper, to a wire rack and let cool completely. Store in an airtight tin at room temperature for up to 2 weeks.

Nutrients per 4 crackers	
Calories	191
Fat	13 g
Carbohydrate	14 g
Fiber	7 g
Protein	7 g
Vitamin B_6	0.1 mg
Magnesium	103 mg
Zinc	2.1 mg

Moroccan Anise Crackers

Making dough doesn't get much easier or faster than this. The hands-on preparation is less than 15 minutes. Dip these crackers in hummus or a vegetable dip.

Tips

For a milder flavor, decrease the anise seeds to 2 tsp (10 mL).

Make lots of holes with the fork, as this gives an interesting finish to the top crust.

Variation

Substitute an equal quantity of cumin seeds for the anise seeds.

Nutrients per 3 crackers

Calories	72
Fat	2 g
Carbohydrate	12 g
Fiber	1 g
Protein	1 g
Vitamin B$_6$	0.1 mg
Magnesium	17 mg
Zinc	0.3 mg

- **Baking sheet, sprinkled with cornmeal**

¾ cup	sorghum flour	175 mL
⅓ cup	teff flour	75 mL
2 tbsp	cornmeal	30 mL
¼ cup	tapioca starch	60 mL
½ tsp	granulated sugar	2 mL
1½ tsp	xanthan gum	7 mL
2 tsp	bread machine or instant yeast	10 mL
1 tsp	salt	5 mL
1 tbsp	anise seeds	15 mL
1 cup	water	250 mL
2 tbsp	vegetable oil	30 mL
1 tsp	cider vinegar	5 mL

1. In a bowl or plastic bag, combine sorghum flour, teff flour, cornmeal, tapioca starch, sugar, xanthan gum, yeast, salt and anise seeds. Mix well and set aside.

2. In a separate bowl, using a heavy-duty electric mixer with paddle attachment, combine water, oil and vinegar until well blended. With the mixer on its lowest speed, slowly add the dry ingredients until combined. Stop the machine and scrape the bottom and sides of the bowl with a rubber spatula. With the mixer on medium speed, beat for 1 minute or until smooth.

3. Immediately pour dough onto prepared baking sheet. Using a moistened rubber spatula, spread evenly into a 10-inch (25 cm) round, leaving the top rough. Let rise, uncovered, in a warm, draft-free place for 10 to 15 minutes. Meanwhile, preheat oven to 400°F (200°C).

4. Using a fork, pierce the dough all over, pressing all the way down to the baking sheet.

5. Bake in preheated oven for 15 minutes or until firm. Remove from pan and place directly on oven rack. Bake for 8 to 10 minutes or until crisp. Remove from the oven immediately and let cool completely on a rack. Break into pieces.

Chocolate Date Protein Bars

These dense treats are perfect for midday hunger and take very little time to prepare. Try making a double batch and freezing some of the mixture for future use.

Tips

To soak the dates for this recipe, place them in a bowl and cover with 4 cups (1 L) water. Cover and set aside to soak for 30 minutes. Drain, discarding any remaining water.

Dates provide iron, fiber and potassium and they are also a good source of antioxidants. Although dates are a healthy whole food, they are high in sugar. When you find yourself craving refined sugar, reach for one or two dates and you will find the craving goes away.

If caffeine is a concern, substitute raw carob powder in place of the cacao.

Nutrients per bar (1 of 8)	
Calories	232
Fat	8 g
Carbohydrate	41 g
Fiber	5 g
Protein	7 g
Vitamin B$_6$	0.2 mg
Magnesium	148 mg
Zinc	2.0 mg

- **Food processor**

2 cups	pitted dates, soaked (see tip, at left)	500 mL
1/4 cup	freshly squeezed orange juice	60 mL
1/4 cup	raw agave nectar	60 mL
1/2 cup	raw cacao powder	125 mL
1 cup	raw shelled hemp seeds	250 mL

1. In food processor, combine dates, orange juice, agave nectar and cacao powder; process until smooth, stopping once to scrape down the sides of the work bowl. Add hemp seeds and pulse several times until well integrated.

2. Transfer onto a baking sheet and, using your hands, press out until approximately 8 inches (20 cm) square and 1 inch (2.5 cm) thick. Refrigerate for 1 hour to firm up. Remove and cut into bars. Transfer to an airtight container and store, refrigerated, for up to 7 days.

Multi-Seed Energy Bars

Makes 12 bars

You've never had an energy bar quite like this one: a medley of seeds — quinoa, sunflower and sesame — coalesce in a crisp-chewy base. Stow one away for a mid-morning energy boost.

Tips

Any dried fruit, or a combination of dried fruits, may be used. Try raisins, cranberries, blueberries, cherries and/or chopped apricots.

If you're not following a gluten-free diet, try other puffed grain cereals, such as wheat or barley, in place of the puffed rice.

Nutrients per bar	
Calories	224
Fat	9 g
Carbohydrate	32 g
Fiber	3 g
Protein	5 g
Vitamin B_6	0.2 mg
Magnesium	63 mg
Zinc	1.3 mg

- Preheat oven to 350°F (180°C)
- Large rimmed baking sheet
- 8-inch (20 cm) square metal baking pan, lined with foil (see tip, page 176) and sprayed with nonstick cooking spray

1 cup	quinoa flakes	250 mL
½ cup	sunflower seeds	125 mL
3 tbsp	toasted sesame seeds	45 mL
1 cup	unsweetened puffed rice or millet cereal	250 mL
1 cup	chopped dried fruit	250 mL
¼ cup	natural cane sugar or packed dark brown sugar	60 mL
¼ tsp	fine sea salt	1 mL
⅓ cup	tahini or sunflower seed butter	75 mL
¼ cup	pure maple syrup or brown rice syrup	60 mL
1 tsp	gluten-free vanilla extract	5 mL

1. Spread quinoa flakes, sunflower seeds and sesame seeds on baking sheet. Bake in preheated oven for 8 to 10 minutes, shaking halfway through, until golden and fragrant.

2. Transfer quinoa mixture to a large bowl and stir in cereal and fruit.

3. In a small saucepan, combine sugar, salt, tahini and maple syrup. Heat over medium-low heat, stirring constantly, for 2 to 4 minutes or until sugar is dissolved and mixture is bubbly. Stir in vanilla.

4. Immediately pour tahini mixture over quinoa mixture, stirring with a spatula until quinoa mixture is coated.

5. Using your hands, a spatula or a large piece of waxed paper, press quinoa mixture firmly into prepared pan. Refrigerate for 30 minutes or until firm. Using foil liner, lift mixture from pan and invert onto a cutting board. Peel off foil and cut into 12 bars.

Storage Tip

Store cooled bars in an airtight container at room temperature for up to 5 days. Or wrap them in plastic wrap, then foil, completely enclosing them, and freeze for up to 6 months. Let thaw at room temperature for 1 hour before serving.

Chewy Coconut Quinoa Bars

Makes 15 bars

How could something that tastes so good also be good for you? Eating is believing.

Tips

Any other variety of natural nut or seed butter, such as peanut, sunflower seed or cashew butter, may be used in place of the almond butter.

If the bars crumble while you're cutting them, refrigerate for 15 to 30 minutes, until they are more firm.

- **Preheat oven to 350°F (180°C)**
- **8-inch (20 cm) square metal baking pan, lined with foil (see tip, page 176) and sprayed with nonstick cooking spray**

2 cups	quinoa flakes	500 mL
2 cups	unsweetened flaked coconut	500 mL
1 tsp	ground ginger	5 mL
½ tsp	fine sea salt	2 mL
¾ cup	liquid honey or brown rice syrup	175 mL
6 tbsp	virgin coconut oil, warmed, or vegetable oil	90 mL
⅓ cup	unsweetened natural almond butter	75 mL

1. In a large bowl, combine quinoa flakes, coconut, ginger and salt.

2. In a medium bowl, whisk together honey, coconut oil and almond butter until blended.

3. Add the honey mixture to the quinoa mixture and stir until evenly coated. Using your hands, a spatula or a large piece of waxed paper, press mixture firmly into prepared pan.

4. Bake in preheated oven for 30 to 40 minutes or until browned at the edges but still slightly soft at the center. Let cool completely in pan on a wire rack. Using foil liner, lift mixture from pan and invert onto a cutting board. Peel off foil and cut into 15 bars.

Storage Tip

Store cooled bars in an airtight container at room temperature for up to 5 days. Or wrap them in plastic wrap, then foil, completely enclosing them, and freeze for up to 6 months. Let thaw at room temperature for 1 hour before serving.

Nutrients per bar	
Calories	254
Fat	13 g
Carbohydrate	31 g
Fiber	3 g
Protein	5 g
Vitamin B$_6$	0.1 mg
Magnesium	65 mg
Zinc	1.1 mg

Sunflower Quinoa Snack Squares

Makes 16 squares

Peanut butter and oat candies get a modern spin with sunflower seed butter, quinoa flakes and dried apricots and cranberries.

Tips

Substitute 2 cups (500 mL) certified gluten-free large-flake (old-fashioned) rolled oats for half the quinoa flakes.

Use this recipe as a template: use any variety of natural nut or seed butter (such as peanut, cashew, almond or tahini), seeds or nuts and dried fruit of your choice.

- 8-inch (20 cm) square metal or glass baking dish, lined with foil (see tip, page 176) and sprayed with nonstick cooking spray

1 tsp	fine sea salt	5 mL
1 cup	sunflower seed butter	250 mL
½ cup	agave nectar, liquid honey or brown rice syrup	125 mL
2 tsp	gluten-free vanilla extract	10 mL
4 cups	quinoa flakes	1 L
1 cup	lightly salted roasted sunflower seeds	250 mL
¾ cup	chopped dried apricots	175 mL
½ cup	dried cranberries	125 mL

1. In a large bowl, combine salt, sunflower seed butter, agave nectar and vanilla until blended. Stir in quinoa flakes, sunflower seeds, apricots and cranberries until well combined.

2. Using your hands, a spatula or large piece of waxed paper, press quinoa mixture firmly into prepared pan. Refrigerate for 30 minutes or until firm. Using foil liner, lift mixture from pan and invert onto a cutting board. Peel off foil and cut into 16 squares.

Storage Tip

Store squares in an airtight container at room temperature for up to 1 week or in the refrigerator for up to 3 weeks. Or wrap them in plastic wrap, then foil, completely enclosing them, and freeze for up to 6 months. Let thaw at room temperature for 1 hour before serving.

Nutrients per square	
Calories	361
Fat	15 g
Carbohydrate	49 g
Fiber	5 g
Protein	11 g
Vitamin B_6	0.4 mg
Magnesium	146 mg
Zinc	2.6 mg

Nori Pinwheels

Working with raw nori sheets is easier than you might think. Make these delicious pinwheels ahead so you can enjoy them on busy days when you are on the go.

Tips

If you have a sushi mat, feel free to use it for this recipe.

Nori is one of the best sources of natural iodine and also contains an appreciable amount of potassium. Iodine is essential for proper functioning of the thyroid gland, which produces hormones needed for growth, development, reproduction and a healthy metabolism.

To remove the skin from gingerroot with the least amount of waste, use the edge of a teaspoon. With a brushing motion, scrape off the skin to reveal the yellow root.

Nutrients per roll	
Calories	53
Fat	5 g
Carbohydrate	2 g
Fiber	1 g
Protein	2 g
Vitamin B$_6$	0.1 mg
Magnesium	29 mg
Zinc	0.5 mg

- **Food processor**

3	sheets raw nori, divided	3
1 cup	raw sunflower seeds	250 mL
½ cup	chopped celery	125 mL
¼ cup	filtered water	60 mL
¼ cup	freshly squeezed lemon juice	60 mL
1 tbsp	chopped gingerroot	15 mL
½ tsp	fine sea salt	2 mL

1. In food processor, combine 1 sheet nori, sunflower seeds, celery, water, lemon juice, ginger and salt; process until smooth, stopping to scrape down sides of work bowl as necessary. Transfer to a bowl.

2. Lay the remaining nori sheets side by side on a flat surface. Divide sunflower seed mixture into two equal parts and spread evenly on each sheet. Starting at the bottom of the sheet, roll each up to form a cylinder. Cut each roll into 8 equal pieces. Serve immediately or cover and refrigerate for up to 2 days.

Variation

Pumpkin Red Pepper Nori Pinwheels: Substitute pumpkin seeds for the sunflower seeds, chopped red bell pepper for the celery and 2 cloves garlic for the ginger.

Avocado Cucumber Hand Rolls

Makes 2 rolls

These hand rolls are refreshing, healthy and packed with protein.

Tips

To soak the sunflower seeds, place in a bowl and add 2 cups (500 mL) warm water. Cover and set aside for 10 minutes. Drain, discarding soaking water and any bits of shell or unwanted particles. Rinse under cold running water until the water runs clear.

Be sure to use high-quality nori that is labeled "raw." Purchase your nori from a reputable source such as your favorite raw foods retailer, health food store or well-stocked grocery store.

- **Food processor**

1 cup	raw sunflower seeds, soaked (see tip, at left)	250 mL
¼ cup	freshly squeezed lemon juice	60 mL
¼ cup	filtered water	60 mL
¼ tsp	fine sea salt	1 mL
1	sheet raw nori, cut in half lengthwise	1
½	cucumber, seeded and thinly sliced lengthwise	½
½	avocado, thinly sliced lengthwise	½

1. In food processor, combine soaked sunflower seeds, lemon juice, water and salt; process until smooth.

2. Place 1 piece of nori, shiny side down, in the palm of your left hand (if you are right-handed), long edge facing you. Place half the sunflower mixture on a diagonal starting from the upper left corner. Top with half the cucumber and avocado slices. Fold bottom left corner of nori over filling and roll into a cone shape. Repeat with second piece of nori. Enjoy immediately.

Variations

Substitute finely sliced red bell pepper for the cucumber.

For some added crunch, add 1 tsp (5 mL) raw white sesame seeds to each roll.

Nutrients per roll	
Calories	502
Fat	44 g
Carbohydrate	22 g
Fiber	10 g
Protein	16 g
Vitamin B$_6$	1.1 mg
Magnesium	250 mg
Zinc	3.9 mg

Maki Rolls with Carrot Rice and Avocado

Makes 2 rolls

You'll be surprised by how similar the carrot in these rolls is to traditional sushi rice when it is processed and combined with vinegar and raw agave nectar.

Tip

If you don't have a sushi mat, use a sheet of waxed paper. However, be aware that your maki rolls will not be as tight as when made using a sushi mat. It takes some time to get used to working with a sushi mat, but once you do, it is very simple.

- **Food processor**
- **Sushi mat (see tip, at left)**

2 cups	finely chopped carrots	500 mL
2 tbsp	unpasteurized apple cider vinegar	30 mL
1 tbsp	raw agave nectar	15 mL
½ tsp	fine sea salt	2 mL
2	sheets raw nori (see tip, page 207)	2
½	avocado, thinly sliced lengthwise	½

1. In food processor, process carrots just until rice-like in consistency (be careful not to overprocess or they will become soft and mushy).

2. In a bowl, combine processed carrots, vinegar, agave nectar and salt. Mix well.

3. Place sushi mat on a flat surface, with bamboo strips running crosswise. Place 1 sheet nori on mat, shiny side down. Spread half the carrot mixture over nori, pressing it to about ¼ inch (0.5 cm) thick, leaving a border of 1½ inches (4 cm) along the edge farthest from you. Place half the avocado slices on top, in a crosswise row about ½ inch (1 cm) from the closest edge.

Nutrients per roll	
Calories	167
Fat	8 g
Carbohydrate	25 g
Fiber	7 g
Protein	2 g
min B6	0.3 mg
	31 mg
	0.7 mg

4. Place your thumb underneath sushi mat and index finger on top. Using your remaining fingers to hold filling in place, gently roll nori with mat, tucking in edges as you roll, to make a cylinder shape. Continue to roll sushi, taking care to tuck in nori — but not the mat itself — as you roll. Using both hands, grab mat and roll it a few times to tighten. Repeat several times during rolling process to make sushi as tight as possible.

5. Once you have rolled all the way to the top, wet your finger with a little water and lightly moisten free top edge of nori. Make one final roll to seal edge. Remove mat and cut cylinder crosswise into 8 equal slices. Repeat with second nori sheet. If not serving immediately, leave roll whole (do not cut) and cover and refrigerate for up to 2 days.

Kale Spring Rolls

These delicious spring rolls are perfect for busy days when you don't have much time to eat. Make them ahead so you can pack them for a quick meal on the go.

Tips

If the stems of the kale leaves are thick, remove them with a small paring knife.

Hemp seeds are considered a complete protein, meaning that they contain all eight essential amino acids. One tablespoon (15 mL) raw shelled hemp seeds provides up to 5 grams of protein. Two tablespoons (30 mL) hemp seeds meets your daily requirement for omega-3 essential fatty acids.

4	large leaves black kale, trimmed (see tip, at left)	4
¼ cup	freshly squeezed lemon juice, divided	60 mL
½ tsp	fine sea salt, divided	2 mL
1 cup	shredded carrots	250 mL
1 cup	shredded beets	250 mL
½ cup	raw shelled hemp seeds	125 mL

1. In a bowl, combine kale, 2 tbsp (30 mL) lemon juice and ⅛ tsp (0.5 mL) salt. Toss until well combined. Cover and set aside for 5 minutes, until softened.

2. In another bowl, combine carrots, beets, hemp seeds and the remaining lemon juice and salt. Toss until well combined. Cover and set aside for 5 minutes, until softened.

3. Remove kale from marinade, pat each leaf dry and place on a flat surface. Discard marinade. Divide carrot-beet filling into 4 equal portions. Place one portion on the bottom third of each kale leaf. Starting at the bottom of the leaf, roll up around the filling, making a tight cylinder. Transfer to a serving dish. Serve immediately or cover and refrigerate for up to 2 days.

Variation

Substitute 4 large collard or Swiss chard leaves for the kale leaves.

Nutrients per roll	
Calories	121
Fat	8 g
Carbohydrate	10 g
Fiber	3 g
Protein	6 g
Vitamin B$_6$	0.2 mg
Magnesium	123 mg
Zinc	1.7 mg

Dips, Spreads and Sauces

Avocado Spinach Dip. 212

Spicy Black Bean Dip 213

Garlicky White Bean Spread. 214

Roasted Vegetable Hummus 215

Country-Style Eggplant. 216

Herbed Vegetable Spread. 217

Avocado Mayonnaise. 218

Luscious Apple Butter 219

Apricot Tamarind Marmalade .220

Avocado, Orange and Quinoa Salsa 221

Classic Pesto Sauce 222

Pumpkin Seed Chimichurri 223

Basic Gravy. 224

Creamy White Sauce 225

Butternut Squash Spaghetti Sauce 226

Avocado Spinach Dip

This creamy dip is delightful. It is sure to fool any dedicated dairy-lovers — they won't believe it doesn't contain cream cheese, mascarpone or heavy cream. The key to making it perfect is to use perfectly ripe avocados. Serve with fresh veggies as dippers, or as a dressing on salad greens.

Tips

Spinach contains about 90% water. When cooking or marinating spinach, a good amount of the water will come out of it. Make sure to drain off the excess moisture before adding it to your recipe.

Nutritional yeast is a source of vitamin B_{12} and adds a deep, umami-like flavor to many dishes.

Nutrients per $\frac{1}{4}$ cup (60 mL)	
Calories	97
Fat	10 g
Carbohydrate	3 g
Fiber	1 g
Protein	1 g
Vitamin B_6	0.1 mg
Magnesium	13 mg
Zinc	0.2 mg

- **Food processor**

2 cups	chopped trimmed spinach	500 mL
$\frac{1}{2}$ cup	cold-pressed extra virgin olive oil, divided	125 mL
$\frac{1}{4}$ cup	freshly squeezed lemon juice	60 mL
2 tbsp	nutritional yeast	30 mL
3	cloves garlic, minced	3
2 tsp	fine sea salt, divided	10 mL
2	small avocados, chopped (about 2 cups/500 mL)	2
3 tbsp	chopped red onion	45 mL

1. In a bowl, toss spinach, $\frac{1}{4}$ cup (60 mL) oil, lemon juice, nutritional yeast, garlic and 1 tsp (5 mL) salt. Set aside for 30 minutes to soften. Once it is soft, drain the spinach.

2. In food processor, process marinated spinach for 30 seconds, until broken down. Add avocados and onion and process until smooth. With the motor running, slowly add the remaining oil through the feed tube, until mixture is creamy. Add the remaining salt and pulse to blend.

Spicy Black Bean Dip

Makes about 3 cups (750 mL)

Simple, yet delicious and nutritious to boot. What more could you want? Serve with blue corn tortilla chips for a great starter or snack.

Tips

For this quantity of beans, soak, cook and drain 1 cup (250 mL) dried black beans or drain and rinse 1 can (14 to 19 oz/398 to 540 mL) black beans.

For a smoother dip, purée the beans in a food processor or mash with a potato masher before adding to stoneware.

- **Small to medium (1½- to 3½-quart) slow cooker**
- **Food processor**

1	small red or sweet onion, coarsely chopped	1
2	cloves garlic, chopped	2
1 to 2	canned chipotle pepper(s) in adobo sauce	1 to 2
2 cups	cooked black beans (see tips, at left)	500 mL
2 tsp	ground cumin (see tip, page 266)	10 mL
1 tsp	finely grated lime zest	5 mL
1 tsp	salt	5 mL
½ tsp	freshly cracked black pepper	2 mL
2 cups	shredded vegan Monterey Jack cheese alternative (about 8 oz/250 g)	500 mL
	Finely chopped fresh cilantro	

1. In food processor, combine onion, garlic and chipotle pepper; process until finely chopped. Add beans, cumin, lime zest, salt and pepper; process until desired consistency is achieved.

2. Transfer to slow cooker stoneware. Stir in cheese alternative. Cover and cook on High for 1 hour. Stir well. Cover and cook on High for 30 minutes, until mixture is hot and bubbly. Garnish with cilantro. Serve immediately or set temperature at Warm until ready to serve.

Nutrients per ¼ cup (60 mL)	
Calories	117
Fat	6 g
Carbohydrate	8 g
Fiber	3 g
Protein	7 g
Vitamin B$_6$	0.1 mg
Magnesium	27 mg
Zinc	0.9 mg

Garlicky White Bean Spread

Tips

If using a 19-oz (540 mL) can of beans, drain and measure out 1⅔ cups (400 mL) beans.

This spread may also be served as a dip.

- **Food processor**

3	cloves garlic, minced	3
1	can (14 to 15 oz/398 to 425 mL) cannellini (white kidney) beans, drained and rinsed	1
⅔ cup	cooked quinoa, cooled	150 mL
1 tbsp	dried Italian seasoning	15 mL
½ tsp	fine sea salt	2 mL
¼ cup	freshly squeezed lemon juice	60 mL
1 tbsp	extra virgin olive oil	15 mL
¼ cup	packed fresh flat-leaf (Italian) parsley, chopped	60 mL

1. In food processor, combine garlic, beans, quinoa, Italian seasoning, salt, lemon juice and oil; process until smooth. Transfer to a serving dish and stir in parsley. Store tightly covered in the refrigerator for up to 3 days.

Nutrients per ¼ cup (60 mL)	
Calories	79
Fat	2 g
Carbohydrate	12 g
Fiber	3 g
Protein	3 g
Vitamin B$_6$	0.1 mg
Magnesium	25 mg
Zinc	0.4 mg

Roasted Vegetable Hummus

Makes
2½ cups (625 mL)

Cinnamon gives a spicy nudge to this Middle Eastern staple. This is a fairly thick dip that is best made in a food processor.

Tips

To use a blender, add ¼ cup (60 mL) apple juice before processing in step 2.

You can use 2 cups (500 mL) cooked chickpeas, drained and rinsed, instead of canned.

- **Preheat oven to 400°F (200°C)**
- **Rimmed baking sheet**
- **Food processor (see tip, at left)**

6	cloves garlic	6
2	onions, quartered	2
2	carrots, cut into 1-inch (2.5 cm) pieces	2
1	red bell pepper, quartered	1
5 tbsp	olive oil, divided	75 mL
1	can (14 to 19 oz/398 to 540 mL) chickpeas, drained and rinsed	1
2 tbsp	freshly squeezed lemon juice	30 mL
2 tbsp	tahini	30 mL
½ tsp	ground cinnamon	2 mL
½ tsp	sea salt	2 mL

1. On baking sheet, combine garlic, onions, carrots and red pepper. Drizzle with 2 tbsp (30 mL) oil and toss well to coat. Roast in preheated oven for 40 minutes or until soft and browned. Edges of vegetables may be slightly burnt and crisp. Let cool.

2. In food processor, combine roasted vegetables, the remaining oil, chickpeas, lemon juice, tahini, cinnamon and salt; process until smooth.

3. Transfer mixture to a clean container with lid. Store hummus tightly covered in the refrigerator for up to 3 days.

Nutrients per
¼ cup (60 mL)

Calories	143
Fat	9 g
Carbohydrate	14 g
Fiber	3 g
Protein	3 g
Vitamin B6	0.3 mg
Magnesium	19 mg
Zinc	0.7 mg

Country-Style Eggplant

This easy chunky mix is a quick and great-tasting dip for raw veggies or as a spread on crackers, or it can be served with radicchio leaves as a first course. It may be made one day in advance but tends to darken during storage.

Tip

For a smoother dip, blend in a food processor or blender.

3 tbsp	olive oil, divided	45 mL
1½ cups	finely chopped onions	375 mL
4 cups	diced eggplant (about 1 medium)	1 L
3 tbsp	freshly squeezed lemon juice	45 mL
2	cloves garlic, minced	2
½ tsp	sea salt	2 mL
2 tbsp	pure maple syrup	30 mL
1	jar (6 oz/175 g) marinated artichokes, drained and coarsely chopped	1
1 cup	green olives, pitted and chopped (optional)	250 mL
	Toast points or radicchio leaves (optional)	

1. In a saucepan, heat 2 tbsp (30 mL) oil over medium heat. Add onions and cook, stirring occasionally, for 6 to 8 minutes or until soft.

2. Add the remaining oil and heat. Stir in eggplant, lemon juice, garlic and salt. Cover, reduce heat to low and cook, stirring occasionally, for 15 minutes. Check periodically and add small amounts of water by the tablespoon (15 mL) if eggplant appears to be sticking. Eggplant should be very soft.

3. Add maple syrup, artichokes and olives (if using) and cook, stirring occasionally, for 5 minutes. Serve with toast points (if using).

Nutrients per ¼ cup (60 mL)	
Calories	93
Fat	5 g
Carbohydrate	12 g
Fiber	4 g
Protein	1 g
Vitamin B$_6$	0.1 mg
Magnesium	19 mg
Zinc	0.3 mg

Herbed Vegetable Spread

Vegetable or fruit spreads offer a lower-fat alternative to butter or mayonnaise. Fresh herbs are the key to the great flavor.

Tips

Use chives, thyme, oregano, basil, sage or savory in this spread. Chives were used in the nutrient analysis.

You can use 2 cups (500 mL) cooked chickpeas, drained and rinsed, instead of canned.

- **Food processor or blender**
- **Ramekins or custard cups**

1 lb	parsnips or carrots, cut into chunks	500 g
1	can (19 oz/540 mL) chickpeas, drained and rinsed	1
2 tbsp	butter	30 mL
1 tbsp	chopped fresh herbs (see tip, at left)	15 mL
1 tbsp	liquid honey	15 mL

1. In a pot, cover parsnips with water. Bring to a boil over high heat. Cover, reduce heat and simmer for 10 minutes or until soft. Drain and let cool.

2. In food processor, process parsnips, chickpeas, butter, herb and honey for about 30 seconds or until smooth. Pack into ramekins or custard cups and cover with plastic wrap. Store tightly covered in the refrigerator for up to 2 weeks.

Variations

Use cannellini beans in place of the chickpeas.

For a vegan version, use 1 tbsp (15 mL) olive oil in place of the butter.

Nutrients per 1 tbsp (15 mL)	
Calories	38
Fat	1 g
Carbohydrate	7 g
Fiber	1 g
Protein	1 g
Vitamin B$_6$	0.1 mg
Magnesium	9 mg
Zinc	0.3 mg

Avocado Mayonnaise

**Makes
1 cup (250 mL)**

This no-egg mayonnaise also works as a spread.

Tips

To determine if your avocado is ripe, hold it in the palm of your hand and press. It should feel like a tomato that has a little "give."

If your food processor has a feed tube with the drip feature (a small hole in the bottom of the tube), fill the tube with oil and let it drizzle in, refilling the tube with oil as it drains until all of the oil is incorporated. Alternatively, pour a thin, steady stream of oil slowly into the feed tube. Adding the oil too quickly can cause the mayonnaise to separate.

- **Food processor**

1	ripe avocado, cut into quarters	1
2 tbsp	freshly squeezed lime juice	30 mL
2 tbsp	chopped fresh cilantro	30 mL
¼ tsp	sea salt	1 mL
¼ tsp	freshly ground black pepper	1 mL
2 tbsp	extra virgin olive oil	30 mL

1. In food processor, combine avocado, lime juice, cilantro, salt and pepper; process until smooth.

2. With the motor running, slowly drizzle oil through the small hole in the feed tube until it has been incorporated into mayonnaise (see tip, at left). Use within a few hours.

Nutrients per 1 tbsp (15 mL)	
Calories	33
Fat	3 g
Carbohydrate	1 g
Fiber	1 g
Protein	0 g
Vitamin B_6	0 mg
Magnesium	4 mg
Zinc	0.1 mg

Luscious Apple Butter

This delicious old-fashioned spread has lots of appeal. Serve it on toast for breakfast, on nut butter sandwiches for lunch or as a snack or dessert topping. You can also forgo the puréeing and serve a warm, chunky version as an accompaniment to puddings or vanilla-flavor soy yogurt.

- Preheat oven to 400°F (200°C)
- 13- by 9-inch (33 by 23 cm) baking dish, ungreased
- Food processor or blender

¼ cup	water	60 mL
10	small to medium cooking apples (such as McIntosh), peeled and thinly sliced	10
⅓ cup	packed dark brown sugar	75 mL
¼ tsp	ground cinnamon	1 mL
¼ tsp	ground cloves	1 mL
⅛ tsp	ground allspice	0.5 mL
Pinch	ground nutmeg	Pinch
3 tbsp	light (fancy) molasses	45 mL
1 tbsp	freshly squeezed lemon juice	15 mL

1. Pour water into baking dish. Add apples and brown sugar. Stir until sugar is dissolved. Sprinkle cinnamon, cloves, allspice and nutmeg over top and mix well.

2. Drizzle molasses and lemon juice over top. Stir well.

3. Bake, uncovered, in preheated oven, stirring every 20 minutes, for 1 hour or until apples are deep brown, soft and coated with syrup. Let cool in baking dish on a rack for 5 to 10 minutes.

4. Transfer cooled apple mixture to food processor and purée until smooth. Store in a glass jar or airtight container in the refrigerator for up to 6 weeks.

Variation

For convenience, make this recipe using one 26-oz (700 mL) jar unsweetened applesauce instead of the apples. Omit the water and bake at 375°F (190°C) for 1 hour. No puréeing is needed.

Nutrients per 1 tbsp (15 mL)	
Calories	37
Fat	0 g
Carbohydrate	10 g
Fiber	1 g
Protein	0 g
Vitamin B$_6$	0 mg
Magnesium	7 mg
Zinc	0 mg

Apricot Tamarind Marmalade

Fruity and tart-sweet, this spread makes a healthy accompaniment to savory baked and roasted dishes.

Tips

Be sure to check the tamarind for seeds. They are very smooth and hard and easy to miss but a hazard for teeth in a finished dish.

Jaggery is a coarse, unrefined sugar found throughout South and Southeast Asia. It is sometimes available at Indian markets or natural food stores and comes in solid cakes or blocks that range from rock-hard to crumbly. Use jaggery as you would brown sugar in recipes.

¾ cup	freshly squeezed orange juice	175 mL
2 tbsp	freshly squeezed lemon juice	30 mL
1 tbsp	rice vinegar	15 mL
¾ cup	chopped dried apricots	175 mL
¼ cup	chopped pitted tamarind (see tip, at left)	60 mL
¼ cup	chopped dates	60 mL
2 tbsp	jaggery or brown sugar (see tip, at left)	30 mL
½ tsp	ground cinnamon	2 mL
½ tsp	ground turmeric	2 mL
¼ tsp	ground mace	1 mL
	Sea salt and freshly ground black pepper	

1. In a heavy-bottomed saucepan, combine orange juice, lemon juice and vinegar. Bring to a boil over high heat. Add apricots, tamarind, dates, jaggery, cinnamon, turmeric and mace. Stir well to combine and bring to a boil, stirring constantly. Reduce heat to medium-low and simmer, stirring occasionally, for 40 minutes or until mixture is soft and thick. Season to taste with salt and pepper.

2. Let cool and transfer mixture to a clean container with lid. Store marmalade in the refrigerator for up to 3 weeks.

Nutrients per 1 tbsp (15 mL)	
Calories	25
Fat	0 g
Carbohydrate	6 g
Fiber	1 g
Protein	0 g
Vitamin B$_6$	0 mg
Magnesium	4 mg
Zinc	0 mg

Avocado, Orange and Quinoa Salsa

A foundation of sunny oranges and nutty quinoa is the perfect destination for those perfectly firm-ripe avocados sitting on your counter.

Tip

If you can only find 10-oz (287 mL) cans of mandarin oranges, use 1½ cans.

2	small firm-ripe Hass avocados, diced	2
1	can (15 oz/425 mL) mandarin oranges packed in juice, drained and coarsely chopped	1
1 cup	cooked black, red or white quinoa, cooled	250 mL
⅓ cup	finely chopped red onion	75 mL
⅓ cup	packed fresh cilantro leaves, chopped	75 mL
¼ tsp	chipotle chile powder or cayenne pepper	1 mL
1 tbsp	freshly squeezed lime juice	15 mL
	Fine sea salt	

1. In a large bowl, combine avocados, mandarin oranges, quinoa, red onion, cilantro, chipotle chile powder and lime juice, tossing gently. Season to taste with salt. Cover and refrigerate for at least 30 minutes, until chilled, or for up to 2 hours.

Nutrients per ¼ cup (60 mL)	
Calories	88
Fat	5 g
Carbohydrate	10 g
Fiber	3 g
Protein	2 g
Vitamin B$_6$	0.1 mg
Magnesium	24 mg
Zinc	0.6 mg

Classic Pesto Sauce

A classic pesto is always so versatile and should be prominently included in everyone's recipe repertoire. Add a spoonful to soups, stews, curries and sauces or toss it with steamed vegetables, roasted potatoes and, of course, pasta.

Tip

Drizzling olive oil over top of pesto during storage helps prevent discoloration.

• **Food processor or blender**

6 cups	packed fresh basil leaves	1.5 L
1 tsp	salt	5 mL
½ tsp	freshly ground black pepper	2 mL
½ cup	olive oil	125 mL
¼ cup	pine nuts	60 mL

1. In food processor, combine basil, salt and pepper and pulse until finely chopped, 3 to 4 times. With motor running, slowly add oil through the feed tube and process until just smooth, scraping down sides as necessary. Add pine nuts and pulse to incorporate, 2 to 4 times. Use immediately or refrigerate in an airtight container for up to 5 days.

Nutrients per ¼ cup (60 mL)

Calories	207
Fat	22 g
Carbohydrate	2 g
Fiber	1 g
Protein	2 g
Vitamin B$_6$	0.1 mg
Magnesium	41 mg
Zinc	0.7 mg

Pumpkin Seed Chimichurri

This South American–inspired dip bursts with flavor on your tongue. In addition to being a great dip for veggies such as leaves of romaine hearts, it makes a fabulous chunky dressing for salad.

Variation

Substitute 1½ cups (375 mL) sunflower seeds or ¾ cup (175 mL) almonds for the pumpkin seeds in this recipe. Soak either for 30 minutes in 2 cups (500 mL) water. Cover and set aside. Drain and discard any remaining water.

Nutrients per ¼ cup (60 mL)	
Calories	193
Fat	18 g
Carbohydrate	5 g
Fiber	2 g
Protein	7 g
Vitamin B6	0.1 mg
Magnesium	135 mg
Zinc	1.8 mg

- **Food processor**

1 cup	raw pumpkin seeds, soaked (see tip, below)	250 mL
3 tbsp	freshly squeezed lemon juice	45 mL
3 tbsp	cold-pressed extra virgin olive oil	45 mL
1 tbsp	apple cider vinegar	15 mL
2 tbsp	chopped gingerroot	30 mL
3	cloves garlic	3
1 tbsp	chili powder	15 mL
1 tsp	ground cumin	5 mL
½ tsp	sea salt	2 mL
Pinch	cayenne pepper	Pinch
1 cup	chopped fresh cilantro	250 mL
½ cup	chopped fresh flat-leaf (Italian) parsley	125 mL
	Filtered water (optional)	

1. In food processor, combine lemon juice, oil, vinegar, ginger, garlic, chili powder, cumin, salt and cayenne; process until smooth. Using a rubber spatula, scrape down the sides of the work bowl.

2. Add cilantro, parsley and soaked pumpkin seeds and pulse just until mixture is chopped and blended (you want the result to be a bit chunky, not smooth). If the mixture seems dry, add water through the feed tube in increments of 1 tbsp (15 mL) and pulse to integrate. Serve immediately or cover and refrigerate for up to 5 days.

Tips

To soak the pumpkin seeds for this recipe, combine with 2 cups (500 mL) water in a bowl. Cover and set aside for 30 minutes. Drain, rinse and discard any remaining water.

Pumpkin seeds provide an impressive array of nutrients. They contain healthy polyunsaturated and monounsaturated fats, protein, fiber, iron, magnesium, potassium, zinc, manganese, thiamine (vitamin B_1) and vitamin E — not bad for the seeds of a common squash.

Parsley comes in two different varieties: flat-leaf (also called Italian parsley) and curly. Both are very good for you. Flat-leaf parsley has more flavor when it is left in a roughly chopped state.

Basic Gravy

This generic curry sauce enhancer speeds up curry recipes and works every time. It comes to us courtesy of Chef Prasannan of the Lonely Planet restaurant in Kovalam Beach, Kerala.

Tips

If you don't have a food processor, you can use a blender. Just add enough of the tomato purée to the onion mixture to help the blender purée more easily.

Let extra gravy cool completely, then transfer to an airtight container, cover and refrigerate for up to 1 week. Or divide into ½-cup (125 mL) and/ or 1-cup (250 mL) portions in airtight containers and freeze for up to 2 months. Thaw overnight in the refrigerator or defrost in the microwave.

Nutrients per ¼ cup (60 mL)	
Calories	41
Fat	2 g
Carbohydrate	6 g
Fiber	1 g
Protein	1 g
Vitamin B$_6$	0.1 mg
Magnesium	13 mg
Zinc	0.2 mg

- **Food processor**

1	can (28 oz/796 mL) tomatoes, with juice (see tip, page 282)	1
2 cups	coarsely chopped onions	500 mL
⅓ cup	whole garlic cloves (about 12)	75 mL
⅓ cup	thinly sliced gingerroot	75 mL
2 tbsp	vegetable oil	30 mL
¼ cup	ground coriander	60 mL
1 tbsp	ground turmeric	15 mL
1 tbsp	garam masala	15 mL
2 tsp	salt	10 mL
1 tsp	cayenne pepper	5 mL

1. In food processor, purée tomatoes until smooth. Pour back into the can or into a bowl and set aside.

2. Add onions, garlic and ginger to food processor and pulse until very finely chopped but not juicy.

3. In a skillet, heat oil over medium heat. Add onion mixture and cook, stirring, until onions start to release their liquid, about 3 minutes. Stir in coriander, turmeric, garam masala, salt and cayenne. Cook, stirring, until well blended and mixture is starting to dry and get thick and paste-like, about 3 minutes.

4. Stir in puréed tomatoes and bring to a simmer, scraping up bits stuck to pan. Reduce heat and boil gently, stirring often, until slightly thickened and flavors are blended, about 5 minutes. Use as directed in recipes.

Creamy White Sauce

A very easy sauce that is useful in main-course dishes. This basic white sauce is light and silky with a roasted, nutty taste. Use it in pasta and roasted vegetable dishes.

- Preheat oven to 400°F (200°C)
- Rimmed baking sheet
- Blender or food processor

½	eggplant	½
½	butternut squash	½
1	apple, cut in half	1
4 tbsp	olive oil, divided	60 mL
1	whole head garlic, ¼ inch (0.5 cm) of the top removed	1
1½ cups	rice milk or soy milk	375 mL

1. Arrange eggplant, squash and apple cut side down on baking sheet and drizzle with 3 tbsp (45 mL) oil. Place garlic head cut side up on baking sheet and drizzle with the remaining oil.

2. Bake in preheated oven for 30 minutes. Using a slotted spoon, remove apple halves and transfer to a bowl. Bake remaining vegetables for 15 minutes or until eggplant is tender. Transfer eggplant to a bowl. Continue to bake squash and garlic for 15 minutes, for a total of 1 hour, or until tender. Let cool slightly. Scoop apple, eggplant and squash flesh out of their skins and discard skins.

3. In blender, combine rice milk, apple, eggplant and squash. Squeeze garlic flesh out of the skin and add to the blender. Blend until sauce is liquefied and smooth. Store tightly covered in the refrigerator for up to 3 days.

Nutrients per ¼ cup (60 mL)	
Calories	56
Fat	4 g
Carbohydrate	6 g
Fiber	1 g
Protein	0 g
Vitamin B$_6$	0.1 mg
Magnesium	8 mg
Zinc	0.1 mg

Butternut Squash Spaghetti Sauce

Makes 2 servings

For those who cannot eat tomato-based spaghetti sauce, this is a good alternative. Serve over rice pasta.

Storage Tip

This sauce can be stored in an airtight container in the refrigerator for up to 3 days. Reheat on the stovetop over low heat, stirring constantly and adding a little water as needed for the desired consistency.

- **Blender**

1	butternut squash (about 3½ lbs/1.75 g), diced	1
2 tbsp	olive oil	30 mL
1	onion, sliced	1
1	stalk celery, chopped	1
1	clove garlic, minced	1
¼ tsp	salt	1 mL

1. Bring a pot of water to a boil over high heat. Add squash, reduce heat and simmer for 20 minutes until tender. Drain and transfer squash to blender.

2. In a saucepan, heat oil over medium heat. Add onion, celery and garlic; cook, stirring, for 5 to 10 minutes or until tender.

3. Add onion mixture and salt to blender and blend until smooth.

Nutrients per serving	
Calories	496
Fat	14 g
Carbohydrate	97 g
Fiber	17 g
Protein	9 g
Vitamin B$_6$	1.3 mg
Magnesium	276 mg
Zinc	1.3 mg

Salads and Dressings

Cauliflower and Zucchini Slaw 228

Mixed Green Salad with Zesty Herb Dressing 229

Greens and Vegetable Salad with Lemon Dressing 230

Summer Greens and Berries
  with Apple Cider Vinaigrette. 230

Watercress, Raspberry and Avocado Salad 231

Artichoke Heart Salad. 232

Avocado Salad 232

Warm Beet Salad 233

Asian-Style Quinoa Salad
  with Chili-Orange Dressing 234

Sweet Potato, Quinoa and Black Bean Salad. 235

Black Bean and Rice Salad 236

Middle Eastern Balela Salad 237

Mediterranean Bean Salad 238

Chickpea Salad 240

Apple Cider Vinaigrette 241

Berry Vinaigrette. 241

Easy Italian Dressing 242

Creamy Herb Dressing 243

Spicy Lime Avocado Dressing 244

Zesty Herb Dressing 245

Lemon Dressing. 245

Caesar Salad Dressing. 246

Cauliflower and Zucchini Slaw

Fresh and crisp green and white fruit and vegetables offer a united and striking presentation. Flecks of almonds and black poppy seeds with a zippy dressing make this salad a standout.

3	zucchini, grated	3
1	green apple, unpeeled and grated	1
½	head cauliflower, grated	½
2	green onions, white and green parts, chopped	2
½ cup	toasted slivered almonds	125 mL
¼ cup	chopped fresh cilantro	60 mL
1 tbsp	poppy seeds	15 mL

Dressing

¼ cup	freshly squeezed lime juice	60 mL
¼ cup	olive oil	60 mL
½ tsp	salt	2 mL
¼ tsp	freshly ground white pepper	1 mL

1. In a large bowl, combine zucchini, apple, cauliflower, green onions, almonds and cilantro.

2. *Dressing:* In a small bowl, whisk together lime juice, oil, salt and white pepper. Taste and adjust seasonings. Pour dressing over salad. Add poppy seeds and toss to combine. Serve immediately or refrigerate in an airtight container for up to 2 days.

Nutrients per serving (1 of 10)	
Calories	108
Fat	9 g
Carbohydrate	7 g
Fiber	2 g
Protein	2 g
Vitamin B6	0.1 mg
Magnesium	30 mg
Zinc	0.4 mg

Mixed Green Salad with Zesty Herb Dressing

Makes 4 servings

This salad is full of nutrients that aid in liver detoxification. The carrots are high in flavonoids that help the first phase of liver detoxification, and artichokes help the liver produce bile.

4 cups	mixed baby greens	1 L
2	large carrots, chopped	2
2 cups	trimmed sugar snap peas	500 mL
1 cup	broccoli florets	250 mL
1 cup	pickled red cabbage	250 mL
1 cup	chopped drained marinated artichoke hearts	250 mL
½ cup	sunflower seeds	125 mL
½ cup	Zesty Herb Dressing (page 245)	125 mL

1. In a large bowl, combine greens, carrots, peas, broccoli, cabbage, artichokes and sunflower seeds. Drizzle with dressing and toss to coat.

Nutrients per serving	
Calories	328
Fat	28 g
Carbohydrate	16 g
Fiber	6 g
Protein	8 g
Vitamin B6	0.4 mg
Magnesium	83 mg
Zinc	1.3 mg

Greens and Vegetable Salad with Lemon Dressing

This salad is a great way to detoxify the liver with antioxidants and lemon.

Nutrients per serving	
Calories	213
Fat	18 g
Carbohydrate	12 g
Fiber	3 g
Protein	2 g
Vitamin B$_6$	0.2 mg
Magnesium	27 mg
Zinc	0.4 mg

4 cups	mixed greens	1 L
1 cup	chopped cucumber	250 mL
1 cup	halved cherry tomatoes	250 mL
1 cup	chopped green beans	250 mL
1 cup	chopped carrots	250 mL
½ cup	Lemon Dressing (page 245)	125 mL

1. In a large bowl, combine greens, cucumber, tomatoes, green beans and carrots. Drizzle with dressing and toss to coat.

Tip

The chlorophyll in dark green leafy vegetables helps the body eliminate environmental toxins and metals.

Summer Greens and Berries with Apple Cider Vinaigrette

Berries are full of antioxidants, to help the liver detoxify.

Nutrients per serving	
Calories	333
Fat	29 g
Carbohydrate	16 g
Fiber	6 g
Protein	7 g
Vitamin B$_6$	0.1 mg
Magnesium	119 mg
Zinc	1.8 mg

4 cups	mixed baby greens	1 L
1 cup	blueberries	250 mL
1 cup	raspberries	250 mL
1 cup	blackberries	250 mL
½ cup	green pumpkin seeds (pepitas)	125 mL
½ cup	Apple Cider Vinaigrette (page 241)	125 mL

1. In a large bowl, combine greens, blueberries, raspberries, blackberries and pumpkin seeds. Drizzle with vinaigrette and toss to coat.

Watercress, Raspberry and Avocado Salad

Watercress grows in and around shallow water and is often gathered from the wild. The only caution if wild-crafting is that the water should not be standing and should be clear of any field run-off.

Nutrients per serving	
Calories	275
Fat	25 g
Carbohydrate	13 g
Fiber	9 g
Protein	3 g
Vitamin B$_6$	0.3 mg
Magnesium	44 mg
Zinc	0.8 mg

**Makes
¼ cup (60 mL)**

Nutrients per 1 tbsp (15 mL)	
Calories	93
Fat	11 g
Carbohydrate	0 g
Fiber	0 g
Protein	0 g
Vitamin B$_6$	0 mg
Magnesium	0 mg
Zinc	0 mg

2	firm ripe avocados	2
2 tbsp	freshly squeezed lemon juice	30 mL
4 cups	tender watercress sprigs, torn	1 L
1 cup	fresh raspberries	250 mL
¼ cup	Raspberry Dressing (see recipe, below)	60 mL

1. Slit avocados lengthwise from stem end around base and back to stem. Twist the two halves apart. Remove pit from one half and skin from both halves. Slice flesh into a small bowl. Sprinkle lemon juice over top.

2. Line a serving platter with watercress. Arrange avocado slices and raspberries over watercress. Drizzle dressing over top and serve immediately.

Variations

Use 2 kiwifruits or 1 cup (250 mL) sliced mango, melon or papaya in place of the avocados.

Tender young spinach leaves may be used to replace the watercress.

Raspberry Dressing

3 tbsp	canola oil	45 mL
1 tbsp	raspberry vinegar or purée	15 mL
1 tbsp	liquid honey (optional)	15 mL
1 tbsp	chopped fresh chervil or parsley	15 mL
	Salt and freshly ground black pepper	

1. In a jar with lid or small bowl, combine oil, vinegar, honey (if using) and chervil. Shake or whisk to mix well. Season to taste with salt and pepper, and extra vinegar, if required.

Tip

Use fresh pressed raspberry purée when raspberries are in season.

Artichoke Heart Salad

Artichoke hearts contain cynarine and silymarin, which help the liver produce bile and help protect and regenerate liver cells.

Nutrients per serving	
Calories	245
Fat	19 g
Carbohydrate	12 g
Fiber	5 g
Protein	13 g
Vitamin B$_6$	0.1 mg
Magnesium	198 mg
Zinc	2.6 mg

2 cups	mixed baby greens	250 mL
1 cup	chopped marinated artichoke hearts	250 mL
½ cup	green pumpkin seeds (pepitas)	125 mL

1. In a large bowl, combine greens, artichokes (with marinade) and pumpkin seeds, tossing to combine.

Avocado Salad

The avocado dressing, together with the beans and sunflower seeds, contributes fiber and protein to fill you up.

Nutrients per serving	
Calories	280
Fat	14 g
Carbohydrate	31 g
Fiber	14 g
Protein	11 g
Vitamin B$_6$	0.4 mg
Magnesium	98 mg
Zinc	1.6 mg

1	avocado, sliced	1
4 cups	mixed baby greens	1 L
2 cups	rinsed drained canned black beans	500 mL
¼ cup	sunflower seeds	60 mL
½ cup	Spicy Lime Avocado Dressing (page 244)	125 mL

1. In a large bowl, combine avocado, greens, black beans and sunflower seeds. Drizzle with dressing and toss to coat.

Warm Beet Salad

Slightly sweet, this salad is often enjoyed by ardent beet haters.

Tip

If you don't have home-made stock on hand, you can use ready-to-use reduced-sodium vegetable broth in its place. Check the label to make sure ingredients containing gluten have not been added.

4	medium beets	4
2 tbsp	olive oil	30 mL
½ cup	chopped onion	125 mL
½ cup	sliced fennel bulb or celery	125 mL
½ cup	Vegetable Stock (page 248)	125 mL
⅓ cup	apple juice	75 mL
2	apples, quartered	2
¼ cup	quartered dried apricots	60 mL
2 tbsp	rice vinegar	30 mL
1 to	liquid honey	15 to
2 tbsp		30 mL

Salt and freshly ground black pepper

1. Trim and scrub beets. Cut into wedges.

2. In a large saucepan with a lid, heat oil over medium heat. Add onion and cook, stirring, for 5 minutes or until soft. Add beets, fennel, stock and apple juice. Bring to a boil over high heat. Cover, reduce heat and simmer for about 20 minutes or until beets are tender.

3. Stir in apples, apricots, vinegar and honey. Simmer for about 7 minutes or until apples are soft and sauce is reduced slightly. Season to taste with salt and pepper. Serve warm.

Nutrients per serving (1 of 6)	
Calories	137
Fat	5 g
Carbohydrate	24 g
Fiber	4 g
Protein	1 g
Vitamin B$_6$	0.1 mg
Magnesium	21 mg
Zinc	0.3 mg

Asian-Style Quinoa Salad with Chili-Orange Dressing

Perhaps surprisingly, since quinoa is a "New World" grain, it takes very well to Asian ingredients such as water chestnuts. This is a nice light salad that is perfect for summer dining or a buffet.

Tip
The chili sauce adds a pleasant bit of zest, but if you're heat averse you can omit it. Heat seekers can increase the quantity to taste.

Chili-Orange Dressing

1 tsp	finely grated orange zest	5 mL
1/4 cup	freshly squeezed orange juice	60 mL
1 tbsp	gluten-free reduced-sodium soy sauce	15 mL
1 tbsp	liquid honey or agave nectar	15 mL
2 tsp	sesame oil	10 mL
1/2 tsp	Asian chili sauce (such as sambal oelek)	2 mL
	Freshly ground black pepper	

Salad

3 cups	cooked quinoa, cooled	750 mL
1	can (8 oz/227 g) water chestnuts, drained and chopped	1
1	red bell pepper, chopped	1
1 1/2 cups	chopped snow peas, cooked until tender-crisp and cooled	375 mL
4	green onions, white part with a bit of green, thinly sliced	4

1. *Chili-Orange Dressing:* In a small bowl, whisk together orange zest and juice, soy sauce, honey, sesame oil, chili sauce and pepper to taste. Set aside.

2. *Salad:* In a serving bowl, combine quinoa, water chestnuts, red pepper, snow peas and green onions. Add dressing and toss until combined. Chill thoroughly.

Variation
Substitute 3 cups (750 mL) cooked toasted millet for the quinoa.

Nutrients per serving	
Calories	178
Fat	3 g
Carbohydrate	32 g
Fiber	5 g
Protein	6 g
Vitamin B$_6$	0.3 mg
Magnesium	72 mg
Zinc	1.3 mg

Sweet Potato, Quinoa and Black Bean Salad

**Makes
4 main-dish
servings**

These sweet potatoes caramelize slightly in the oven, which gives them a sweet crunch even as their flesh remains creamy. Quinoa and black beans balance their sweetness while making this dish supper-worthy, and a lime dressing lends addictive acid and tart notes.

- Preheat oven to 400°F (200°C)
- Large rimmed baking sheet, lined with foil and sprayed with nonstick cooking spray

1 lb	sweet potatoes, peeled and cut into 1/2-inch (1 cm) cubes	500 g
3 tbsp	extra virgin olive oil, divided	45 mL
1 tbsp	chili powder	15 mL
	Fine sea salt and freshly cracked black pepper	
1 1/2 cups	cooked quinoa, cooled slightly	375 mL
1	large red bell pepper, chopped	1
1/2 cup	thinly sliced green onions	125 mL
1	can (14 to 19 oz/398 to 540 mL) black beans, drained and rinsed	1
1 tbsp	ground cumin	15 mL
3 tbsp	freshly squeezed lime juice	45 mL
1 tbsp	liquid honey or agave nectar	15 mL

1. Place sweet potatoes on prepared baking sheet. Drizzle with 1 tbsp (15 mL) oil and sprinkle with chili powder. Season with salt and pepper. Gently toss to coat. Spread in a single layer. Roast in preheated oven for 20 to 25 minutes or until golden brown and tender. Let cool completely in pan.

2. In a large bowl, combine sweet potatoes, quinoa, red pepper, green onions and beans.

3. In a small bowl, whisk together cumin, lime juice, honey and the remaining oil. Add to sweet potato mixture and gently toss to coat. Season to taste with salt and pepper.

Nutrients per serving	
Calories	408
Fat	13 g
Carbohydrate	64 g
Fiber	14 g
Protein	12 g
Vitamin B_6	0.6 mg
Magnesium	125 mg
Zinc	2.0 mg

Black Bean and Rice Salad

Makes 8 servings

This colorful salad makes a great summer meal or portable potluck offering. It's also very Western, with Tex-Mex overtones and earthy black beans.

1 cup	dried black beans, soaked overnight in enough water to cover	250 mL
8 cups	cold water	2 L
1	onion, halved	1
2	cloves garlic, chopped	2
1	small carrot	1
1	sprig fresh parsley	1
1¾ cups	water	425 mL
1 cup	white rice	250 mL
1 tbsp	canola oil	15 mL
1 tsp	ground turmeric	5 mL
1 tsp	ground cumin, divided	5 mL
½ tsp	salt	2 mL
3 tbsp	olive oil	45 mL
3 tbsp	freshly squeezed lime juice	45 mL
2	tomatoes, seeded and diced	2
1	small red onion, finely chopped	1
1	red bell pepper, finely chopped	1
1	jalapeño pepper, seeded and minced	1
¼ cup	chopped fresh cilantro	60 mL
	Cayenne pepper	

1. In a saucepan, combine drained beans with 8 cups (2 L) cold water, onion, garlic, carrot and parsley; bring to a boil. Reduce heat and simmer for 1½ hours or until tender. Drain and let cool. Discard onion, carrot and parsley.

2. Meanwhile, in a small saucepan, combine 1¾ cups (425 mL) cold water, rice, oil, turmeric, ½ tsp (2 mL) cumin and salt; bring to a boil. Reduce heat to low and simmer, covered, for 30 minutes. Fluff rice and let cool to room temperature.

3. In a small bowl, whisk together oil, lime juice and the remaining cumin.

4. In a large bowl, toss cooled beans and rice with tomatoes, red onion, red pepper, jalapeño, cilantro and dressing. Season to taste with cayenne and, if desired, additional salt. Chill.

Nutrients per serving	
Calories	251
Fat	7 g
Carbohydrate	39 g
Fiber	7 g
Protein	8 g
Vitamin B$_6$	0.2 mg
Magnesium	56 mg
Zinc	1.1 mg

Middle Eastern Balela Salad

This colorful bean salad makes use of canned beans and throws together in minutes. The next time you cook up a pot of chickpeas, be sure to make extra with this recipe in mind.

Tip

Tuck balela salad into a pita or wrap in a spinach tortilla for a quick lunch or dinner.

2	cans (each 14 to 19 oz/398 to 540 mL) chickpeas, drained and rinsed	2
1 cup	diced tomatoes	250 mL
1	small red onion, chopped	1
1/4 cup	minced fresh parsley	60 mL
2 tbsp	minced fresh mint	30 mL
1	clove garlic, minced	1
1/4 cup	olive oil	60 mL
1/2 cup	apple cider vinegar	125 mL
1/2 tsp	salt	2 mL
1/2 tsp	freshly ground black pepper	2 mL

1. In a serving bowl, toss together chickpeas, tomatoes, red onion, parsley, mint and garlic.

2. In a liquid measuring cup or small bowl, combine oil, vinegar, salt and pepper. Add to salad, tossing gently to combine. Taste and adjust seasonings. Let salad stand for at least 1 hour before serving to combine flavors.

Variations

Use sun-dried tomatoes instead of fresh tomato.

Swap 1 can of the chickpeas with drained and rinsed black, kidney or cannellini beans.

Nutrients per serving	
Calories	374
Fat	16 g
Carbohydrate	48 g
Fiber	10 g
Protein	10 g
Vitamin B$_6$	1.0 mg
Magnesium	67 mg
Zinc	2.3 mg

Mediterranean Bean Salad

Make this salad your own by adding your favorite vegetables. In the winter, 1 cup (250 mL) shredded cabbage or root vegetables add texture and vitamins. Summer squash or peas or beans, steamed just until they crunch, make great warm-weather ingredients.

Tip

You can substitute 2 cups (500 mL) cooked cannellini, navy or Great Northern beans for the canned cannellini beans.

1	can (19 oz/540 mL) cannellini beans, drained and rinsed	1
½ cup	cooked red lentils	125 mL
½ cup	coarsely chopped drained canned artichoke halves or hearts of palm	125 mL
½ cup	diced red onion	125 mL
¼ cup	chopped fresh parsley	60 mL
¼ cup	coarsely chopped black or green olives	60 mL
¼ cup	Mediterranean Dressing (see recipe, opposite)	60 mL

1. In a large bowl, combine beans, lentils, artichokes, onion, parsley and olives. Toss with dressing. Cover and let stand for at least 30 minutes or refrigerate overnight. Serve at room temperature.

Variations

Use chopped nuts for the lentils but add just before serving.

Chopped red or green bell pepper may replace the olives.

Add 1 cup (250 mL) cooked green beans or ½ cup (125 mL) cherry tomato halves.

Nutrients per serving	
Calories	281
Fat	8 g
Carbohydrate	40 g
Fiber	12 g
Protein	14 g
Vitamin B$_6$	0.3 mg
Magnesium	68 mg
Zinc	1.8 mg

Olive oil, lemons and garlic are classic Mediterranean ingredients. The light and zippy dressing complements other ingredients of the area such as olives, artichokes, legumes and red pepper.

Mediterranean Dressing

2 tbsp	olive oil	30 mL
2 tbsp	apple cider vinegar	30 mL
1 tbsp	freshly squeezed lemon juice	15 mL
1	clove garlic, minced	1
2 tsp	miso	10 mL
	Freshly ground black pepper	

1. In a jar with lid or small bowl, combine oil, vinegar, lemon juice, garlic, miso and pepper. Shake or whisk to mix well. Taste and add more lemon juice, if required.

Nutrients per 1 tbsp (15 mL)	
Calories	55
Fat	6 g
Carbohydrate	1 g
Fiber	0 g
Protein	0 g
Vitamin B$_6$	0 mg
Magnesium	2 mg
Zinc	0.1 mg

Chickpea Salad

This is an excellent take-along salad for the beach or a picnic. It also makes a delicious, healthy snack when you get peckish.

Tip

A 19-oz (540 mL) can of chickpeas will yield about 2 cups (500 mL) once the beans are drained and rinsed, so you'll need 2 cans of that size for this recipe. If you have smaller or larger cans, you can use the volume called for or just add the amount from the can.

4 cups	drained rinsed canned chickpeas	1 L
½ cup	chopped onion	125 mL
½ cup	chopped red bell pepper	125 mL
8	cherry tomatoes, quartered	8
2	cloves garlic, minced	2
2	carrots, chopped	2
3 tbsp	freshly squeezed lemon juice	45 mL
3 tbsp	rosemary-flavored vinegar	45 mL
2 tbsp	extra virgin olive oil	30 mL
1 tbsp	gluten-free prepared mustard	15 mL
1 tsp	dried parsley	5 mL
1 tsp	dried basil	5 mL
½ tsp	dried oregano	2 mL
½ tsp	dried rosemary	2 mL
	Salt and freshly ground black pepper	

1. In a large bowl, combine chickpeas, onion, red pepper, tomatoes, garlic and carrots.

2. In a small bowl, whisk together lemon juice, vinegar, oil, mustard, parsley, basil, oregano and rosemary. Drizzle over salad and toss to coat. Season to taste with salt and pepper. Cover and refrigerate for 1 hour to blend the flavors.

Nutrients per serving (1 of 8)	
Calories	194
Fat	5 g
Carbohydrate	32 g
Fiber	6 g
Protein	7 g
Vitamin B$_6$	0.7 mg
Magnesium	43 mg
Zinc	1.4 mg

Apple Cider Vinaigrette

This sweet and tangy vinaigrette is perfect for a baby lettuce salad.

Nutrients per 1 tbsp (15 mL)	
Calories	86
Fat	10 g
Carbohydrate	0 g
Fiber	0 g
Protein	0 g
Vitamin B$_6$	0 mg
Magnesium	0 mg
Zinc	0 mg

¼ cup	apple cider vinegar	60 mL
1 tsp	liquid honey	5 mL
¾ cup	extra virgin olive oil	175 mL

1. In a medium bowl, whisk together vinegar and honey; gradually pour in oil, while whisking, until incorporated.

2. Store in an airtight container in the refrigerator for up to 3 days.

Berry Vinaigrette

**Makes
1¾ cups (425 mL)**

Few things say "summer" more than fresh berries.

Nutrients per 1 tbsp (15 mL)	
Calories	56
Fat	6 g
Carbohydrate	1 g
Fiber	0 g
Protein	0 g
Vitamin B$_6$	0 mg
Magnesium	1 mg
Zinc	0 mg

• Blender

¾ cup	cold-pressed extra virgin olive oil	175 mL
½ cup	filtered water	125 mL
¼ cup	freshly squeezed lemon juice	60 mL
1 cup	blueberries	250 mL
½ cup	raspberries	125 mL
¼ tsp	fine sea salt	1 mL

1. In blender, combine oil, water, lemon juice, blueberries, raspberries and salt. Blend at high speed until smooth. Serve immediately or cover and refrigerate for up to 2 days.

Variation
Substitute an equal amount of chopped hulled strawberries for the blueberries.

Easy Italian Dressing

This healthier Italian salad dressing is made with unpasteurized apple cider vinegar, which may aid in digestion and provide healthy bacteria to improve the health status of your gut. Try it over a big bowl of crisp romaine lettuce and juicy tomatoes.

Tips

You may substitute 3 tbsp (45 mL) fresh oregano leaves for the dried.

Organic sea salt is classified as a whole food and is said to contain many trace minerals. If you are concerned about your salt intake, feel free to use less salt or omit it completely.

Nutrients per 1 tbsp (15 mL)	
Calories	46
Fat	5 g
Carbohydrate	1 g
Fiber	0 g
Protein	0 g
Vitamin B$_6$	0 mg
Magnesium	0 mg
Zinc	0 mg

- **Blender**

¾ cup	cold-pressed extra virgin olive oil	175 mL
¼ cup	unpasteurized apple cider vinegar	60 mL
2 tbsp	filtered water	30 mL
1 tbsp	raw agave nectar	15 mL
1 tbsp	dried oregano	15 mL
1 tsp	fine sea salt	5 mL
2	cloves garlic	2

1. In blender, combine oil, vinegar, water, agave nectar, oregano, salt and garlic. Blend at high speed until smooth. Serve immediately or cover and refrigerate for up to 7 days.

Variation

Substitute ⅓ cup (75 mL) freshly squeezed lemon juice for the vinegar.

Creamy Herb Dressing

Soft herbs such as basil and cilantro infuse bold flavor into dressings, dips and sauces. Serve this creamy dressing with some crisp fresh watercress.

Tips

To store fresh herbs, rinse well in cool water to remove any dirt, then dry in a salad spinner. Wrap in slightly damp paper towels and refrigerate for up to 1 week.

A medium lemon will typically yield about 3 tbsp (45 mL) juice.

• **Blender**

1 cup	cold-pressed extra virgin olive oil	250 mL
1/2 cup	filtered water	125 mL
1/4 cup	freshly squeezed lemon juice	60 mL
2 tsp	fine sea salt	10 mL
2	bunches fresh basil, roughly chopped	2
1	bunch fresh flat-leaf (Italian) parsley, stems removed, roughly chopped	1
1	bunch fresh cilantro, roughly chopped	1

1. In blender, combine oil, water, lemon juice, salt, basil, parsley and cilantro. Blend at high speed until smooth. Serve immediately or cover and refrigerate for up to 4 days.

Variation

For a healthy boost of omega-3 fatty acids, substitute an equal amount of cold-pressed hemp oil for the olive oil, or use 1/2 cup (125 mL) olive oil and 1/2 cup (125 mL) flax oil.

Nutrients per 1 tbsp (15 mL)

Calories	59
Fat	7 g
Carbohydrate	0 g
Fiber	0 g
Protein	0 g
Vitamin B$_6$	0 mg
Magnesium	1 mg
Zinc	0 mg

Spicy Lime Avocado Dressing

Makes
1 cup (250 mL)

This dressing combines aromatic spices, rich avocado and tart lime. Toss it with crisp romaine lettuce and juicy wedges of tomato and cucumber.

Variation

Summery Lemon Avocado Dressing: Substitute freshly squeezed lemon juice for the lime juice and ½ cup (125 mL) fresh basil leaves for the chili powder.

- **Blender**

¾ cup	filtered water	175 mL
¼ cup	freshly squeezed lime juice	60 mL
½	avocado	½
1 tbsp	raw agave nectar	15 mL
2 tsp	chili powder	10 mL
1 tsp	fine sea salt	5 mL
1	clove garlic	1

1. In blender, combine water, lime juice, avocado, agave nectar, chili powder, salt and garlic. Blend at high speed until smooth. Serve immediately or cover and refrigerate for up to 3 days.

Tips

The texture of this dressing will depend on the ripeness of the avocado. If it's not thick enough for your liking, add 1 tbsp (15 mL) chopped avocado and blend at high speed until smooth. Continue to add avocado until you reach the desired consistency.

To remove the pit from an avocado, use a paring knife to remove the nib at the top. Insert the blade of the knife where the nib was and turn the avocado from top to bottom to cut it in half lengthwise. Twist the two halves apart. Stick the knife into the pit and, with one motion, turn it 90 degrees, pulling out the pit as you twist the knife.

Nutrients per 1 tbsp (15 mL)	
Calories	15
Fat	1 g
Carbohydrate	2 g
Fiber	1 g
Protein	0 g
Vitamin B$_6$	0 mg
Magnesium	3 mg
Zinc	0.1 mg

Zesty Herb Dressing

This dressing is great
to make in the summer.

Nutrients per 1 tbsp (15 mL)	
Calories	73
Fat	8 g
Carbohydrate	0 g
Fiber	0 g
Protein	0 g
Vitamin B$_6$	0 mg
Magnesium	0 mg
Zinc	0 mg

1 tsp	chopped fresh thyme	5 mL
1 tsp	chopped fresh oregano	5 mL
⅛ tsp	freshly ground black pepper	0.5 mL
¼ cup	apple cider vinegar	60 mL
1 tsp	grated lemon zest	5 mL
3 tbsp	freshly squeezed lemon juice	45 mL
¾ cup	extra virgin olive oil	175 mL

1. In a bowl, whisk together thyme, oregano, pepper, vinegar, lemon zest and lemon juice. Gradually whisk in oil until incorporated.

Storage Tip
This dressing is best when served immediately, but can be stored in an airtight container in the refrigerator for up to 3 days.

Lemon Dressing

**Makes
½ cup (125 mL)**

Nutrients per 1 tbsp (15 mL)	
Calories	87
Fat	9 g
Carbohydrate	2 g
Fiber	0 g
Protein	0 g
Vitamin B$_6$	0 mg
Magnesium	1 mg
Zinc	0 mg

⅓ cup	olive oil	75 mL
1 tsp	grated lemon zest	5 mL
2 tbsp	freshly squeezed lemon juice	30 mL
1 tbsp	natural cane sugar	15 mL
1 tbsp	fresh lemon thyme leaves	15 mL
1 tbsp	chopped fresh lemon balm	15 mL
½ tsp	salt (or to taste)	2 mL

1. In a jar with lid or small bowl, combine oil, lemon zest and juice, sugar, thyme, lemon balm and salt. Shake or whisk to mix well. Taste and adjust seasonings, if required.

Variation
When fresh lemon herbs are not available, use 1 tbsp (15 mL) each chopped fresh parsley and an additional 1 tbsp (15 mL) grated lemon zest.

Caesar Salad Dressing

Use this classic, garlicky sauce to dress raw and cooked greens and vegetables.

• Blender

2 tbsp	ground flax seeds (flaxseed meal)	30 mL
¼ cup	soy milk or rice milk	60 mL
3	large cloves garlic	3
2 tbsp	freshly squeezed lemon juice	30 mL
1 tsp	balsamic vinegar	5 mL
½ tsp	dry mustard	2 mL
½ cup	olive oil	125 mL

1. In blender, combine flax seeds and soy milk. Let stand for at least 10 minutes or until gelatinous.

2. Add garlic, lemon juice, vinegar and mustard. Blend until smooth. With the motor running, slowly pour oil through the opening in the lid. Blend until oil is incorporated into the dressing.

3. Transfer dressing to a clean jar with lid. Store tightly covered in the refrigerator for up to 5 days.

Nutrients per 1 tbsp (15 mL)	
Calories	90
Fat	10 g
Carbohydrate	1 g
Fiber	0 g
Protein	0 g
Vitamin B$_6$	0 mg
Magnesium	6 mg
Zinc	0.1 mg

Soups

Vegetable Stock. 248

Borscht. 249

Creamy Onion Soup with Kale 250

Green Pea Soup. 251

Hearty Potato and Leek Soup. 252

Pumpkin Curry Soup 253

Butternut Squash and Apple Soup with Ginger. 254

Spinach and Sea Vegetable Soup 255

Spicy Squash and Fennel Soup 256

Curried Sweet Potato Soup. 257

Curried Sweet Potato and Millet Soup. 258

Fennel-Scented Tomato and Wild Rice Soup. 259

Spinach, Quinoa and Broccoli Bisque. 260

Hearty Black and White Bean Soup 261

Kale and Quinoa Minestrone 262

Harira 263

Roasted Garlic and Lentil Soup. 264

Vegetable Stock

Makes about 16 cups (4 L), or 4 cups (1 L) reduced

Make sure to use or freeze this stock soon after you make it, as vegetable stock loses its flavor quickly. This light stock makes a suitable substitute for chicken stock.

Tip

Save the white part of the leeks for another recipe.

3	onions, quartered	3
3	leeks (green tops only)	3
3	stalks celery, quartered	3
3	carrots, quartered	3
3	tomatoes, coarsely chopped	3
2	cloves garlic, crushed	2
1	parsnip, quartered	1
1	bulb fennel, quartered	1
1 cup	mushrooms (including stems)	250 mL
6	sprigs parsley	6
6	whole black peppercorns	6
2	bay leaves	2
20 cups	water	5 L

1. In a large stockpot, combine onions, leeks, celery, carrots, tomatoes, garlic, parsnip, fennel, mushrooms, parsley, peppercorns, bay leaves and water; bring to a boil over medium heat. Reduce heat and simmer for 1 hour.

2. Set up a large pot with a fine-mesh strainer over it and ladle the stock through the strainer, dumping out the solids after you've pushed as much liquid from them as possible with the back of the ladle. If desired, reduce stock (see box, below).

Reducing and Storing Stock

Stock is reduced for two reasons: so you can store it efficiently and for a richer, fuller flavor. Return the stock to medium heat and boil it until the volume is reduced by about three-quarters. That sounds like a lot, but the more the stock is reduced, the more space you'll have in your freezer. Stock can be made ahead and refrigerated for up to 4 days or frozen for up to 4 months. When you want to use it, just add water in increments until it tastes right to you. Begin by adding 2 parts water to 1 part stock. If that tastes too strong, add a little more water until you get the flavor just right.

Nutrients per ½ cup (125 mL) unreduced	
Calories	20
Fat	0 g
Carbohydrate	5 g
Fiber	1 g
Protein	1 g
Vitamin B$_6$	0.1 mg
Magnesium	10 mg
Zinc	0.1 mg

Borscht

Beets are high in plant flavonoids that help the first phase of liver detoxification.

Tip

If you don't have home-made stock on hand, you can use ready-to-use reduced-sodium vegetable broth in its place. Check the label to make sure ingredients containing gluten have not been added.

5	beets (about 1 lb/500 g)	5
2 tbsp	olive oil	30 mL
1	large onion, chopped	1
4 cups	Vegetable Stock (see recipe, opposite)	1 L
2 tsp	apple cider vinegar	10 mL
	Salt (optional)	

1. Scrub beets and trim off long roots and stems. Place in a large pot and add enough water to cover. Bring to a boil over high heat. Reduce heat and simmer for about 1 hour or until tender. Drain and let cool, then rub beets to remove the skins. Chop beets.

2. In a clean large pot, heat oil over medium heat. Add onion and cook, stirring, for 5 minutes or until tender.

3. Stir in beets and stock; bring to a boil. Reduce heat and simmer for 5 minutes. Stir in apple cider vinegar. Taste soup and, if desired, season to taste with salt.

Nutrients per serving

Calories	132
Fat	7 g
Carbohydrate	17 g
Fiber	4 g
Protein	2 g
Vitamin B$_6$	0.2 mg
Magnesium	33 mg
Zinc	0.5 mg

Creamy Onion Soup with Kale

Makes 6 servings

The creaminess in this delicious soup is achieved by the addition of potatoes, which are puréed into the soup, providing it with a velvety texture.

Tips

If you don't have home-made stock on hand, you can use ready-to-use reduced-sodium vegetable broth in its place. Check the label to make sure ingredients containing gluten have not been added.

You can use any kind of paprika in this recipe: regular or sweet; hot, which produces a nicely peppery version; or smoked, which adds a delicious note of smokiness to the soup. If you have regular paprika and would like a bit of heat, dissolve ¼ tsp (1 mL) cayenne pepper in the lemon juice along with the paprika.

Nutrients per serving	
Calories	144
Fat	3 g
Carbohydrate	29 g
Fiber	5 g
Protein	5 g
Vitamin B$_6$	0.3 mg
Magnesium	36 mg
Zinc	0.5 mg

- **Medium to large (3½- to 5-quart) slow cooker**
- **Food processor, blender or immersion blender**

1 tbsp	olive oil	15 mL
4	onions, thinly sliced	4
2	cloves garlic, minced	2
4	whole allspice	4
1	bay leaf	1
1 tsp	grated lemon zest	5 mL
½ tsp	freshly cracked black pepper	2 mL
4 cups	Vegetable Stock (page 248)	1 L
3	potatoes, peeled and diced	3
1 tsp	paprika dissolved in 2 tbsp (30 mL) freshly squeezed lemon juice (see tip, at left)	5 mL
4 cups	chopped kale	1 L

1. In a skillet, heat oil over medium heat. Add onions and cook, stirring, until softened, about 5 minutes. Add garlic, allspice, bay leaf, lemon zest and pepper; cook, stirring, for 1 minute. Transfer to slow cooker stoneware. Stir in stock.

2. Add potatoes and stir well. Cover and cook on Low for 8 hours or on High for 4 hours, until potatoes are tender. Discard allspice and bay leaf. Stir in paprika solution and add kale, in batches, stirring after each to submerge the leaves in the liquid. Cover and cook on High for 20 minutes, until kale is tender.

3. Working in batches, transfer soup to food processor (or use immersion blender in pot) and purée until smooth. Serve immediately.

Green Pea Soup

Green peas contain vitamin A and protein, and onions and leeks provide bioflavonoids. Serve this velvety soup with gluten-free bread for dipping.

Tip

If you don't have home-made stock on hand, you can use ready-to-use reduced-sodium vegetable broth in its place. Check the label to make sure ingredients containing gluten have not been added.

• **Food processor, blender or immersion blender**

1 tbsp	olive oil	15 mL
3	leeks (white part only), thinly sliced	3
1	onion, thinly sliced	1
3	white potatoes, peeled and diced	3
3 cups	frozen green peas	750 mL
1 tsp	salt	5 mL
5 cups	Vegetable Stock (page 248)	1.25 L

1. In a large pot, heat oil over medium heat. Add leeks and onion; cook, stirring often, for about 10 minutes or until tender.

2. Stir in potatoes, peas, salt and stock; bring to a boil. Reduce heat and simmer for 20 minutes or until potatoes are tender.

3. Working in batches, transfer soup to food processor (or use immersion blender in pot) and purée until smooth. Return soup to pot (if necessary). Heat over medium heat until warmed through.

Nutrients per serving	
Calories	156
Fat	2 g
Carbohydrate	31 g
Fiber	5 g
Protein	5 g
Vitamin B$_6$	0.4 mg
Magnesium	48 mg
Zinc	0.8 mg

Hearty Potato and Leek Soup

Tomato is an unusual ingredient in potato and leek soup, but in the fall when tomatoes are abundant, they add a cheery note to this winter favorite. Omit them in the winter when fresh ripe organic tomatoes are not available.

Tips

If you don't have home-made stock on hand, you can use ready-to-use reduced-sodium vegetable broth in its place. Check the label to make sure ingredients containing gluten have not been added.

You can use 2 cups (500 mL) cooked chickpeas, drained and rinsed, instead of canned.

Nutrients per serving (1 of 8)	
Calories	141
Fat	4 g
Carbohydrate	25 g
Fiber	4 g
Protein	3 g
Vitamin B$_6$	0.4 mg
Magnesium	39 mg
Zinc	0.5 mg

• **Blender**

2 tbsp	olive oil	30 mL
3	onions, chopped	3
2	leeks (white and light green parts only), sliced	2
3	cloves garlic, finely chopped	3
2	tomatoes, seeded and chopped (optional)	2
4 cups	Vegetable Stock (page 248) or water (approx.)	1 L
4 to 5	potatoes, cut into 1-inch (2.5 cm) cubes (about 4 cups/1 L)	4 to 5
1 tsp	crushed dried rosemary	5 mL
	Sea salt and freshly ground black pepper	
1	can (14 to 19 oz/398 to 540 mL) chickpeas, with liquid (optional)	1
2 cups	trimmed spinach (optional)	500 mL

1. In a large saucepan, heat oil over medium heat. Add onions and cook, stirring occasionally, for 3 minutes or until slightly soft. Stir in leeks and cook, stirring occasionally, for 6 minutes or until soft. Add garlic and cook, stirring occasionally, for 3 minutes. Add tomatoes (if using).

2. Add vegetable stock, potatoes and rosemary. Stir and bring to a boil over medium-high heat. Cover, reduce heat to low and cook for 20 minutes or until potatoes are tender when pierced with the tip of a knife.

3. Using a ladle, transfer 3 cups (750 mL) of the soup mixture to blender. Blend until mixture is smooth. Return to saucepan and season to taste with salt and pepper. Stir in chickpeas with liquid and spinach (if using). Cook over low heat for about 2 minutes, until chickpeas are heated and spinach is wilted. Add more vegetable stock or water if a thinner soup is desired.

Pumpkin Curry Soup

Makes 4 servings

This thick, hearty soup is full of nutrients. Spinach contains glutathione, to help the liver detoxify, and chlorophyll, which helps get rid of environmental toxins and metals. Pumpkin contains vitamins A, B, C and E, as well as magnesium and iron.

Tip

If you don't have home-made stock on hand, you can use ready-to-use reduced-sodium vegetable broth in its place. Check the label to make sure ingredients containing gluten have not been added.

1 cup	brown rice	250 mL
3 cups	water, divided	750 mL
1 tbsp	vegetable oil	15 mL
1	onion, chopped	1
2½ lbs	pumpkin, peeled and chopped (about 10 cups/2.5 L)	1.25 kg
1	can (14 to 19 oz/398 to 540 mL) chickpeas, drained and rinsed	1
1 cup	Vegetable Stock (page 248)	250 mL
¼ cup	mild curry paste	60 mL
1 cup	baby spinach	250 mL
½ cup	chopped fresh cilantro	125 mL

1. In a medium saucepan, combine rice and 2 cups (500 mL) water. Bring to a boil over high heat. Reduce heat to low, cover and simmer for 15 to 20 minutes or until rice is tender and water is absorbed.

2. Meanwhile, in a large pot, heat oil over medium heat. Add onion and cook, stirring, for 5 minutes or until tender.

3. Stir in pumpkin, chickpeas, stock, curry paste and the remaining water; bring to a boil. Reduce heat to medium-low, cover and boil gently for 10 minutes or until pumpkin is tender. Stir in spinach and boil gently, uncovered, for 2 minutes. Stir in cilantro and serve over rice.

Nutrients per serving	
Calories	413
Fat	6 g
Carbohydrate	81 g
Fiber	8 g
Protein	12 g
Vitamin B$_6$	1.0 mg
Magnesium	145 mg
Zinc	3.1 mg

Butternut Squash and Apple Soup with Ginger

This is a crowd-pleaser, and it's equally delicious served hot or cold. It makes a refreshing summer lunch or a light dinner served with salad and bread.

Tips

If you prefer, substitute fresh gingerroot for the ground ginger. Use a 2- by 1-inch (5 by 2.5 cm) piece, peeled and finely grated.

If you are not using an immersion blender and time permits, let the soup cool before puréeing. Use caution as you blend hot soup, particularly if using a blender. Fill the blender container only half-full to avoid the buildup of steam, which can cause the lid to pop off.

Nutrients per serving (1 of 10)	
Calories	123
Fat	3 g
Carbohydrate	25 g
Fiber	3 g
Protein	1 g
Vitamin B$_6$	0.2 mg
Magnesium	39 mg
Zinc	0.2 mg

- **Preheat oven to 450°F (230°C)**
- **Baking sheet, greased**
- **Food processor, blender or immersion blender**

1	butternut squash (about 2 lbs/1 kg)	1
2 tbsp	vegetable oil	30 mL
1	onion, coarsely chopped	1
2	tart apples (such as Granny Smith), peeled and coarsely chopped	2
2	cloves garlic, thinly sliced (about 2 tsp/10 mL)	2
5 cups	water	1.25 L
3 cups	unsweetened apple cider	750 mL
1 tsp	ground ginger	5 mL
Pinch	cayenne pepper	Pinch
	Salt and freshly ground black pepper	
	Hot pepper sauce (optional)	

1. Cut squash in half lengthwise. Scrape out seeds with a spoon. Place squash, cut side down, on prepared baking sheet. Bake in preheated oven for 30 to 40 minutes or until soft.

2. Meanwhile, in a large pot, heat oil over medium heat. Add onion and cook, stirring, for 3 minutes or until softened. Add apples and garlic; cook, stirring, for 2 to 3 minutes or until apples are softened but not browned. Stir in water, cider, ginger and cayenne; bring to a boil. Reduce heat to medium-low and simmer, uncovered, for 25 minutes to blend the flavors.

3. Using a large spoon, scoop cooked squash out of skin and add to pot, discarding skin. Increase heat to medium and simmer for 5 minutes longer.

4. Working in batches, transfer soup to food processor (or use immersion blender in pot) and purée until smooth. Return soup to pot (if necessary). Reheat until steaming. Season to taste with salt, black pepper and hot pepper sauce (if using).

Variation

Garnish with thin slices of apple with skin, cut into thin sticks. Place on top of each serving and sprinkle with freshly cracked black pepper.

Spinach and Sea Vegetable Soup

A thick purée is the perfect foil for the slightly crisp, nutty-tasting strands of wakame in this soup. Serve with a salad and bread for a hearty lunch.

Tip

To clean leeks, fill a sink full of lukewarm water. Split leeks in half lengthwise and submerge in water, swishing them around to remove all traces of dirt. Transfer to a colander and rinse under cold water.

Nutrients per serving	
Calories	123
Fat	5 g
Carbohydrate	18 g
Fiber	5 g
Protein	3 g
Vitamin B6	0.3 mg
Magnesium	69 mg
Zinc	0.7 mg

- **Food processor or blender**

2 tbsp	olive oil	30 mL
1 cup	chopped onion	250 mL
2	cloves garlic, finely chopped	2
1	carrot, chopped	1
1	leek (white and light green parts only), chopped	1
1	turnip, chopped	1
6 cups	Vegetable Stock (page 248), divided	1.5 L
8 oz	spinach, trimmed	250 g
½ cup	wakame or arame	125 mL
2 tbsp	fresh thyme leaves	30 mL

1. In a large saucepan, heat oil over medium heat. Add onion and cook, stirring, for 7 minutes or until soft. Stir in garlic, carrot, leek, turnip and ½ cup (125 mL) stock. Bring to a boil. Cover, reduce heat and simmer, stirring occasionally, for 10 minutes.

2. Stir in 4 cups (1 L) stock. Bring to a boil. Cover, reduce heat and simmer for 10 minutes or until vegetables are tender. Stir in spinach. Cook for 2 minutes or until wilted. Let cool slightly.

3. Using a slotted spoon, lift out half the vegetables and transfer to food processor. Process for 30 seconds or until smooth. Pour into a bowl. Repeat with the remaining vegetables. Keep the remaining cooking liquids hot in the saucepan over low heat.

4. Return purée to the saucepan. Add wakame and thyme. Stir in the remaining stock, a small amount at a time, until desired consistency is achieved. Cover and simmer over medium heat for 10 minutes or until wakame is tender. Serve immediately.

Spicy Squash and Fennel Soup

Makes 6 to 8 servings

This deeply flavorful soup delivers a rich, creamy texture. Serve as a main course, accompanied by bread and salad. For those with more adventurous palates, pass hot pepper sauce at the table.

Tips

If you can't find mushroom stock, use additional vegetable stock and add 4 oz (125 g) sliced mushrooms.

If you don't have home-made stock on hand, you can use ready-to-use reduced-sodium vegetable broth in its place. Check the label to make sure ingredients containing gluten have not been added.

Nutrients per serving (1 of 8)	
Calories	128
Fat	4 g
Carbohydrate	23 g
Fiber	5 g
Protein	3 g
Vitamin B6	0.4 mg
Magnesium	62 mg
Zinc	0.5 mg

- **Food processor, blender or immersion blender**

2 tbsp	olive oil (approx.)	30 mL
1	large onion, finely chopped	1
3	cloves garlic, coarsely chopped	3
1 tbsp	all-purpose flour	15 mL
4 cups	mushroom stock (see tip, at left)	1 L
4 cups	Vegetable Stock (page 248)	1 L
1	butternut squash (about 2 lbs/1kg), peeled and cut into 1-inch (2.5 cm) cubes	1
½	head Chinese cabbage, coarsely chopped (about 4 cups/1 L)	½
½	bulb fennel, coarsely chopped	½
1¼ tsp	ground cumin	6 mL
1 tsp	mustard seeds	5 mL
½ tsp	fennel seeds	2 mL
	Hot pepper flakes	
	Salt and freshly ground black pepper	

1. In a large saucepan, heat oil over medium heat for 30 seconds. Add onion and cook, stirring, for 3 minutes or until softened. Add garlic and cook, stirring, for 1 minute. Add flour and cook, stirring, for 1 minute, adding more oil if necessary to make a stiff, doughy texture.

2. Gradually whisk in mushroom stock and vegetable stock; bring to a boil. Add squash, Chinese cabbage and fennel; simmer, uncovered, for 20 minutes or until vegetables are tender.

3. Stir in cumin, mustard seeds, fennel seeds and hot pepper flakes, salt and black pepper to taste. Cook for 10 minutes to blend the flavors. Remove from heat and let cool for 10 minutes.

4. Working in batches, transfer soup to food processor (or use immersion blender in pot) and purée until smooth. Return soup to pot (if necessary). Reheat until steaming.

Curried Sweet Potato Soup

The taste combination of the curry and the sweet potatoes along with the coconut milk makes this complex and mildly flavorful soup a great starter for a lunch meal or for a soup-salad combo.

Tips

Check to make sure your curry powder doesn't contain gluten. Some blends may contain wheat or are processed in a facility where wheat is present, thus being potentially contaminated.

If you don't have home-made stock on hand, you can use ready-to-use reduced-sodium vegetable broth in its place. Check the label to make sure ingredients containing gluten have not been added.

2 tbsp	olive oil	30 mL
1 cup	chopped onion	250 mL
1 tbsp	yellow or red curry powder (see tip, at left)	15 mL
2	sweet potatoes, peeled and cut into large dice	2
1 cup	chopped carrot	250 mL
3 cups	Vegetable Stock (page 248)	750 mL
1/4 cup	chopped raisins	60 mL
1 tsp	salt	5 mL
1	can (14 oz/400 mL) coconut milk	1
1/3 cup	chopped red bell pepper	75 mL

1. In a large saucepan, heat oil over medium low heat. Add onion and curry spice; cook, stirring occasionally, for 6 minutes. Stir in sweet potatoes and carrot. Cook, stirring constantly, for 3 minutes.

2. Stir in stock. Increase heat and bring to a boil. Reduce heat and simmer for 15 minutes. Add raisins and salt. Cook for 5 minutes or until all vegetables are soft. Remove from the heat.

3. Using a potato masher, roughly mash sweet potato mixture. Stir in coconut milk and return to medium-high heat and heat through. Ladle soup into four bowls. Float 1 tbsp (15 mL) red pepper on top of each bowl. Serve immediately.

Nutrients per serving	
Calories	406
Fat	29 g
Carbohydrate	38 g
Fiber	6 g
Protein	5 g
Vitamin B$_6$	0.4 mg
Magnesium	93 mg
Zinc	1.2 mg

Curried Sweet Potato and Millet Soup

Makes 6 servings

This lovely soup has a mild curry taste, enhanced by the addition of orange and a hint of sweetness. The toasted walnuts add an appealing crunch.

Tips

To get this quantity of puréed sweet potato, bake, peel and mash 2 medium sweet potatoes, each about 6 oz (175 g). You can also use a can (14 oz/398 mL) sweet potato purée.

If you don't have home-made stock on hand, you can use ready-to-use reduced-sodium vegetable broth in its place. Check the label to make sure ingredients containing gluten have not been added.

To toast millet, heat it in a dry skillet over medium heat, stirring constantly, until it crackles and releases its aroma, about 5 minutes.

Nutrients per serving	
Calories	365
Fat	8 g
Carbohydrate	69 g
Fiber	8 g
Protein	7 g
Vitamin B$_6$	0.6 mg
Magnesium	89 mg
Zinc	1.2 mg

1 tbsp	vegetable oil	15 mL
2	onions, finely chopped	2
2	carrots, diced	2
2	stalks celery, diced	2
2	cloves garlic, minced	2
2 tsp	minced gingerroot	10 mL
2 tsp	curry powder (see tip, page 257)	10 mL
1 tsp	grated orange zest	5 mL
2 cups	sweet potato purée (see tip, at left)	500 mL
6 cups	Vegetable Stock (page 248)	1.5 L
¾ cup	millet, toasted (see tip, at left)	175 mL
1 cup	freshly squeezed orange juice	250 mL
¼ cup	pure maple syrup	60 mL
	Salt and freshly ground black pepper	
	Toasted chopped walnuts or sliced almonds	
	Plain yogurt (optional)	

1. In a large saucepan or stockpot, heat oil over medium heat for 30 seconds. Add onions, carrots and celery; cook, stirring, until carrots have softened, about 7 minutes.

2. Add garlic, ginger, curry powder and orange zest; cook, stirring, for 1 minute. Add sweet potato and stock, stirring well. Bring to a boil. Stir in millet. Reduce heat to low. Cover and simmer until millet is tender and flavors have blended, about 30 minutes.

3. Add orange juice and maple syrup and heat through. Season to taste with salt and pepper. Ladle into bowls and garnish with toasted walnuts and a drizzle of yogurt (if using).

Variation

Curried Sweet Potato and Quinoa Soup: Substitute an equal quantity of quinoa for the millet. Do not toast it, but rinse thoroughly before adding to the soup.

Fennel-Scented Tomato and Wild Rice Soup

Makes 8 servings

This soup is especially welcome in the winter, when fresh tomatoes are hard to find. The fennel adds an intriguing licorice flavor that complements the tomatoes.

Tips

To clean leeks, fill a sink full of lukewarm water. Split leeks in half lengthwise and submerge in water, swishing them around to remove all traces of dirt. Transfer to a colander and rinse under cold water.

If you don't have home-made stock on hand, you can use ready-to-use reduced-sodium vegetable broth in its place. Check the label to make sure ingredients containing gluten have not been added.

Nutrients per serving

Calories	151
Fat	3 g
Carbohydrate	30 g
Fiber	6 g
Protein	5 g
Vitamin B$_6$	0.4 mg
Magnesium	72 mg
Zinc	1.4 mg

• **Food processor, blender or immersion blender**

1 tbsp	olive oil	15 mL
2	leeks (white and light green parts only), sliced	2
1	bulb fennel, base and leafy stems discarded, bulb thinly sliced on the vertical	1
3	cloves garlic, sliced	3
1 tsp	fennel seeds, toasted (see tip, page 281) and ground	5 mL
½ tsp	salt (optional)	2 mL
½ tsp	freshly ground black pepper	2 mL
5 cups	Vegetable Stock (page 248), divided	1.25 L
1	can (28 oz/796 mL) crushed tomatoes (see tip, page 266)	1
¾ cup	wild rice, rinsed and drained	175 mL
	Finely chopped fresh parsley	

1. In a large saucepan or stockpot, heat oil over medium heat for 30 seconds. Add leeks and fennel; cook, stirring, until vegetables are softened, about 7 minutes. Add garlic, fennel seeds, salt (if using) and pepper; cook, stirring, for 1 minute. Stir in 2 cups (500 mL) stock and tomatoes.

2. Working in batches, transfer soup to food processor (or use immersion blender in pot) and purée until smooth. Return soup to pot (if necessary). Add wild rice and the remaining stock; bring to a boil over medium heat. Reduce heat to low, cover and cook until rice is tender and grains have begun to split, about 1 hour. (Cooking times for wild rice vary. Expect your grains to be cooked anywhere from 50 minutes to more than 1 hour.)

3. Ladle into bowls and garnish with parsley.

Spinach, Quinoa and Broccoli Bisque

This gorgeous green soup is so velvety, it's hard to believe there's neither cream nor butter in it. Quinoa flakes are the secret, adding richness and complexity in one fell swoop.

Tips

For best results, use a vegetable peeler to peel the thick outer layer off the broccoli stems before chopping.

If you don't have home-made stock on hand, you can use ready-to-use reduced-sodium vegetable broth in its place. Check the label to make sure ingredients containing gluten have not been added.

When puréeing soup in a food processor or blender, fill the bowl no more than halfway full at a time.

Nutrients per serving	
Calories	160
Fat	3 g
Carbohydrate	28 g
Fiber	7 g
Protein	7 g
Vitamin B$_6$	0.4 mg
Magnesium	75 mg
Zinc	1.0 mg

- **Food processor, blender or immersion blender**

1 tbsp	olive oil	15 mL
1½ cups	chopped onions	375 mL
2	cloves garlic, minced	2
2½ tsp	dried basil	12 mL
¼ tsp	freshly ground black pepper	1 mL
1½ lbs	broccoli, coarsely chopped (florets and peeled stems)	750 g
½ cup	quinoa flakes or quinoa flour	125 mL
6 cups	Vegetable Stock (page 248)	1.5 L
1½ cups	water	375 mL
6 cups	packed trimmed spinach	1.5 L
	Fine sea salt and freshly ground black pepper	

1. In a large pot, heat oil over medium-high heat. Add onions and cook, stirring, for 5 to 6 minutes or until softened. Add garlic, basil and pepper; cook, stirring, for 30 seconds.

2. Stir in broccoli, quinoa flakes, stock and water; bring to a boil. Reduce heat and simmer, stirring occasionally, for 15 minutes. Stir in spinach and simmer for 3 to 4 minutes or until broccoli is tender.

3. Working in batches, transfer soup to food processor (or use immersion blender in pot) and purée until smooth. Return soup to pot (if necessary). Warm over medium heat, stirring, for 1 minute. Season to taste with salt and pepper.

Hearty Black and White Bean Soup

Here's a thick, chunky and tasty soup the whole family can enjoy.

Tips

If you can only find 19-oz (540 mL) cans of beans, add an additional 2 cups (500 mL) vegetable stock, 2 tsp (10 mL) red wine vinegar and a pinch more dried basil and chili powder.

If you don't have home-made stock on hand, you can use ready-to-use reduced-sodium vegetable broth in its place. Check the label to make sure ingredients containing gluten have not been added.

Nutrients per serving (1 of 8)	
Calories	228
Fat	4 g
Carbohydrate	40 g
Fiber	13 g
Protein	12 g
Vitamin B$_6$	0.4 mg
Magnesium	90 mg
Zinc	1.6 mg

- **Food processor or blender**

1½ tbsp	olive oil	22 mL
1	large onion, finely chopped	1
3	cloves garlic, minced (about 1 tbsp/15 mL)	3
2	carrots, thinly sliced	2
2	stalks celery, coarsely chopped	2
4 cups	Vegetable Stock (page 248)	1 L
1	can (28 oz/796 mL) diced tomatoes, with juice (see tip, page 266)	1
2	cans (each 14 oz/398 mL) black beans, drained and rinsed	2
1	can (14 oz/398 mL) white beans, drained and rinsed	1
2 tbsp	red wine vinegar	30 mL
1½ tbsp	chili powder	22 mL
1 tbsp	dried basil	15 mL
	Salt and freshly ground black pepper	

1. In a large pot, heat oil over medium heat for 30 seconds. Add onion and garlic; cook, stirring, for 3 minutes or until softened. Add carrots and celery; cook, stirring, for 3 minutes.

2. Stir in vegetable stock and tomatoes; bring to a boil. Reduce heat to medium-low and cook, uncovered, for 10 minutes or until vegetables are tender.

3. Meanwhile, in food processor, process half of the black beans to achieve a thick paste-like consistency. Stir into soup. Add the remaining black beans and white beans.

4. Add red wine vinegar, chili powder, basil, and salt and pepper to taste. Stir well. Reduce heat to low, cover and simmer for 15 minutes or until the flavors meld.

Variations

Purée the entire soup to completely blend flavors. This will give you a thick, rich result.

Add two sliced smoked soy sausages, thawed if frozen, after the soup has finished cooking. Cook for 5 minutes longer or until sausages are heated through. Garnish with chopped fresh basil or cilantro leaves to taste.

Kale and Quinoa Minestrone

Makes 8 servings

Everyone needs a few recipes that meet the trifecta of busy weeknight meal requirements: easy, fast and fabulous. Add this soup, which is super-healthy to boot, to your pile.

Tip

If you don't have home-made stock on hand, you can use ready-to-use reduced-sodium vegetable broth in its place. Check the label to make sure ingredients containing gluten have not been added.

1 tbsp	extra virgin olive oil	15 mL
1½ cups	chopped onions	375 mL
1½ cups	chopped carrots	375 mL
1 cup	chopped celery	250 mL
4	cloves garlic, minced	4
8 cups	chopped kale (tough stems and center ribs removed)	2 L
1½ tbsp	dried Italian seasoning	22 mL
¾ cup	quinoa, rinsed	175 mL
1	jar (26 oz/700 mL) marinara sauce	1
8 cups	Vegetable Stock (page 248)	2 L
1	can (14 to 19 oz/398 to 540 mL) white beans, drained and rinsed	1
	Fine sea salt and freshly ground black pepper	

1. In a large pot, heat oil over medium-high heat. Add onions, carrots and celery; cook, stirring, for 6 to 8 minutes or until softened. Add garlic, kale and Italian seasoning; cook, stirring, for 1 minute.

2. Stir in quinoa, marinara sauce and stock; bring to a boil. Reduce heat, cover, leaving lid ajar, and simmer, stirring occasionally, for 20 minutes or until quinoa is tender.

3. In a small bowl, mash half the beans with a fork. Stir mashed beans and whole beans into the pot. Simmer, stirring occasionally, for 5 to 10 minutes or until soup is slightly thickened. Season to taste with salt and pepper.

Storage Tip

Store the cooled soup in an airtight container in the refrigerator for up to 2 days or in the freezer for up to 6 months. Thaw overnight in the refrigerator or in the microwave using the Defrost function. Warm soup in a medium saucepan over medium-low heat.

Nutrients per serving	
Calories	309
Fat	6 g
Carbohydrate	55 g
Fiber	11 g
Protein	12 g
Vitamin B$_6$	0.7 mg
Magnesium	127 mg
Zinc	2.3 mg

Harira

Makes 6 servings

This traditional Moroccan soup is finished with a dollop of harissa, a spicy North African sauce that adds flavor and punch.

Tips

If you prefer, you can use 1 cup (250 mL) dried chickpeas, soaked, cooked and drained, instead of the canned chickpeas.

If you don't have home-made stock on hand, you can use ready-to-use reduced-sodium vegetable broth in its place. Check the label to make sure ingredients containing gluten have not been added.

- **Large (minimum 5-quart) slow cooker**

1 tbsp	olive oil	15 mL
4	stalks celery, diced	4
2	onions, coarsely chopped	2
2	cloves garlic, minced	2
1 tbsp	ground turmeric	15 mL
1 tbsp	grated lemon zest	15 mL
½ tsp	freshly cracked black pepper	2 mL
1	can (28 oz/796 mL) diced tomatoes, with juice (see tip, page 266)	1
4 cups	Vegetable Stock (page 248)	1 L
1 cup	dried red lentils, rinsed	250 mL
1	can (14 to 19 oz/398 to 540 mL) chickpeas, drained and rinsed	1
½ cup	finely chopped fresh parsley	125 mL
	Harissa	

1. In a skillet, heat oil over medium heat for 30 seconds. Add celery and onions; cook, stirring, until celery is softened, about 5 minutes. Add garlic, turmeric, lemon zest and pepper; cook, stirring, for 1 minute. Add tomatoes and bring to a boil. Transfer to slow cooker stoneware.

2. Stir in stock, lentils and chickpeas. Cover and cook on Low for 6 to 8 hours or on High for 3 to 4 hours, until mixture is hot and bubbly and lentils are tender. Stir in parsley.

3. Ladle into bowls and pass the harissa at the table.

Nutrients per serving

Calories	285
Fat	4 g
Carbohydrate	51 g
Fiber	11 g
Protein	14 g
Vitamin B_6	0.8 mg
Magnesium	82 mg
Zinc	2.5 mg

Roasted Garlic and Lentil Soup

Use fresh tomatoes in season and substitute 1 cup (250 mL) of crushed canned tomatoes in winter.

Tips

Designer rice (mahogany, black, red; short- and long-grain varieties) is becoming very popular and widely available. Look for red rice in gourmet food or natural food stores.

If you don't have home-made stock on hand, you can use ready-to-use reduced-sodium vegetable broth in its place. Check the label to make sure ingredients containing gluten have not been added.

- **Preheat oven to 375°F (190°C)**
- **10-inch (25 cm) pie plate or baking dish**
- **Blender**

10	small tomatoes (2 inches/5 cm in diameter)	10
12	cloves garlic	12
4 tbsp	olive oil, divided	60 mL
1 tbsp	chopped fresh rosemary	15 mL
1 cup	chopped onion	250 mL
1 tsp	ground cumin	5 mL
½ tsp	crushed fennel seeds	2 mL
½ tsp	sea salt	2 mL
Pinch	ground ginger	Pinch
Pinch	ground nutmeg	Pinch
1 cup	red or brown rice (see tip, at left)	250 mL
3 cups	Vegetable Stock (page 248) or water (approx.), divided	750 mL
1	can (19 oz/540 mL) lentils, with liquid	1

1. In pie plate, combine tomatoes and garlic and toss with 2 tbsp (30 mL) oil and rosemary. Bake in preheated oven for 40 minutes or until garlic is soft. Let cool.

2. Meanwhile, in a large saucepan, heat the remaining oil over medium heat. Add onion and cook, stirring occasionally, for 6 to 8 minutes or until soft. Add cumin, fennel, salt, ginger, nutmeg and rice. Cook, stirring constantly, for 1 minute. Add 2 cups (500 mL) stock, increase heat to high and bring to a boil. Cover, reduce heat to low and simmer for 40 minutes or until rice is tender.

3. When tomatoes and garlic are cool enough to handle, transfer to blender and add the remaining stock. Blend until smooth. Add tomato purée and lentils with liquid to rice in saucepan. Bring to a simmer and cook for 1 to 2 minutes or until heated through. Add more stock or water if a thinner soup is desired. Serve immediately.

Nutrients per serving	
Calories	367
Fat	11 g
Carbohydrate	57 g
Fiber	12 g
Protein	13 g
Vitamin B$_6$	0.6 mg
Magnesium	109 mg
Zinc	2.3 mg

Beans, Peas and Lentils

Two-Bean Chili with Zucchini 266

Squash and Black Bean Chili 268

Black Bean Burgers 269

Navy Bean Sloppy Joes 270

Red Beans and Red Rice 271

Caribbean Red Bean, Spinach and Potato Curry 272

Zucchini Chickpea Tagine with Cilantro Quinoa 274

Chickpeas in Tomato Curry 275

Chickpeas and Cauliflower in Tomato Curry 276

Curried Chickpeas 277

Black-Eyed Peas with Vegetables 278

Golden Cauliflower with Split Peas 279

Potato and Pea Coconut Curry 280

Peas and Greens 281

Sweet Potato Shepherd's Pie 282

Yellow Lentil Curry with Vegetables 283

Sindhi Spinach 284

Yellow Curry Dal 286

Two-Bean Chili with Zucchini

Makes 6 servings

This delicious version of vegetarian chili combines fresh green beans with dried beans and adds corn kernels and sautéed zucchini for a tasty finish.

Tips

For the best flavor, toast cumin seeds and grind them yourself. Place seeds in a dry skillet over medium heat and cook, stirring, until fragrant, about 3 minutes. Immediately transfer to a spice grinder or mortar and grind finely.

When using any canned product, such as tomatoes, check the label to make sure ingredients containing gluten have not been added.

Nutrients per serving	
Calories	265
Fat	10 g
Carbohydrate	34 g
Fiber	9 g
Protein	12 g
Vitamin B$_6$	0.6 mg
Magnesium	68 mg
Zinc	1.4 mg

- **Medium to large (4- to 5-quart) slow cooker**
- **Blender**

1 tbsp	vegetable oil	15 mL
2	small zucchini, cut into ½-inch (1 cm) lengths and sweated	2
2	onions, finely chopped	2
2	cloves garlic, minced	2
1 tbsp	ground cumin (see tip, at left)	15 mL
1 tbsp	dried oregano	15 mL
1 tsp	salt	5 mL
½ tsp	freshly cracked black pepper	2 mL
1	can (28 oz/796 mL) tomatoes, with juice, coarsely chopped (see tip, at left)	1
2 cups	Vegetable Stock (page 248)	500 mL
2 cups	green beans, cut into 2-inch (5 cm) lengths	500 mL
2 cups	rinsed drained canned or cooked pinto beans (see tips, opposite)	500 mL
2	dried ancho chile peppers	2
2 cups	boiling water	500 mL
1	jalapeño pepper, seeded and coarsely chopped (optional)	1
½ cup	coarsely chopped fresh cilantro	125 mL
1½ cups	corn kernels	375 mL
1 cup	shredded vegan Monterey Jack cheese alternative (optional)	250 mL
	Vegan sour cream alternative (optional)	

1. In a skillet, heat oil over medium heat. Add zucchini and cook, stirring, until it begins to brown. Transfer to a bowl using a slotted spoon, cover and refrigerate.

2. In same skillet, add onions and cook, stirring, until softened, about 3 minutes. Add garlic, cumin, oregano, salt and pepper; cook, stirring, for 1 minute. Add tomatoes and bring to a boil. Transfer to slow cooker stoneware.

If you don't have home-made stock on hand, you can use ready-to-use reduced-sodium vegetable broth in its place. Check the label to make sure ingredients containing gluten have not been added.

For this quantity of beans, use 1 can (14 to 19 oz/398 to 540 mL) drained and rinsed, or cook 1 cup (250 mL) dried beans.

Substitute cranberry, Romano or red kidney beans for the pinto beans, if desired.

3. Add stock, green beans and pinto beans and stir to combine. Cover and cook on Low for 6 hours or on High for 3 hours, until mixture is hot and bubbly.

4. About an hour before the chili has finished cooking, in a heatproof bowl, soak ancho chiles in boiling water for 30 minutes, weighing down with a cup to ensure they remain submerged. Drain and set soaking water aside. Discard stems and chop peppers coarsely. Transfer to blender. Add jalapeño (if using), cilantro and $\frac{1}{2}$ cup (125 mL) of the chile soaking liquid (discard remainder). Purée.

5. Add chile mixture to stoneware and stir well. Stir in corn and reserved zucchini. Cover and cook on High for 30 minutes, until corn is tender and flavors meld. Ladle into bowls and garnish with cheese alternative and/or sour cream alternative (if using).

Squash and Black Bean Chili

Nicely flavored with hot, smoky chipotle pepper and a hint of cinnamon, this luscious chili makes a fabulous weeknight meal. Add a tossed green salad and some whole-grain rolls, relax and enjoy.

Tip

Try substituting virgin coconut oil for the olive oil. It adds a hint of coconut flavor to this chili that is quite appealing.

- **Medium to large (3½- to 5-quart) slow cooker**

1 tbsp	vegetable oil	15 mL
2	onions, finely chopped	2
4	cloves garlic, minced	4
2 tsp	chili powder	10 mL
1 tsp	dried oregano	5 mL
1 tsp	ground cumin (see tip, page 266)	5 mL
1 tsp	salt	5 mL
1	3-inch (7.5 cm) cinnamon stick	1
1	can (28 oz/796 mL) tomatoes, with juice, coarsely chopped (see tip, page 266)	1
2 cups	rinsed drained canned or cooked black beans	500 mL
4 cups	cubed peeled butternut squash (1-inch/2.5 cm cubes)	1 L
2	green bell peppers, finely chopped	2
1	can (4½ oz/127 mL) chopped mild green chiles	1
1	finely chopped canned chipotle pepper in adobo sauce (optional)	1
	Finely chopped fresh cilantro	

1. In a skillet, heat oil over medium heat. Add onions and cook, stirring, until softened, about 3 minutes. Add garlic, chili powder, oregano, cumin, salt and cinnamon stick; cook, stirring, for 1 minute. Add tomatoes and bring to a boil. Transfer to slow cooker stoneware.

2. Add beans and squash and stir well. Cover and cook on Low for 6 hours or on High for 3 hours, until squash is tender. Add bell peppers, chiles, and chipotle pepper (if using). Cover and cook on High for 20 minutes, until bell pepper is tender. Discard cinnamon stick. When ready to serve, ladle into bowls and garnish with cilantro.

Nutrients per serving	
Calories	186
Fat	3 g
Carbohydrate	36 g
Fiber	11 g
Protein	8 g
Vitamin B$_6$	0.5 mg
Magnesium	83 mg
Zinc	0.9 mg

Black Bean Burgers

These tasty burgers are quick and easy to make and are full of fiber. Serve on gluten-free dinner rolls (store-bought or see recipe, page 188) and top with your favorite toppings.

Tip

If you can only find 14-oz (398 mL) or 15-oz (425 mL) cans of black beans, buy two, drain and rinse the beans and measure out 2 cups (500 mL) for this recipe. The remaining beans can be stored in an airtight container in the refrigerator for up to 3 days.

1	slice gluten-free bread (store-bought or see recipes, pages 186–187)	1
1	can (19 oz/540 mL) black beans, drained and rinsed	1
2 tbsp	finely chopped onion	30 mL
3 tbsp	ground chia seeds	45 mL
1/2 tsp	salt	2 mL
1 tsp	water	5 mL
3 tbsp	olive oil	45 mL

1. Toast bread until dry, then crumble into coarse bread crumbs.

2. In a large bowl, using a potato masher, coarsely mash beans. Stir in bread crumbs, onion, chia seeds, salt and water until evenly blended. Let stand for 2 minutes before forming into 4 patties, each about 1/2 inch (1 cm) thick.

3. In a large skillet, heat oil over medium heat. Cook patties for 5 to 10 minutes per side, turning once, until lightly browned on both sides.

Nutrients per burger	
Calories	278
Fat	13 g
Carbohydrate	31 g
Fiber	13 g
Protein	10 g
Vitamin B$_6$	0.1 mg
Magnesium	48 mg
Zinc	1.0 mg

Navy Bean Sloppy Joes

This is a recipe that is sure to please the whole family. Navy beans are full of potassium and fiber.

1 tbsp	olive oil	15 mL
1	onion, chopped	1
1	green bell pepper, chopped	1
2 tbsp	gluten-free ketchup	30 mL
1	can (14 to 19 oz/398 to 540 mL) navy beans	1
1	can (8 oz/227 mL) gluten-free tomato sauce	1
1 tsp	apple cider vinegar	5 mL
4	gluten-free dinner rolls (store-bought or see page 188), split	4

1. In a medium skillet, heat oil over medium heat. Add onion and green pepper; cook, stirring, for 5 to 10 minutes or until tender.

2. Stir in ketchup until combined, then stir in beans, tomato sauce and vinegar. Reduce heat and simmer, stirring often, for 5 to 10 minutes or until sauce is thickened. Serve on dinner rolls.

Nutrients per serving	
Calories	306
Fat	8 g
Carbohydrate	51 g
Fiber	8 g
Protein	11 g
Vitamin B$_6$	0.3 mg
Magnesium	67 mg
Zinc	1.0 mg

Red Beans and Red Rice

Makes 8 servings

Here's a fresh twist on the classic Southern dish of red beans and rice. Bulked up with muscular red rice, this is very hearty — with the addition of salad, it's a meal in itself. The green peas add a burst of color, making this a visually attractive dish that looks good on a buffet. It is particularly tasty as an accompaniment to a platter of roasted vegetables.

Tip

Wehani rice, grown by Lundberg Family Farms, is robust and chewy and is widely available in well-stocked supermarkets or natural foods stores. Bhutanese, Thai or Camargue red rice can be substituted, although the cooking times vary.

Nutrients per serving	
Calories	209
Fat	3 g
Carbohydrate	39 g
Fiber	6 g
Protein	8 g
Vitamin B$_6$	0.2 mg
Magnesium	32 mg
Zinc	1.4 mg

1 tbsp	olive oil	15 mL
1	onion, finely chopped	1
1	green bell pepper, finely chopped	1
4	stalks celery, diced	4
4	cloves garlic, minced	4
1 tsp	dried thyme	5 mL
½ tsp	salt	2 mL
½ tsp	freshly cracked black pepper	2 mL
¼ tsp	cayenne pepper	1 mL
1 cup	Wehani rice, rinsed and drained (see tip, at left)	250 mL
2 cups	water	500 mL
2 cups	rinsed drained canned or cooked red beans	500 mL
2 cups	cooked green peas	500 mL

1. In a Dutch oven, heat oil over medium heat for 30 seconds. Add onion, green pepper, celery and garlic; cook, stirring, until pepper is softened, about 5 minutes. Add thyme, salt, black pepper and cayenne; cook, stirring, for 1 minute.

2. Add rice and toss to coat. Add water and bring to a boil. Reduce heat to low. Cover and simmer until rice is tender and most of the water is absorbed, about 1 hour. Stir in beans and peas; cook, covered, until heated through, about 10 minutes.

Variation

Substitute brown rice or a mixture of brown rice and wild rice for the Wehani rice.

Caribbean Red Bean, Spinach and Potato Curry

To combine the Caribbean staples of beans, potato and greens is to invite the sunshine of the islands to dinner or lunch. Bring on the reggae!

Tip

There are several varieties of curry powder from the Caribbean that vary in spices from island to island. Any will work nicely in this recipe. If using a stronger, Indian curry powder, reduce the amount to 1½ to 2 tsp (7 to 10 mL) or according to taste.

2 lbs	baby new potatoes, halved (or quartered if large)	1 kg
	Cold water	
1 tsp	salt, divided	5 mL
2 tbsp	vegetable oil	30 mL
1	onion, sliced lengthwise	1
½	hot chile pepper, preferably Scotch bonnet, minced	½
1 tbsp	minced gingerroot	15 mL
1 tbsp	curry powder, preferably Caribbean-style (see tips, at left and opposite)	15 mL
1 tsp	ground coriander	5 mL
¼ tsp	ground allspice	1 mL
1	can (14 to 19 oz/398 to 540 mL) red kidney beans, drained and rinsed	1
½ cup	water or Vegetable Stock (page 248)	125 mL
2 tbsp	freshly squeezed lemon juice	30 mL
2 cups	shredded fresh spinach	500 mL

1. In a pot, cover potatoes with cold water. Add ½ tsp (2 mL) salt and bring to a boil over high heat. Reduce heat and boil gently until potatoes are fork-tender, about 15 minutes. Drain well and transfer to a large bowl; set aside.

2. Meanwhile, in a skillet, heat oil over medium heat. Add onion, chile pepper, ginger, curry powder, coriander, allspice and the remaining salt; cook, stirring, until onion is softened, about 3 minutes.

Nutrients per serving (1 of 6)	
Calories	214
Fat	5 g
Carbohydrate	37 g
Fiber	8 g
Protein	7 g
Vitamin B$_6$	0.4 mg
Magnesium	64 mg
Zinc	1.7 mg

Tip

Check to make sure your curry powder doesn't contain gluten. Some blends may contain wheat or are processed in a facility where wheat is present, thus being potentially contaminated.

3. Stir in beans until coated with spices. Pour in water and bring to a boil, scraping up bits stuck to pan. Reduce heat and boil gently, stirring occasionally, until liquid is almost evaporated, about 5 minutes. Remove from heat and stir in lemon juice. Season to taste with salt. Pour over potatoes in bowl and stir in spinach just until wilted. Serve hot or let cool.

Variation

Replace spinach with Swiss chard, callaloo or another hearty green. Add with beans in step 3, increasing time as necessary to make sure greens are tender.

Zucchini Chickpea Tagine with Cilantro Quinoa

Makes 4 servings

A hearty yet refined mingling of sweet and spicy, this easy Moroccan-inspired meal is reason enough to keep peas on hand — both protein-rich chickpeas and vitamin-packed spring peas.

Tips

If you don't have home-made stock on hand, you can use ready-to-use reduced-sodium vegetable broth in its place. Check the label to make sure ingredients containing gluten have not been added.

Other varieties of tender squash, such as yellow crookneck or a small pattypan, may be used in place of the zucchini.

1 cup	quinoa, rinsed	250 mL
3 cups	Vegetable Stock (page 248), divided	750 mL
½ cup	packed fresh cilantro leaves, chopped	125 mL
1 tbsp	olive oil	15 mL
2 cups	chopped onions	500 mL
2 tsp	ground cumin	10 mL
1 tsp	ground cinnamon	5 mL
1 tsp	ground coriander	5 mL
3	small zucchini, trimmed and diced	3
1	can (14 to 15 oz/398 to 425 mL) diced tomatoes, with juice (see tip, page 266)	1
1	can (14 to 19 oz/398 to 540 mL) chickpeas, drained and rinsed	1
¼ cup	golden or dark raisins	60 mL
1 cup	frozen petite peas, thawed	250 mL

1. In a medium saucepan, combine quinoa and 2 cups (500 mL) stock. Bring to a boil over medium-high heat. Reduce heat to low, cover and simmer for 12 to 15 minutes or until liquid is absorbed. Remove from heat and let stand, covered, for 5 minutes. Fluff with a fork, then gently stir in cilantro.

2. Meanwhile, in a large saucepan, heat oil over medium-high heat. Add onions and cook, stirring, for 6 to 8 minutes or until softened. Add cumin, cinnamon and coriander; cook, stirring, for 30 seconds.

3. Stir in zucchini, tomatoes, chickpeas, raisins and the remaining stock; bring to a boil. Reduce heat to medium-low, cover and simmer, stirring occasionally, for 10 minutes or until zucchini is tender. Stir in peas and simmer for 1 minute. Serve over quinoa.

Nutrients per serving	
Calories	455
Fat	8 g
Carbohydrate	83 g
Fiber	14 g
Protein	17 g
Vitamin B$_6$	1.1 mg
Magnesium	178 mg
Zinc	3.5 mg

Chickpeas in Tomato Curry

A very easy recipe for a rightfully popular legume, this chickpea dish works well as a simple lunch alongside rice or naan or as part of a complex meal. The meaty taste of the chickpea marries the tartness of tomato seamlessly.

Tip

If very ripe, flavorful fresh tomatoes aren't available, substitute drained canned diced tomatoes. When using any canned product, check the label to make sure ingredients containing gluten have not been added.

1 tbsp	vegetable oil	15 mL
½ tsp	cumin seeds	2 mL
1 cup	diced tomatoes (see tip, at left)	250 mL
8	curry leaves	8
½ cup	Basic Gravy (page 224)	125 mL
¼ cup	water	60 mL
2 cups	rinsed drained canned or cooked chickpeas	500 mL

1. In a skillet, heat oil over medium heat until hot but not smoking. Add cumin seeds and cook, stirring, until starting to pop, about 1 minute. Add tomatoes and curry leaves; cook, stirring, until tomatoes are softened, about 2 minutes.

2. Add gravy and cook, stirring, for 1 minute. Add water and bring to a boil, stirring. Reduce heat and boil gently for 3 minutes. Add chickpeas and cook, stirring gently, until heated through and flavorful, about 5 minutes.

Nutrients per serving	
Calories	202
Fat	6 g
Carbohydrate	32 g
Fiber	6 g
Protein	7 g
Vitamin B$_6$	0.7 mg
Magnesium	47 mg
Zinc	1.5 mg

Chickpeas and Cauliflower in Tomato Curry

**Makes
4 to 6 servings**

This hearty dish with the protein of chickpeas and the appeal of al dente cauliflower is great for a breezy lunch.

Tips

If perfectly ripe fresh tomatoes are not available, substitute drained canned diced tomatoes. When using any canned product, check the label to make sure ingredients containing gluten have not been added.

If using dried chickpeas, soak and cook 1 cup (250 mL). One 19-oz (540 mL) can of chickpeas yields 2 cups (500 mL).

1 tbsp	vegetable oil	15 mL
1½ tsp	mustard seeds	7 mL
1 tsp	cumin seeds	5 mL
2 cups	small cauliflower florets	500 mL
¼ cup	water	60 mL
1½ cups	chopped tomatoes	375 mL
1 tsp	minced hot green chile pepper (or to taste)	5 mL
8	curry leaves	8
½ cup	Basic Gravy (page 224)	125 mL
2 cups	rinsed drained canned or cooked chickpeas	500 mL
½ tsp	salt (or to taste)	2 mL

1. In a saucepan, heat oil over medium heat until hot but not smoking. Add mustard seeds and cumin seeds; cook, stirring, until starting to pop, about 1 minute. Add cauliflower and water; cover pan quickly. Cook, covered, until cauliflower starts to soften, about 5 minutes.

2. Uncover and add tomatoes, chile pepper and curry leaves. Cook, stirring, until tomatoes are softened, about 2 minutes. Add gravy and cook, stirring, for 1 minute. Stir in chickpeas until well coated. Cover and cook, stirring once, until cauliflower is tender, about 5 minutes. Season with salt.

Nutrients per serving (1 of 6)	
Calories	150
Fat	4 g
Carbohydrate	24 g
Fiber	5 g
Protein	6 g
Vitamin B6	0.5 mg
Magnesium	42 mg
Zinc	1.1 mg

Curried Chickpeas

This recipe requires very little effort, takes less than half an hour from stovetop to table and makes a quick family supper. Served with steamed or sticky rice and a salad, it's a particular favorite of kids.

Tips

Although coconut milk adds the best flavor to this dish, you can replace all or a portion of it with almond milk or any other non-dairy beverage.

In place of the frozen bell peppers, you can use fresh bell peppers, cut into 2-inch by ¼-inch (5 cm by 0.5 cm) strips.

2 tbsp	vegetable oil	30 mL
1	Spanish onion, thinly sliced	1
3	garlic cloves, minced	3
1 tbsp	curry powder (see tip, page 273)	15 mL
1	can (14 oz/400 mL) coconut milk	1
1	can (14 to 19 oz/398 to 540 mL) chickpeas, drained and rinsed	1
1 lb	frozen mixed bell peppers, thawed	500 g
2 tbsp	tomato paste	30 mL
1 tbsp	packed brown sugar or granulated natural cane sugar	15 mL
1 tbsp	freshly squeezed lemon juice	15 mL
1 tsp	salt (or to taste)	5 mL
Pinch	hot pepper flakes (or dash hot pepper sauce)	Pinch
2 tbsp	chopped fresh cilantro or parsley (optional)	30 mL

1. In a large skillet, heat oil over medium heat for about 30 seconds. Add onion and cook, stirring, for 3 minutes or until softened. Add garlic and curry powder; cook, stirring, for 1 minute.

2. Stir in coconut milk, chickpeas, bell peppers, tomato paste, brown sugar, lemon juice, salt and hot pepper flakes; bring to a boil. Reduce heat and simmer, uncovered, for 20 to 25 minutes or until sauce is thickened and vegetables are tender. Serve sprinkled with cilantro (if using).

Nutrients per serving (1 of 4)	
Calories	425
Fat	30 g
Carbohydrate	37 g
Fiber	7 g
Protein	9 g
Vitamin B6	0.7 mg
Magnesium	92 mg
Zinc	1.8 mg

Black-Eyed Peas with Vegetables

This hearty stew is a perfect vegetarian entrée.

Tip

The important thing in Indian cooking is to use a chile pepper with spirit. Fresh cayenne peppers, or any similar ones, would work very well. If using fresh Thai peppers, now readily available in North America, use only half the amount called for in the recipe. At a pinch, jalapeños could also be used.

1½ tbsp	vegetable oil	22 mL
1 tsp	mustard seeds	5 mL
½ tsp	cumin seeds	2 mL
¼ tsp	fenugreek seeds (methi)	1 mL
1 cup	finely chopped onion	250 mL
2½ tsp	sambar powder	12 mL
1 tsp	garam masala	5 mL
2 to 3	green chile peppers (see tip, at left)	2 to 3
1	package (11 oz/330 g) fresh or frozen black-eyed peas	1
1 tsp	minced gingerroot	5 mL
1 tsp	minced garlic	5 mL
3 cups	water	750 mL
1½ tsp	salt (or to taste)	7 mL
½ cup	cubed potatoes (1-inch/2.5 cm cubes)	125 mL
½ cup	sliced carrots (½ inch/1 cm thick)	125 mL
½ cup	chopped green beans (½ inch/1 cm thick)	125 mL

1. In a medium saucepan, heat oil over high heat until a couple of mustard seeds thrown in start to sputter. Add the remaining mustard seeds and cover quickly.

2. When the seeds stop popping, in a few seconds, uncover, reduce heat to medium and add cumin and fenugreek seeds; cook, stirring, for 10 seconds. Add onion and cook, stirring, until golden, 5 to 7 minutes.

3. Add sambar powder, garam masala and green chile. Mix well. Cook for 2 minutes. Add black eyed-peas, ginger and garlic. Mix well. Add water, cover and bring to a boil. Reduce heat to low. Simmer until peas are slightly softened, about 20 minutes. Stir in salt.

4. Add potatoes, carrots and beans; cook until vegetables are tender, 12 to 15 minutes. If necessary, add ½ cup (125 mL) hot water to allow for a thick gravy.

5. Serve with rice or an Indian bread.

Nutrients per serving	
Calories	67
Fat	3 g
Carbohydrate	10 g
Fiber	1 g
Protein	2 g
Vitamin B6	0.2 mg
Magnesium	35 mg
Zinc	0.3 mg

Golden Cauliflower with Split Peas

Any fresh summer vegetable will work well in this lower-fat recipe.

Tip

If you don't have home-made stock on hand, you can use ready-to-use reduced-sodium vegetable broth in its place. Check the label to make sure ingredients containing gluten have not been added.

¾ cup	dried split green peas	175 mL
2 cups	water	500 mL
2 tbsp	olive oil	30 mL
1	1-inch (2.5 cm) cinnamon stick, crushed	1
2 tsp	whole cumin seeds	10 mL
2 tsp	whole fennel seeds	10 mL
2 tsp	ground turmeric	10 mL
1 tbsp	minced gingerroot	15 mL
1	small cauliflower, cut into small florets	1
½ cup	Vegetable Stock (page 248)	125 mL
1 cup	chopped green onions	250 mL

1. In a saucepan, cover split peas with water. Bring to a boil over medium-high heat. Cover, reduce heat and simmer for 15 to 20 minutes or until peas are tender. Drain and set aside.

2. Meanwhile, in a large skillet or wok, heat oil over medium heat. Add cinnamon, cumin and fennel seeds. Toast, stirring, for 1 minute or until seeds turn brown. Add turmeric, ginger, cauliflower and stock. Bring to a boil over high heat. Reduce heat and cook, stirring occasionally, for 10 minutes. Stir in peas and heat through. Sprinkle green onions over top. Serve immediately.

Variation

Use mung beans in place of the dried split green peas.

Nutrients per serving (1 of 6)	
Calories	153
Fat	5 g
Carbohydrate	21 g
Fiber	8 g
Protein	8 g
Vitamin B$_6$	0.2 mg
Magnesium	48 mg
Zinc	1.1 mg

Potato and Pea Coconut Curry

Sweet and white potatoes cooked in an aromatic sauce make a simple but very tasty combination. Serve over hot rice.

Tips

If you don't have homemade stock on hand, you can use ready-to-use reduced-sodium vegetable broth in its place. Check the label to make sure ingredients containing gluten have not been added.

Some curry pastes contain products such as shrimp paste or fish sauce, so if you're a vegetarian, check the label to ensure that yours is fish- and seafood-free.

If you're a heat seeker, you can increase the quantity of curry paste.

- Medium to large (3½- to 5-quart) slow cooker

1 tbsp	vegetable oil	15 mL
2	onions, finely chopped	2
4	cloves garlic, minced	4
1 tbsp	minced gingerroot	15 mL
½ tsp	freshly cracked black pepper	2 mL
1 cup	Vegetable Stock (page 248)	250 mL
2	large sweet potatoes (each about 8 oz/250 g), peeled and cut into 1-inch (2.5 cm) cubes	2
2	potatoes, peeled and diced	2
2 tsp	Thai red curry paste (see tips, at left)	10 mL
1 cup	coconut milk, divided	250 mL
2 cups	sweet green peas, thawed if frozen	500 mL
	Finely chopped fresh cilantro	

1. In a skillet, heat oil over medium heat. Add onions and cook, stirring, until softened, about 3 minutes. Add garlic, ginger and pepper; cook, stirring, for 1 minute. Add stock and bring to a boil. Transfer to slow cooker stoneware.

2. Stir in sweet potatoes and potatoes. Cover and cook on Low for 6 to 8 hours or on High for 3 to 4 hours, until potatoes are tender.

3. In a small bowl, combine curry paste and ¼ cup (60 mL) coconut milk. Stir until blended. Add to stoneware, along with the remaining coconut milk, and stir well. Stir in peas. Cover and cook on High for 15 minutes, until peas are tender and flavors have melded. When serving, garnish with cilantro.

Nutrients per serving	
Calories	240
Fat	11 g
Carbohydrate	33 g
Fiber	6 g
Protein	6 g
Vitamin B$_6$	0.4 mg
Magnesium	66 mg
Zinc	1.3 mg

Peas and Greens

This delicious combination of black-eyed peas and greens is a great dish for busy weeknights.

Tips

Before removing the fennel bulb's core, chop off the top shoots (which resemble celery) and discard. If desired, save the feathery green fronds to use as a garnish. If the outer sections of the bulb seem old and dry, peel them with a vegetable peeler before using.

To toast fennel seeds, place them in a dry skillet over medium heat and stir until fragrant, about 3 minutes. Immediately transfer to a mortar or spice grinder and grind.

- **Medium to large (3½- to 5-quart) slow cooker**

1 tbsp	vegetable oil	15 mL
2	onions, finely chopped	2
1	bulb fennel, trimmed, cored and thinly sliced on the vertical	1
4	cloves garlic, minced	4
½ tsp	salt (or to taste)	2 mL
½ tsp	freshly cracked black pepper	2 mL
¼ tsp	fennel seeds, toasted and ground (see tip, at left)	1 mL
1	can (14 oz/398 mL) diced tomatoes, with juice (see tip, page 282)	1
2 cups	rinsed drained canned or cooked black-eyed peas	500 mL
1 tsp	paprika, dissolved in 2 tbsp (30 mL) freshly squeezed lemon juice	5 mL
4 cups	chopped spinach or Swiss chard (about 1 bunch), stems removed	1 L

1. In a skillet, heat oil over medium heat. Add onions and fennel; cook, stirring, until fennel is softened, about 5 minutes. Add garlic, salt, pepper and fennel seeds; cook, stirring, for 1 minute. Add tomatoes and bring to a boil. Transfer to slow cooker stoneware.

2. Stir in peas. Cover and cook on Low for 8 hours or on High for 4 hours, until peas are tender. Stir in paprika solution. Add spinach, in batches, stirring after each to submerge the leaves in the liquid. Cover and cook on High for 20 minutes, until spinach is tender.

Nutrients per serving	
Calories	111
Fat	4 g
Carbohydrate	18 g
Fiber	4 g
Protein	4 g
Vitamin B$_6$	0.4 mg
Magnesium	71 mg
Zinc	0.7 mg

Sweet Potato Shepherd's Pie

This vegetarian version of shepherd's pie contains lots of antioxidant nutrients from the vegetables and protein and fiber from the beans. Sweet potato provides beta-carotene, potassium and manganese.

Tip

When using any canned product, such as tomatoes, check the label to make sure ingredients containing gluten have not been added.

- **Preheat oven to 400°F (200°C)**
- **6-cup (1.5 L) shallow baking dish**

4	large sweet potatoes, peeled and cut into cubes	4
1 tbsp	olive oil	15 mL
1	onion, finely chopped	1
1	large carrot, diced	1
1	green bell pepper, finely chopped	1
1	zucchini, diced	1
2	cans (each 14 oz/398 mL) diced tomatoes, with juice (see tip, at left)	2
1	can (14 to 19 oz/398 to 540 mL) pinto beans, drained and rinsed	1
1	can (14 to 19 oz/398 to 540 mL) chickpeas, drained and rinsed	1
1 cup	frozen green peas	250 mL
1/4 tsp	salt	1 mL

1. Place sweet potatoes in a large saucepan and add enough water to cover. Bring to a boil over high heat. Reduce heat and boil gently for 20 minutes or until tender. Drain sweet potatoes, return to pot and mash until smooth.

2. Meanwhile, in a large skillet, heat oil over medium heat. Add onion, carrot, green pepper and zucchini; cook, stirring often, for about 10 minutes or until tender.

3. Stir in tomatoes, pinto beans, chickpeas, green peas and salt; bring to a boil, stirring often. Reduce heat and simmer, stirring occasionally, for 10 minutes.

4. Spread onion mixture in baking dish, then spread mashed sweet potatoes on top, smoothing top.

5. Bake in preheated oven for 30 minutes or until filling is bubbling and topping is lightly browned.

Nutrients per serving	
Calories	433
Fat	6 g
Carbohydrate	82 g
Fiber	18 g
Protein	16 g
Vitamin B$_6$	1.3 mg
Magnesium	134 mg
Zinc	3.0 mg

Yellow Lentil Curry with Vegetables

This meal-in-one-dish combines the protein of lentils with the comfort of flavorful vegetables. Add some rice, and you're all set for a casual but enjoyable lunch or dinner.

Tip
Simmering the lentils slowly and uncovered allows them to hold their shape and soften nicely, but be sure not to let them dry out.

1 cup	small yellow lentils (toor dal), rinsed	250 mL
½ tsp	salt	2 mL
	Cold water	
2 tbsp	vegetable oil	30 mL
1 cup	finely chopped onion	250 mL
½ cup	chopped green bell pepper	125 mL
½ cup	small cauliflower florets	125 mL
½ cup	cubed eggplant (½-inch/1 cm cubes)	125 mL
½ cup	thinly sliced carrot	125 mL
1	hot green chile pepper, minced	1
½ cup	chopped tomato	125 mL
1 tbsp	minced gingerroot	15 mL
1 tbsp	minced garlic	15 mL
1 tsp	ground cumin	5 mL
1 tsp	garam masala	5 mL
2½ cups	boiling water, divided (approx.)	625 mL

1. In a bowl, combine lentils and salt. Add enough cold water to cover by about 1 inch (2.5 cm). Let stand at room temperature for 1 hour.

2. In a skillet, heat oil over medium-high heat. Add onion, green pepper, cauliflower, eggplant and carrot; cook, stirring, until starting to brown, about 5 minutes. Add chile, tomato, ginger, garlic, cumin and garam masala; cook, stirring, until tomato is softened, about 2 minutes.

3. Drain lentils and add to skillet. Add 1 cup (250 mL) boiling water. Reduce heat and simmer, stirring occasionally and adding more boiling water, about ½ cup (125 mL) at a time, as mixture becomes dry, until lentils are very soft, about 20 minutes.

Nutrients per serving	
Calories	272
Fat	8 g
Carbohydrate	39 g
Fiber	8 g
Protein	14 g
Vitamin B$_6$	0.4 mg
Magnesium	56 mg
Zinc	2.2 mg

Sindhi Spinach

This is the most popular vegetable dish in Sindhi cuisine. A light and nutritious combination of greens, vegetables and split yellow peas, it is served daily in most Sindhi homes in the summer, along with rice and plain yogurt.

1 cup	split yellow peas (chana dal)	250 mL
4½ cups	water, divided	1.125 L
1 tbsp	vegetable oil	15 mL
1½ tsp	cumin seeds	7 mL
2 tbsp	chopped green chile pepper (see tip, page 278)	30 mL
1 tbsp	minced gingerroot	15 mL
1 tbsp	chopped garlic	15 mL
1	onion, chopped	1
1	red or green bell pepper, chopped	1
1	piece eggplant (3 inches/7.5 cm), cut into 1-inch (2.5 cm) dice	1
15	green beans, cut into ½-inch (1 cm) pieces	15
1	carrot, cut into ½-inch (1 cm) pieces	1
1	potato, cut into 1-inch (2.5 cm) dice	1
2	plum (Roma) tomatoes, chopped	2
1 tsp	ground turmeric	5 mL
2	packages (each 10 oz/300 g) frozen spinach, preferably thawed	2
½ cup	packed fresh dill, chopped (or 2 tbsp/30 mL dried dillweed)	125 mL
2½ tsp	salt (or to taste)	12 mL
¼ cup	Thai tamarind paste (or 2 tbsp/30 mL Indian tamarind concentrate)	60 mL

1. Clean and pick through peas for any small stones and grit. Rinse several times in cold water until water is fairly clear. Soak in 3 cups (750 mL) water in a bowl for 30 minutes. Drain.

2. In a large saucepan, heat oil over medium heat. Add cumin seeds and cook, stirring, for 30 seconds. Add chile, ginger and garlic; cook, stirring, for 1 minute. Add onion, red pepper, eggplant, beans, carrot, potato, tomatoes and turmeric. Mix well.

Nutrients per serving (1 of 12)	
Calories	113
Fat	2 g
Carbohydrate	19 g
Fiber	7 g
Protein	7 g
Vitamin B$_6$	0.2 mg
Magnesium	64 mg
Zinc	0.9 mg

Storage Tip

Sindhi Spinach freezes well in an airtight container for up to 6 months. If it appears too thick and dry after reheating, stir in 2 to 3 tbsp (30 to 45 mL) water to loosen it.

3. Add spinach, dill and drained peas. Pour in the remaining water. Mix well. Increase heat to medium-high. Cover and bring to a boil. Reduce heat to medium and cook until peas and vegetables are softened, about 30 minutes.

4. Stir in salt and tamarind. Mash with potato masher or with back of spoon so vegetables and peas are well mixed. Continue to cook, uncovered, until mixture is thick, 10 to 15 minutes. Vegetables should be almost completely mashed and about half of the peas should also be mashed. Consistency will be thick but not dry. Serve with rice.

Yellow Curry Dal

Look for small yellow lentils in Middle Eastern supermarkets or use the widely available red lentils in this dish. Save leftover Yellow Curry Dal for use in soups.

Tips

Check to make sure your curry powder doesn't contain gluten. Some blends may contain wheat or are processed in a facility where wheat is present, thus being potentially contaminated.

If you don't have home-made stock on hand, you can use ready-to-use reduced-sodium vegetable broth in its place. Check the label to make sure ingredients containing gluten have not been added.

2 tbsp	olive oil	30 mL
1 cup	chopped onion	250 mL
2	cloves garlic, finely chopped	2
1 tbsp	yellow curry powder (see tip, at left)	15 mL
1 tsp	grated gingerroot	5 mL
1¼ cups	dried yellow lentils, rinsed	300 mL
2 cups	Vegetable Stock (page 248) or water	500 mL
	Sea salt and freshly ground black pepper	

1. In a saucepan, heat oil over medium heat. Add onion and garlic; cook, stirring occasionally, for 6 to 8 minutes or until soft. Stir in curry and ginger. Cook, stirring frequently, for 1 minute.

2. In a strainer, pick over and remove any small stones or grit from lentils. Add lentils and vegetable stock to saucepan. Stir well and bring to a boil. Reduce heat and simmer for 15 minutes, stirring occasionally for the first 10 minutes and frequently during the last 5 minutes of cooking. Cook only until water is absorbed and lentils are soft. Season to taste with salt and pepper. Serve warm or at room temperature.

Nutrients per serving (1 of 6)	
Calories	207
Fat	6 g
Carbohydrate	30 g
Fiber	6 g
Protein	11 g
Vitamin B$_6$	0.3 mg
Magnesium	41 mg
Zinc	1.8 mg

Vegetables and Grains

Vegetable Paella 288

Mixed Vegetable Coconut Curry 289

Whole Baked Masala Cauliflower 290

Citrus Beets 292

Garlic-Scented Zucchini 292

Zucchini Spaghetti with Lemon and Herbs 293

Curried Zucchini Strips 294

Spiced Root Vegetables 295

Roasted Spice-Glazed Root Vegetables. 296

Potatoes in Tomato Gravy. 297

Onion-Braised Potatoes with Spinach 298

Potato and Spinach Curry. 299

Butternut Squash with Snow Peas and Red Pepper . . . 299

Spaghetti Squash 300

Squash with Quinoa and Apricots. 301

Basil and Roasted Pepper Quinoa 302

Fragrant Coconut Rice 303

Chile Rice 304

Brown Rice. 305

Wild Rice. 305

Indonesian-Style Yellow Rice Pilaf 306

Sweet Potato Wild Rice Cakes 307

Wild Rice Stuffing with Cranberries. 308

Vegetable Paella

With the colors of a Spanish landscape, this richly flavored one-pan meal is fun and festive. Dinner on the deck and a pitcher of sangria; now that's relaxing. As cooking with seasonal vegetables produces superior flavors, use green beans if asparagus is unavailable.

Tips

When garlic is browned too quickly, it becomes bitter. If sautéing with other vegetables, add garlic toward the end of the browning process.

To ensure time with your guests, make the paella up to 1 day ahead. Refrigerate cooled paella in an airtight container for up to 2 days. Spread in paella pan, cover and reheat in a 350°F (180°C) oven for 25 to 30 minutes.

Nutrients per serving (1 of 8)	
Calories	325
Fat	7 g
Carbohydrate	51 g
Fiber	4 g
Protein	7 g
Vitamin B$_6$	0.2 mg
Magnesium	34 mg
Zinc	0.9 mg

- **Preheat oven to 350°F (180°C)**
- **Paella pan or large ovenproof skillet**

3 tbsp	olive oil	45 mL
1	onion, finely chopped	1
1	large fennel bulb, trimmed and cut into bite-size pieces	1
4	cloves garlic, chopped	4
2 cups	short- or medium-grain white rice	500 mL
2 cups	warm water	500 mL
1½ cups	dry white wine	375 mL
½ tsp	paprika	2 mL
¾ tsp	saffron threads or ground turmeric	3 mL
1 tsp	salt	5 mL
1	can (14 oz/400 mL) artichoke hearts in water, drained	1
¾ cup	sliced drained oil-packed sun-dried tomatoes	175 mL
8 oz	thin asparagus or green beans, trimmed and halved	250 g
⅓ cup	green olives	75 mL
3 tbsp	chopped fresh flat-leaf (Italian) parsley	45 mL

1. Place paella pan over medium heat and let pan get hot. Add oil and tip pan to coat. Add onion and fennel; cook, stirring frequently, until vegetables begin to soften, 4 to 5 minutes. Add garlic and cook, stirring frequently, until onions and fennel are lightly browned, 3 to 5 minutes. Mix in rice, lightly coating all grains with oil. Stir in water, wine, paprika, saffron, salt, artichoke hearts and sun-dried tomatoes. Gently shake pan to distribute rice evenly. Reduce heat and simmer for 10 minutes.

2. Remove pan from heat and scatter asparagus and green olives over rice. Cover pan and bake in preheated oven until rice is tender with a slightly crusted bottom, about 30 minutes. Serve hot, garnished with parsley.

Mixed Vegetable Coconut Curry

Vegetables and a flavorful sauce softened by silken coconut milk become a great asset to any curry meal. A standard in Indian cuisine, vegetable khurma is a snap to make, allowing more time for you to concoct additional dishes.

1 tbsp	vegetable oil	15 mL
1	large tomato, chopped	1
8	curry leaves	8
½ cup	Basic Gravy (page 224)	125 mL
¼ cup	water	60 mL
4 cups	cooked chopped vegetables (potatoes, peas, cauliflower florets, green beans, carrots, in any combination)	1 L
1 cup	coconut milk	250 mL
½ tsp	salt	2 mL

1. In a large skillet, heat oil over medium heat. Add tomato and curry leaves; cook, stirring, until tomato starts to soften, about 2 minutes. Add gravy and cook, stirring for 1 minute. Add water and bring to a boil, stirring.

2. Stir in vegetables and return to a boil. Stir in coconut milk and salt; simmer, stirring gently, until vegetables are heated through and sauce is flavorful, about 5 minutes.

Nutrients per serving	
Calories	248
Fat	17 g
Carbohydrate	22 g
Fiber	5 g
Protein	6 g
Vitamin B$_6$	0.4 mg
Magnesium	69 mg
Zinc	1.2 mg

Whole Baked Masala Cauliflower

Makes 8 servings

This elegant dish from north India is particularly wonderful in the cooler months, when cauliflower is at its best.

- **Preheat oven to 350°F (180°C)**
- **13- by 9-inch (33 by 23 cm) baking dish**

1	head cauliflower (about 1½ lbs/750 g)	1
3 tbsp	vegetable oil, divided	45 mL
2 cups	finely chopped onions	500 mL
2 tsp	minced green chile pepper (see tip, page 278)	10 mL
1 tsp	minced gingerroot	5 mL
1 tsp	minced garlic	5 mL
1 cup	finely chopped tomatoes	250 mL
1½ tsp	ground coriander	7 mL
¾ tsp	ground cumin	3 mL
½ tsp	ground turmeric	2 mL
1½ tsp	salt (or to taste)	7 mL
¾ cup	water	175 mL
2 tbsp	coarsely chopped garlic	30 mL

1. Remove leaves from cauliflower. In a large saucepan filled with about 3 inches (7.5 cm) water, place cauliflower, stem side down. Cover and bring to a boil over medium-high heat. Reduce heat to medium and cook for 2 minutes. Remove from heat and let stand, covered, for 3 minutes longer to steam. Remove cauliflower carefully from water and place in a colander under cool running water to stop further cooking. Set aside to drain. Cauliflower should be tender-crisp.

2. Meanwhile, in a small saucepan, heat 2 tbsp (30 mL) oil over medium-high heat. Add onions and cook, stirring, until golden, about 10 minutes. Stir in chile, ginger and garlic. Reduce heat to medium and cook, stirring, until onions are browned, 5 to 8 minutes longer.

4. Stir in tomatoes. Cook until tomatoes can be mashed with back of spoon, about 5 minutes.

Nutrients per serving	
Calories	88
Fat	5 g
Carbohydrate	9 g
Fiber	3 g
Protein	2 g
Vitamin B$_6$	0.2 mg
Magnesium	20 mg
Zinc	0.4 mg

Tip

Cauliflower and gravy can be prepared a day ahead and refrigerated. Let cauliflower come to room temperature and warm gravy before assembling for baking.

5. Stir in coriander, cumin, turmeric and salt. Cook for 2 to 3 minutes. Add water. Reduce heat to low. Cover and simmer for 10 minutes. Gravy should be thick.

6. Place cauliflower in baking dish. Spoon gravy in between florets, taking care cauliflower does not break apart. Cover completely with the remaining gravy. Bake in preheated oven until cauliflower is tender, about 20 minutes.

7. In a small saucepan, heat the remaining oil over medium heat. Add garlic and cook, stirring, until golden, about 2 minutes. Pour on top of cauliflower just before serving.

8. Serve either in baking dish or transfer carefully, without breaking, to a serving platter.

Citrus Beets

Chill and serve as a condiment or spoon directly from the pan for a colorful side dish or salad.

4 cups	shredded beets (about 1½ lbs/750 g)	1 L
1 cup	freshly squeezed orange juice	250 mL
¼ cup	freshly squeezed lemon juice	60 mL
2 tbsp	agave nectar	30 mL
1 tbsp	rice vinegar	15 mL
1 tbsp	finely chopped candied ginger (optional)	15 mL
	Sea salt and freshly ground black pepper	

1. In a saucepan or skillet, combine beets, orange juice and lemon juice. Bring to a boil over medium heat. Stir in agave nectar, vinegar and ginger. Reduce heat to medium-low and simmer, stirring occasionally, until liquid is nearly evaporated, sauce is syrupy and beets are tender, about 1 hour. Season to taste with salt and pepper.

Nutrients per serving	
Calories	122
Fat	0 g
Carbohydrate	29 g
Fiber	4 g
Protein	3 g
Vitamin B6	0.1 mg
Magnesium	39 mg
Zinc	0.5 mg

Garlic-Scented Zucchini

Tip
If you can only find large zucchini, cut them in half lengthwise, then slice them into half-moon shapes.

1 lb	small zucchini (about 4)	500 g
2 tbsp	vegetable oil	30 mL
2 tsp	chopped garlic	10 mL
1 tsp	salt (or to taste)	5 mL
½ tsp	granulated sugar	2 mL

1. Trim both ends from each zucchini and slice into thin rounds. You will need about 3 cups (750 mL).

2. Heat a wok or a large deep skillet over high heat. Add oil and swirl to coat pan. Add garlic and toss well, until fragrant, about 15 seconds.

3. Add zucchini and spread into a single layer. Cook, undisturbed, for 1 minute. Toss once.

4. Add salt and sugar and toss well. Reduce heat to medium and cook, tossing occasionally, until zucchini are tender-crisp, 2 to 3 minutes more. Transfer to a serving plate. Serve hot or warm.

Nutrients per serving	
Calories	83
Fat	7 g
Carbohydrate	5 g
Fiber	1 g
Protein	1 g
Vitamin B6	0.2 mg
Magnesium	21 mg
Zinc	0.4 mg

Zucchini Spaghetti with Lemon and Herbs

In this dish, versatile zucchini noodles are tossed with rich olive oil, aromatic fresh herbs and zesty lemon.

Tips

A spiralizer (spiral vegetable slicer) is one of the most common tools used in raw food preparation. The smallest blade will make spaghetti-sized noodles, the medium blade will make half-moon noodles and the largest blade will make thick, dense noodles.

Organic sea salt is classified as a whole food and is said to contain many trace minerals. If you are concerned about your salt intake, feel free to use less salt or omit it completely.

- Spiralizer, fitted with the smallest blade (see tip, at left)
- Food processor

2	large zucchini	2
2	bunches fresh flat-leaf (Italian) parsley, stems removed, roughly chopped	2
¼ cup	cold-pressed extra virgin olive oil	60 mL
1 tbsp	grated lemon zest	15 mL
¼ cup	freshly squeezed lemon juice	60 mL
½ tsp	fine sea salt	2 mL

1. Using a sharp chef's knife, remove a small portion from each end of the zucchini to create a flat surface. Using spiralizer fitted with the smallest blade, secure zucchini on prongs. Rotate crank while gently pushing zucchini toward blade to create long strands of "pasta." Transfer noodles to a bowl.

2. In food processor, combine parsley, oil, lemon zest and juice and salt. Process until smooth, stopping motor to scrape down sides of work bowl as necessary. Add to zucchini noodles and toss until well coated. Serve immediately.

Variations

Try spiralizing other vegetables or fruits — such as carrots, parsnips, beets, apples or squash — in place of the zucchini.

Substitute 3 bunches of fresh cilantro, roughly chopped, for the parsley and add other vegetables, such as broccoli florets, cauliflower florets or shredded carrot.

For a boost of protein, add ¼ cup (60 mL) raw shelled hemp seeds.

Nutrients per serving	
Calories	302
Fat	28 g
Carbohydrate	13 g
Fiber	3 g
Protein	4 g
Vitamin B_6	0.6 mg
Magnesium	61 mg
Zinc	1.1 mg

Curried Zucchini Strips

Makes 4 servings

Fast, easy and delicious, these zucchini strips go well with any meal. They can also be eaten cold as a snack.

Tips

Check to make sure your curry powder doesn't contain gluten. Some blends may contain wheat or are processed in a facility where wheat is present, thus being potentially contaminated.

Leftovers of this dish are delicious. Eat them on their own or cut them into chunks and add to a salad or stir-fry.

3	zucchini	3
1 tbsp	vegetable oil	15 mL
¼ tsp	curry powder (see tip, at left)	1 mL
	Salt	

1. Cut ends off zucchini. Cut in half lengthwise, then cut each half in half crosswise. Cut each quarter lengthwise into two or three strips of equal size. These will vary depending on the size of your zucchini.

2. In a large nonstick skillet, heat oil over medium-high heat until hot but not smoking. Add zucchini and cook, stirring occasionally, for 5 minutes or until soft. Stir in curry powder and salt to taste. Cover and cook for 2 minutes or until tender and fragrant.

Nutrients per serving	
Calories	55
Fat	4 g
Carbohydrate	5 g
Fiber	1 g
Protein	2 g
Vitamin B$_6$	0.2 mg
Magnesium	27 mg
Zinc	0.5 mg

Spiced Root Vegetables

Some dishes just simmer away without attention and this is one. Once the ingredients are in the pot, it can be left virtually on its own to gently bubble and that makes it a great recipe for company dinners — a half hour more will not harm either the taste or the presentation.

Variation

For a vegan version, use 2 tbsp (30 mL) olive oil in place of the butter.

- **Flameproof tagine or Dutch oven**

2	cloves garlic, chopped	2
1 tsp	cumin seeds, crushed	5 mL
1 tsp	coriander seeds, crushed	5 mL
3 tbsp	butter	45 mL
1½ cups	orange juice	375 mL
2 tbsp	freshly squeezed lemon juice	30 mL
¼ cup	chopped dates	60 mL
½ tsp	salt	2 mL
3	carrots, cut into thick matchsticks	3
3	parsnips, cut into thick matchsticks	3
3	¼-inch (0.5 cm) slices rutabaga, trimmed and cut into thick matchsticks	3

1. In bottom of tagine, combine garlic, cumin, coriander and butter. Cook gently over medium heat for 3 minutes. Stir in orange juice, lemon juice, dates and salt. Bring to a gentle simmer. Cover and cook for 10 minutes.

2. Stir in carrots, parsnips and rutabaga. Cover, reduce heat to low and cook for about 30 minutes or until vegetables are tender and sauce is thick. Add more orange juice if cooking time is extended or if vegetables get too dry. Serve immediately.

Nutrients per serving	
Calories	260
Fat	10 g
Carbohydrate	44 g
Fiber	8 g
Protein	3 g
Vitamin B$_6$	0.3 mg
Magnesium	62 mg
Zinc	0.6 mg

Roasted Spice-Glazed Root Vegetables

Makes 4 servings

Adding garlic to the roasted vegetables gives them extra sweetness. This side dish is very easy to prepare.

- **Preheat oven to 400°F (200°C)**
- **Rimmed baking sheet, lightly oiled**

6	cloves garlic	6
2	onions, quartered	2
2	carrots, quartered lengthwise and cut in half	2
2	parsnips, quartered lengthwise and cut in half	2
1	sweet potato, cut lengthwise into wedges	1
½	rutabaga, cut in half lengthwise, then cut into wedges	½
3 tbsp	olive oil	45 mL
	Sea salt and freshly ground black pepper	
3 tbsp	pure maple syrup	45 mL

1. On prepared baking sheet, arrange garlic, onions, carrots, parsnips, sweet potato and rutabaga in one layer. Drizzle with oil and season to taste with salt and pepper.

2. Bake in preheated oven for 45 minutes or until tender when pierced with the tip of a knife. Transfer to a bowl and toss with maple syrup.

Nutrients per serving	
Calories	255
Fat	11 g
Carbohydrate	40 g
Fiber	6 g
Protein	3 g
Vitamin B$_6$	0.3 mg
Magnesium	48 mg
Zinc	0.8 mg

Potatoes in Tomato Gravy

Makes 8 servings

Indians consider
the potato to be a
vegetable, so serving
potato curry with rice
is perfectly logical.
Alternatively, serve
with an Indian bread to
scoop up the gravy.

Tips

The important thing in
Indian cooking is to use
a chile pepper with spirit.
Fresh cayenne peppers,
or any similar ones, would
work very well. If using fresh
Thai peppers, now readily
available in North America,
use only half the amount
called for in the recipe. At a
pinch, jalapeños could also
be used.

When using any canned
product, such as tomatoes,
check the label to make
sure ingredients containing
gluten have not been
added.

1 tbsp	vegetable oil	15 mL
1½ tsp	cumin seeds	7 mL
1½ tbsp	finely sliced green chile pepper (see tip, at left)	22 mL
1	can (28 oz/796 mL) crushed tomatoes (see tip, at left)	1
¾ tsp	ground turmeric	3 mL
2 lbs	potatoes, peeled and cut into 1-inch (2.5 cm) cubes	1 kg
2 tsp	salt (or to taste)	10 mL
5 tbsp	chopped fresh cilantro, divided	75 mL

1. In a saucepan, heat oil over medium-high heat. Add cumin seeds and green chile; cook, stirring, until cumin is fragrant and slightly darker, about 1 minute.

2. Add tomatoes and turmeric. Mix well. Bring to a boil. Cook for 2 minutes.

3. Add potatoes, salt and 4 tbsp (60 mL) cilantro; return to a boil. Reduce heat to low. Cover and simmer until potatoes are soft, 12 to 15 minutes. If gravy is too thin, mash a few potatoes with back of spoon and cook for 3 to 4 minutes longer to thicken. Serve garnished with the remaining cilantro.

Variation

Add 1½ cups (375 mL) peas for a variation. Small boiling onions, 1½ to 2 cups (375 to 500 mL), are also a good addition.

Nutrients per serving	
Calories	147
Fat	2 g
Carbohydrate	30 g
Fiber	4 g
Protein	4 g
Vitamin B$_6$	0.5 mg
Magnesium	44 mg
Zinc	0.6 mg

Onion-Braised Potatoes with Spinach

Makes 8 servings

Served with brown rice and a salad, this tasty braise makes a great weeknight dinner. It also works well as part of a multi-dish Indian meal.

Tips

If you don't have homemade stock on hand, you can use ready-to-use reduced-sodium vegetable broth in its place. Check the label to make sure ingredients containing gluten have not been added.

Before adding the final ingredients in this recipe, check to make sure the potatoes are tender. If not, continue cooking until the potatoes are cooked, increasing the temperature to High, if necessary.

Nutrients per serving	
Calories	148
Fat	2 g
Carbohydrate	29 g
Fiber	6 g
Protein	5 g
Vitamin B$_6$	0.5 mg
Magnesium	89 mg
Zinc	0.9 mg

- **Medium to large (3½- to 5-quart) slow cooker**

1 tbsp	vegetable oil	15 mL
4	onions, thinly sliced on the vertical	4
4	cloves garlic, minced	4
1 tbsp	minced gingerroot	15 mL
1 tbsp	ground cumin (see tip, page 266)	15 mL
1 tsp	salt	5 mL
1 tsp	freshly cracked black pepper	5 mL
2	black cardamom pods, crushed	2
1	can (14 oz/398 mL) diced tomatoes, with juice (see tip, page 282)	1
1 cup	Vegetable Stock (page 248)	250 mL
2 lbs	new potatoes, quartered (about 24 potatoes)	1 kg
1 lb	spinach leaves, trimmed	500 g
¼ tsp	cayenne pepper, dissolved in 2 tbsp (30 mL) freshly squeezed lemon juice	1 mL

1. In a skillet, heat oil over medium heat. Add onions and cook, stirring, until softened, about 3 minutes. Add garlic, ginger, cumin, salt, black pepper and cardamom; cook, stirring, for 1 minute. Add tomatoes and stock; bring to a boil. Transfer to slow cooker stoneware.

2. Add potatoes and stir well. Cover and cook on Low for 8 hours or on High for 4 hours, until potatoes are tender. Discard cardamom pods. Add spinach, in batches, stirring after each addition until all the leaves are submerged in the liquid. Add cayenne pepper solution to slow cooker and stir well. Cover and cook on High for 10 minutes, until spinach is wilted and flavors have melded.

Potato and Spinach Curry

Makes 4 servings

This curry, traditionally known as *aloo palak*, is a tasty way to fill up on spinach.

Nutrients per serving	
Calories	100
Fat	5 g
Carbohydrate	13 g
Fiber	2 g
Protein	2 g
Vitamin B$_6$	0.2 mg
Magnesium	27 mg
Zinc	0.4 mg

1 tbsp	vegetable oil	15 mL
1 cup	sliced tomato	250 mL
½ cup	Basic Gravy (page 224)	125 mL
1 cup	cooked cubed potato (½-inch/1 cm cubes)	250 mL
1 cup	lightly packed finely chopped fresh spinach	250 mL
¼ cup	milk	60 mL
	Salt	

1. In a skillet, heat oil over medium heat. Add tomato and cook, stirring, until starting to soften, about 2 minutes. Add gravy and cook, stirring, for 1 minute.

2. Stir in potato and spinach; bring to a simmer, stirring gently. Add milk and cook, stirring, until potatoes are heated through and sauce is flavorful, about 3 minutes. Season to taste with salt.

Butternut Squash with Snow Peas and Red Pepper

Makes 4 servings

This easy stir-fry can be made in a flash.

Nutrients per serving	
Calories	143
Fat	4 g
Carbohydrate	28 g
Fiber	5 g
Protein	3 g
Vitamin B$_6$	0.4 mg
Magnesium	71 mg
Zinc	0.4 mg

1 tbsp	vegetable oil	15 mL
5 cups	julienned butternut squash	1.25 L
4 oz	snow peas, ends trimmed	125 g
1	red bell pepper, cut into thin strips	1
1 tbsp	packed brown sugar	15 mL
1½ tsp	grated gingerroot	7 mL
	Salt and freshly ground black pepper	

1. In a large nonstick skillet, heat oil over medium-high heat. Cook squash, stirring, for 3 to 4 minutes or until almost tender.

2. Add snow peas, red pepper, brown sugar and ginger. Cook, stirring often, for 2 minutes or until vegetables are tender-crisp. Season to taste with salt and pepper.

Spaghetti Squash

This plump, yellow wintry squash naturally cooks into long, slender strands with a warm color and delicate flavor. Use as you would noodles, lightly seasoning it as a base for robustly flavored stir-fried dishes.

- **Preheat oven to 375°F (190°C)**

1	small spaghetti squash, about 1½ lbs (750 g)	1
¾ cup	water	175 mL
2 tbsp	Asian sesame oil	30 mL
1 tsp	salt (or to taste)	5 mL
¼ cup	chopped fresh cilantro or parsley	60 mL

1. Cut spaghetti squash in half lengthwise and scoop out seeds. Place both pieces in a baking pan, cut side down. Add water to pan around squash.

2. Bake squash in preheated oven, until tender and easily pierced with a fork, 30 to 45 minutes. Remove from oven and carefully turn each half cut side up to cool on a platter.

3. When squash is no longer steaming, scrape the flesh gently with a large fork, pulling the naturally shredded squash out of the two husks. Transfer squash strands to a bowl, and add sesame oil and salt. Toss well. Add cilantro and toss well. Transfer the tumble of seasoned squash strands to a serving bowl. Serve hot or warm.

Nutrients per serving	
Calories	113
Fat	8 g
Carbohydrate	12 g
Fiber	0 g
Protein	1 g
Vitamin B$_6$	0.2 mg
Magnesium	21 mg
Zinc	0.3 mg

Squash with Quinoa and Apricots

Makes 8 servings

Banish the blahs with this robust combination of fruits, vegetables and a nutritious whole grain seasoned with ginger, orange and a hint of cinnamon. In season, accompany with a serving of watercress tossed in a simple vinaigrette.

Tips

If you don't have home-made stock on hand, you can use ready-to-use reduced-sodium vegetable broth in its place. Check the label to make sure ingredients containing gluten have not been added.

If you prefer, you can use 2 cups (500 mL) frozen chopped butternut squash in this recipe.

You'll know your quinoa is cooked when a white line forms around the seeds.

Nutrients per serving

Calories	221
Fat	4 g
Carbohydrate	43 g
Fiber	6 g
Protein	6 g
Vitamin B$_6$	0.3 mg
Magnesium	86 mg
Zinc	1.3 mg

- **Medium to large (3½- to 5-quart) slow cooker**

1 tbsp	vegetable oil	15 mL
2	onions, finely chopped	2
2	cloves garlic, minced	2
1 tbsp	minced gingerroot	15 mL
1 tbsp	ground cumin (see tip, page 266)	15 mL
2 tsp	finely grated orange zest	10 mL
1	2-inch (5 cm) cinnamon stick	1
1 tsp	ground turmeric	5 mL
1 tsp	salt	5 mL
½ tsp	freshly cracked black pepper	2 mL
1 cup	Vegetable Stock (page 248)	250 mL
½ cup	orange juice	125 mL
4 cups	cubed peeled winter squash (1-inch/2.5 cm cubes)	1 L
2	apples, peeled and sliced	2
½ cup	chopped dried apricots	125 mL
1½ cups	quinoa, rinsed	375 mL

1. In a skillet, heat oil over medium heat. Add onions and cook, stirring, until softened, about 3 minutes. Add garlic, ginger, cumin, orange zest, cinnamon stick, turmeric, salt and pepper; cook, stirring, for 1 minute. Add stock and orange juice; bring to a boil. Transfer to slow cooker stoneware.

2. Add squash, apples and apricots to stoneware and stir well. Cover and cook on Low for 6 hours or on High for 3 hours, until vegetables are tender. Discard cinnamon stick.

3. In a pot, bring 3 cups (750 mL) of water to a boil. Add quinoa in a steady stream, stirring to prevent lumps, and return to a boil. Cover, reduce heat to low and simmer for 15 minutes, until tender and liquid is absorbed. Add to slow cooker and stir well. Serve immediately.

Basil and Roasted Pepper Quinoa

Chipotle is the name given to jalapeño peppers that have been smoked and dried. The thick flesh is free of peel and lends a distinctly smoky flavor to dishes. They are most commonly available canned in adobo sauce.

1 cup	chopped red onion	250 mL
2	cloves garlic, finely chopped	2
2 tbsp	olive oil	30 mL
2 cups	drained roasted red bell peppers, coarsely chopped	500 mL
¼ cup	chopped drained canned chipotle peppers	60 mL
2 cups	cooked quinoa	500 mL
1 tbsp	shredded fresh basil or basil pesto	15 mL
1 tbsp	rice vinegar	15 mL
½ tsp	salt	2 mL

1. In a skillet, combine onion, garlic and oil. Gently simmer over medium heat for 7 minutes or until soft. Add roasted peppers, chipotle peppers, quinoa, basil, vinegar and salt. Heat through and serve hot.

Variations

Use a whole roasted garlic head in place of the raw garlic.

Substitute 1 cup (250 mL) chopped fresh red bell peppers for the roasted red bell peppers.

Nutrients per serving	
Calories	219
Fat	9 g
Carbohydrate	30 g
Fiber	5 g
Protein	5 g
Vitamin B$_6$	0.4 mg
Magnesium	73 mg
Zinc	1.3 mg

Fragrant Coconut Rice

This is a deliciously rich rice — perhaps a bit too much for every day, but a wonderful treat now and again. Serve it as an accompaniment to a spicy curry.

Tip

Coconut milk should be suitable for people who are allergic to gluten. However, some brands contain guar gum, which although it does not contain gluten, is not recommended for people with celiac disease. Also it may be processed in a facility where gluten is present. Check the label.

1½ cups	coconut milk (see tip, at left)	375 mL
1 cup	water	250 mL
1	2-inch (5 cm) cinnamon stick	1
1 cup	brown basmati or brown long-grain rice, rinsed and drained	250 mL

1. In a saucepan over medium-high heat, bring coconut milk, water and cinnamon stick to a rapid boil. Stir in rice and return to a boil. Reduce heat to low. Cover and simmer until rice is tender and liquid is absorbed, about 50 minutes. Discard cinnamon stick.

Nutrients per serving	
Calories	339
Fat	19 g
Carbohydrate	39 g
Fiber	2 g
Protein	5 g
Vitamin B6	0.3 mg
Magnesium	106 mg
Zinc	1.4 mg

Chile Rice

This robust rice makes a great accompaniment to a platter of roasted vegetables. Use 2 chiles if you're a heat seeker and 1 if you prefer a tamer result. Either way, this is a winner.

Tip

Unless you have a stove with a true simmer, after reducing the heat to low, place a heat diffuser under the pot to prevent the mixture from boiling. This device also helps to ensure the rice will cook evenly and prevents hot spots, which might cause scorching, from forming. Heat diffusers are available at kitchen supply and hardware stores and are made to work on gas or electric stoves.

1 tbsp	olive oil	15 mL
1	onion, thinly sliced on the vertical	1
2	cloves garlic, minced	2
1 tbsp	minced gingerroot	15 mL
1 to 2	long red or green chile peppers, seeded and minced	1 to 2
2	bay leaves	2
1 tsp	ground cumin	5 mL
	Salt and freshly ground black pepper	
1 cup	brown basmati or brown long-grain rice, rinsed and drained	250 mL
1	can (28 oz/796 mL) no-salt-added diced tomatoes, with juice (see tip, page 282)	1
1 cup	water	250 mL
½ cup	finely chopped fresh parsley	125 mL

1. In a large saucepan with a tight-fitting lid, heat oil over medium-high heat for 30 seconds. Add onion and cook, stirring, until well browned, about 10 minutes. Add garlic, ginger, chile, bay leaves, cumin, and salt and black pepper to taste; cook, stirring, for 1 minute.

2. Add rice and toss until coated. Stir in tomatoes and water. Bring to a boil. Reduce heat to low. Cover and simmer until rice is tender, about 1 hour. Remove from heat and let stand for 5 minutes. Fluff with a fork and garnish with parsley.

Variation

For variety, try adding some red rice to the brown rice when cooking it. Two tablespoons (30 mL) per cup (250 mL) adds a visual and textural spark to the dish.

Nutrients per serving	
Calories	170
Fat	4 g
Carbohydrate	32 g
Fiber	3 g
Protein	4 g
Vitamin B$_6$	0.4 mg
Magnesium	67 mg
Zinc	0.9 mg

Brown Rice

A nutty flavor, robust texture and wholesome benefits make brown rice worth the extra bit of cooking time it requires.

Nutrients per serving	
Calories	188
Fat	3 g
Carbohydrate	36 g
Fiber	2 g
Protein	4 g
Vitamin B$_6$	0.2 mg
Magnesium	68 mg
Zinc	1.0 mg

- **2- to 3-quart (2 to 3 L) saucepan with tight-fitting lid**

2¼ cups	water	550 mL
1 cup	long-grain brown rice	250 mL
2 tsp	butter or olive oil	10 mL
½ tsp	salt	2 mL

1. In a saucepan, combine water, brown rice, butter and salt and stir well. Place over medium-high heat and bring to a rolling boil.

2. Stir well. Reduce heat to maintain a gentle but visible simmer. Cover and cook until rice is tender and cooked through, 30 to 40 minutes. Uncover and stir gently to fluff rice. Serve hot or warm.

Wild Rice

This gorgeous grain makes a delicious companion to stir-fried dishes.

Nutrients per serving	
Calories	214
Fat	1 g
Carbohydrate	45 g
Fiber	4 g
Protein	9 g
Vitamin B$_6$	0.2 mg
Magnesium	109 mg
Zinc	3.6 mg

- **2- to 3-quart (2 to 3 L) saucepan with tight-fitting lid**

4½ cups	water	1.125 L
1½ cups	wild rice	375 mL
1 tsp	salt	5 mL

1. In a saucepan over medium-high heat, combine water, wild rice and salt. Bring to a rolling boil and stir well.

2. Reduce heat to maintain a gentle boil, cover and cook until rice is plump, cracked open and tender, about 45 minutes. Remove from heat and let stand, covered, for 10 minutes. Uncover and stir well. Serve hot or warm.

Variation
You could add butter or olive oil to the rice after removing it from the stove. Or stir in finely chopped fresh herbs, such as cilantro or Italian parsley.

Indonesian-Style Yellow Rice Pilaf

Makes 4 servings

This traditional rice dish, known in Indonesia as *nasi kuning*, provides a lovely and delicious centerpiece for a stir-fry meal. Its flavor and color are unique, but it is quite simple to make.

Tips

To prepare lemongrass, trim the end to make a smooth base, and trim tops, leaving a 6-inch (15 cm) stalk. Quarter it lengthwise.

A 2-quart (2 L) or 3-quart (3 L) saucepan with a tight-fitting lid is perfect for cooking rice. The rice needs plenty of room since it triples in volume in the course of cooking. If your pan is too small, rice will probably boil over. The tight-fitting lid captures the steam, cooking the rice to tender perfection after its initial boiling stage.

Nutrients per serving	
Calories	259
Fat	10 g
Carbohydrate	39 g
Fiber	1 g
Protein	4 g
Vitamin B$_6$	0.2 mg
Magnesium	34 mg
Zinc	0.7 mg

- **2- to 3-quart (2 to 3 L) saucepan with tight-fitting lid**

1 cup	long-grain parboiled white rice	250 mL
¾ cup	unsweetened coconut milk	175 mL
¾ cup	water	175 mL
3	slices gingerroot	3
½ tsp	salt (or to taste)	2 mL
½ tsp	ground turmeric or curry powder	2 mL
1	stalk fresh lemongrass, trimmed and quartered (optional)	1

1. Place rice in a saucepan and add water to cover by about 3 inches (7.5 cm). Stir rice with your hand to rinse thoroughly and then drain well.

2. Add coconut milk, water, ginger, salt and turmeric. Stir well. Add lemongrass pieces to pan. Bring rice mixture to a rolling boil over high heat, stirring well. Reduce heat to maintain a gentle boil and cook, covered, for 20 minutes. Remove from heat and let stand, covered, for 10 minutes.

3. Uncover and stir gently to fluff rice. Discard ginger and lemongrass. Serve hot or warm.

Sweet Potato Wild Rice Cakes

These cakes are so delicious they become the focus of the meal.

Tips

Stainless steel baking rings are available at restaurant supply and kitchen specialty stores. Rings with a minimum 1-inch (2.5 cm) depth are the most popular. Handles are not easy to work with because they prevent the ring (and the food in it) from being flipped to brown the other side.

If you don't have homemade stock on hand, you can use ready-to-use reduced-sodium vegetable broth in its place. Check the label to make sure ingredients containing gluten have not been added.

The sticky rice should be moist and very sticky.

Nutrients per cake	
Calories	142
Fat	7 g
Carbohydrate	18 g
Fiber	2 g
Protein	2 g
Vitamin B$_6$	0.1 mg
Magnesium	27 mg
Zinc	0.7 mg

- **Eight 4-inch (10 cm) baking rings, lightly oiled (see tip, at left)**

1⅓ cups	Vegetable Stock (page 248) or water	325 mL
⅓ cup	wild rice	75 mL
⅓ cup	sticky rice	75 mL
1	medium-large sweet potato, peeled and cut into large chunks	1
1 cup	shredded rutabaga or carrot	250 mL
2	sprigs fresh thyme	2
1	sprig fresh rosemary	1
3 tbsp	olive oil, divided	45 mL
1 tbsp	toasted sesame oil	15 mL
	Sea salt and freshly ground black pepper	

1. In a saucepan over high heat, bring stock to a boil. Add wild rice, stir and cover. Reduce heat to low and cook for 10 minutes. Quickly stir in sticky rice. Cover and cook for 30 minutes. Remove from heat and fluff with a fork. Cover and set aside.

2. Meanwhile, in a steamer basket set over a pot of boiling water, steam sweet potato, covered, for 15 to 20 minutes, until tender. Let cool. Coarsely chop and place in a large bowl. Add rutabaga, thyme, rosemary and 1 tbsp (15 mL) olive oil. Add rice and stir gently to combine. Drizzle with sesame oil and season to taste with salt and pepper. Stir well.

3. In one large or two medium skillets, heat the remaining olive oil over medium heat. Arrange metal rings in skillet and reduce heat to low. Press sweet potato-rice mixture into rings and cook for 5 minutes. Flip cakes and cook for 5 minutes. Flip and cook for about 5 minutes on each side one more time or until cakes are lightly browned on both sides and cooked through.

Wild Rice Stuffing with Cranberries

This stuffing is different enough to satisfy any needs for something exotic, yet traditionally North American in terms of its ingredients. Use it to stuff baked squash or bell peppers.

2 cups	cooked wild rice, cooled	500 mL
1 cup	dry gluten-free bread crumbs	250 mL
6	green onions, white part only, finely chopped	6
2	stalks celery, diced	2
½ cup	dried cranberries	125 mL
½ cup	toasted chopped pecans (see tip, below)	125 mL
1	jalapeño pepper, seeded and minced (optional)	1
1 tbsp	fresh thyme leaves (or 1 tsp/5 mL dried)	15 mL
1 tbsp	grated orange zest	15 mL
½ cup	freshly squeezed orange juice	125 mL
2 tbsp	melted butter or extra virgin olive oil	30 mL
	Salt and freshly ground black pepper	

1. In a bowl, combine wild rice, bread crumbs, green onions, celery, cranberries, pecans, jalapeño (if using), thyme and orange zest. Mix well. Add orange juice and butter, stirring well. Season to taste with salt and pepper.

Tips

Look for gluten-free bread crumbs in well-stocked supermarkets. Natural foods stores will stock whole-grain versions.

To toast pecans, preheat oven to 350°F (180°C). Place chopped nuts on a baking sheet and bake, stirring occasionally, until fragrant, about 10 minutes.

If you prefer, rather than using this to stuff squash or peppers, bake it in a greased covered baking dish at 350°F (180°C) for 1 hour.

Nutrients per ½ cup (125 mL)	
Calories	123
Fat	6 g
Carbohydrate	17 g
Fiber	2 g
Protein	2 g
Vitamin B$_6$	0.1 mg
Magnesium	17 mg
Zinc	0.6 mg

Desserts

Chocolate, Lime and Coconut Cake. 310

Make Your Own Cupcake Mix 312

No-Bake Chocolate Quinoa Cookies 313

Gingerbread Amaranth Cookies 314

Maple Cinnamon Cookies 315

Summer Fruit Compote. 316

Seasonal Fruit Parfaits. 317

Black Sticky Rice Pudding 318

Chocolate Teff Pudding. 319

Coconut Milk Ice Cream 320

Coco-Cocoa Chia Gelato. . . . , ... 321

Lemon-Lime Sorbet. 322

Polka-Dot Mango Ice Pops 323

Vanilla Raspberry Ice Cream 324

Chocolate, Lime and Coconut Cake

Makes 8 servings

Easy to make, grand to eat and (yes, really!) good for you, too, this is a recipe you will make again and again.

Storage Tip

Store the cooled, unfrosted cake, loosely wrapped in foil or waxed paper, at room temperature for up to 3 days or in the refrigerator for up to 1 week. Alternatively, wrap the unfrosted cake in plastic wrap, then foil, completely enclosing it, and freeze for up to 6 months. Let thaw at room temperature for 4 to 6 hours before serving.

Nutrients per serving	
Calories	315
Fat	19 g
Carbohydrate	36 g
Fiber	3 g
Protein	4 g
Vitamin B$_6$	0.2 mg
Magnesium	75 mg
Zinc	0.9 mg

- **Preheat oven to 350°F (180°C)**
- **8-inch (20 cm) square metal baking pan, greased**

1 cup	amaranth flour	250 mL
½ cup	unsweetened natural cocoa powder	125 mL
¼ cup	potato starch	60 mL
1 tbsp	ground flax seeds (flaxseed meal)	15 mL
¾ tsp	baking soda	3 mL
½ tsp	fine sea salt	2 mL
¾ cup	fine crystal cane sugar	175 mL
½ cup	well-stirred coconut milk (full-fat)	125 mL
½ cup	melted virgin coconut oil	125 mL
½ cup	water	125 mL
1 tbsp	finely grated lime zest	15 mL
1 tbsp	freshly squeezed lime juice	15 mL

Suggested Topping

Whipped Coconut Cream
(see recipe, opposite)

1. In a large bowl, whisk together amaranth flour, cocoa powder, potato starch, flax seeds, baking soda and salt.

2. In a medium bowl, whisk sugar, coconut milk, coconut oil, water, lime zest and lime juice until blended.

3. Add the coconut milk mixture to the flour mixture and stir until just blended.

4. Spread batter evenly in prepared pan.

5. Bake in preheated oven for 27 to 32 minutes or until a tester inserted in the center comes out with moist crumbs attached. Let cool completely in pan on a wire rack.

6. If desired, spread coconut cream over cooled cake, or serve it alongside.

Whipped Coconut Cream

This lush, snow-white whip is likely to become your new favorite dessert topping. It also makes a great instant frosting for cakes and cupcakes.

Storage Tip

Store any unused whipped coconut cream in an airtight container in the refrigerator for up to 2 weeks. Rewhip with an electric mixer before using.

- **Electric mixer**

1	can (14 oz/400 mL) coconut milk (full-fat)	1

1. Place the can of coconut milk in the refrigerator. Refrigerate for at least 24 hours.

2. Just before whipping the coconut cream, place a medium bowl (preferably metal) and the beaters from the electric mixer in the freezer for 5 minutes.

3. Remove can from refrigerator and flip upside down. Open can and pour off liquid (store liquid in an airtight container in the refrigerator for another use). Scoop thick coconut cream into chilled bowl.

4. Whip the coconut cream with the electric mixer on high until soft peaks form. Use immediately.

Variations

Whipped Lemon Coconut Cream: Add 2 tsp (10 mL) coconut sugar, 1½ tsp (7 mL) finely grated lemon zest and 1 tbsp (15 mL) freshly squeezed lemon juice near the end of whipping in step 4.

Whipped Vanilla Coconut Cream: Add 2 tsp (10 mL) coconut sugar and 1 tsp (5 mL) vanilla extract near the end of whipping in step 4.

Whipped Maple Coconut Cream: Add 1 tbsp (15 mL) pure maple syrup near the end of whipping in step 4.

Tips

Some brands of coconut milk now add emulsifiers to their products to prevent separation of the coconut fats and liquid. Making whipped coconut cream is not possible with these brands because the cream will not solidify properly when chilled. Be sure to check the ingredients on the coconut milk label; if emulsifiers are included on the list, opt for a different brand.

Flipping the can upside down places the solidified cream at the bottom and the milky coconut water on top; this makes it easier to pour off the liquid and scoop out the cream.

Nutrients per 1 tbsp (15 mL)	
Calories	65
Fat	7 g
Carbohydrate	1 g
Fiber	0 g
Protein	1 g
Vitamin B$_6$	0 mg
Magnesium	15 mg
Zinc	0.2 mg

Make Your Own Cupcake Mix

<table>
<tr><td>Makes about
4½ cups
(1.125 L), enough
for 18 cupcakes</td></tr>
</table>

Makes about 4½ cups (1.125 L), enough for 18 cupcakes

This easy mix is the basis for many different cupcakes.

Tips

Stir the mix before spooning very lightly into the dry measures in step 2. Do not pack.

Be sure to divide the mix into 3 equal portions. Depending on how much air you incorporate into the mix and the texture of the individual gluten-free flours, the total volume of the mix can vary slightly.

1¼ cups	sorghum flour	300 mL
⅔ cup	amaranth flour	150 mL
⅔ cup	brown rice flour	150 mL
¼ cup	quinoa flour	60 mL
2 tbsp	potato starch	30 mL
2 tbsp	tapioca starch	30 mL
1⅓ cups	granulated sugar	325 mL
1 tbsp	gluten-free baking powder	15 mL
1½ tsp	baking soda	7 mL
¾ tsp	xanthan gum	3 mL
¾ tsp	salt	3 mL

1. In a large bowl, combine sorghum flour, amaranth flour, brown rice flour, quinoa flour, potato starch, tapioca starch, sugar, baking powder, baking soda, xanthan gum and salt. Mix well.

2. Immediately divide into 3 equal portions of about 1½ cups (375 mL) each. Seal tightly in plastic bags, removing as much air as possible. Store at room temperature for up to 3 days or in the freezer for up to 3 months. Let warm to room temperature and mix well before using.

Nutrients per ¼ cup (60 mL)

Calories	141
Fat	1 g
Carbohydrate	33 g
Fiber	2 g
Protein	2 g
Vitamin B$_6$	0.1 mg
Magnesium	37 mg
Zinc	0.3 mg

No-Bake Chocolate Quinoa Cookies

Makes 24 cookies

Chocolate no-bake cookies are made brand-new with the help of an ancient grain. Good luck eating just one!

Storage Tip

Store the cookies in an airtight container, separating layers between sheets of parchment paper, in the refrigerator for up to 1 week or in the freezer for up to 3 months.

- **Large rimmed baking sheet, lined with parchment paper**

¼ cup	unsweetened natural cocoa powder	60 mL
½ cup	pure maple syrup, liquid honey or brown rice syrup	125 mL
¼ cup	warmed virgin coconut oil	60 mL
½ tsp	fine sea salt	2 mL
½ cup	unsweetened creamy nut or seed butter	125 mL
1 tsp	gluten-free vanilla extract	5 mL
3 cups	cooked quinoa, cooled	750 mL

1. In a large saucepan, combine cocoa, maple syrup and coconut oil. Melt over medium heat, whisking until blended and smooth. Bring to a boil and let boil for 1 minute. Remove from heat and stir in salt, nut butter and vanilla until blended and smooth. Stir in quinoa until combined.

2. Drop mixture by small scoopfuls onto prepared baking sheet. Refrigerate for 2 to 3 hours or until firm and set.

Nutrients per cookie	
Calories	101
Fat	6 g
Carbohydrate	11 g
Fiber	1 g
Protein	2 g
Vitamin B$_6$	0 mg
Magnesium	31 mg
Zinc	0.5 mg

Gingerbread Amaranth Cookies

Makes 24 cookies

Tender and spicy, these homey cookies are everything you want a cookie with "gingerbread" in the title to be.

Tip

An equal amount of quinoa flour can be used in place of the amaranth flour, and cooked quinoa, cooled, can be used in place of the amaranth.

Storage Tip

Store the cooled cookies in an airtight container at room temperature for up to 3 days or in the freezer for up to 3 months.

- **Preheat oven to 350°F (180°C)**
- **Large baking sheets, lined with parchment paper**

1 cup	amaranth flour	250 mL
1/2 cup	ground flax seeds (flaxseed meal)	125 mL
2 1/2 tsp	ground ginger	12 mL
1 tsp	ground cinnamon	5 mL
1/2 tsp	baking soda	2 mL
1/4 tsp	ground nutmeg	1 mL
1/4 tsp	ground cloves	1 mL
1/4 tsp	fine sea salt	1 mL
1/4 cup	fine crystal cane sugar	60 mL
1/4 cup	dark (cooking) molasses	60 mL
1/4 cup	unsweetened applesauce	60 mL
3 tbsp	olive oil	45 mL
1 tsp	gluten-free vanilla extract	5 mL
2 cups	cooked amaranth, cooled	500 mL

1. In a large bowl, whisk together amaranth flour, flax seeds, ginger, cinnamon, baking soda, nutmeg, cloves and salt. Stir in sugar, molasses, applesauce, oil and vanilla until just blended. Stir in amaranth until blended.

2. Drop dough by tablespoonfuls (15 mL) onto prepared baking sheets, spacing cookies 2 inches (5 cm) apart. Flatten slightly with your fingertips.

3. Bake, one sheet at a time, in preheated oven for 16 to 21 minutes or until just set at the center. Let cool on pan on a wire rack for 10 minutes, then transfer to the rack to cool completely.

Nutrients per cookie	
Calories	87
Fat	3 g
Carbohydrate	13 g
Fiber	2 g
Protein	2 g
Vitamin B6	0.1 mg
Magnesium	51 mg
Zinc	0.5 mg

Maple Cinnamon Cookies

These aromatic cookies may bring to mind winter holidays, but they are worth baking — and eating — throughout the year.

Storage Tip

Store the cooled cookies in an airtight container in the refrigerator for up to 5 days.

- **Preheat oven to 350°F (180°C)**
- **Large baking sheet, lined with parchment paper**

2 cups	quinoa flakes	500 mL
1 cup	quinoa flour	250 mL
1½ tsp	ground cinnamon	7 mL
¼ tsp	fine sea salt	1 mL
¼ tsp	baking soda	1 mL
½ cup	vegetable oil	125 mL
½ cup	pure maple syrup	125 mL
2 tsp	gluten-free vanilla extract	10 mL

1. In a large bowl, whisk together quinoa flakes, quinoa flour, cinnamon, salt and baking soda. Stir in oil, maple syrup and vanilla until just blended.

2. Drop dough by tablespoonfuls (15 mL) onto prepared baking sheet, spacing them 2 inches (5 cm) apart. Flatten slightly with your fingertips.

3. Bake in preheated oven for 12 to 15 minutes or until just set at the center. Let cool on pan on a wire rack for 5 minutes, then transfer to the rack to cool.

4. Repeat steps 2 and 3 with the remaining dough.

Variation

Honey Cardamom Cookies: Replace the maple syrup with liquid honey and replace the cinnamon with 1 tsp (5 mL) ground cardamom.

Nutrients per cookie	
Calories	95
Fat	4 g
Carbohydrate	12 g
Fiber	1 g
Protein	2 g
Vitamin B$_6$	0 mg
Magnesium	23 mg
Zinc	0.4 mg

Summer Fruit Compote

With its blend of fresh summer fruits, vanilla and lime juice, this is no ordinary light dessert.

Tips

To get extra duty from vanilla beans, lightly rinse and air-dry them, then add the split pieces to a jar of sugar to make vanilla sugar. The split bean can stay indefinitely in the sugar jar, as you use and replenish your supply.

Add the firmest fruit, such as apples, peaches and pears, to the hot syrup first, then continue in order of the fruit's texture, ending with the most fragile fruits, such as raspberries or pieces of melon. Mix carefully so that the tender fruit doesn't break or bruise.

3½ cups	water	875 mL
1 cup	granulated natural cane sugar	250 mL
1	vanilla bean, split lengthwise (or 2 tsp/10 mL gluten-free vanilla extract)	1
4	2- by ½-inch (5 by 1 cm) strips lime zest	4
2 cups	diced peeled pitted peaches, nectarines or apricots	500 mL
1 cup	diced pitted plums (about 2)	250 mL
1 cup	fresh cherries, pitted and halved	250 mL
2 cups	fresh berries (see tip, at left)	500 mL
2 cups	cantaloupe or honeydew melon balls (1-inch/2.5 cm balls)	500 mL
⅓ cup	freshly squeezed lime juice (about 3 limes)	75 mL

1. In a large pot, bring water and sugar to a boil over high heat, stirring until sugar is dissolved. Add vanilla bean and lime zest. Remove from heat, cover and let stand for 6 to 8 minutes or until fragrant.

2. Add peaches, plums, cherries, berries, then melon to syrup and stir to combine. Add lime juice and mix well. Let stand at room temperature for at least 3 hours to develop full flavor. Transfer to an airtight container and refrigerate for up to 3 days. Remove vanilla bean and lime zest before serving.

Variation

Use lemons or oranges instead of limes.

Nutrients per serving (1 of 10)	
Calories	141
Fat	0 g
Carbohydrate	34 g
Fiber	2 g
Protein	1 g
Vitamin B$_6$	0.1 mg
Magnesium	15 mg
Zinc	0.2 mg

Seasonal Fruit Parfaits

Sweet but not cloying, filling but not heavy, fresh with a bit of crunch and distinctive tropical vibe, these ever-so-simple parfaits can be assembled the night before.

Tips

An equal amount of well-stirred coconut milk (full-fat) can be used in place of the coconut yogurt. If desired, whisk 1 tbsp (15 mL) freshly squeezed lemon or lime juice into the coconut milk first, to give it some tang.

You can also assemble these parfaits in small mason jars, for a portable breakfast extraordinaire.

- **2 parfait glasses**

½ cup	assorted raw seeds (green pumpkin, sunflower seeds, hemp hearts, sesame seeds), toasted	125 mL
½ cup	unsweetened flaked or shredded coconut, toasted	125 mL
1 cup	plain regular or Greek-style coconut yogurt	250 mL
3 tbsp	coconut nectar or coconut sugar	45 mL
1½ cups	assorted diced seasonal fruit and/or berries	375 mL

1. In a small bowl, combine seeds and coconut.

2. Spoon half the coconut yogurt into each parfait glass. Drizzle 1 tbsp (15 mL) coconut nectar into each glass. Top each with half the seed mixture and half the fruit. Drizzle with the remaining nectar.

Nutrients per serving	
Calories	448
Fat	24 g
Carbohydrate	50 g
Fiber	8 g
Protein	16 g
Vitamin B$_6$	0.3 mg
Magnesium	202 mg
Zinc	3.9 mg

Black Sticky Rice Pudding

Makes 6 servings

Although this black sticky rice pudding is high in saturated fat, it comes from the coconut milk, which may have healthful benefits.

Tips

Thai black sticky rice is available in Asian markets.

If you prefer, cook the rice in your rice cooker on the brown rice setting.

1½ cups	water	375 mL
¾ cup	cooked Thai black sticky rice (see tip, at left)	175 mL
1	can (14 oz/400 mL) coconut milk	1
½ cup	packed demerara or other raw cane sugar	125 mL
½ tsp	salt	2 mL
1 cup	sliced strawberries or kiwifruit or chopped peaches or mango	250 mL
¼ cup	toasted shredded sweetened coconut	60 mL
	Finely chopped mint (optional)	

1. In a bowl, combine water and rice. Set aside to soak for at least 4 hours or overnight. When you're ready to cook, transfer rice and soaking water to a heavy pot with a tight-fitting lid. Bring to a rapid boil over medium heat. Reduce heat to low and simmer until rice is tender, 30 to 45 minutes. (Don't lift the lid.)

2. In a saucepan, combine coconut milk, demerara sugar and salt. Bring to a boil over medium heat and cook, stirring, until sugar dissolves. Stir in cooked rice and cook, stirring, until thickened, about 10 minutes. Transfer to a serving bowl and chill, if desired.

3. When you're ready to serve, top with fruit and garnish with coconut and mint (if using).

Nutrients per serving	
Calories	256
Fat	16 g
Carbohydrate	29 g
Fiber	1 g
Protein	2 g
Vitamin B6	0 mg
Magnesium	37 mg
Zinc	0.5 mg

Chocolate Teff Pudding

Not only does this chocolate pudding trump any and all store-bought varieties, but it is also rich in antioxidants and other nutrients. Go ahead, have seconds.

Storage Tip

Store leftover pudding in an airtight container in the refrigerator for up to 2 days.

* **Blender**

½ cup	teff	125 mL
¼ cup	unsweetened natural cocoa powder	60 mL
¼ cup	fine crystal cane sugar	60 mL
⅛ tsp	fine sea salt	0.5 mL
1⅓ cups	water	325 mL
1 cup	well-stirred coconut milk (full-fat)	250 mL
1 tsp	gluten-free vanilla extract	15 mL

1. In a medium saucepan, whisk together teff, cocoa powder, sugar, salt, water and coconut milk. Bring to a gentle boil over medium heat. Reduce heat to medium-low, cover, leaving lid ajar, and simmer, stirring occasionally, for 15 to 20 minutes or until teff is very soft and mixture is thickened. Remove from heat and stir in vanilla.

2. Transfer teff mixture to a medium heatproof bowl and let cool to room temperature.

3. Transfer cooled mixture to blender and blend until smooth.

4. Divide mixture among four ramekins or dessert cups. Cover loosely and refrigerate until cold.

Nutrients per serving	
Calories	271
Fat	13 g
Carbohydrate	34 g
Fiber	3 g
Protein	5 g
Vitamin B6	0.1 mg
Magnesium	71 mg
Zinc	1.2 mg

Coconut Milk Ice Cream

Makes 4 servings

This is a simple and delicious recipe that everyone will love.

- **Ice cream maker**

2	cans (each 14 oz/400 mL) unsweetened coconut milk	2
½ cup	granulated sugar	125 mL
½ cup	dairy-free, gluten-free semi-sweet chocolate chips	125 mL

1. In a saucepan, whisk together coconut milk and sugar. Heat over medium-low heat, stirring constantly to dissolve the sugar.

2. Transfer to a bowl, cover and refrigerate for at least 15 minutes or until chilled.

3. Pour into ice cream maker and freeze according to manufacturer's directions. Add chocolate chips in the last 2 minutes.

4. Transfer to a chilled freezer-safe container, cover and freeze until firm. Store in the freezer for up to 2 weeks.

Nutrients per serving	
Calories	589
Fat	49 g
Carbohydrate	44 g
Fiber	1 g
Protein	5 g
Vitamin B$_6$	0.1 mg
Magnesium	115 mg
Zinc	1.5 mg

Coco-Cocoa Chia Gelato

Makes 6 servings

This is a sublime chocolate ice cream–like frozen dessert. The processed chia seeds help thicken the ice cream, resulting in a particularly rich, velvety texture.

- Blender
- Ice cream maker

½ cup	unsweetened natural cocoa powder	125 mL
⅓ cup	packed pitted soft dates	75 mL
¼ cup	chia seeds	60 mL
1	can (14 oz/400 mL) coconut milk (full-fat)	1
¼ cup	pure maple syrup or liquid honey	60 mL
1 tsp	gluten-free vanilla extract	5 mL

1. In blender, combine cocoa powder, dates, chia seeds, coconut milk, maple syrup and vanilla; process until smooth. Cover and refrigerate for at least 4 hours or until cold.

2. Pour into ice cream maker and freeze according to manufacturer's instructions.

3. Spoon into an airtight container, cover and freeze for 4 hours, until firm, or for up to 3 days.

Nutrients per serving	
Calories	251
Fat	17 g
Carbohydrate	24 g
Fiber	5 g
Protein	4 g
Vitamin B$_6$	0 mg
Magnesium	37 mg
Zinc	0.8 mg

Lemon-Lime Sorbet

**Makes
12 servings**

This very citrusy sorbet
is a great-tasting,
low-fat alternative to
ice cream.

- Ice cream maker

4 cups	lime-flavored club soda, divided	1 L
1 cup	granulated sugar	250 mL
1 cup	Key lime preserves (without peel)	250 mL
	Juice of 2 lemons	
	Juice of 2 limes	

1. In a medium saucepan over low heat, stir together
   1 cup (250 mL) club soda, sugar and preserves until
   sugar has dissolved and preserves have melted. Stir in
   lemon juice, lime juice and the remaining soda. Pour
   into an airtight container and seal. Refrigerate for 2 to
   3 hours or until thoroughly chilled.

2. Transfer to ice cream maker and process according to
   the manufacturer's instructions until mixture is the
   consistency of firm slush. Return to airtight container,
   seal and freeze for 1 hour or until mixture resembles
   sorbet.

Nutrients per serving	
Calories	139
Fat	0 g
Carbohydrate	35 g
Fiber	0 g
Protein	0 g
Vitamin B$_6$	0 mg
Magnesium	2 mg
Zinc	0.1 mg

Polka-Dot Mango Ice Pops

These ice pops are a serious ode to summer fruit.

Tips

Taste the mango before blending; depending on its sweetness, you may not need to add any sugar.

You can use 4-oz (125 mL) paper cups as ice-pop molds. Place them on a baking sheet, then fill until almost full. Cover with foil, then make a small slit to insert ice-pop sticks or small bamboo skewers and freeze as directed.

- Blender
- 8-serving ice-pop mold

3½ cups	fresh or frozen mango chunks	875 mL
2 tbsp	fine crystal cane sugar (see tip, at left)	30 mL
2 tbsp	chia seeds	30 mL

1. In blender, purée mango and sugar until smooth.

2. Transfer mango purée to a bowl and let stand for 5 minutes to allow sugar to dissolve. Stir in chia seeds.

3. Pour purée into ice-pop molds, insert sticks and freeze for 4 to 6 hours, until solid, or for up to 3 days. If necessary, briefly dip bases of mold in hot water to loosen and unmold.

Nutrients per pop

Calories	68
Fat	1 g
Carbohydrate	15 g
Fiber	2 g
Protein	1 g
Vitamin B$_6$	0.1 mg
Magnesium	7 mg
Zinc	0.2 mg

Vanilla Raspberry Ice Cream

This simple and tasty dessert can be whipped up in a flash. If you don't have time to freeze it, serve it as a dessert smoothie (see variation).

Tips

Substitute vanilla-flavored coconut ice cream or vanilla rice milk frozen dessert for the soy milk frozen dessert.

Transfer the blended mixture to a single container and use a scoop to serve, if desired. Increase the freezing time.

- Blender
- Four 6-oz (175 mL) ramekins

2 cups	softened organic vanilla soy milk frozen dessert	500 mL
1 cup	raspberries (fresh or thawed frozen)	250 mL

1. In blender, on high speed, blend frozen dessert and raspberries until thoroughly combined.
2. Transfer to ramekins, dividing equally. Cover tightly with plastic wrap and freeze until firm, about 1 hour.

Variation

Vanilla Raspberry Dessert Smoothie: If you don't have time to freeze the raspberry mixture, scoop it into glasses, add a straw and serve as a dessert smoothie.

Nutrients per serving	
Calories	136
Fat	3 g
Carbohydrate	26 g
Fiber	5 g
Protein	2 g
Vitamin B$_6$	1.4 mg
Magnesium	25 mg
Zinc	0.3 mg

Library and Archives Canada Cataloguing in Publication

Barnes, Karen, 1968-, author
The complete 10-day detox : diet plan & cookbook / Karen Barnes, MSc, ND.

Includes index.
ISBN 978-0-7788-0536-6 (paperback)

1. Detoxification (Health). 2. Natural foods. 3. Cooking (Natural foods). 4. Cookbooks.
I. Title. II. Title: Complete ten-day detox.

RA784.5.B37 2016   641.5'63   C2016-901992-6

Contributing Authors

Alexandra Anca with Theresa Santandrea-Cull
Complete Gluten-Free Diet & Nutrition Guide
A recipe from this book is found on page 240.

Byron Ayanoglu and Jennifer MacKenzie
Complete Curry Cookbook
Recipes from this book are found on pages 224, 272–73, 275, 276, 283, 289 and 299 (top).

Karen Barnes
Recipes by this author, developed for this book, are found on pages 170, 174, 184 (top and bottom), 226, 229, 230 (top and bottom), 232 (top and bottom), 241 (top), 245 (top), 249, 251, 253, 269, 270, 282 and 320.

Johanna Burkhard
500 Best Comfort Food Recipes
A recipe from this book is found on page 299 (bottom).

Pat Crocker
The Vegan Cook's Bible
Recipes from this book are found on pages 183 (bottom), 198, 216, 220, 225, 246, 286, 292 (top), 296 and 307.

Pat Crocker
The Vegetarian Cook's Bible
Recipes from this book are found on pages 217, 231, 233, 238–39, 245 (bottom), 255, 257, 279, 295 and 302.

Maxine Effenson-Chuck and Beth Gurney
125 Best Vegan Recipes
Recipes from this book are found on pages 254, 256, 261, 277, 294 and 316.

Judith Finlayson
A recipe by this author, developed for this book, is found on page 324.

Judith Finlayson, ed.
250 Best Beans, Lentils and Tofu Recipes
Recipes from this book are found on pages 215, 236, 252, 263 and 264.

Judith Finlayson
The Complete Gluten-Free Whole Grains Cookbook
Recipes from this book are found on pages 163, 165, 234, 258, 259, 271, 303, 304, 308 and 318.

Judith Finlayson
The Vegetarian Slow Cooker
Recipes from this book are found on pages 213, 250, 266–68, 280, 281, 298 and 301.

George Geary
350 Best Salads & Dressings
A recipe from this book is found on page 218.

Nancie McDermott
300 Best Stir-Fry Recipes
Recipes from this book are found on pages 292 (bottom), 300 and 305–6.

Douglas McNish
Eat Raw, Eat Well
Recipes from this book are found on
pages 178–82, 183 (top), 202, 212 and 223.

Douglas McNish
Raw, Quick & Delicious!
Recipes from this book are found on
pages 164, 206–9, 210, 241 (bottom),
242–44 and 293.

**Dr. Maitreyi Raman, Angela Sirounis
& Jennifer Shrubsole**
The Complete IBS Health & Diet Guide
A recipe from this book is found on
page 322.

Deb Roussou
350 Best Vegan Recipes
Recipes from this book are found on
pages 219, 222, 228, 237 and 288.

Camilla V. Saulsbury
500 Best Quinoa Recipes
Recipes from this book are found on
pages 203–5, 214, 221, 235, 260, 262, 274
and 315.

Camilla V. Saulsbury
Bob's Red Mill Everyday Gluten-Free Cookbook
Recipes from this book are found on
pages 162, 166, 199, 200, 310–11, 313,
314, 319, 321 and 323.

Camilla V. Saulsbury
Complete Coconut Cookbook
Recipes from this book are found on
pages 167–69, 171–73, 175, 176, 191, 192
and 317.

Camilla V. Saulsbury
The Total Food Allergy Health and Diet Guide
Recipes by this author from this book are
found on pages 193–96.

Carla Snyder and Meredith Deeds
300 Sensational Soups
A recipe from this book is found on
page 248.

Suneeta Vaswani
Easy Indian Cooking, Second Edition
Recipes from this book are found on
pages 278, 284–85, 290–91 and 297.

Donna Washburn & Heather Butt
The Gluten-Free Baking Book
Recipes from this book are found on
pages 186–90, 201 and 312.

References

Agency for Toxic Substances & Disease Registry. Arsenic toxicity. What is the biologic fate of arsenic in the body? Oct 1, 2009. Accessed Jan 4, 2016. Available at www.atsdr.cdc.gov/csem/csem.asp?csem=1&po=9.

Agency for Toxic Substances & Disease Registry. Lead toxicity. What is the biological fate of lead? Aug 20, 2007. Accessed Jan 4, 2015. Available at www.atsdr.cdc.gov/csem/csem.asp?csem=7&po=9.

Alavanja, MC. Introduction: pesticides use and exposure extensive worldwide. *Rev Environ Health*. 2009 Oct–Dec; 24 (4): 303–9.

Alexander J, Kowdley KV. HFE-associated hereditary hemochromatosis. *Genet Med*. 2009 May; 11 (5): 307–13.

Alternative Daily. Detoxify your liver with artichokes. Accessed Oct 7, 2015. Available at www.thealternativedaily.com/cleanse-liver-artichokes.

American Academy of Allergy Asthma & Immunology. Oral allergy syndrome (OAS): Available at www.aaaai.org/conditions-and-treatments/library/allergy-library/outdoor-allergies-and-food-allergies-can-be-relate.aspx.

American Academy of Dermatology. Sunscreen FAQs. 2015. Accessed Dec 2, 2015. Available at www.aad.org/media-resources/stats-and-facts/prevention-and-care/sunscreen-faqs.

American Diabetes Association. What foods have gluten? March 11, 2014. Accessed March 25, 2016. Available at www.diabetes.org/food-and-fitness/food/planning-meals/gluten-free-diets/what-foods-have-gluten.html.

Anderson, DW. Effect of DDT on wildlife. *Epidemiology*. 2005 Sept; 16 (5): S163–4.

Antunes P, Gil O. PCB and DDT contamination in cultivated and wild sea bass from Ria de Aveiro, Portugal. *Chemosphere*. 2004 Mar; 54 (10): 1503–7.

Ascherio A, Willett W, Rimm EB, et al. Dietary iron intake and risk of coronary disease among men. *Circulation*. 1994 Mar; 89 (3): 969–74.

Ask a Naturopath. Does eating garlic kill off the good bacteria in the gut? *Ask a Naturopath*. Mar 15, 2002. Accessed Sept 2015. Available at www.askanaturopath.com/faqs/garlic/p/324.

Australian Government Department of the Environment. Bromonated flame retardants. Accessed Nov 17. 2015. Available at www.environment.gov.au/protection/chemicals-management/brominated-flame-retardants.

Axe, J. 75% of sunscreens are toxic: what to do instead. *Dr. Axe Food Is Medicine*. 2014. Accessed Nov 2015. Available at draxe.com/75-of-sunscreens-are-toxic-what-to-do-instead.

Aydinlar EI, Dikmen PY, Tiftikci A, et al. IgG-based elimination diet in migraine plus irritable bowel syndrome. *Headache*. 2013 Mar; 53 (3): 514–25.

Baad-Hansen L, Cairns B, Ernberg M, et al. Effect of systemic monosodium glutamate (MSG) on headache and pericranial muscle sensitivity. *Cephalalgia*. 2010 Jan; 30 (1): 68–76.

Bacon BR, Britton RS. Hepatic injury in chronic iron overload. Role of lipid peroxidation. *Chem Biol Interact*. 1989; 70 (3–4): 183–226.

Balamtekin N, Uslu N, Baysoy G, et al. The presentation of celiac disease in 220 Turkish children. *Turk J Pediatr*. 2010 May–Jun; 52 (3): 239–44.

Ballmer-Weber BK. Cutaneous symptoms after ingestion of pollen-associated foodstuffs. [Article in German.] *Hautarzt*. 2006 Feb; 57 (2): 108–15.

Bellisle F. Experimental studies of food choices and palatability responses in European subjects exposed to the Umami taste. *Asia Pac J Clin Nutr*. 2008; 17 Suppl 1: 376–9.

Berntssen MHG, Lundebye A, Torstensen BE. Reducing the levels of dioxins and dioxin-like PCBs in farmed Atlantic salmon by substitution of fish oil with vegetable oil in the feed. *Aquaculture Nutrition*. 2005 Jun; 11 (3): 219–31.

Beyond Pesticides. Pyrethroids/pyrethrins. Beyond Pesticides rating: toxic. Accessed Apr 5, 2015, from www.beyondpesticides.org/infoservices/pesticidefactsheets/toxic/pyrethroid.php.

Biello D. Fertilizer runoff overwhelms streams and rivers — creating vast "dead zones." *Scientific American*. Mar 14, 2008. Accessed Mar 22, 2015. Available at www.scientificamerican.com/article/fertilizer-runoff-overwhelms-streams.

Biesiekierski JR, Rosella O, Rose R, et al. Quantification of fructans, galacto-oligosaccharides and other short-chain carbohydrates in processed grains and cereals. *J Hum Nutr Diet*. 2011 Apr; 24 (2): 154–76.

Böhn L, Störsrud S, Törnblom H, et al. Self-reported food-related gastrointestinal symptoms of IBS are common and associated with more severe symptoms and reduced quality of life. *Amer J Gastroenterol*. 2013 May; 108 (5): 634–41.

Bonner MR, Coble J, Blair A, et al. Malathion exposure and the incidence of cancer in the agricultural health study. *Am J Epidemiol*. 2007 Nov 1; 166 (9): 1023–34.

Bouchard MF, Bellinger DC, Wright RO, et al. Attention-deficit/hyperactivity disorder and urinary metabolites of organophosphate pesticides. *Pediatrics*. 2010 Jun; 125 (6): e1270–7.

Bousquet P, Ciais P, Miller JB, et al. Contribution of anthropogenic and natural sources to atmospheric methane variability. *Nature*. 2006 Sept 28; 443 (7110): 439–43.

Bradberry SM, Proudfoot AT, Vale JA. Glyphosate poisoning. *Toxicol Rev*. 2004; 23 (3): 159–67.

Bray GA. How bad is fructose? *Am J Clin Nutr*. 2007 Oct; 86 (4): 895–6.

Brooks M. Organophosphate pesticides linked to ADHD. *Medscape Medical News*. May 17, 2010. Available at www.medscape.com/viewarticle/721892.

Buchanan S, Targos L, Nagy KL, et al. Fish consumption and hair mercury among Asians in Chicago. *J Occup Environ Med*. 2015 Dec; 57 (12): 1325–30.

Canada History. Canadian history: modern Canada. 2012. Accessed Sept 24, 2014. Available at www.canadahistory.com/sections/eras/eras.html.

Canadian Food Inspection Agency. Arsenic speciation in rice and pear products. Government of Canada, Nov 12, 2014. Accessed Jan 4, 2016. Available at www.inspection.gc.ca/food/chemical-residues-microbiology/chemical-residues/arsenic/eng/1348168297496/1348168708519.

Canadian Food Inspection Agency. Canada organic regime: a certified choice. Government of Canada. Available at www.inspection.gc.ca/food/organic-products/labelling-and-general-information/certified-choice/eng/1328082717777/1328082783032.

Canadian Food Inspection Agency. Testing of arsenic in various products determines no health risk to consumers. Government of Canada, Nov 18, 2013. Accessed Jan 3, 2016. Available at www.inspection.gc.ca/about-the-cfia/newsroom/news-releases/2013-11-18/eng/1384697508388/1384697518948.

Canadian Hemochromatosis Society. How common is it? Available at www.toomuchiron.ca/hemochromatosis/how-common-is-it.

Cançado R, Melo MR, de Moraes Bastos R, et al. Deferasirox in patients with iron overload secondary to hereditary hemochromatosis: results of a 1-yr Phase 2 study. *Eur J Haematol*. 2015 Dec; 95 (6): 545–50.

Cancer Research UK. Smoking and cancer: what's in a cigarette? Sept 2014. Accessed Mar 1, 2015, from www.cancerresearchuk.org/cancer-info/healthyliving/smoking-and-cancer/whats-in-a-cigarette/smoking-and-cancer-whats-in-a-cigarette.

Carlsson-Kanyama A, González AD. Potential contributions of food consumption patterns to climate change. *Am J Clin Nutr*. 2009 May; 89 (5): 1704S–9S.

Carocci A, Rovito N, Sinicropi MS, et al. Mercury toxicity and neurodegenerative effects. *Rev Environ Contam Toxicol*. 2014; 229: 1–18.

Carter, JS. Complementary protein and diet. University of California-Clermont College, Jan 13, 2014. Available at biology.clc.uc.edu/courses/bio104/compprot.htm.

Charnley G, Doull J. Human exposure to dioxins from food, 1999–2002. *Food Chem Toxicol*. 2005 May; 43 (5): 671–9.

Chen A, Kim SS, Chung E, et al. Thyroid hormones in relation to lead, mercury, and cadmium exposure in the National Health and Nutrition Examination Survey, 2007–2008. *Environ Health Perspect*. 2013 Feb; 121 (2): 181–6.

Chiang SS, Pan TM. Beneficial effects of *Lactobacillus paracasei* subsp. *paracasei* NTU 101 and its fermented products. *Appl Microbiol Biotechnol*. 2012 Feb; 93 (3): 903–16.

Christensen KY, Thompson BA, Werner M, et al. Levels of persistent contaminants in relation to fish consumption among older male anglers in Wisconsin. *Int J Hyg Environ Health*. 2016 Mar; 219 (2): 184–94.

Cogliano VJ. Assessing the cancer risk from environmental PCBs. *Environ Health Perspect*. 1998 Jun; 106 (6): 317–23.

Concern over excessive DDT use in Jiribam fields. *The Imphal Free Press*. May 5, 2008.

Cutler N. Top 4 liver detox foods. *Liversupport.com*, Oct 18, 2013. Accessed Oct 6, 2015. Available at www.liversupport.com/top-4-liver-detox-foods.

Department of Economic and Social Affairs, Population Division. The world at six billion: introduction. United Nations, 1999. Accessed Jul 14, 2013. Available at www.un.org/esa/population/publications/sixbillion/sixbillion.htm.

DesRoches A, Infante-Rivard C, Paradis L, et al. Peanut allergy: is maternal transmission of antigens during pregnancy and breastfeeding a risk factor? *J Investig Allergol Clin Immunol*. 2010; 20 (4): 289–94.

Dharam Kaur S. *The Complete Natural Medicine Guide to Breast Cancer*. Toronto: Robert Rose, 2003.

Diamanti-Kandarakis E, Bourguignon JP, Giudice LC, et al. Endocrine-disrupting chemicals: an Endocrine Society scientific statement. *Endocr Rev*. 2009 Jun; 30 (4): 293–342.

Diet & Fitness Today. Niacin content in sweet potato. Accessed Mar 27, 2016. Available at www.dietandfitnesstoday.com/niacin-in-sweet-potato.php.

Diet & Fitness Today. Niacin content in baked potato. Accessed Mar 27, 2016. Available at www.dietandfitnesstoday.com/niacin-in-baked-potato.php.

Dietitians of Canada. "Food sources of magnesium." May 8, 2014. Accessed Dec 19, 2015. Available at www.dietitians.ca/Your-Health/Nutrition-A-Z/Minerals/Food-Sources-of-Magnesium.aspx.

Doney S, Balch W, Fabry V, et al. Ocean acidification: A critical emerging problem for the ocean sciences. *Oceanography*. 2009 Dec; 22 (4): 16–25.

Drake SL, Carunchia Whetstine ME, Drake MA, et al. Sources of umami taste in Cheddar and Swiss cheeses. *J Food Sci*. 2007 Aug; 72 (6): S360–6.

Earle, S. Personal communication with author. Blue Ocean Conference, 2014.

EatRight Ontario. What you need to know about sugar. Available at www.eatrightontario.ca/en/Articles/Carbohydrate/What-you-need-to-know-about-sugar.aspx.

Ecoffet, AL. How many chickens, cows, pigs and fish does an average human consume in a year? *Quora*. Accessed Apr 2015. Available at www.quora.com/How-many-chickens-cows-pigs-and-fish-does-an-average-human-consume-in-a-year.

Ecology Action. Grow biointensive: a sustainable solution for growing food. Accessed Mar 30, 2016. Available at www.growbiointensive.org/grow_main.html.

Elbert A, Haas M, Springer B, et al. Applied aspects of neonicotinoid uses in crop protection. *Pest Manag Sci*. 2008 Nov; 64 (11): 1099–105.

El-Demerdash FM. Antioxidant effect of vitamin E and selenium on lipid peroxidation, enzyme activities and biochemical parameters in rats exposed to aluminium. *J Trace Elem Med Biol*. 2004; 18 (1): 113–21.

Ellsworth R, Mamula K, Costantino NS, et al. Abundance and distribution of polychlorinated biphenyls (PCBs) in breast tissue. *Environ Res*. 2015 Apr; 138: 291–7.

Elobeid MA, Allison DB. Putative environmental-endocrine disruptors and obesity: a review. *Curr Opin Endocrinol Diabetes Obes*. 2008 Oct; 15 (5): 403–8.

Environment and Human Health. Risks from lawn care pesticides. Accessed Sept 21, 2015. Available at www.ehhi.org/reports/lcpesticides/summary.shtml.

Environmental Working Group. The trouble with sunscreen chemicals. Accessed Dec 2, 2015. Available at www.ewg.org/2015sunscreen/report/the-trouble-with-sunscreen-chemicals.

Erwin EA, James HR, Gutekunst HM, et al. Serum IgE measurement and detection of food allergy in pediatric patients with eosinophilic esophagitis. *Ann Allergy Asthma Immunol.* 2010 Jun; 104 (6): 496–502.

Evers DC, Wiener JG, Basu N, et al. Mercury in the Great Lakes region: bioaccumulation, spatiotemporal patterns, ecological risks, and policy. *Ecotoxicology.* 2011 Oct; 20 (7): 1487–99.

Extension Toxicology Network. Parathion. *Pesticide Information Profiles.* Sept 1993. Available at extoxnet.orst.edu/pips/parathio.htm.

Eybl V, Kotyzová D, Cerná P. Effect of melatonin, curcumin, quercetin, and resveratrol on acute ferric nitrilotriacetate (Fe-NTA)-induced renal oxidative damage in rats. *Hum Exp Toxicol.* 2008 Apr; 27 (4): 347–53.

Eybl V, Kotyzova D, Koutensky J. Comparative study of natural antioxidants — curcumin, resveratrol and melatonin — in cadmium-induced oxidative damage in mice. *Toxicology.* 2006 Aug 15; 225 (2–3): 150–6.

Eysink PE, De Jong MH, Bindels PJ, et al. Relation between IgG antibodies to foods and IgE antibodies to milk, egg, cat, dog and/or mite in a cross-sectional study. *Clin Exp Allergy.* 1999 May; 29 (5): 604–10.

Faniband M, Lindh CH, Jönsson BA. Human biological monitoring of suspected endocrine-disrupting compounds. *Asian J Androl.* 2014 Jan–Feb; 16 (1): 5–16.

Farombi EO, Onyema OO. Monosodium glutamate-induced oxidative damage and genotoxicity in the rat: modulatory role of vitamin C, vitamin E and quercetin. *Hum Exp Toxicol.* 2006 May; 25 (5): 251–9.

Fedewa A, Rao SS. Dietary fructose intolerance, fructan intolerance and FODMAPs. *Curr Gastroenterol Rep.* 2014 Jan; 16 (1): 370.

Filocamo A, Nueno-Palop C, Bisignano C, et al. Effect of garlic powder on the growth of commensal bacteria from the gastrointestinal tract. *Phytomedicine.* 2012 Jun 15; 19 (8–9): 707–11.

Fine KD, Do K, Schulte K, et al. High prevalence of celiac sprue-like HLA-DQ genes and enteropathy in patients with the microscopic colitis syndrome. *Am J Gastroenterol.* 2000 Aug; 95 (8): 1974–82.

Fine KD, Lafon G, Ogunji F, et al. The genetic and histopathologic relationship of microscopic colitis and celiac sprue or refractory sprue. (Abstract). *Gastroenterology.* 1999; 116; A879.

Fine KD, Lee EL, Meyer RL. Colonic histopathology in untreated celiac sprue or refractory sprue: is it lymphocytic colitis or colonic lymphocytosis? *Hum Pathol.* 1998 Dec; 29 (12): 1433–40.

Fine KD, Meyer RL, Lee E. The prevalence and causes of chronic diarrhea in patients with celiac sprue treated with a gluten-free diet. *Gastroenterology.* 1997 Jun; 112 (6): 1830–8.

Flora SJ, Mittal M, Mehta A. Heavy metal induced oxidative stress & its possible reversal by chelation therapy. *Indian J Med Res.* 2008 Oct; 128 (4): 501–23.

Flora SJ, Pande M, Kannan G, et al. Lead induced oxidative stress and its recovery following co-administration of melatonin or N-acetylcysteine during chelation with succimer in male rats. *Cell Mol Biol* (Noisy-le-grand). 2004; 50 Online Pub: OL543–51.

Food Allergy Facts and Statistics for the U.S. Food Allergy Research & Education. Accessed Sept 20, 2014. Available at www.foodallergy.org/document.doc?id=194.

Food and Agriculture Organization of the United Nations. *Food Outlook: Biannual Report on Global Food Markets.* Oct 2015. Accessed Mar 25, 2016. Available at www.globalagriculture.org/fileadmin/files/weltagrarbericht/GlobalAgriculture/02Hunger/Oktober2015.pdf.

Food and Agriculture Organization of the United Nations. *International Code of Conduct on the Distribution and Use of Pesticides.* Rome: FAO of the United Nations, 1986.

Food and Environmental Hygiene Department. Pesticides. Jan 1, 2013. Accessed Nov 25, 2015. Available at www.fehd.gov.hk/english/safefood/pesticides.html.

Formiga A. Celebrate the three sisters: corn, beans and squash. *Renee's Garden.* 2014. Accessed Mar 22, 2015. Available at www.reneesgarden.com/articles/3sisters.html.

Fraga CG, Oteiza PI. Iron toxicity and antioxidant nutrients. *Toxicology.* 2002 Oct 30; 180 (1): 23–32.

Frei B. Reactive oxygen species and antioxidant vitamins: mechanisms of action. *Am J Med.* 1994 Sept 26; 97 (3A): 5S–13S; discussion 22S–28S.

Frost DV, Lish PM. Selenium in biology. *Annu Rev Pharmacol.* 1975; 15: 259–84.

Furrie E. Probiotics and allergy. *Proc Nutr Soc.* 2005 Nov; 64 (4): 465–9.

Gaetke LM, Chow CK. Copper toxicity, oxidative stress, and antioxidant nutrients. *Toxicology.* 2003 Jul 15; 189 (1–2): 147–63.

Gamboa PM, Sánchez-Monge R, Díaz-Perales A, et al. Latex-vegetable syndrome due to custard apple and aubergine: new variations of the hevein symphony. *J Investig Allergol Clin Immunol.* 2005; 15 (4): 308–11.

García-Niño WR, Pedraza-Chaverrí J. Protective effect of curcumin against heavy metals-induced liver damage. *Food Chem Toxicol.* 2014 Jul; 69: 182–201.

Garelick H, Jones H, Dybowska A, et al. Arsenic pollution sources. *Rev Environ Contam Toxicol.* 2008; 197: 17–60.

Gasull M, Bosch de Basea M, Puigdomènech E, et al. Empirical analyses of the influence of diet on human concentrations of persistent organic pollutants: a systematic review of all studies conducted in Spain. *Environ Int.* 2011 Oct; 37 (7): 1226–35.

Genetics Home Reference. Hereditary fructose intolerance. U.S. National Library of Medicine, Jun 2011. Accessed Apr 22, 2015. Available at ghr.nlm.nih.gov/condition/hereditary-fructose-intolerance.

George R. Dateline 2006: 90% of fish gone, rest to disappear by 2048 → 2013: A solution demonstrated. May 10, 2013. Accessed Mar 22, 2015. Available at russgeorge.net/2013/05/10/fish-to-disappear-by-2050.

Ghisari M, Long M, Tabbo A, et al. Effects of currently used pesticides and their mixtures on the function of thyroid hormone and aryl hydrocarbon receptor in cell culture. *Toxicol Appl Pharmacol.* 2015 May 1; 284 (3): 292–303.

Glaser, LC. "Organophosphates and carbamate pesticides." *Field Manual of Wildlife Disease: General Field Procedures and Diseases of Birds.* U.S. Department of the Interior, May 21, 2013. Accessed Dec 6, 2015. Available at www.nwhc.usgs.gov/publications/field_manual/chapter_39.pdf.

Glickman LT, Raghavan M, Knapp DW, et al. Herbicide exposure and the risk of transitional cell carcinoma of the urinary bladder in Scottish Terriers. *J Am Vet Med Assoc.* 2004 Apr 15; 224 (8): 1290–7.

Global Footprint Network. World footprint: do we fit on the planet? Accessed Dec 2015. Available at www.footprintnetwork.org/en/index.php/GFN/page/world_footprint.

Goldman LR, Shannon MW; American Academy of Pediatrics: Committee on Environmental Health. Technical Report: Mercury in the Environment: Implications for Pediatricians. *Pediatrics.* 2001 Jul; 108 (1): 197–205.

González-Estecha M, Bodas-Pinedo A, Guillén-Pérez, et al. Methylmercury exposure in the general population: toxicokinetics: differences by gender, nutritional and genetic factors. [Article in Spanish.] *Nutr Hosp.* 2014 Nov 1; 30 (5): 969–88.

González-Estecha M, Bodas-Pinedo A, Rubio-Herrera MÁ, et al. The effects of methylmercury on health in children and adults: national and international studies. [Article in Spanish.] *Nutr Hosp.* 2014 Nov 1; 30 (5): 989–1007.

Goodland R, Anhang J. Livestock and climate change: what if the key actors in climate change are … cows, pigs, and chickens? *World Watch Magazine.* 2009 Nov–Dec; 22 (6).

Goodman B. Arsenic in food: FAQ. *WebMD.* Dec 5, 2011. Accessed Jan 3, 2016. Available at www.webmd.com/diet/arsenic-food-faq?page=3.

Grossman E. What do we really know about Roundup weed killer? *National Geographic.* Apr 23, 2015. Accessed Dec 1, 2015. Available at news.nationalgeographic.com/2015/04/150422-glyphosate-roundup-herbicide-weeds.

Group E. 10 foods that detox the body. Global Healing Center, Jul 8, 2009. Accessed Oct 6, 2015. Available at www.globalhealingcenter.com/natural-health/foods-that-detox-the-body.

Grube A, Donaldson D, Kiely T, et al. Pesticides industry sales and usage: 2006 and 2007 market estimates. Environmental Protection Agency, Feb 2011. Accessed 2011. Available at www.panna.org/sites/default/files/EPA%20market_estimates2007.pdf.

Gruber SJ, Munn MD. Organochlorine pesticides and PCBs in aquatic ecosystems of the Central Columbia Plateau. U.S. Geological Survey Department of the Interior, Sept 1996. Available at wa.water.usgs.gov/pubs/fs/fs170-96.

Grün F, Blumberg B. Endocrine disrupters as obesogens. *Mol Cell Endocrinol.* 2009 May 25; 304 (1–2): 19–29.

Hajoway M. Alpha lipoic acid: a true antioxidant! Jul 7, 2006. Accessed Mar 27, 2016. Available at www.bodybuilding.com/fun/ala2.htm.

Haldeman-Englert C. Hereditary fructose intolerance. Medline Plus U.S. National Library of Medicine, Apr 20, 2015. Accessed Dec 27, 2015. Available at www.nlm.nih.gov/medlineplus/ency/article/000359.htm.

Halpern GM, Scott JR. Non-IgE antibody mediated mechanisms in food allergy. *Ann Allergy.* 1987; 58: 14–27.

Hämäläinen P, Saltevo J, Kautiainen H, et al. Serum ferritin levels and the development of metabolic syndrome and its components: a 6.5-year follow-up study. *Diabetol Metab Syndr.* 2014 Oct 26; 6 (1): 114.

Hanson EH, Imperatore G, Burke W. HFE gene and hereditary hemochromatosis: a HuGE review. Human Genome Epidemiology. *Am J Epidemiol.* 2001 Aug 1; 154 (3): 193–206.

Hardell L, Vanbavel B, Lindstrom G, et al. Higher concentrations of specific polychlorinated biphenyl congeners in adipose tissue from non-Hodgkin's lymphoma patients compared with controls without a malignant disease. *Int J Oncol.* 1996 Oct 9 (4): 603–8.

Hayden K, Norton M, Darcey D, et al. Occupational exposure to pesticides increases the risk of incident AD: the Cache County study. *Neurology.* 2010 May 11; 74 (19): 1524–30.

Health Canada. Consumer product safety: safety of cosmetic ingredients. May 28, 2015. Accessed Dec 2, 2015. Available at www.hc-sc.gc.ca/cps-spc/cosmet-person/labelling-etiquetage/ingredients-eng.php.

Health Canada. Monosodium glutamate (MSG): questions and answers. Jun 27, 2008. Accessed Jan 1, 2016. Available at www.hc-sc.gc.ca/fn-an/securit/addit/msg_qa-qr-eng.php.

Health Canada. Sulphites: one of the ten priority food allergens. 2012. Accessed Jan 1, 2016. Available at www.hc-sc.gc.ca/fn-an/pubs/securit/2012-allergen_sulphites-sulfites/index-eng.php.

Health Canada Mercury Issues Task Group. Mercury: your health and the environment. 2004. Accessed Sept 7, 2015. Available at www.hc-sc.gc.ca/ewh-semt/pubs/contaminants/mercur/index-eng.php#q-12.

Hecht DW. *Bacteroides* species. *Antimicrobe.* Accessed Dec 19, 2015. Available at www.antimicrobe.org/b85.asp.

Heindel J, Newbold R, Schug T. Endocrine disruptors and obesity. *Nat Rev Endocrinol* 2015; 11: 653–61.

Hernández-Lahoz C, Rodríguez S, Tuñón A, et al. Sustained clinical remission in a patient with remittent-recurrent multiple sclerosis and celiac disease gluten-free diet for 6 years. [Article in Spanish.] *Neurologia.* 2009 Apr; 24 (3): 213–5.

Higdon J. Flavanoids. Linus Pauling Institute, Oregon State University, 2005. Accessed Sept 27, 2015. Available at lpi.oregonstate.edu/mic/dietary-factors/phytochemicals/flavonoids.

Hizli S, Karabulut H, Ozdemir O, et al. Sensorineural hearing loss in pediatric celiac patients. *Int J Pediatr Otorhinolaryngol.* 2011 Jan; 75 (1): 65–8.

Holmgren D. *Permaculture: Principles and Pathways Beyond Sustainability.* Sydney: Holmgren Design Services, 2002.

Holzhammer J, Wöber C. Alimentary trigger factors that provoke migraine and tension-type headache. [Article in German.] *Schmerz.* 2006 Apr; 20 (2): 151–9.

Hotchkiss AK, Rider CV, Blystone CR, et al. Fifteen years after "Wingspread" — environmental endocrine disrupters and human and wildlife health: where we are today and where we need to go. *Toxicol Sci.* 2008 Oct; 105 (2): 235–59.

Hozyasz KK. Promising [sic] role of probiotics in prevention of smoking-related diseases. [Article in Polish.] *Przegl Lek.* 2008; 65 (10): 706–8.

Huwe JK, Larsen GL. Polychlorinated dioxins, furans, and biphenyls, and polybrominated diphenyl ethers in a U.S. meat market basket and estimates of dietary intake. *Environ Sci Technol.* 2005 Aug 1; 39 (15): 5606–11.

Ibrahim F, Halttunen T, Tahvonen R, et al. Probiotic bacteria as potential detoxification tools: assessing their heavy metal binding isotherms. *Can J Microbiol.* 2006 Sept; 52 (9): 877–85.

Ingre C, Roos PM, Piehl F, et al. Risk factors for amyotrophic lateral sclerosis. *Clin Epidemiol.* 2015 Feb 12; 7: 181–93.

Institute of Medicine Food and Nutrition Board. *Dietary Reference Intakes for Vitamin A, Vitamin K, Arsenic, Boron, Chromium, Copper, Iodine, Iron, Manganese, Molybdenum, Nickel, Silicon, Vanadium, and Zinc: A Report of the Panel on Micronutrients.* Washington, DC: National Academies Press, 2001.

International Cadmium Association. Cadmium exposure and human health. Accessed Mar 21, 2015. Available at www.cadmium.org/environment/cadmium-exposure-and-human-health.

Jaeger C, Hatziagelaki E, Petzoldt R, et al. Comparative analysis of organ-specific autoantibodies and celiac disease: associated antibodies in type 1 diabetic patients, their first-degree relatives, and healthy control subjects. *Diabetes Care.* 2001 Jan; 24 (1): 27–32.

Järup L. Hazards of heavy metal contamination. *Br Med Bull.* 2003; 68: 167–82.

Jiang R, Manson JE, Meigs JB, et al. Body iron stores in relation to risk of type 2 diabetes in apparently healthy women. *JAMA.* 2004 Feb 11; 291 (6): 711–7.

Johnston P, McCrea I. *Death in Small Doses: The Effects of Organochlorines on Aquatic Ecosystems.* Amsterdam: Greenpeace International, 1992.

Jomova K, Valko M. Advances in metal-induced oxidative stress and human disease. *Toxicology.* 2011 May 10; 283 (2–3): 65–87.

Jomova K, Vondrakova D, Lawson M, et al. Metals, oxidative stress and neurodegenerative disorders. *Mol Cell Biochem.* 2010 Dec; 345 (1–2): 91–104.

Karaytug S, Sevgiler Y, Karayakar F. Comparison of the protective effects of antioxidant compounds in the liver and kidney of Cd- and Cr-exposed common carp. *Environ Toxicol.* 2014 Feb; 29 (2): 129–37.

Kell DB, Pretorius E. Serum ferritin is an important inflammatory disease marker, as it is mainly a leakage product from damaged cells. *Metallomics.* 2014 Apr; 6 (4): 748–73.

Kids Health. Blood test: immunoglobulins (IgA, IgG, IgM). Aug 2014. Accessed Sept 20, 2015. Available at kidshealth.org/parent/system/medical/test_immunoglobulins.html.

Kim MH, Bae YJ. Postmenopausal vegetarians' low serum ferritin level may reduce the risk for metabolic syndrome. *Biol Trace Elem Res.* 2012 Oct; 149 (1): 34–41.

Kjeldsen LS, Ghisari M, Bonefeld-Jørgensen EC. Currently used pesticides and their mixtures affect the function of sex hormone receptors and aromatase enzyme activity. *Toxicol Appl Pharmacol.* 2013 Oct 15; 272 (2): 453–64.

Klein S. Study: ADHD linked to pesticide exposure. CNN, May 17, 2010. Available at www.cnn.com/2010/HEALTH/05/17/pesticides.adhd.

Knapp DW, Peer WA, Conteh A, et al. Detection of herbicides in the urine of pet dogs following home lawn chemical application. *Sci Total Environ.* 2013 Jul 1; 456–57: 34–41.

Kniker, WT. Immunologically mediated reactions to food: state of the art. *Ann Allergy.* 1987 Nov; 59 (5 Pt 2): 60–70.

Konefes JL, McGee MK. Old cemeteries, arsenic, and health safety. *Water Industry News.* Accessed Mar 28, 2015. Available at waterindustry.org/arsenic-3.htm.

Koulaouzidis A, Cottier R, Bhat S, et al. A ferritin level >50 microg/L is frequently consistent with iron deficiency. *Eur J Intern Med.* 2009 Mar; 20 (2): 168–70.

Kurihara K. Glutamate: from discovery as a food flavor to role as a basic taste (umami). *Am J Clin Nutr.* 2009 Sept; 90 (3): 719S–722S.

Kurppa K, Lindfors K, Collin P, et al. Antibodies against deamidated gliadin peptides in early-stage celiac disease. *J Clin Gastroenterol.* 2011 Sept; 45 (8): 673–8.

Kurtzman L. Exposures to some phthalates fall after federal ban: UCSF study finds widespread exposure to these endocrine disrupters. University of California San Francisco, Jan 14, 2014. Accessed Nov 2015. Available at www.ucsf.edu/news/2014/01/111066/exposures-some-phthalates-fall-after-federal-ban.

Lah K. History of lead use. *Toxipedia.* May 8, 2011. Accessed Mar 22, 2015. Available at www.toxipedia.org/display/toxipedia/History+of+Lead+Use.

Lappé FM. *Diet for a Small Planet* (20th anniversary edition). New York: Ballantine Books, 1991.

LaRocca C, Martovani A. From environment to food: the case of PCB. *Ann Ist Super Sanità.* 2006; 42 (4): 410–6.

Lawrence T, Sheppard W. Neonicotinoid pesticides and honey bees: fact sheet FS122E. Washington State University Extension, Nov 2013. Available at cru.cahe.wsu.edu/CEPublications/FS122E/FS122E.pdf

Lawson A, West J, Aithal GP, et al. Autoimmune cholestatic liver disease in people with coeliac disease: a population-based study of their association. *Aliment Pharmacol Ther.* 2005 Feb 15; 21 (4): 401–5.

Le LT, Sabate J. Beyond meatless, the health effects of vegan diets: findings from the Adventist cohorts. *Nutrients.* 2014 May 27; 6 (5): 2131–47.

Lee BK, Kim Y, Kim YI. Association of serum ferritin with metabolic syndrome and diabetes mellitus in the South Korean general population according to the Korean National Health and Nutrition Examination Survey 2008. *Metabolism.* 2011 Oct; 60 (10): 1416–24.

Lee YJ, Hwang IC. Relationship between serum ferritin level and blood mercury concentration using data from the Korean national health and nutrition examination survey (2010–2012). *Environ Res.* 2014 Nov; 135: 271–5.

Lester MR. Sulfite sensitivity: significance in human health. *J Am Coll Nutr.* 1995 Jun; 14 (3): 229–32.

Levin, S. EPA considers ban on hazardous pesticide widely used in California. *East Bay Express.* Jul 1, 2015. Accessed Sept 21, 2015. Available at www.eastbayexpress.com/SevenDays/archives/2015/07/01/epa-considers-ban-on-hazardous-pesticide-widely-used-in-california.

Levine A, Domanov S, Sukhotnik I, et al. Celiac-associated peptic disease at upper endoscopy: how common is it? *Scand J Gastroenterol.* 2009; 44 (12): 1424–8.

Li MM, Wu MQ, Zu J, et al. Body burden of Hg in different bio-samples of mothers in Shenyang city, China. *PLoS One*. 2014 May 23; 9 (5): e98121.

Lioe HN, Apriyantono A, Takara K, et al. Low molecular weight compounds responsible for savory taste of Indonesian soy sauce. *Agric Food Chem*. 2004 Sept 22; 52 (19): 5950–6.

Liu AH, Jaramillo R, Sicherer SH, et al. National prevalence and risk factors for food allergy and relationship to asthma: results from the National Health and Nutrition Examination Survey 2005–2006. *Allergy Clin Immunol*. 2010 Oct; 126 (4): 798–806. e13.

Lomer MC, Parkes GC, Sanderson JD. Review article: lactose intolerance in clinical practice — myths and realities. *Aliment Pharmacol Ther*. 2008 Jan 15; 27 (2): 93–103.

Looker, AC. Iron deficiency: United States, 1999–2000. Centers for Disease Control and Prevention, Oct 11, 2002. Accessed Dec 16, 2015. Available at www.cdc.gov/mmwr/preview/mmwrhtml/mm5140a1.htm.

Lordan S, Ross RP, Stanton C. Marine bioactives as functional food ingredients: potential to reduce the incidence of chronic diseases. *Mar Drugs*. 2011; 9 (6): 1056–100.

Lutteri L, Sagot C, Chapelle JP. Anti-deamidated gliadin peptides antibodies and coeliac disease: state of art and analysis of false-positive results from five assays. [Article in French.] *Ann Biol Clin* (Paris). 2010 Mar–Apr; 68 (2): 149–56.

Maffini MV, Rubin BS, Sonnenschein C, et al. Endocrine disruptors and reproductive health: the case of bisphenol-A. *Mol Cell Endocrinol*. 2006 Jul 25; 254–5: 179–86.

Makris KC, Quazi S, Punamiya P, et al. Fate of arsenic in swine waste from concentrated animal feeding operations. *J Environ Qual*. 2008 Jun 23; 37 (4): 1626–33.

Malisch R, Kotz A. Dioxins and PCBs in feed and food: review from European perspective. *Sci Total Environ*. 2014 Sept 1; 491–2: 2–10.

Mallick HN. Understanding safety of glutamate in food and brain. *Indian J Physiol Pharmacol*. 2007 Jul–Sept; 51 (3): 216–34.

Mangalgiri KP, Adak A, Blaney L. Organoarsenicals in poultry litter: detection, fate, and toxicity. *Environ Int*. 2015 Feb; 75: 68–80.

Mansueto P, Montalto G, Pacor ML, et al. Food allergy in gastroenterologic diseases: review of literature. *World J Gastroenterol*. 2006 Dec 28; 12 (48): 7744–52.

Marks AR, Harley K, Bradman A, et al. Organophosphate pesticide exposure and attention in young Mexican-American children: the CHAMACOS study. *Environ Health Perspect*. 2010 Dec; 118 (12): 1768–74.

Martins C, Vasco E, Paixão E, et al. Total mercury in infant food, occurrence and exposure assessment in Portugal. *Food Addit Contam Part B Surveill*. 2013; 6 (3): 151–7.

McDowell MA, Dillon CF, Osterloh J, et al. Hair mercury levels in U.S. children and women of childbearing age: reference range data from NHANES 1999–2000. *Environ Health Perspect*. 2004 Aug; 112 (11): 1165–71.

McGough N, Cummings JH. Coeliac disease: a diverse clinical syndrome caused by intolerance of wheat, barley and rye. *Proc Nutr Soc*. 2005 Nov; 64 (4): 434–50.

Mendel RR, Bittner F. Cell biology of molybdenum. *Biochim Biophys Acta*. 2006 Jul; 1763 (7): 621–35.

Mercola. Broccoli sprouts. Accessed Dec 19, 2015. Available at www.mercola.com/article/diet/broccoli_sprouts.htm.

Mercola. Monsanto to keep selling pesticide-coated seeds EPA says don't help yields — and may harm bees. Nov 4, 2014. Available at articles.mercola.com/sites/articles/archive/2014/11/04/neonicotinoid-pesticide-use.aspx.

Mercola. What are the health benefits of oregano? Feb 1, 2014. Accessed Sept 27, 2015. Available at articles.mercola.com/sites/articles/archive/2014/02/01/oregano-health-benefits.aspx.

Mercola. What is chlorella good for? Jan 28, 2013. Accessed Dec 19, 2015. Available at articles.mercola.com/sites/articles/archive/2013/01/28/chlorella-for-mercury-poisoning.aspx.

Mesnage R, Defarge N, Spiroux de Vendômois J, et al. Major pesticides are more toxic to human cells than their declared active principles. *Biomed Res Int*. 2014; 2014: 179691.

Messenger S. Half the rainforest could be lost by 2050, says study. *Treehugger*, May 4, 2010. Accessed Mar 2015. Available at www.treehugger.com/natural-sciences/half-the-amazon-could-be-lost-by-2050-says-study.html.

Michelozzi P, Lapucci E, Farchi S. Meat consumption reduction policies: benefits for climate change mitigation and health. [Article in Italian.] *Recenti Prog Med*. 2015 Aug; 106 (8): 354–7.

Michielan A, D'Incà R. Intestinal permeability in inflammatory bowel disease: pathogenesis, clinical evaluation, and therapy of leaky gut. *Mediators Inflamm*. 2015; 2015: 628157.

Miedico O, Iammarino M, Pompa C, et al. Assessment of lead, cadmium and mercury in seafood marketed in Puglia and Basilicata (Italy) by inductively coupled plasma mass spectrometry. *Food Addit Contam Part B Surveill*. 2015; 8 (2): 85–92.

Millichap JG, Yee MM. The diet factor in pediatric and adolescent migraine. *Pediatr Neurol*. 2003 Jan; 28 (1): 9–15.

Minnesota Department of Health. Formaldehyde in your home. 2011. Accessed Mar 19, 2015. Available at www.health.state.mn.us/divs/eh/indoorair/voc/formaldehyde.htm.

Mnif W, Hassine AI, Bouaziz A, et al. Effect of endocrine disruptor pesticides: a review. *Int J Environ Res Public Health*. 2011 Jun; 8 (6): 2265–303.

Mohr N. Average and total numbers of land animals who died to feed Americans in 2011. *United Poultry Concerns*. Jan 12, 2011. Accessed Apr 2015. Available at www.upc-online.org/slaughter/2009americans.html.

Moore C Jr, Ormseth M, Fuchs H. Causes and significance of markedly elevated serum ferritin levels in an academic medical center. *J Clin Rheumatol*. 2013 Sept; 19 (6): 324–8.

Moreno-Jiménez E, Esteban E, Peñalosa JM. The fate of arsenic in soil-plant systems. *Rev Environ Contam Toxicol*. 2012; 215: 1–37.

Morris CR, Agin MC. Syndrome of allergy, apraxia, and malabsorption: characterization of a neurodevelopmental phenotype that responds to omega 3 and vitamin E supplementation. *Altern Ther Health Med*. 2009 Jul–Aug; 15 (4): 34–43.

Morris WL, Ross HA, Ducreux LJ, et al. Umami compounds are a determinant of the flavor of potato (*Solanum tuberosum L.*). *J Agric Food Chem.* 2007 Nov 14; 55 (23): 9627–33.

Moshfegh AJ, Friday JE, Goldman JP, et al. Presence of inulin and oligofructose in the diets of Americans. *J Nutr.* 1999 Jul; 129 (7 Suppl): 1407S–11S.

Mrema EJ, Rubino FM, Brambilla G, et al. Persistent organoclorinated pesticides and mechanisms of their toxicity. *Toxicology.* 2013 May 10; 307: 74–88.

Mucchetti G, Locci F, Massara P, et al. Production of pyroglutamic acid by thermophilic lactic acid bacteria in hard-cooked mini-cheeses. *J Dairy Sci.* 2002 Oct; 85 (10): 2489–96.

Muhammad A, Pitchumoni CS. Newly detected celiac disease by wireless capsule endoscopy in older adults with iron deficiency anemia. *J Clin Gastroenterol.* 2008 Oct; 42 (9): 980–3.

Muir P. II. Trends in pesticide use. Oregon State University, Oct 22, 2012. Accessed Feb 21, 2015. Available at people.oregonstate.edu/~muirp/pesttren.htm.

Myers RA, Worm B. Rapid worldwide depletion of predatory fish communities. *Nature.* 2003 May 15; 423 (6937): 280–3.

Myllyvirta L. Comment: new coal power plant in China — a (carbon) bubble waiting to burst. Energy Desk Greenpeace, Feb 23, 2015. Accessed Apr 5, 2015. Available at energydesk. greenpeace.org/2015/02/23/comment-new-coal-power-plants-china-carbon-bubble-waiting-burst.

Nadal I, Donat E, Ribes-Koninckx C, et al. Imbalance in the composition of the duodenal microbiota of children with coeliac disease. *J Med Microbiol.* 2007 Dec; 56 (Pt 12): 1669–74.

Nakayama S, Harada K, Inoue K, et al. Distributions of perfluorooctanoic acid (PFOA) and perfluorooctane sulfonate (PFOS) in Japan and their toxicities. *Environ Sci.* 2005; 12 (6): 293–313.

National Heart, Lung, and Blood Institute. What is hemochromatosis? Feb 1, 2011. Available at www.nhlbi.nih.gov/health/health-topics/topics/hemo.

National Institute of Environmental Health Sciences. Dioxins. National Institutes of Health, 2015. Accessed Nov 14, 2015. Available at www.niehs.nih.gov/health/topics/agents/dioxins.

National Institute of Environmental Health Sciences. Perfluorinated chemicals (PFCs). National Institutes of Health. Accessed Nov 17, 2015. Available at www.niehs.nih.gov/health/topics/agents/pfc/index.cfm.

National Oceanic and Atmospheric Administration. What is a dead zone? National Ocean Service, Sept 3, 2014. Accessed Mar 28, 2015. Available at oceanservice.noaa.gov/facts/deadzone.html.

National Pesticide Information Center. Arsenic. Accessed Mar 22, 2015. Available at npic.orst.edu/ingred/ptype/treatwood/arsenic.html.

National Pesticide Information Center. Chlorpyrifos general fact sheet. Apr 2010. Accessed Nov 2015. Available at npic.orst.edu/factsheets/chlorpgen.html.

National Pesticide Information Center. Types of pesticides. 2015. Accessed Nov 25, 2015. Available at www.npic.orst.edu/ingred/ptype/index.html.

National Research Council (US) Committee on the Toxicological Effects of Methylmercury, Board on Environmental Studies and Toxicology; Commission on Life Sciences; Division on Earth and Life Studies; National Research Council. *Toxicological Effects of Methylmercury.* Washington, DC: National Academies Press, 2000.

Natural Resources Defense Council. EPA will not protect public from dioxins in land-applied sewage sludge. Oct 17, 2003. Accessed Nov 14, 2015. Available at www.nrdc.org/media/pressreleases/031017.asp.

Natural Resources Defense Council. Healthy milk, healthy baby: chemical pollution and mother's milk. May 22, 2001. Accessed Nov 14, 2015. Available at www.nrdc.org/media/2001/010522.

Natural Resources Defense Council. Mercury contamination in fish: know where it's coming from. 2014. Accessed Dec 2, 2015. Available at www.nrdc.org/health/effects/mercury/sources.asp.

Natural Resources Defense Council. Protect yourself and your family: consumer guide to mercury in fish. Accessed Mar 1, 2015. Available at www.nrdc.org/health/effects/mercury/guide.asp.

Natural Resources Defense Council. The story of silent spring. How a courageous woman took on the chemical industry and raised important questions about humankind's impact on nature. Aug 13, 2015. Available at www.nrdc.org/health/pesticides/hcarson.asp.

Neuhausen SL, Steele L, Ryan S, et al. Co-occurrence of celiac disease and other autoimmune diseases in celiacs and their first-degree relatives. *J Autoimmun.* 2008 Sept; 31 (2): 160–5.

Neumann, J. Food safety: FDA and USDA should strengthen pesticide residue monitoring programs and further disclose monitoring limitations. U.S. Government Accountability Office. Nov 6, 2014. Available at www.gao.gov/products/GAO-15-38.

NOAA Fisheries. Basic questions about aquaculture. 2012. Accessed Feb 9, 2016. Available at www.nmfs.noaa.gov/aquaculture/faqs/faq_aq_101.html#4howmuch.

Odom Health and Wellness. Natural liver detox: how to support natural liver detoxification. Mar 4, 2013. Accessed Apr 5, 2015. Available at odomhealthandwellness.com/natural-liver-detox-how-to-support-natural-liver-detoxification.

Orangutan Conservancy. Threats to orangutans. Orangutans face possible extinction. 2014. Accessed Apr 8, 2015. Available at www.orangutan.com/threats-to-orangutans.

Ozdemir C, Akdis M, Akdis CA. T-cell response to allergens. *Chem Immunol Allergy.* 2010; 95: 22–44.

Paganelli R, Quinti I, D'Offizi GP, et al. Immune complexes in food allergy: a critical reappraisal. *Ann Allergy.* 1987 Nov; 59 (5 Pt 2):157–61.

Palmer DS, O'Toole J, Montreuil T, et al. Screening of Canadian Blood Services donors for severe immunoglobulin A deficiency. *Transfusion.* 2010 Jul; 50 (7): 1524–31.

Pastorelli AA, Baldini M, Stacchini P, et al. Human exposure to lead, cadmium and mercury through fish and seafood product consumption in Italy: a pilot evaluation. *Food Addit Contam Part A Chem Anal Control Expo Risk Assess.* 2012; 29 (12): 1913–21.

Pelé F, Bajeux E, Gendron H, et al. Maternal fish and shellfish consumption and wheeze, eczema and food allergy at age two: a prospective cohort study in Brittany, France. *Environ Health.* 2013 Dec 2; 12: 102.

Pongracic J. Patterns of allergy in North America. Presentation at Symposium on Frontiers in Food Allergen Risk Assessment, Oct 2010. Accessed Sept 20, 2015. Available at www.ilsi.org/Europe/Documents/Food%20Allergy%20Symposium/Present%20Pongracic%20Nice.pdf.

Pozniakov SP. Mechanism of action of vitamin A on cell differentiation and function. [Article in Russian.] *Ontogenez.* 1986 Nov–Dec; 17 (6): 578–86.

Prescott J. Effects of added glutamate on liking for novel food flavors. *Appetite.* 2004 Apr; 42 (2): 143–50.

Proctor, RN. The history of the discovery of the cigarette–lung cancer link: evidentiary traditions, corporate denial, global toll. *Tob Control.* 2012; 21: 87–91.

Rainforest Action Network. Your supermarket is selling rainforest destruction! Get the facts on palm oil and the U.S. snack food industry. May 16, 2013. Accessed Mar 28, 2015. Available at www.ran.org/your_supermarket_is_selling_rainforest_destruction_get_the_facts_on_palm_oil_and_the_us_snack_food_industry.

Ralston NV, Raymond LJ. Dietary selenium's protective effects against methylmercury toxicity. *Toxicology.* 2010 Nov 28; 278 (1): 112–23.

Ramakrishnan U, Kuklina E, Stein AD. Iron stores and cardiovascular disease risk factors in women of reproductive age in the United Sates. *Am J Clin Nutr.* 2002 Dec; 76 (6): 1256–60.

Ramm GA, Ruddell RG. Hepatotoxicity of iron overload: mechanisms of iron-induced hepatic fibrogenesis. *Semin Liver Dis.* 2005 Nov; 25 (4): 433–49.

Rasyid A, Rahman AR, Jaalam K, et al. Effect of different curcumin dosages on human gall bladder. *Asia Pac J Clin Nutr.* 2002; 11 (4): 314–8.

Reijnders L, Soret S. Quantification of the environmental impact of different dietary protein choices. *Am J Clin Nutr.* 2003 Sept; 78 (3 Suppl): 664S–668S.

Rice KM, Walker EM Jr, Wu M, et al. Environmental mercury and its toxic effects. *J Prev Med Public Health.* 2014 Mar; 47 (2): 74–83.

Rich Vegan Foods. Methionine: richest foods for vegans (per portion). *Rich Vegan Foods.* 2014. Accessed Sept 26, 2015. Available at methionine.rich-vegan-foods.com/100g.html.

Richard L. Antifungals: caprylic acid. *The Candida Diet.* Accessed Sept 27, 2015. Available at www.thecandidadiet.com/caprylicacid.htm.

Rivero J, Luzardo OP, Henríquez-Hernández LA, et al. In vitro evaluation of oestrogenic/androgenic activity of the serum organochlorine pesticide mixtures previously described in a breast cancer case-control study. *Sci Total Environ.* 2015 Dec 15; 537: 197–202.

Robbins J. *Diet for a New America: How Your Food Choices Affect Your Health, Happiness and the Future of Life on Earth.* Walpole, NH: Stillpoint Publishing, 1987.

Rostami Nejad M, Rostami K, Pourhoseingholi MA, et al. Atypical presentation is dominant and typical for coeliac disease. *J Gastrointestin Liver Dis.* 2009 Sept; 18 (3): 285–91.

Rothman N, Cantor KP, Blair A, et al. A nested case-control study of non-Hodgkin lymphoma and serum organochlorine residues. *Lancet.* 1997 Jul 26; 350 (9073): 240–4.

Roy D, Morgan M, Yoo C, et al. Integrated bioinformatics, environmental epidemiologic and genomic approaches to identify environmental and molecular links between endometriosis and breast cancer. *Int J Mol Sci.* 2015 Oct 23; 16 (10): 25285–322.

Rush T, Hjelmhaug J, Lobner D. Effects of chelators on mercury, iron, and lead neurotoxicity in cortical culture. *Neurotoxicology.* 2009 Jan; 30 (1): 47–51.

Sabaté J, Soret S. Sustainability of plant-based diets: back to the future. *Am J Clin Nutr.* 2014 Jul; 100 Suppl 1: 476S–82S.

Sass J. Why we need bees: nature's tiny workers put food on our tables. Natural Resources Defense Council, Mar 2011. Accessed Mar 19, 2015. Available at www.nrdc.org/wildlife/animals/files/bees.pdf.

Schecter A, Wallace D, Pavuk M, et al. Dioxins in commercial United States baby food. *J Toxicol Environ Health A.* 2002 Dec 13; 65 (23): 1937–43.

Schell LM, Gallo MV, Cook K. What's NOT to eat: food adulteration in the context of human biology. *Am J Hum Biol.* 2012 Mar–Apr; 24 (2): 139–48.

Schlesinger D. Dealing with yeast die-off reactions. *Modern Herbalist.* 2013. Accessed Dec 19, 2015. Available at www.modernherbalist.com/dieoff.html.

Science Daily. Low concentrations of pesticides can become toxic mixture for amphibians. *Science Daily.* Nov 18, 2008. Accessed Dec 11, 2012. Available at www.sciencedaily.com/releases/2008/11/081111183041.htm.

Scrimshaw NS, Murray EB. The acceptability of milk and milk products in populations with a high prevalence of lactose intolerance. *Am J Clin Nutr.* 1988 Oct; 48 (4 Suppl): 1079–159.

Sears ME, Kerr KJ, Bray RI. Arsenic, cadmium, lead, and mercury in sweat: a systematic review. *J Environ Public Health.* 2012; 2012: 184745.

Séralini GE, Clair E, Mesnage R, et al. Republished study: long-term toxicity of a Roundup herbicide and a Roundup-tolerant genetically modified maize. Environmental Sciences Europe, Jun 24, 2014. Available at www.enveurope.com/content/26/1/14.

Settipane GA. The restaurant syndromes. *N Engl Reg Allergy Proc.* 1987 Jan–Feb; 8 (1): 39–46.

Sevgiler Y, Karaytug S, Karayakar F. Antioxidative effects of N-acetylcysteine, lipoic acid, taurine, and curcumin in the muscle of Cyprinus carpio L. exposed to cadmium. *Arh Hig Rada Toksikol.* 2011 Mar; 62 (1): 1–9.

Shepherd SJ, Gibson PR. Fructose malabsorption and symptoms of irritable bowel syndrome: guidelines for effective dietary management. *J Amer Diet Assoc.* 2006 Oct; 106: 1631–9.

Simon RA. Adverse reactions to food additives. *N Engl Reg Allergy Proc.* 1986 Nov–Dec; 7 (6): 533–42.

Smil V. Harvesting the biosphere: the human impact. *Popul Dev Rev.* 2011; 37 (4): 613–36.

Smith JD, Terpening CM, Schmidt SO, et al. Relief of fibromyalgia symptoms following discontinuation of dietary excitotoxins. *Ann Pharmacother.* 2001 Jun; 35 (6): 702–6.

Smith LN. Monarch butterfly's reign threatened by milkweed decline. *National Geographic*. Aug 20, 2002. Accessed Mar 21, 2015. Available at news.nationalgeographic.com/news/2014/08/140819-monarch-butterfly-milkweed-environment-ecology-science.

Smith TM, Stratton GW. Effects of synthetic pyrethroid insecticides on nontarget organisms. *Residue Rev*. 1986; 97: 93–120.

Soldin OP, O'Mara DM, Aschner M. Thyroid hormones and methylmercury toxicity. *Biol Trace Elem Res*. 2008 Winter; 126 (1–3): 1–12.

Sorrequieta A, Ferraro G, Boggio SB, et al. Free amino acid production during tomato fruit ripening: a focus on L-glutamate. *Amino Acids*. 2010 May; 38 (5): 1523–32.

Sourcewatch. Arsenic. *Sourcewatch*. Jan 4, 2012. Accessed Mar 28, 2015. Available at www.sourcewatch.org/index.php/Arsenic.

Srogi K. Levels and congener distributions of PCDDs, PCDFs and dioxin-like PCBs in environmental and human samples: a review. *Environ Chem Lett*. 2008; 6: 1–28.

Stern D. Citricidal side effects. *Livestrong*. Aug 16, 2013. Accessed Sept 28, 2015. Available at www.livestrong.com/article/27614-citricidal-side-effects.

Sturniolo GC, Di Leo V, Ferronato A, et al. Zinc supplementation tightens leaky gut in Crohn's disease. *Inflamm Bowel Dis*. 2001 May; 7 (2): 94–8.

Suja F, Pramanik BK, Zain SM. Contamination, bioaccumulation and toxic effects of perfluorinated chemicals (PFCs) in the water environment: a review paper. *Water Sci Technol*. 2009; 60 (6): 1533–44.

Sun HJ, Rathinasabapathi B, Wu B, et al. Arsenic and selenium toxicity and their interactive effects in humans. *Environ Int*. 2014 Aug; 69: 148–58.

Sun-Edelstein C, Mauskop A. Foods and supplements in the management of migraine headaches. *Clin J Pain*. 2009 Jun; 25 (5): 446–52.

Suzuki D. Food and climate change. David Suzuki Foundation, 2014. Accessed Mar 20, 2015. Available at www.davidsuzuki.org/what-you-can-do/food-and-our-planet/food-and-climate-change.

Suzuki D. Help bring bees and butterflies back! David Suzuki Foundation, 2015. Available at www.davidsuzuki.org/issues/wildlife-habitat/projects/save-the-bees-and-butterflies.

Suzuki D. Highlights of Ontario's cosmetic pesticide ban. David Suzuki Foundation, 2014. Accessed Dec 6, 2015. Available at www.davidsuzuki.org/issues/health/science/pesticides/highlights-of-ontarios-cosmetic-pesticide-ban.

Suzuki D. Ontario restricts bee-killing neonic pesticides. David Suzuki Foundation, Sept 2015. Accessed Dec 6, 2015. Available at davidsuzuki.org/publications/finding-solutions/2015/fall/ontario-restricts-bee-killing-neonic-pesticides.

Suzuki D. Parabens. David Suzuki Foundation, 2015. Available at davidsuzuki.org/issues/health/science/toxics/chemicals-in-your-cosmetics—-parabens.

Suzuki D, Roberts J. Help solve an orange-and-black mystery. David Suzuki Foundation, Oct 17, 2013. Accessed Mar 19, 2016. Available at www.davidsuzuki.org/blogs/science-matters/2013/10/help-solve-an-orange-and-black-mystery.

Tahiliani AG, Beinlich CJ. Pantothenic acid in health and disease. *Vitam Horm*. 1991; 46: 165–228.

Takashima-Uebelhoer BB, Barber LG, Zagarins SE, et al. Household chemical exposures and the risk of canine malignant lymphoma, a model for human non-Hodgkin's lymphoma. *Environ Res*. 2012 Jan; 112: 171–6.

Thornton, PK. Livestock production: recent trends, future prospects. *Philos Trans R Soc Lond B Biol Sci*. 2010 Sept 27; 365 (1554): 2853–67.

Tolins M, Ruchirawat M, Landrigan P. The developmental neurotoxicity of arsenic: cognitive and behavioral consequences of early life exposure. *Ann Glob Health*. 2014 Jul–Aug; 80 (4): 303–14.

Toraason M, Sussman G, Biagini R, et al. Latex allergy in the workplace. *Toxicol Sci*. 2000 Nov; 58 (1): 5–14.

Tupper K. At long last: EPA releases pesticide use statistics. Pesticide Action Network, 2011. Accessed Sept 5, 2015. Available at www.panna.org/blog/long-last-epa-releases-pesticide-use-statistics.

UN News Centre. Rearing cattle produces more greenhouse gases than driving cars, UN report warns. Nov 29, 2006. Accessed Mar 19, 2014. Available at www.un.org/apps/news/story.asp?newsID=20772#.VwZRZce06t8.

University of Maryland Medical Center. Alpha-lipoic acid. 2014. Accessed Sept 27, 2015. Available at umm.edu/health/medical/altmed/supplement/alphalipoic-acid.

University of Maryland Medical Centre. Cysteine. Jun 26, 2014. Accessed Dec 19, 2015. Available at umm.edu/health/medical/altmed/supplement/cysteine.

Unsworth J. History of pesticide use. International Union of Pure and Applied Chemistry, May 10, 201. Accessed Mar 19, 2015. Available at agrochemicals.iupac.org/index.php?option=com_sobi2&sobi2Task=sobi2Details&catid=3&sobi2Id=31.

Urban Farmer. Permaculture design. Accessed Mar 22, 2015. Available at www.theurbanfarmer.ca/permaculture-design.

U.S. Census Bureau. U.S. and world population clock. Accessed Jul 2013. Available at www.census.gov/popclock.

U.S. Department of Agriculture, Agricultural Research Service. USDA National Nutrient Database for Standard Reference, Release 26 external link disclaimer. Nutrient Data Lab, 2013. Available at https://ndb.nal.usda.gov/.

U.S. Environmental Protection Agency. Cleaner power plants. 2014. Accessed Jan 26, 2015. Available at www.epa.gov/mats/powerplants.html.

U.S. Environmental Protection Agency. Polychlorinated biphenyl (PCBs). Apr 8, 2013. Available at www.epa.gov/wastes/hazard/tsd/pcbs/about.htm.

U.S. Environmental Protection Agency. Types of pesticide ingredients. 2015. Accessed Nov 22, 2015. Available at www2.epa.gov/ingredients-used-pesticide-products/types-pesticide-ingredients.

U.S. Environmental Protection Agency. Understanding PCB risks at the GE-Pittsfield/Housatonic river site. 2015. Accessed Apr 2, 2015. Available at www.epa.gov/housatonic/understandingpcbrisks.html#WildlifeHumanHealthEffects.

U.S. Food and Drug Administration. Arsenic in rice and rice products. 2012. Accessed Jan 6, 2016. Available at www.fda.gov/Food/FoodborneIllnessContaminants/Metals/ucm319870.htm.

U.S. Food and Drug Administration. Questions and answers on lead-glazed traditional pottery. Nov 2010. Accessed Sept 7, 2015. Available at www.fda.gov/Food/FoodborneIllnessContaminants/Metals/ucm233281.htm.

U.S. Food and Drug Administration. Questions and answers on monosodium glutamate (MSG). Nov 19, 2012. Accessed Jan 1, 2016. Available at www.fda.gov/Food/IngredientsPackagingLabeling/FoodAdditivesIngredients/ucm328728.htm.

U.S. Food and Drug Administration. Questions and answers regarding 3-Nitro (Roxarsone). Apr 1, 2015. Accessed Jan 3, 2016. Available at www.fda.gov/AnimalVeterinary/SafetyHealth/ProductSafetyInformation/ucm258313.htm#What_did_FDA_announce_.

U.S. Geological Survey. Mercury in the environment. Feb 19, 2009. Accessed Dec 11, 2015. Available at www.usgs.gov/themes/factsheet/146-00.

Uttara B, Singh AV, Zamboni P, et al. Oxidative stress and neurodegenerative diseases: a review of upstream and downstream antioxidant therapeutic options. *Curr Neuropharmacol.* 2009 Mar; 7 (1): 65–74.

Vahter M, Akesson A, Lidén C, et al. Gender differences in the disposition and toxicity of metals. *Environ Res.* 2007 May; 104 (1): 85–95.

Vahter M, Berglund M, Akesson A, et al. Metals and women's health. *Environ Res.* 2002 Mar; 88 (3): 145–55.

Vahter M, Berglund M, Akesson A. Toxic metals and the menopause. *J Br Menopause Soc.* 2004 Jun; 10 (2): 60–4.

Valenti L, Dongiovanni P, Fargion S. Diagnostic and therapeutic implications of the association between ferritin level and severity of nonalcoholic fatty liver disease. *World J Gastroenterol.* 2012 Aug 7; 18 (29): 3782–6.

Valenti L, Fracanzani AL, Dongiovanni P, et al. A randomized trial of iron depletion in patients with nonalcoholic fatty liver disease and hyperferritinemia. *World J Gastroenterol.* 2014 Mar 21; 20 (11): 3002–10.

Vally H, Misso NL, Madan V. Clinical effects of sulfite additives. *Clin Exp Allergy.* 2010 Apr; 40 (4): 688; author reply: 689–90.

Vally H, Thompson PJ. Allergic and asthmatic reactions to alcoholic drinks. *Addict Biol.* 2003 Mar; 8 (1): 3–11.

Van den Berg H. Global status of DDT and its alternatives for use in vector control to prevent disease. *Environ Health Perspect.* 2009 Nov; 117 (11): 1656–63.

Van den Berg KJ, van Raaij JA, Bragt PC, et al. Interactions of halogenated industrial chemicals with transthyretin and effects on thyroid hormone levels in vivo. *Arch Toxicol.* 1991; 65: 15–19.

Vázquez M, Calatayud M, Vélez D, et al. Intestinal transport of methylmercury and inorganic mercury in various models of Caco-2 and HT29-MTX cells. *Toxicology.* 2013 Sept 15; 311 (3): 147–53.

Vázquez M, Devesa V, Vélez D. Characterization of the intestinal absorption of inorganic mercury in Caco-2 cells. *Toxicol In Vitro.* 2015 Feb; 29 (1): 93–102.

Vázquez M, Vélez D, Devesa V. In vitro evaluation of inorganic mercury and methylmercury effects on the intestinal epithelium permeability. *Food Chem Toxicol.* 2014 Dec; 74: 349–59.

Vigh É, Colombo A, Benfenati E, et al. Individual breast milk consumption and exposure to PCBs and PCDD/Fs in Hungarian infants: a time-course analysis of the first three months of lactation. *Sci Total Environ.* 2013 Apr 1; 449: 336–44.

Vojdani A, O'Bryan T, Green JA, et al. Immune response to dietary proteins, gliadin and cerebellar peptides in children with autism. *Nutr Neurosci.* 2004 Jun; 7 (3): 151–61.

Volta U, Granito A, Parisi C, et al. Deamidated gliadin peptide antibodies as a routine test for celiac disease: a prospective analysis. *J Clin Gastroenterol.* 2010 Mar; 44 (3): 186–90.

Wagner S, Breiteneder H. The latex-fruit syndrome. *Biochem Soc Trans.* 2002 Nov; 30 (Pt 6): 935–40.

Walker DM, Gore AC. Transgenerational neuroendocrine disruption of reproduction. *Nat Rev Endocrinol.* 2011 Apr; 7 (4): 197–207.

Walker R, Lupien JR. The safety evaluation of monosodium glutamate. *J Nutr.* 2000 Apr; 130 (4S Suppl): 1049S–52S.

Wang IC, Lee WJ. Polychlorinated dibenzo-p-dioxin, polychlorinated dibenzofurans and polychlorinated biphenyls in farmed fish, water, sediment, and feed. *J Environ Sci Health A Tox Hazard Subst Environ Eng.* 2010; 45 (2): 201–10.

Wang IJ, Wang JY. Children with atopic dermatitis show clinical improvement after *Lactobacillus* exposure. *Clin Exp Allergy.* 2015 Apr; 45 (4): 779–87.

Wang J, Sampson HA. Food allergy. *J Clin Invest.* 2011 Mar; 121 (3): 827–35.

Wasserman M, Nogueira DP, Tomatis L, et al. Organochlorine compounds in neoplastic and adjacent apparently normal breast tissue. *Bull Environ Contam Toxicol.* 1976 Apr; 15 (4): 478–84.

WebMD. Arsenic in food: FAQ. Accessed Mar 22, 2015. Available at www.webmd.com/diet/arsenic-food-faq?page=2.

WebMD. Chlorella. Accessed Sept 27, 2015. Available at www.webmd.com/vitamins-supplements/ingredientmono-907-chlorella.aspx?activeingredientid=907&activeingredientname=chlorella.

WebMD. Vitamin E. Accessed Sept 20, 2015. Available at www.webmd.com/vitamins-supplements/ingredientmono-954-vitamin%20e.aspx?activeingredientid=954&activeingredientname=vitamin%20e.

WebMD. Women's health: hypothyroidism (underactive thyroid). Accessed Mar 5, 2016. Available at www.webmd.com/women/hypothyroidism-underactive-thyroid-symptoms-causes-treatments?page=2.

Weeds S. *Breast Cancer? Breast Health! The Wise Women Way.* Woodstock, NY: Ash Tree Publishing, 1996.

Weil A. Foods you don't have to buy organic. *Dr. Weil.* Nov 2015. Available at www.drweil.com/drw/u/ART02984/Foods-You-Dont-Have-to-Buy-Organic.html.

Weil A. Foods you should always buy organic. *Dr. Weil.* Nov 2015. Available at www.drweil.com/drw/u/ART02985/Foods-You-Should-Always-Buy-Organic.html.

Whales Online. Are St-Lawrence belugas contaminated? 2015. Accessed Dec 4, 2015. Available at baleinesendirect. org/en/scientific-exploration/research-projects/st-lawrence-beluga/are-st-lawrence-belugas-contaminated-2015.

Whales Online. Do PAHs (toxic contaminants) cause cancer in St. Lawrence beluga whales? 2015. Accessed Dec 4, 2015. Available at baleinesendirect.org/en/scientific-exploration/research-projects/st-lawrence-beluga/do-pahs-toxic-contaminants-cause-cancer-in-st-lawrence-beluga-whales.

Whitbread D. Top 10 foods highest in cysteine. *HealthAliciousNess.com.* Accessed Sept 27, 2015. Available at www.healthaliciousness.com/articles/high-cysteine-foods.php.

Whitbread D. Top 10 foods highest in selenium. *HealthAliciousNess.com.* Accessed Mar 27, 2016. Available at www.healthaliciousness.com/articles/foods-high-in-selenium.php.

Whitbread D. Top 10 foods highest in vitamin B5 (pantothenic acid). *HealthAliciousNess.com.* Accessed Sept 27, 2015. Available at www. healthaliciousness.com/articles/foods-high-in-pantothenic-acid-vitamin-B5. php.

Whitbread D. Top 10 foods highest in vitamin B6. *HealthAliciousNess.com.* Accessed Mar 27, 2016. Available at www.healthaliciousness.com/articles/foods-high-in-vitamin-B6.php.

Whitbread D. Top 10 foods highest in vitamin B9 (folate). *HealthAliciousNess. com.* Accessed Mar 27, 2016. Available at www.healthaliciousness. com/articles/foods-high-in-folate-vitamin-B9.php.

Whitbread D. Top 10 foods highest in vitamin C. *HealthAliciousNess.com.* Accessed Mar 27, 2016. Available at www.healthaliciousness.com/articles/vitamin-C.php.

Whitbread D. Top 10 high magnesium foods you can't miss. *HealthAliciousNess.com.* Accessed Sept 27, 2015. Available at www. healthaliciousness.com/articles/foods-high-in-magnesium.php.

Whitehorn PR, O'Connor S, Wackers FL, et al. Neonicotinoid pesticide reduces bumble bee colony growth and queen production. *Science.* 2012 Apr 20; 336 (6079): 351–2.

Williams CM, Barker JC, Sims JT. Management and utilization of poultry wastes. *Rev Environ Contam Toxicol.* 1999; 162: 105–57.

Winters D, Cleverly D, Lorber M, et al. Coplanar polychlorinated biphenyls (PCBs) in a national sample of beef in the United States: preliminary results. *Organohalogen Compounds.* 1996; 28: 350–4.

Wolff MS, Toniolo PG, Lee EW, et al. Blood levels of organochlorine residues and risk of breast cancer. *J Natl Cancer Inst.* 1993 Apr 21; 85 (8): 648–52.

World Health Organization. Dioxins and their effects on human health. Jun 2014. Accessed Nov 14, 2015. Available at www.who.int/mediacentre/factsheets/fs225/en.

World Health Organization. Exposure to arsenic: a major public health concern. 2010. Accessed Jan 3, 2016. Available at www.who.int/ipcs/features/arsenic.pdf?ua=1.

World Health Organization. Obesity and overweight. Fact sheet N°311. Jan 2015. Accessed Mar 25, 2016. Available at www.who.int/mediacentre/factsheets/fs311/en/.

Wüthrich B. Food allergy: definition, diagnosis, epidemiology, clinical aspects. [Article in German.] *Schweiz Med Wochenschr.* 1996 May 4; 126 (18): 770–6.

Xiong JS, Branigan D, Li M. Deciphering the MSG controversy. *Int J Clin Exp Med.* 2009 Nov 15; 2 (4): 329–36.

Yang WH, Drouin MA, Herbert M, et al. The monosodium glutamate symptom complex: assessment in a double-blind, placebo-controlled, randomized study. *J Allergy Clin Immunol.* 1997 Jun; 99 (6 Pt 1): 757–62.

Yasawy MI, Folsch UR, Schmidt WE, et al. Adult hereditary fructose intolerance. *World J Gastroenterol.* 2009 May 21; 15 (19): 2412–3.

Yassa HA. Autism: a form of lead and mercury toxicity. *Environ Toxicol Pharmacol.* 2014 Nov; 38 (3): 1016–24.

Yeap BB, Divitini ML, Gunton JE, et al. Higher ferritin levels, but not serum iron or transferrin saturation, are associated with Type 2 diabetes mellitus in adult men and women free of genetic haemochromatosis. *Clin Endocrinol* (Oxford). 2015 Apr; 82 (4): 525–32.

Yeast Infection Advisor. Mercury poisoning, candida yeast, or is it both? Accessed Dec 10, 2015. Available at www.yeastinfectionadvisor.com/mercurypoisoning.html.

Yoon CK. Exposure to pesticides is lowered when young children go organic. *New York Times.* Mar 25, 2003. Available at www.nytimes.com/2003/03/25/science/exposure-to-pesticides-is-lowered-when-young-children-go-organic.html.

Yu HY, Guo Y, Zeng EY. Dietary intake of persistent organic pollutants and potential health risks via consumption of global aquatic products. *Environ Toxicol Chem.* 2010 Oct; 29 (10): 2135–42.

Zacharski LR, Chow BK, Howes PS, et al. Decreased cancer risk after iron reduction in patients with peripheral arterial disease: results from a randomized trial. *J Natl Cancer Inst.* 2008 Jul 16; 100 (14): 996–1002.

Zamani F, Mohamadnejad M, Shakeri R, et al. Gluten sensitive enteropathy in patients with iron deficiency anemia of unknown origin. *World J Gastroenterol.* 2008 Dec 28; 14 (48): 7381–5.

Zhai Q, Narbad A, Chen W. Dietary strategies for the treatment of cadmium and lead toxicity. *Nutrients.* 2015 Jan 14; 7 (1): 552–71.

Zhang J, Jiang Y, Zhou J, et al. Concentrations of PCDD/PCDFs and PCBs in retail foods and an assessment of dietary intake for local population of Shenzhen in China. *Environ Int.* 2008 Aug; 34 (6): 799–803.

Zhang L, Wong MH. Environmental mercury contamination in China: sources and impacts. *Environ Int.* 2007 Jan; 33 (1): 108–21.

Zheng HX, Yan S, Qin ZD, et al. MtDNA analysis of global populations support that major population expansions began before Neolithic Time. *Sci Rep.* 2012; 2: 745.

Zwicker JD, Dutton DJ, Emery JC. Longitudinal analysis of the association between removal of dental amalgam, urine mercury and 14 self-reported health symptoms. *Environ Health.* 2014 Nov 18; 13: 95.

Zwolińska-Wcisło M, Galicka-Latała D, Rudnicka-Sosin L, et al. Coeliac disease and other autoimmunological disorders coexistence. [Article in Polish.] *Przegl Lek.* 2009; 66 (7): 370–2.

Resources

Books

Heinberg R. *Afterburn: Society Beyond Fossil Fuels.* Gabriola Island, BC: New Society Publishers, 2015.

Heinberg R. *Peak Everything: Waking Up to the Century of Declines.* Gabriola Island, BC: New Society Publishers, 2007.

Oppenlander RA. *Comfortably Unaware: What We Choose to Eat Is Killing Us and Our Planet.* New York: Beaufort Books, 2012.

Oppenlander RA. *Food Choice and Sustainability: Why Buying Local, Eating Less Meat and Taking Baby Steps Won't Work.* Minneapolis, MN: Langdon Street Press, 2013.

Smil V. *Harvesting the Biosphere: What We Have Taken from Nature.* Cambridge MA: MIT Press, 2012.

Stewart R. *Save the Humans.* Toronto: Penguin Random House, 2013.

Documentary Films

Acid Test: The Global Challenge of Ocean Acidification

Cowspiracy: The Sustainability Secret

Dive! The Film — Living Off America's Waste

Food, Inc.

Forks over Knives

GMO OMG

Just Eat It: A Food Waste Story

Racing Extinction

Revolution

What a Way to Go: Life at the End of Empire Movie

What the Health?

Environmental Groups

David Suzuki Foundation: davidsuzuki.org

Earth System Governance Project: earthsystemgovernance.org

EnteroLab: enterolab.com

Environmental Working Group: ewg.org

Global Environment Facility: thegef.org

Greenpeace: greenpeace.org

Intergovernmental Panel on Climate Change: ipcc.ch

International POPs Elimination Network: ipen.org

Jane Goodall Institute of Canada: janegoodall.ca

Natural Resources Defense Council: nrdc.org

Ocean Conservancy: oceanconservancy.org

Orangutan Conservancy: orangutan.com

Pesticide Action Network International: pan-international.org

Pesticide Action Network North America: panna.org

Rainforest Action Network: ran.org

Sierra Club Canada Foundation: sierraclub.ca

United Conservationists: unitedconservationists.org

United Nations Environment Programme: unep.org

Wildlife Conservation Society: wcs.org

World Nature Organization: wno.org

World Wildlife Fund: worldwildlife.org

Growing Food

Big Sky Permaculture (Calgary): bigskypermaculture.ca

Ecology Action: growbiointensive.org/grow_main.html

Ecovillage Network of Canada (National): ecovillagenetworkcanada.ning.com

Edmonton Permaculture Guild (Edmonton): edmontonpermaculture.ca

Environmental Design Collaborative (Ontario): bradpeterson.ca/permaculture.htm

Kootenay Permaculture Institute (Winlaw, BC): telus.net/permaculture

Montreal Permaculture Guild (Montreal): montrealpermaculture.wordpress.com

OUR Ecovillage (Shawnigan Lake, BC): ourecovillage.org

P3 Permaculture Design (Montreal): p3permaculture.ca

Pacific Permaculture (Denman Island, BC): pacificpermaculture.ca

Permaculture Activist (North America): permacultureactivist.net

Permaculture BC (Victoria): permaculturebc.com

Permaculture Institute of Eastern Ontario (Ottawa): eonpermaculture.ca

Permaculture Ottawa (Ottawa): permacultureottawa.ca

Permaculture Powell River (Powell River, BC): permaculturepowellriver.ca

The Permaculture Project of GTA (Toronto): www.tppgta.com

Permaculture School (Edmonton): permacultureschool.ca

Seven Ravens Permaculture Academy and Eco Forest (Saltspring Island, BC): seven-ravens.com

Sustainable Living Network (Ontario): sustainablelivingnetwork.org

Urban Farmer (Powell River, BC): theurbanfarmer.ca

Verge Permaculture (Calgary): vergepermaculture.ca

Health Index

A

agriculture, 25–27
  biointensive, 35–37, 38, 39
  environmental impacts, 26–27, 144–47
  genetically engineered crops, 28, 34, 151
  organic, 28, 34, 37–38, 145
  pesticide use in, 25–27, 35–39
air pollution, 41, 47
ALA (alpha-lipoic acid), 98–99
allergies
  in children, 32, 76, 130
  to foods, 105–11, 134–41
  to latex, 141
  to pollen, 134–36
  skin reactions, 77
  to sulfites, 136–37, 138
aloe vera gel, 84
anaphylaxis, 106, 107–8, 110, 132
anemia, 66, 125
animal foods, 13, 14
  environmental impact, 26, 68, 144–45, 146
  as iron source, 62, 63, 65
anthocyanins, 93, 94
antibiotics, 82
antibodies, 106–7, 123, 130–32. *See also* allergies
antioxidants, 43, 61, 140. *See also specific antioxidants*
apples, 72, 88
arsenic, 41, 43–46, 47
  sources, 43, 44–45, 46, 47
arthritis (rheumatoid), 123
artichokes, 72, 88
asparagus, 88

aspartame, 140
asthma, 140
autism, 124
autoimmune diseases, 123–24

B

baby food, 15
bacteria, 79, 145. *See also* gut bacteria
bees, 32–33, 39, 151
beets, 88
beluga whales, 148
bioaccumulation, 11, 13, 21, 54
birds, 148, 149, 150
bisphenol A (BPA), 16, 18, 21, 22
blood pressure, 139
bone loss, 48
bowel. *See also* celiac disease; gut bacteria
  detoxification of, 71–85
breast cancer, 12, 13, 16, 32
breast milk, 11, 13, 14
broccoli, 88
Brussels sprouts, 88
butterflies, 39, 150–51

C

cabbage, 88
cadmium, 49–50, 58, 76
caffeine, 156
calcium, 48, 66, 158
cancer. *See also specific types of cancer*
  arsenic and, 46
  dioxins and, 15
  iron and, 64, 65
  PCBs and, 12
  pesticides and, 16–17, 30
Candida albicans, 55–56
caprylic acid, 80
carbamates, 31–32, 149–50

carbon dioxide, 42, 152
cardiovascular disease, 65
carnosine, 158
carrots, 88
Carson, Rachel, 27–28
celiac disease, 79, 120–25
children
  allergies in, 32, 76, 130
  toxins and, 20, 31, 32, 48–49, 54, 55
chlorella (*Chlorella vulgaris*), 99–100
chlorine. *See* organochlorides
chlorpyrifos, 31, 149
cholangitis (primary sclerosing), 124
cholesterol, 43
choline, 98
cigarette smoking, 49–50
cilantro, 72
cirrhosis, 124
Citricidal (grapefruit seed extract), 80
coal, 45, 47, 55
constipation, 74
corn syrup (high-fructose), 117
cosmetics, 19, 22
Crohn's disease, 83, 130
curcumin (turmeric), 72, 101
cysteine, 95

D

DDE (dichlorodiphenyl-dichloroethylene), 16
DDT (dichlorodiphenyl-trichloroethane), 16, 21, 27–28, 30, 149
dental fillings, 57
dermatitis (allergic), 77
detoxification
  adverse effects, 71, 89
  of bowel, 71–85

cautions, 73–74
definition, 71
diet and, 72–73, 81
of liver, 85–102
nutrients for, 81–84,
   87–107
phases, 71–72, 87, 90–98
supplements for, 72,
   81–83
10-day diet for, 156–59
DGL (deglycyrrhizinated
   licorice), 83
diabetes, 18, 64, 123, 124
diet. *See also* foods
   and detoxification, 72–73,
   81
   elimination/challenge,
   132–34
   FODMAP, 119–20
   vegan, 11, 158
   vegetarian, 66, 67, 68, 72,
   158
digestive (GI) tract, 78,
   81–84. *See also* bowel;
   gut bacteria
dioxins, 12–15, 16, 21

E

endocrine disruptors, 16–17,
   18–19, 20–21, 30, 32
endocrine system, 11, 17.
   See also endocrine
   disruptors; hormones
endometriosis, 16, 20
environment, 143–44, 154.
   See also toxins
Environmental Working
   Group (EWG), 20, 35
estrogen, 12, 14–15
estrogen mimics, 16, 19,
   20. *See also* endocrine
   disruptors

F

ferritin, 61–64, 68, 69.
   See also iron
fiber, 72, 75
fibromyalgia, 140
fish, 26, 153–54

mercury in, 54, 56, 58–59
other to xins in, 10–11,
   14, 149
fishing industry, 145,
   152–53
flame retardants
   (brominated), 18–19, 22
flavonoids, 93, 94
flax oil, 158
FODMAP diet, 119–20
folic acid, 92
foods. *See also* diet; *specific*
   reactions to (below)
   allergy/sensitivity-
   provoking, 134–41
   detoxifying, 72
   fiber sources, 75
   fructose sources, 118,
   119
   glutamate sources, 140
   gluten sources, 126–27
   iron sources, 67
   lactose sources, 115, 120
   liver-cleansing, 88–89
   magnesium sources, 86,
   95–96
   nutrient sources, 90–102
   organic, 36–37
   palm oil sources, 147
   polyphenol sources, 94
   reintroducing, 133–34
   sulfite sources, 137
food allergies, 105–11
   immune system response,
   106–10
   testing for, 111
   triggers, 109, 134–41
food intolerances, 111,
   113–25
   diagnosing, 114, 115, 121,
   123
food sensitivities, 111,
   125–27, 129–54
   diet changes and, 132–34
   immune system response,
   129–32
   testing for, 125–26,
   130–34
   triggers, 134–41
formaldehyde, 17–18

fossil fuels, 50, 53, 144,
   145. *See also* coal;
   gasoline
free radicals, 43, 71–72
fructans, 119–20
fructose, 116–18
fungicides, 21, 29, 30, 35.
   See also pesticides

G

galactans, 120
gallbladder, 124
gardening, 37–39
garlic, 80, 81, 88
gasoline, 47–48
gastrointestinal (GI) tract,
   78, 81–84. *See also*
   gut bacteria
glutamate. *See* MSG
glutamine, 81, 98
glutathione, 43, 81, 82,
   92–93
gluten, 125–27. *See also*
   celiac disease
glycine, 97
glyphosate (Roundup), 29,
   33–34, 35, 150–51
grains, 119
grapefruit seed extract
   (Citricidal), 80
greenhouse gas emissions,
   42, 144, 145, 152
gut bacteria, 55–56, 76–77,
   79–81

H

headaches, 129, 130, 139
hemochromatosis (genetic),
   61, 63–64
herbicides, 29, 33–34
herbs, 83–84
high-fructose corn syrup,
   117
homosalate, 20
hormones, 11, 12, 14–15.
   See also endocrine
   system; *specific*
   hormones
hypothyroidism, 123

I

IBS (irritable bowel
  syndrome), 119, 130
immune system, 106–7,
  123–24
  and food allergies,
    106–10
  and food sensitivities,
    129–32
inflammation, 64, 79
inflammatory bowel disease
  (IBD), 76
iodine, 56
iron, 61–69. See also ferritin
  from animal sources, 62,
    63, 65
  deficiency of, 66, 67, 125
  excess levels of, 62,
    63–66, 69
  plant sources, 67, 68

L

lactase deficiency, 115
Lactobacillus probiotics, 77,
  82
lactose intolerance, 114–15
latex allergy, 141
laxatives, 84–85
lead, 46–49, 58, 76
lemons, 89
L-glutamine. See glutamine
licorice (deglycyrrhizinated),
  83
liver
  cleansing foods for,
    88–89
  detoxification of, 85–102
  detoxification phase 1,
    90–94
  diseases of, 124
  iron toxicity and, 65
  toxicity symptoms, 86
lung cancer, 49–50

M

magnesium, 48, 84, 85, 86,
  95–96
Malthus, Thomas, 26
marshmallow root, 83

meat, 13, 14, 26. See also
  animal foods
mercury, 53–59
  in fish, 54, 56, 58–59
  health effects, 43, 54–57,
    59
  sources, 41, 53–54, 57
  yeast die-off and, 80, 81
metabolic syndrome,
  64, 68
metals (heavy), 41–51, 148.
  See also specific metals
  sources, 41–42
  toxicity of, 42–43
  toxicity prevention/
    treatment, 98–102
methane, 145
methionine, 95
methylmercury, 54.
  See also mercury
migraines, 129, 130
Monarch butterflies,
  150–51
MSG (monosodium
  glutamate), 137–41
multiple sclerosis, 123

N

neonicotinoids, 32–33, 151
nervous system, 46,
  122–23
nuts, 135

O

obesity, 21
oceans, 42, 59, 152–54
octyl methoxycinnamate,
  20
oral allergy syndrome,
  134–36
oregano, 80
organochlorides, 15–17,
  30. See also DDE; DDT;
  PCBs
organophosphates, 30–31,
  150
oxidative damage, 42–43,
  59, 65
oxybenzone, 20

P

PAHs (polyaromatic
  hydrocarbons), 12, 148
palm oil, 146, 147
pantothenic acid
  (vitamin B5), 82, 96
parabens, 19, 22
PBBs (polybrominated
  biphenyls), 21
PCBs (polychlorinated
  biphenyls), 9–12, 21,
  22, 148
perchloroethylene, 20, 22
permaculture, 35–37, 38, 39
pesticides, 25–39
  in agriculture, 25–27,
    35–39
  arsenic-containing, 44
  bans on, 28–30, 33, 44
  and children, 31, 32
  as endocrine disruptors,
    21, 30, 32
  history of, 27–30
  testing for, 34–35
  types, 30–31
  wildlife impacts, 21,
    27–28, 149–57
PFCs (perfluorinated
  compounds), 19, 22
phthalates (plasticizers), 16,
  19, 21, 22
phytoplankton, 59
pollen allergies, 134–36
polyols, 120
polyphenols, 93, 94
POPs (persistent organic
  pollutants), 10, 28–
  29. See also specific
  pollutants
poultry, 13, 14, 44
power plants, 41–42, 47, 55
pregnancy, 11, 12, 54–55
proanthocyanidins, 93, 94
probiotics, 76–77, 82
produce, 35, 36, 37–38. See
  also specific fruits and
  vegetables
progesterone, 12
prostate cancer, 30
pyrethroids, 32, 150

Q

quercetin, 82

R

rainforests, 144, 146–47
rice, 44–45
Roundup (glyphosate), 29, 33–34, 35, 150–51

S

salmon, 11
seaweed, 89
selenium, 54–55, 82, 100–101
senna, 84
Silent Spring (Carson), 27–28
slippery elm, 83
soil erosion, 146
solvents (organic), 20, 22
spinach, 89
sprouts, 88
styrene, 20, 22
sugar, 117, 118
sulfites, 136–37, 138
sulfoxaflor, 33
sunscreens, 19–20, 22
supplements
    Detox Diet and, 156, 157, 158
    for detoxification, 72, 81–83
sustainability, 145. *See also* permaculture

T

taurine, 97
tea (green), 72, 88
10-Day Detox Diet, 156–59
thyroid, 123
    toxins and, 11, 12, 14, 30, 56–57
toluene, 20, 22
toxins (environmental), 9–23, 146, 151. *See also specific toxins*
    as endocrine disruptors, 16–17, 18–19, 20–21
    in fish, 10–11, 14, 54, 56, 58–59, 149
transferrin, 64
Trowbridge, J., 56
turmeric (curcumin), 72, 101

U

UV (ultraviolet) filters, 19–20, 22

V

vitamin A, 82
vitamin B_1, 96
vitamin B_2, 90
vitamin B_3, 90–91
vitamin B_5 (pantothenic acid), 82, 96
vitamin B_6, 91
vitamin B_{12}, 92, 158
vitamin C, 48, 84, 96–97
vitamin D, 20, 158
vitamin E, 96

W

watercress, 72
weight loss programs, 9
whales, 148, 154
wildlife, 143, 145, 146, 147, 148–53
    pesticide impact on, 21, 27–28, 149–57

X

xenoestrogens, 32
xylene, 20, 22

Y

yeast infections, 55–56, 79–81, 156
The Yeast Syndrome (Trowbridge), 56

Z

zinc, 82–83, 102, 158

Recipe Index

A

almonds and almond flour
  Breakfast Porridge (variation), 164
  Cauliflower and Zucchini Slaw, 228
  Flax Bread (Egg-Free, Corn-Free, Dairy-Free, Soy-Free), 187
  Pumpkin Seed Chimichurri (variation), 223
amaranth. *See also* amaranth flour
  Ancient Grains Granola, 162
  Carrot Cake Baked Amaranth, 166
  Gingerbread Amaranth Cookies, 314
  Multi-Seed Quinoa Crackers (tip), 200
amaranth flour. *See also* amaranth
  Chocolate, Lime and Coconut Cake, 310
  Make Your Own Cupcake Mix, 312
  Swedish Wraps, 190
  White Dinner Rolls (Egg-Free, Corn-Free, Dairy-Free, Soy-Free), 188
Ancient Grains Granola, 162
Apple Cider Vinaigrette, 241
apples and applesauce
  Applesauce Raisin Muffins, 194
  Beta-Carotene Burst, 179
  Bitter Detoxifier, 182
  Blueberry Muffins, Favorite, 193
  Butternut Squash and Apple Soup with Ginger, 254
  Cauliflower and Zucchini Slaw, 228
  Coconut Pancakes, Essential (variation), 167
  Creamy White Sauce, 225
  Grasshopper Juice, 181
  Iron-Builder Juice, 180
  Luscious Apple Butter, 219
  Multigrain Cereal with Fruit, 163
  Squash with Quinoa and Apricots, 301
  Warm Beet Salad, 233
apricots (dried)
  Apricot Breakfast Bites, 175
  Apricot Tamarind Marmalade, 220
  Squash with Quinoa and Apricots, 301
  Sunflower Quinoa Snack Squares, 205
  Warm Beet Salad, 233
artichokes
  Artichoke Heart Salad, 232
  Country-Style Eggplant, 216
  Mediterranean Bean Salad, 238
  Mixed Green Salad with Zesty Herb Dressing, 229
  Vegetable Paella, 288
Asian-Style Quinoa Salad with Chili-Orange Dressing, 234
avocado
  Avocado, Orange and Quinoa Salsa, 221
  Avocado Cucumber Hand Rolls, 207
  Avocado Mayonnaise, 218
  Avocado Salad, 232
  Avocado Spinach Dip, 212
  Maki Rolls with Carrot Rice and Avocado, 208
  Spicy Lime Avocado Dressing, 244
  Super Protein Shake, 184
  Watercress, Raspberry and Avocado Salad, 231

B

bananas
  Blueberry Muffins, Favorite, 193
  Pumpkin Latte Waffles (variation), 172
bars and squares, 176, 202–5
Basic Gravy, 224
  Chickpeas and Cauliflower in Tomato Curry, 276
  Chickpeas in Tomato Curry, 275
  Mixed Vegetable Coconut Curry, 289
  Potato and Spinach Curry, 299
basil. *See also* herbs
  Basil and Roasted Pepper Quinoa, 302
  Creamy Herb Dressing, 243
  Pesto Sauce, Classic, 222
  Spicy Lime Avocado Dressing (variation), 244
beans. *See also* beans, green; chickpeas
  Avocado Salad, 232
  Beans and Rice, 174
  Black Bean and Rice Salad, 236
  Black Bean Burgers, 269
  Caribbean Red Bean, Spinach and Potato Curry, 272
  Garlicky White Bean Spread, 214
  Golden Cauliflower with Split Peas (variation), 279
  Hearty Black and White Bean Soup, 261
  Kale and Quinoa Minestrone, 262
  Mediterranean Bean Salad, 238
  Navy Bean Sloppy Joes, 270
  Red Beans and Red Rice, 271

Smoky Sweet Potato Hash, 173
Spicy Black Bean Dip, 213
Squash and Black Bean Chili, 268
Sweet Potato, Quinoa and Black Bean Salad, 235
Sweet Potato Shepherd's Pie, 282
Two-Bean Chili with Zucchini, 266
beans, green
Black-Eyed Peas with Vegetables, 278
Greens and Vegetable Salad with Lemon Dressing, 230
Mediterranean Bean Salad (variation), 238
Sindhi Spinach, 284
Two-Bean Chili with Zucchini, 266
Vegetable Paella, 288
beets
Borscht, 249
Citrus Beets, 292
Iron-Builder Juice, 180
Kale Spring Rolls, 210
Warm Beet Salad, 233
berries. See also specific types of berries
Berry Chia Smoothie, 183 .
Berry Vinaigrette, 241
Seasonal Fruit Parfaits, 317
Summer Fruit Compote, 316
Summer Greens and Berries with Apple Cider Vinaigrette, 230
Beta-Carotene Burst, 179
Bitter Detoxifier, 182
Black-Eyed Peas with Vegetables, 278
Black Sticky Rice Pudding, 318
blueberries
Berry Vinaigrette, 241
Coconut Pancakes, Essential (variation), 167
Cranberry Quinoa Porridge (variation), 165
Favorite Blueberry Muffins, 193

Just Peachy Blueberry Picnic, 178
Summer Greens and Berries with Apple Cider Vinaigrette, 230
Super Protein Shake, 184
Borscht, 249
breads, 186–92
Breakfast Porridge, 164
breakfasts, 161–76
broccoli
Mixed Green Salad with Zesty Herb Dressing, 229
Spinach, Quinoa and Broccoli Bisque, 260
Brown Rice, 305
Brown Rice Flour Blend, 195
Applesauce Raisin Muffins, 194
Blueberry Muffins, Favorite, 193
Carrot Cake Muffins, 196
Butternut Squash and Apple Soup with Ginger, 254
Butternut Squash Spaghetti Sauce, 226
Butternut Squash with Snow Peas and Red Pepper, 299

C

cabbage
Mixed Green Salad with Zesty Herb Dressing, 229
Spicy Squash and Fennel Soup, 256
Caesar Salad Dressing, 246
cakes, 310–12
Caribbean Red Bean, Spinach and Potato Curry, 272
carrots. See also vegetables
Beta-Carotene Burst, 179
Carrot Cake Baked Amaranth, 166
Carrot Cake Muffins, 196
Greens and Vegetable Salad with Lemon Dressing, 230
Herbed Vegetable Spread, 217

Iron-Builder Juice, 180
Kale Spring Rolls, 210
Maki Rolls with Carrot Rice and Avocado, 208
Mixed Green Salad with Zesty Herb Dressing, 229
Roasted Spice-Glazed Root Vegetables, 296
Spiced Root Vegetables, 295
cauliflower
Cauliflower and Zucchini Slaw, 228
Chickpeas and Cauliflower in Tomato Curry, 276
Golden Cauliflower with Split Peas, 279
Whole Baked Masala Cauliflower, 290
Yellow Lentil Curry with Vegetables, 283
celery. See also vegetables
Grasshopper Juice, 181
Green Juice Detox, 182
Green Tea Metabolizer, 183
Harira, 263
Nori Pinwheels, 206
cereals, 162–66
chia seeds. See also seeds
Ancient Grains Granola, 162
Berry Chia Smoothie, 183
Black Bean Burgers, 269
Chia Pancakes with Maple Syrup, 170
Coco-Cocoa Chia Gelato, 321
Polka-Dot Mango Ice Pops, 323
Super Protein Shake, 184
chickpea flour. See also chickpeas
Coconut "Corn" Bread, 191
Coconut Pancakes, Essential, 167
Good Morning Grain-Free Waffles, 171
Make-Ahead Coconut Crêpes, 168
Pumpkin Bread, 192
Pumpkin Latte Waffles, 172

chickpeas. *See also* beans; chickpea flour
Chickpea Salad, 240
Chickpeas and Cauliflower in Tomato Curry, 276
Chickpeas in Tomato Curry, 275
Curried Chickpeas, 277
Harira, 263
Herbed Vegetable Spread, 217
Middle Eastern Balela Salad, 237
Pumpkin Curry Soup, 253
Roasted Vegetable Hummus, 215
Sweet Potato Shepherd's Pie, 282
Zucchini Chickpea Tagine with Cilantro Quinoa, 274
Chile Rice, 304
chocolate. *See also* cocoa and cacao powder
Chocolate Chip Breakfast Bars, 176
Coconut Milk Ice Cream, 320
Good Morning Grain-Free Waffles (variation), 171
cilantro. *See also* herbs
Avocado, Orange and Quinoa Salsa, 221
Avocado Mayonnaise, 218
Creamy Herb Dressing, 243
Pumpkin Curry Soup, 253
Pumpkin Seed Chimichurri, 223
Two-Bean Chili with Zucchini, 266
Zucchini Chickpea Tagine with Cilantro Quinoa, 274
Citrus Beets, 292
Classic Pesto Sauce, 222
cocoa and cacao powder. *See also* chocolate
Chocolate, Lime and Coconut Cake, 310
Chocolate Date Protein Bars, 202

Chocolate Teff Pudding, 319
Coco-Cocoa Chia Gelato, 321
No-Bake Chocolate Quinoa Cookies, 313
coconut. *See also* coconut flour; coconut milk
Apricot Breakfast Bites, 175
Chewy Coconut Quinoa Bars, 204
Chocolate Chip Breakfast Bars, 176
Seasonal Fruit Parfaits, 317
coconut flour
Coconut "Corn" Bread, 191
Essential Coconut Pancakes, 167
Good Morning Grain-Free Waffles, 171
Make-Ahead Coconut Crêpes, 168
Pumpkin Bread, 192
Pumpkin Latte Waffles, 172
coconut milk. *See also* coconut flour
Black Sticky Rice Pudding, 318
Breakfast Porridge (variation), 164
Chocolate, Lime and Coconut Cake, 310
Chocolate Teff Pudding, 319
Coco-Cocoa Chia Gelato, 321
Coconut Milk Ice Cream, 320
Curried Chickpeas, 277
Curried Sweet Potato Soup, 257
Fragrant Coconut Rice, 303
Indonesian-Style Yellow Rice Pilaf, 306
Mixed Vegetable Coconut Curry, 289
Potato and Pea Coconut Curry, 280
Whipped Coconut Cream, 311

cookies, 313–15
Country-Style Eggplant, 216
crackers, 200–201
cranberries (dried)
Cranberry Quinoa Porridge, 165
Sunflower Quinoa Snack Squares, 205
Wild Rice Stuffing with Cranberries, 308
cucumber
Avocado Cucumber Hand Rolls, 207
Bitter Detoxifier, 182
Grasshopper Juice, 181
Green Juice Detox, 182
Greens and Vegetable Salad with Lemon Dressing, 230
Green Tea Metabolizer, 183
Cupcake Mix, Make Your Own, 312
Curried Chickpeas, 277
Curried Sweet Potato and Millet Soup, 258
Curried Sweet Potato Soup, 257
Curried Zucchini Strips, 294

D

dates
Apricot Breakfast Bites (tip), 175
Apricot Tamarind Marmalade, 220
Berry Chia Smoothie, 183
Chocolate Date Protein Bars, 202
Coco-Cocoa Chia Gelato, 321
Mango Greens Smoothie, 184
Multigrain Cereal with Fruit, 163
Spiced Root Vegetables, 295
desserts, 309–23
dips and spreads, 212–20

E

Easy Italian Dressing, 242
egg-free, corn-free, dairy-free, soy-free recipes
    Brown Bread, 186
    Flax Bread, 187
    White Dinner Rolls, 188
eggplant
    Country-Style Eggplant, 216
    Creamy White Sauce, 225
    Sindhi Spinach, 284
    Yellow Lentil Curry with Vegetables, 283

F

Favorite Blueberry Muffins, 193
fennel
    Fennel-Scented Tomato and Wild Rice Soup, 259
    Peas and Greens, 281
    Spicy Squash and Fennel Soup, 256
    Vegetable Paella, 288
    Vegetable Stock, 248
    Warm Beet Salad, 233
flax seeds. *See also* seeds
    Brown Bread (Egg-Free, Corn-Free, Dairy-Free, Soy-Free), 186
    Caesar Salad Dressing, 246
    Flax Bread (Egg-Free, Corn-Free, Dairy-Free, Soy-Free), 187
    Gingerbread Amaranth Cookies, 314
    Super Protein Shake, 184
Fragrant Coconut Rice, 303
frozen desserts, 320–24
fruit, dried. *See also* dates; raisins
    Ancient Grains Granola, 162
    Chocolate Chip Breakfast Bars (tip), 176
    Cranberry Quinoa Porridge, 165
    Multi-Seed Energy Bars, 203
    Sunflower Quinoa Snack Squares, 205

    Wild Rice Stuffing with Cranberries, 308
fruit, fresh. *See also* berries; *specific fruits*
    Seasonal Fruit Parfaits, 317
    Summer Fruit Compote, 316

G

garlic
    Basic Gravy, 224
    Basil and Roasted Pepper Quinoa (variation), 302
    Caesar Salad Dressing, 246
    Creamy White Sauce, 225
    Garlicky White Bean Spread, 214
    Garlic-Scented Zucchini, 292
    Nori Pinwheels (variation), 206
    Pumpkin Seed Chimichurri, 223
    Roasted Garlic and Lentil Soup, 264
    Roasted Spice-Glazed Root Vegetables, 296
    Roasted Vegetable Hummus, 215
ginger
    Basic Gravy, 224
    Caribbean Red Bean, Spinach and Potato Curry, 272
    Curried Sweet Potato and Millet Soup, 258
    Gingerbread Amaranth Cookies, 314
    Golden Cauliflower with Split Peas, 279
    Indonesian-Style Yellow Rice Pilaf, 306
    Just Peachy Blueberry Picnic, 178
    Nori Pinwheels, 206
    Onion-Braised Potatoes with Spinach, 298
    Potato and Pea Coconut Curry, 280
    Pumpkin Seed Chimichurri, 223

    Sindhi Spinach, 284
    Squash with Quinoa and Apricots, 301
    Yellow Lentil Curry with Vegetables, 283
Golden Cauliflower with Split Peas, 279
Good Morning Grain-Free Waffles, 171
Grasshopper Juice, 181
Green Juice Detox, 182
Green Pea Soup, 251
greens. *See also* kale; spinach
    Artichoke Heart Salad, 232
    Avocado Salad, 232
    Beta-Carotene Burst, 179
    Bitter Detoxifier, 182
    Greens and Vegetable Salad with Lemon Dressing, 230
    Green Tea Metabolizer, 183
    Iron-Builder Juice, 180
    Mixed Green Salad with Zesty Herb Dressing, 229
    Peas and Greens, 281
    Summer Greens and Berries with Apple Cider Vinaigrette, 230
Green Tea Metabolizer, 183

H

Harira, 263
Hearty Black and White Bean Soup, 261
Hearty Potato and Leek Soup, 252
hemp seeds. *See also* seeds
    Chocolate Chip Breakfast Bars (tip), 176
    Chocolate Date Protein Bars, 202
    Kale Spring Rolls, 210
    Zucchini Spaghetti with Lemon and Herbs (variation), 293
herbs. *See also specific herbs*
    Creamy Herb Dressing, 243
    Herbed Vegetable Spread, 217

herbs *(continued)*
Lemon Dressing, 245
Raspberry Dressing, 231
Sindhi Spinach, 284
Sweet Potato Wild Rice
Cakes, 307
Zesty Herb Dressing, 245
Zucchini Spaghetti with
Lemon and Herbs, 293

I

Ice Cream, Vanilla
Raspberry, 324
Indonesian-Style Yellow Rice
Pilaf, 306
Iron-Builder Juice, 180

J

juices and smoothies, 177–84
Just Peachy Blueberry Picnic,
178

K

kale. *See also* greens
Creamy Onion Soup with
Kale, 250
Grasshopper Juice, 181
Green Juice Detox, 182
Kale and Quinoa
Minestrone, 262
Kale Spring Rolls, 210
kiwifruit
Black Sticky Rice Pudding,
318
Watercress, Raspberry
and Avocado Salad
(variation), 231

L

leeks. *See also* vegetables
Fennel-Scented Tomato
and Wild Rice Soup, 259
Green Pea Soup, 251
Hearty Potato and Leek
Soup, 252
Spinach and Sea Vegetable
Soup, 255
lemon
Bitter Detoxifier, 182
Green Juice Detox, 182

Green Tea Metabolizer,
183
Lemon Dressing, 245
Lemon-Lime Sorbet, 322
Spicy Lime Avocado
Dressing (variation), 244
Summer Fruit Compote
(variation), 316
Super Protein Shake, 184
Whipped Coconut Cream
(variation), 311
Zesty Herb Dressing, 245
Zucchini Spaghetti with
Lemon and Herbs, 293
lentils
Harira, 263
Mediterranean Bean Salad,
238
Roasted Garlic and Lentil
Soup, 264
Yellow Curry Dal, 286
Yellow Lentil Curry with
Vegetables, 283
lettuce. *See* greens
lime
Avocado Mayonnaise, 218
Chocolate, Lime and
Coconut Cake, 310
Lemon-Lime Sorbet, 322
Spicy Lime Avocado
Dressing, 244
Summer Fruit Compote,
316
Luscious Apple Butter, 219

M

Make-Ahead Coconut
Crêpes, 168
Make Your Own Cupcake
Mix, 312
Maki Rolls with Carrot Rice
and Avocado, 208
mango
Black Sticky Rice Pudding,
318
Mango Greens Smoothie,
184
Polka-Dot Mango Ice Pops,
323
Watercress, Raspberry
and Avocado Salad
(variation), 231

maple syrup
Chia Pancakes with Maple
Syrup, 170
Country-Style Eggplant,
216
Curried Sweet Potato and
Millet Soup, 258
Maple Cinnamon Cookies,
315
Roasted Spice-Glazed Root
Vegetables, 296
Whipped Coconut Cream
(variation), 311
Masala Cauliflower, Whole
Baked, 290
Mediterranean Bean Salad,
238
Mediterranean Dressing, 239
melon
Summer Fruit Compote,
316
Watercress, Raspberry
and Avocado Salad
(variation), 231
Middle Eastern Balela Salad,
237
milk (dairy/non-dairy)
Berry Chia Smoothie, 183
Carrot Cake Baked
Amaranth, 166
Chia Pancakes with Maple
Syrup, 170
Creamy White Sauce, 225
Just Peachy Blueberry
Picnic, 178
Super Protein Shake, 184
millet
Ancient Grains Granola,
162
Asian-Style Quinoa Salad
with Chili-Orange
Dressing (variation), 234
Curried Sweet Potato and
Millet Soup, 258
molasses
Gingerbread Amaranth
Cookies, 314
Luscious Apple Butter, 219
Moroccan Anise Crackers, 201
muffins, 193–96
Multigrain Cereal with Fruit,
163

Multi-Seed Energy Bars, 203
Multi-Seed Quinoa Crackers,
    200
mushrooms
    Spicy Squash and Fennel
        Soup (tip), 256
    Vegetable Stock, 248

N

Navy Bean Sloppy Joes, 270
No-Bake Chocolate Quinoa
    Cookies, 313
nori
    Avocado Cucumber Hand
        Rolls, 207
    Maki Rolls with Carrot
        Rice and Avocado, 208
    Nori Pinwheels, 206
nut butters
    Chewy Coconut Quinoa
        Bars, 204
    No-Bake Chocolate
        Quinoa Cookies, 313
    Sunflower Quinoa Snack
        Squares (tip), 205
nuts. See also almonds
    and almond flour;
    nut butters
    Berry Chia Smoothie, 183
    Mediterranean Bean Salad
        (variation), 238
    Wild Rice Stuffing with
        Cranberries, 308

O

oats and oat bran
    Ancient Grains Granola,
        162
    Brown Bread (Egg-Free,
        Corn-Free, Dairy-Free,
        Soy-Free) (variation), 186
    Sunflower Quinoa Snack
        Squares (tip), 205
onions. See also vegetables
    Basic Gravy, 224
    Creamy Onion Soup with
        Kale, 250
    Onion-Braised Potatoes
        with Spinach, 298
    Potatoes in Tomato Gravy
        (variation), 297

Roasted Spice-Glazed
    Root Vegetables, 296
orange
    Apricot Tamarind
        Marmalade, 220
    Asian-Style Quinoa Salad
        with Chili-Orange
        Dressing, 234
    Avocado, Orange and
        Quinoa Salsa, 221
    Chocolate Date Protein
        Bars, 202
    Citrus Beets, 292
    Curried Sweet Potato and
        Millet Soup, 258
    Spiced Root Vegetables,
        295
    Squash with Quinoa and
        Apricots, 301
    Summer Fruit Compote
        (variation), 316
    Wild Rice Stuffing with
        Cranberries, 308

P

pancakes and waffles, 167–72
parsley. See also herbs
    Bitter Detoxifier, 182
    Green Juice Detox, 182
    Pumpkin Seed
        Chimichurri, 223
parsnips
    Herbed Vegetable Spread,
        217
    Roasted Spice-Glazed Root
        Vegetables, 296
    Spiced Root Vegetables,
        295
    Vegetable Stock, 248
peaches
    Black Sticky Rice Pudding,
        318
    Just Peachy Blueberry
        Picnic, 178
    Summer Fruit Compote,
        316
peas, dried. See also
    chickpeas
    Black-Eyed Peas with
        Vegetables, 278
    Golden Cauliflower with
        Split Peas, 279

Peas and Greens, 281
Sindhi Spinach, 284
peas, green
    Asian-Style Quinoa Salad
        with Chili-Orange
        Dressing, 234
    Butternut Squash with
        Snow Peas and Red
        Pepper, 299
    Green Pea Soup, 251
    Mixed Green Salad with
        Zesty Herb Dressing,
        229
    Potato and Pea Coconut
        Curry, 280
    Potatoes in Tomato Gravy
        (variation), 297
    Red Beans and Red Rice,
        271
    Sweet Potato Shepherd's
        Pie, 282
    Zucchini Chickpea Tagine
        with Cilantro Quinoa,
        274
peppers, bell. See also
    vegetables
    Avocado Cucumber Hand
        Rolls (variation), 207
    Basil and Roasted Pepper
        Quinoa, 302
    Black Bean and Rice Salad,
        236
    Butternut Squash with
        Snow Peas and Red
        Pepper, 299
    Curried Chickpeas, 277
    Nori Pinwheels (variation),
        206
    Squash and Black Bean
        Chili, 268
peppers, chile
    Basil and Roasted Pepper
        Quinoa, 302
    Black Bean and Rice Salad,
        236
    Black-Eyed Peas with
        Vegetables, 278
    Caribbean Red Bean,
        Spinach and Potato
        Curry, 272
    Chickpeas and Cauliflower
        in Tomato Curry, 276

peppers, chile (continued)
  Chile Rice, 304
  Potatoes in Tomato Gravy, 297
  Sindhi Spinach, 284
  Spicy Black Bean Dip, 213
  Squash and Black Bean Chili, 268
  Two-Bean Chili with Zucchini, 266
  Whole Baked Masala Cauliflower, 290
  Yellow Lentil Curry with Vegetables, 283
Pesto Sauce, Classic, 222
Pizza Crust, 189
Polka-Dot Mango Ice Pops, 323
potatoes. See also vegetables
  Caribbean Red Bean, Spinach and Potato Curry, 272
  Creamy Onion Soup with Kale, 250
  Green Pea Soup, 251
  Hearty Potato and Leek Soup, 252
  Onion-Braised Potatoes with Spinach, 298
  Potato and Pea Coconut Curry, 280
  Potato and Spinach Curry, 299
  Potatoes in Tomato Gravy, 297
  Sindhi Spinach, 284
puddings, 318–19
pumpkin. See also pumpkin seeds; squash
  Coconut "Corn" Bread, 191
  Pumpkin Bread, 192
  Pumpkin Curry Soup, 253
  Pumpkin Latte Waffles, 172
pumpkin seeds (pepitas)
  Artichoke Heart Salad, 232
  Breakfast Porridge, 164
  Multi-Seed Quinoa Crackers, 200
  Nori Pinwheels (variation), 206

Pumpkin Bread (tip), 192
Pumpkin Seed Chimichurri, 223
Summer Greens and Berries with Apple Cider Vinaigrette, 230
Super Protein Shake, 184
Sweet Toasted Pumpkin Seeds, 198
White Dinner Rolls (Egg-Free, Corn-Free, Dairy-Free, Soy-Free) (variation), 188

Q
quinoa. See also quinoa flakes/flour
  Ancient Grains Granola, 162
  Asian-Style Quinoa Salad with Chili-Orange Dressing, 234
  Avocado, Orange and Quinoa Salsa, 221
  Basil and Roasted Pepper Quinoa, 302
  Carrot Cake Baked Amaranth (variation), 166
  Cranberry Quinoa Porridge, 165
  Curried Sweet Potato and Millet Soup (variation), 258
  Garlicky White Bean Spread, 214
  Kale and Quinoa Minestrone, 262
  Multi-Seed Quinoa Crackers, 200
  No-Bake Chocolate Quinoa Cookies, 313
  Squash with Quinoa and Apricots, 301
  Sweet Potato, Quinoa and Black Bean Salad, 235
  Zucchini Chickpea Tagine with Cilantro Quinoa, 274
quinoa flakes/flour
  Chewy Coconut Quinoa Bars, 204

Make Your Own Cupcake Mix, 312
Maple Cinnamon Cookies, 315
Multi-Seed Energy Bars, 203
Pizza Crust, 189
Spinach, Quinoa and Broccoli Bisque, 260
Sunflower Quinoa Snack Squares, 205

R
raisins. See also fruit, dried
  Applesauce Raisin Muffins, 194
  Carrot Cake Baked Amaranth, 166
  Carrot Cake Muffins, 196
  Curried Sweet Potato Soup, 257
  Zucchini Chickpea Tagine with Cilantro Quinoa, 274
raspberries
  Berry Chia Smoothie, 183
  Berry Vinaigrette, 241
  Summer Greens and Berries with Apple Cider Vinaigrette, 230
  Super Protein Shake, 184
  Vanilla Raspberry Ice Cream, 324
  Watercress, Raspberry and Avocado Salad, 231
Raspberry Dressing, 231
rice. See also rice, wild; rice flour
  Beans and Rice, 174
  Black Bean and Rice Salad, 236
  Black Sticky Rice Pudding, 318
  Brown Rice, 305
  Chile Rice, 304
  Fragrant Coconut Rice, 303
  Indonesian-Style Yellow Rice Pilaf, 306
  Multigrain Cereal with Fruit, 163
  Pumpkin Curry Soup, 253

Red Beans and Red Rice,
271
Roasted Garlic and Lentil
Soup, 264
Sweet Potato Wild Rice
Cakes, 307
Vegetable Paella, 288
rice, wild
Fennel-Scented Tomato
and Wild Rice Soup, 259
Multigrain Cereal with
Fruit, 163
Sweet Potato Wild Rice
Cakes, 307
Wild Rice, 305
Wild Rice Stuffing with
Cranberries, 308
rice flour
Brown Bread (Egg-Free,
Corn-Free, Dairy-Free,
Soy-Free), 186
Brown Rice Flour Blend,
195
Chia Pancakes with Maple
Syrup, 170
Flax Bread (Egg-Free,
Corn-Free, Dairy-Free,
Soy-Free), 187
Make Your Own Cupcake
Mix, 312
White Dinner Rolls (Egg-
Free, Corn-Free, Dairy-
Free, Soy-Free), 188
romaine lettuce. See greens
rutabaga
Roasted Spice-Glazed Root
Vegetables, 296
Spiced Root Vegetables,
295
Sweet Potato Wild Rice
Cakes, 307

S

salads, 228–40
dressings, 241–46
sauces, 221–26
sausage
Hearty Black and White
Bean Soup (variation),
261
Red Beans and Red Rice
(variation), 271

seaweed
Avocado Cucumber Hand
Rolls, 207
Maki Rolls with Carrot
Rice and Avocado, 208
Nori Pinwheels, 206
Spinach and Sea Vegetable
Soup, 255
seed butters
Chewy Coconut Quinoa
Bars (tip), 204
Chocolate Chip Breakfast
Bars, 176
Multi-Seed Energy Bars,
203
No-Bake Chocolate
Quinoa Cookies, 313
Roasted Vegetable
Hummus, 215
Sunflower Quinoa Snack
Squares, 205
Super Protein Shake, 184
seeds. See also seed butters;
specific types of seeds
Apricot Breakfast Bites, 175
Breakfast Porridge, 164
Moroccan Anise Crackers,
201
Multi-Seed Energy Bars,
203
Multi-Seed Quinoa
Crackers, 200
Pesto Sauce, Classic, 222
Seasonal Fruit Parfaits, 317
Swedish Wraps, 190
Wheat-Free Thins, 199
Sindhi Spinach, 284
Smoky Sweet Potato Hash,
173
sorghum flour
Brown Bread (Egg-Free,
Corn-Free, Dairy-Free,
Soy-Free), 186
Make Your Own Cupcake
Mix, 312
Moroccan Anise Crackers,
201
Pizza Crust, 189
Swedish Wraps, 190
Wheat-Free Thins, 199
soups, 247–64
Spaghetti Squash, 300

Spiced Root Vegetables, 295
Spicy Black Bean Dip, 213
Spicy Lime Avocado
Dressing, 244
Spicy Squash and Fennel
Soup, 256
spinach. See also greens
Avocado Spinach Dip, 212
Caribbean Red Bean,
Spinach and Potato
Curry, 272
Mango Greens Smoothie,
184
Onion-Braised Potatoes
with Spinach, 298
Potato and Spinach Curry,
299
Pumpkin Curry Soup, 253
Sindhi Spinach, 284
Spinach, Quinoa and
Broccoli Bisque, 260
Spinach and Sea Vegetable
Soup, 255
Watercress, Raspberry
and Avocado Salad
(variation), 231
squash. See also pumpkin
Butternut Squash and
Apple Soup with Ginger,
254
Butternut Squash Spaghetti
Sauce, 226
Butternut Squash with
Snow Peas and Red
Pepper, 299
Creamy White Sauce, 225
Spaghetti Squash, 300
Spicy Squash and Fennel
Soup, 256
Squash and Black Bean
Chili, 268
Squash with Quinoa and
Apricots, 301
strawberries
Berry Vinaigrette
(variation), 241
Black Sticky Rice Pudding,
318
Summer Fruit Compote, 316
Summer Greens and Berries
with Apple Cider
Vinaigrette, 230

sunflower seeds. *See also* seeds
  Avocado Cucumber Hand Rolls, 207
  Avocado Salad, 232
  Chocolate Chip Breakfast Bars, 176
  Mixed Green Salad with Zesty Herb Dressing, 229
  Nori Pinwheels, 206
  Pumpkin Seed Chimichurri (variation), 223
  Sunflower Quinoa Snack Squares, 205
  White Dinner Rolls (Egg-Free, Corn-Free, Dairy-Free, Soy-Free) (variation), 188
Super Protein Shake, 184
Swedish Wraps, 190
sweet potatoes
  Beta-Carotene Burst (variation), 179
  Curried Sweet Potato and Millet Soup, 258
  Curried Sweet Potato Soup, 257
  Potato and Pea Coconut Curry, 280
  Roasted Spice-Glazed Root Vegetables, 296
  Smoky Sweet Potato Hash, 173
  Sweet Potato, Quinoa and Black Bean Salad, 235
  Sweet Potato Shepherd's Pie, 282
  Sweet Potato Wild Rice Cakes, 307
Sweet Toasted Pumpkin Seeds, 198
Swiss chard. *See* greens

T

tahini. *See* seed butters
tamarind
  Apricot Tamarind Marmalade, 220
  Sindhi Spinach, 284

teff and teff flour
  Ancient Grains Granola, 162
  Chocolate Teff Pudding, 319
  Moroccan Anise Crackers, 201
  Wheat-Free Thins, 199
tomato. *See also* vegetables
  Basic Gravy, 224
  Chickpeas and Cauliflower in Tomato Curry, 276
  Chickpeas in Tomato Curry, 275
  Chile Rice, 304
  Fennel-Scented Tomato and Wild Rice Soup, 259
  Greens and Vegetable Salad with Lemon Dressing, 230
  Harira, 263
  Kale and Quinoa Minestrone, 262
  Navy Bean Sloppy Joes, 270
  Peas and Greens, 281
  Potatoes in Tomato Gravy, 297
  Roasted Garlic and Lentil Soup, 264
  Squash and Black Bean Chili, 268
  Sweet Potato Shepherd's Pie, 282
  Zucchini Chickpea Tagine with Cilantro Quinoa, 274
  Two-Bean Chili with Zucchini, 266

V

Vanilla Raspberry Ice Cream, 324
vegetables (mixed). *See also* greens; *specific vegetables*
  Black-Eyed Peas with Vegetables, 278
  Chickpea Salad, 240
  Coconut "Corn" Bread (variation), 191
  Hearty Black and White Bean Soup, 261

  Mediterranean Bean Salad, 238
  Mixed Vegetable Coconut Curry, 289
  Red Beans and Red Rice, 271
  Roasted Vegetable Hummus, 215
  Two-Bean Chili with Zucchini, 266
  Vegetable Paella, 288
  Vegetable Stock, 248
  Wild Rice Stuffing with Cranberries, 308
  Yellow Lentil Curry with Vegetables, 283

W

Warm Beet Salad, 233
Watercress, Raspberry and Avocado Salad, 231
Wheat-Free Thins, 199
Whipped Coconut Cream, 311
White Sauce, Creamy, 225
wild rice. *See* rice, wild

Y

Yellow Curry Dal, 286
Yellow Lentil Curry with Vegetables, 283

Z

Zesty Herb Dressing, 245
zucchini
  Cauliflower and Zucchini Slaw, 228
  Curried Zucchini Strips, 294
  Garlic-Scented Zucchini, 292
  Sweet Potato Shepherd's Pie, 282
  Two-Bean Chili with Zucchini, 266
  Zucchini Chickpea Tagine with Cilantro Quinoa, 274
  Zucchini Spaghetti with Lemon and Herbs, 293